Worlds
of
Music

Worlds of Music

An Introduction to the Music of the World's Peoples

Second Edition

Jeff Todd Titon, *General Editor*

Linda Fujie
James T. Koetting
David P. McAllester
David B. Reck
John M. Schechter
Mark Slobin
R. Anderson Sutton

Schirmer Books
A Division of Macmillan, Inc.
New York
Maxwell Macmillan Canada
Toronto
Maxwell Macmillan International
New York   Oxford   Singapore   Sydney

Copyright © 1992 by Schirmer Books
A Division of Macmillan, Inc.

Schirmer Books
A Division of Macmillan, Inc.
866 Third Avenue, New York, N.Y. 10022

Maxwell Macmillan Canada, Inc.
1200 Eglinton Avenue East, Suite 200
Don Mills, Ontario M3C 3N1

Macmillan, Inc. is part of the Maxwell Communication Group of Companies

Library of Congress Catalog Card Number: 91-6390

Printed in the United States of America

printing number

2   3   4   5   6   7   8   9   10

Library of Congress Cataloging-in-Publication Data

Worlds of music : an introduction to the music of the world's peoples
/ Jeff Todd Titon, general editor.—2nd ed.
    p.   cm.
    Includes bibliographical references and index.
    Contents: The music-culture as a world of music / Mark Slobin and
Jeff Todd Titon—2. North America/native America / David P.
McAllester—3. Africa/Ghana / James T. Koetting—4. North
America/Black America / Jeff Todd Titon—5. Europe/peasant music
cultures of Eastern Europe / Mark Slobin—6. India/South India /
David B. Reck—7. Asia/Indonesia / R. Anderson Sutton—8. East
Asia/Japan / Linda Fujie—9. Latin America/Ecuador / John M.
Schechter—10. Discovering and documenting a world of music /
David B. Reck, Mark Slobin, and Jeff Todd Titon.
    ISBN 0-02-872602-2
    1. Folk music—History and criticism.   2. Music—History and
criticism.   3. Ethnomusicology.   I. Titon, Jeff.
ML3545.W67   1992
781.6—dc20   91-6390
                                                         CIP
                                                         MN

Contents

Recorded Selections

13. "Baganda *Akadinda*: 'Kawuta Yeggalidde' " (0'43"). Source: Field tape collected by Klaus Wachsmann. Uganda, 1949. Used by permission of the collector and the Uganda Museum. [Note: Pitch variations were a fault of the original recording.]

14. "Postal workers cancelling stamps at the University of Ghana post office" (2'57"). Source: Field tape collected by James Koetting. Legon, Ghana, 1975.

15. "Highlife music" (1'32"). Nyakrom Brass Band. Source: Field tape collected by James Koetting. Legon, Ghana, 1975.

16. "Amazing Grace" (2'38"). New Bethel Baptist Church. Source: Field tape collected by Jeff Titon. Detroit, Mich., 1977.

17. "Amazing Grace" (2'51"). Fellowship Independent Baptist Church. Source: Field tape collected by Jeff Titon. Stanley, Va., 1977.

18. "Rosie" (2'48"). Prisoners at Mississippi State Penitentiary. Source: Field tape collected by Alan Lomax. Parchman, Miss., 1947. © Alan Lomax. Used by permission of Alan Lomax.

19. "Poor Boy Blues" (3'14"). Lazy Bill Lucas Trio. Source: Field tape collected by Jeff Titon. Minneapolis, Minn., 1970.

Cassette 2, *Side B*

20. "I Need $100" (2'58"). One-string Sam. Source: *Detroit Blues: The Early 1950s,* Blues Classics 12" LP, BC-12. Detroit, Mich., c. 1956.

21. "Sweet Home Chicago" (3'09"). The Fieldstones. Source: *The Fieldstones,* High Water Records 12" LP, LP-1001. Memphis, Tenn., 1981. ℗ 1983, Memphis State University.

22. "The Score" (4'07"). Robert Cray Band. Source: *Who's Been Talkin',* Charly 12" LP, CRB 1140, 1986. "The Score" by D. Amy, © 1980 Joliet Music Administered by BUG. Used by permission.

23. "Paparuda" (0'25"). Gypsy children. Source: *Folk Music of Rumania,* Columbia Records 12" LP, KL 5799. Gişteşti village, Rumania.

24. "Russian wedding song: 'Na solnechnom vskhode' " (1'44"). Source: Melodiya Records. Varzuga, USSR.

25. "Rumanian wedding song" (2'08"). Gheorghe Moţoi. Source: *Folk Music of Rumania,* Columbia Records 12" LP, KL 5799.

26. "Rumanian communal lament" (1'46"). Source: *Folk Music of Rumania,* Columbia Records 12" LP, KL 5799. Borlovenii Vechi village, Rumania.

27. "Rumanian solo lament" (0'54"). Elisabeta Pavel. Source: *Folk Music of Rumania,* Columbia Records 12" LP, KL 5799. Girişu Negru village, Rumania.

28. Ganga (1'29"). Source: *Traditional Music from Bosnia and Hercegovina,* ed. A. Petrovic. Diskoton 8149.

Compact Disc 2

29. "Jewish dance tune" (2'37"). Dave Tarras, clarinet, with unidentified accompanists. Source: Colonial Records 12" LP, ST-LP–718

30. "Hungarian song, followed by two instrumental versions done by the same musician" (2'40"). 52-year-old swineherd from Somogy County. Source: *Hungarian Folk Music, Vol. 2,* Hungaroton Records 12" LP, LPX 18003. Used by permission of Hungarian Academy of Sciences.

31. "Russian balalaika orchestra playing Andreyev's variations on the Russian folksong, 'The Moon Shines'" (1'30"). Source: Melodiya Records 33D 034435–36(a).

32. "Leningrad Dixieland Band playing variations on the Russian folksong, 'The Moon Shines'" (1'01"). Source: Melodiya Records CM-02787–8.

33. "Vinter iz geveyn a groyser shturem vind" (0'44"). Mariam Nirenberg. Used by permission of Barbara Kirschenblatt-Gimblett.

34. "Engal Kalyanam" ("Our Wedding"), cinema song (3'23"). P. Susheela, T. M. Soundararajan, P. B. Sreenivos, and L. R. Eswari. Music by M. S. Viswanathan, lyrics by Vali. Source: *Hits from Tamil Films,* Vol. 6, EMI Odeon (India) 12" LP, 3AECS 5519. Dum Dum, India, 1969. © Gramophone Company of India, Ltd. Used by permission.

35. "Nagapattu" ("Snake song"), folk song (3'27"). G. P. Saraswathi, voice and *kudam.* Source: Field tape collected by Carol S. Reck. Cheruthurthy, Kerala, 1970. Used by permission of the collector.

36. Panchavadyam" (3'57"). Percussion and wind orchestra. Source: Field tape collected by David B. Reck. Trichur, Kerala, 1970.

Cassette 2, *Side C*

37. Karnataka Sangeeta: performance segment built upon Puliyar Doraisamy Ayyar's composition, "Sarasiruha," Natai raga, Adi tala (15'31"). Ramachandra Iyer, *veena,* accompanied by Ravindran Iyer and David Reck, *veenas,* and David Nelson, *mridangam.* Source: Field tape collected by David Nelson.

38. *Bubaran Kembang Pacar, pélog pathet nem* (3'45"). Central Javanese *gamelan* music in "loud-playing" style, performed by musicians affiliated with the royal palace in Yogyakarta. Source: Field tape collected by R. Anderson Sutton.

39. *Ladrang Wilujeng, pélog pathet barang* (8'50"). Central Javanese *gamelan* music "soft-playing" style, performed by musicians of Ngudya Wirama *gamelan* group, Yogyakarta, under the direction of Ki Suhardi. Source: Field tape collected by René Lysloff. Used by permission.

40. *Playon Lasem, sléndro pathet nem* (1'40"). Central Javanese *gamelan* music for shadow puppetry performed by *gamelan* group of Ki Suparman. (Rendition 1). Source: Field tape collected by R. Anderson Sutton.

41. *Playon Lasem, sléndro pathet nem* (0'35"). Central Javanese *gamelan* music for shadow puppetry, performed by *gamelan* group of Ki Suparman. (Rendition 2). Source: Field tape collected by R. Anderson Sutton.

42. *Tabuh Gari* (6'45"). *Gamelan semar pegulingan* music from Pliatan, Bali. Source: Nonesuch Explorer H–72046. Recorded by Robert E. Brown. Used by permission.

43. Excerpts from a performance of *gondang keteng-keteng* (2'10"), from the Karo Batak highlands of North Sumatra, performed by Tukang Ginting and his Group. Source: Field tape collected by R. Anderson Sutton.

Compact Disc 3

44. Excerpts from *Begadang II* (3'30"), popular *dang-dut* music performed by Rhoma Irama and his Soneta Group. Source: *Begadang II,* Yukawi Indomusic. Used by permission.

45. Excerpts from *Indonesia Maharddhika* (2'20"), performed by "heavy pop" group Guruh Gipsy, under the direction of Guruh Sukarnoputra. Source: *Guruh Gipsy.* Used by permission.

46. "Tsuru no sugomori" (3'40"). Kawase Junsuke. Field tape collected by Linda Fujie, Tokyo, Japan, 1989.

Cassette 2, *Side D*

47. "Hakusen no" (3'22"). Shitaya Kotsuru. Source: Nippon Columbia WK-170. Used by permission

48. "Nikata-bushi" (5'07"). Asano Umewaka and Asano Sanae. Field tape collected by Karl Signell, Washington, D.C., 1986. Used by permission of the collector.

49. "Kiri-bayashi" (1'30"). Ueno Shachū. Field tape collected by Linda Fujie, Tokyo, Japan, 1981.

50. "Nonki-bushi" (2'35"). Ishimatsu Ishida. Source: Nippon Columbia SP-ban fukugen. Used by permission.

51. "Naite Nagasaki" (3'34"). Kanda Fukumaru. Source: Nippon Columbia AH-210. Used by permission.

52. "Pajarillo" (2'27") (*joropo* of Venezuela). Source: Disques OCORA 12" LP, OCR 78. Música Folklórica de Venezuela. Collected by Isabel Aretz, Luis Felipe Ramón y Rivera and Alvaro Fernaud. Song 5 "Golpe (Joropo)"/Ocora Radio France OCR 78 / Distribution Harmonia Mundi. Used by permission.

53. "El Lazo" (3'55") by Victor Jara (Chile). Source: *Victor Jara: Desde Lonquén Hasta Siempre.* Monitor Records, Volume 4, MFS 810. 12" LP, n.d.

54. "Kutirimunapaq" (3'52") (*k'antu* of Bolivia). Source: RUPHAY. Discos Heriba, 12" LP. Bolivia, SLP 2212. Jach'a Marka 1982. Eduardo Ibañez W., Gerente General, Heriba Ltda., P.O. Box 3120, La Paz, Bolivia. Used by permission.

55. "Cascarón" (3′26″) (*sanjuán* of Ecuador, played by Quichua harpist Efraín.) Source: Field tape collected by John Schechter. Outside Cotacachi, Ecuador, April 1980.

56. "Rusa Maria" (2′30″) (*sanjuán* of Ecuador, played by three Quichua musicians.) Source: Field tape collected by John Schechter. Outside Cotacachi, Ecuador, January 1980. [Note: microphone noises in original recording.]

57. "Vacación" (1′30″) (played by Quichua harpist, Sergio, at a child's wake.) Source: Field tape collected by John Schechter. Outside Cotacachi, Ecuador, February 1980.

58. Ecuadorian mother's lament, to her deceased two-year-old girl, the morning after the child's wake (preceded by fifteen seconds of Sergio's "Vacación") (3′11″). Source: Field tape collected by John Schechter. Outside Cotacachi, Ecuador, January 1980.

59. "Toro Barroso" (3′32″) (*albazo* of Ecuador, played by Don César Muquinche). Source: Field tape collected by John Schechter. Outside Ambato, Ecuador, 1980.

60. "Lowland Quichua [Ecuador] Shaman Curing Song" (1′40″). Source: *Soul Vine Shaman.* 12″ LP, in situ, recording made in 1976 by Dan Weaks and Neelon Crawford; LP was recorded and was produced and distributed by Neelon Crawford. This song [#1 on the recording] is excerpted from SOUL VINE SHAMAN, a recording made by Neelon Crawford in Ecuador in 1976. This recording is Copyright © 1976. All rights are reserved by Neelon Crawford. No portion of this recording may be reproduced and / or transmitted through any medium without specific written permission from Neelon Crawford. Further information about this recording may be obtained by writing Neelon Crawford, 10 East 23rd Street, Suite 600, New York, NY 10010. Used by permission.

61. "Vamos pa' Manabi" (3′00″) (*bomba* of Ecuador, played by Fabián and Eleuterio Congo). Source: Field tape collected by John Schechter. Chota Valley, Ecuador, March 1980.

The Authors

LINDA K. FUJIE received the Ph.D. in ethnomusicology from Columbia University, where she was a student of Dieter Christensen and Adelaida Reyes Schramm. She has conducted field research in Japan under grants from the National Endowment for the Humanities, Columbia University, and Colby College. Interest in overseas Japanese culture has also resulted in research on Japanese-American and Japanese-Brazilian communities, the latter funded by the German Music Council. Her research has been published in articles in the *Yearbook for Traditional Music,* publications on popular music, and in Japanese journals. She has taught at Colby College as Assistant Professor and currently resides in Berlin, Germany.

JAMES T. KOETTING received the Ph.D. in ethnomusicology from U.C.L.A., where he was a student of Mantle Hood, J. H. Kwabena Nketia, and Klaus Wachsmann. He undertook field research in Uganda and Ghana. He performed professionally with Ashanti and Ewe master drummers, the Aman Folk Ensemble, Mariachi Uclatán, Los Tigres de la Sierra, and Conjunto Jarocho Los Angeles; and he published articles on West African and Mexican music. He held various positions in the Society for Ethnomusicology, including Treasurer, Council Secretary, business manager of its journal, *Ethnomusicology,* and President of its Northeast Chapter. From 1973–1975 he taught ethnomusicology at the University of Ghana in Legon. After 1975 he taught ethnomusicology at Brown University and directed the West African Drum Ensemble. He died in 1984.

DAVID P. MCALLESTER received the Ph.D. in anthropology from Columbia University, where he studied with George Herzog. He has been a student of American Indian music since 1938. He has undertaken field work among the Comanches, Hopis, Apaches, Navajos, Penobscots, and Passamaquoddies. He is the author of such classic works in ethnomusicology as *Peyote Music, Enemy Way Music, Myth of the Great Star Chant,* and *Navajo Blessingway Singer* (coedited with Charlotte J. Frisbie). He is one of the founders of the Society for Ethnomusicology, and he has served as its president and editor of its journal, *Ethnomusicology*. He is Professor Emeritus of Anthropology and Music at Wesleyan University.

DAVID B. RECK received the Ph.D. in ethnomusicology from Wesleyan University where he was a student of Mark Slobin and David P. McAllester. He has studied and traveled in India, Southeast Asia, and the Far East under grants from the American Institute of Indian Studies, the Rockefeller Foundation, the John Simon Guggenheim Memorial Foundation, and the JDR IIIrd Fund. An accomplished musician on the south Indian *veena,* he has performed extensively in the United States, Europe, and India both as a soloist and accompanist and as a member of the group *Kirtana.* As a composer, he has received commissions from the Library of Congress, the Koussevitsky Foundation, and the Fromm Music Foundation, and had performances at Tanglewood and Carnegie Hall. The author of *Music of the Whole Earth,* his research and publications include work on India's music, American popular styles, the music of J. S. Bach, Bartok, and Stravinsky, and cross-influences between the West and the Orient. Currently he is professor of music and of Asian Languages and Civilizations at Amherst College.

JOHN M. SCHECHTER received the Ph.D. in ethnomusicology from The University of Texas at Austin, where he studied ethnomusicology with Gérard Béhague, Andean anthropology with Richard Schaedel, and Quichua with Louisa Stark and Guillermo Delgado. He pursued fieldwork in the Andes of Ecuador in 1979–1980, and again in 1990, under grants from Fulbright-Hays and from the University of California, Santa Cruz. He is the author of *The Indispensable Harp: Historical Development, Modern Roles, Configurations, and Performance Practices in Ecuador and Latin America.* His articles on Quichua music-culture, Inca music-culture, the Latin American child's wake, and Latin American musical instruments have appeared in *Ethnomusicology,* the *Journal of the American Musical Instrument Society, Revista Musical Chilena,* the *Journal of Latin American Lore, Current Musicology,* and *The New Grove Dictionary of Musical Instruments.* A member of the Society for Ethnomusicology, he served as president of its Northern California Chapter in 1988–1990. He has taught ethnomusicology and music theory at The University of California, Santa Cruz, since 1985.

MARK SLOBIN received the Ph.D. in musicology at the University of Michigan. He is the author, editor, or translator of six books—three on the music of Afghanistan and Central Asia, including *Music in the Culture of Northern Afghanistan,* and three on the music of the Eastern European Jews, including *Tenement Songs: The Popular Music of the Jewish Immigrants,* which won the ASCAP-Deems Taylor award. He is a Past President of the Society for Ethnomusicology and the Society for Asian Music and edited the latter's journal, *Asian Music,* from 1971–1988. He is a Research Associate and Consultant to the Music Collections at the YIVO Institute for Jewish Research. He has taught at Wesleyan University since 1971, where he is now Professor of Music.

R. ANDERSON SUTTON received the Ph.D. in musicology from the University of Michigan, where he studied with Judith Becker and William Malm. He was introduced to Javanese music while an undergraduate at Wesleyan University, and made it the focus of his master's study at the University of Hawaii, where he studied gamelan with Hardja Susilo. On numerous occasions since 1973 he has conducted field research in Indonesia, with grants from the East-West Center, Fulbright-Hays, Social Science Research Council, National Endowment for the Humanities, Wenner-Gren Foundation, and the American Philosophical Society.

He is author of *Traditions of Gamelan Music in Java, Variation in Central Javanese Gamelan Music,* and numerous articles on Javanese music. Active as a gamelan musician since 1971, he has performed with several professional groups in Indonesia and directed numerous performances in the United States. He has served as Book Review Editor and Council member for the Society for Ethnomusicology, and as member of the Working Committee on Performing Arts for the Festival of Indonesia (1990–92). He has taught at the University of Hawaii and at the University of Wisconsin–Madison, where he is associate professor of music and director of the Center for Southeast Asian Studies.

JEFF TODD TITON received the Ph.D. in American Studies from the University of Minnesota, where he studied ethnomusicology with Alan Kagan. He has done fieldwork on religious folklife, blues music, and old-time fiddling in the United States and Canada with support from the National Endowment for the Arts and the National Endowment for the Humanities. The author or editor of five books, including *Early Downhome Blues,* which won the ASCAP-Deems Taylor award, he is also a highly regarded documentary photographer and film maker. For two years he was the guitarist in the Lazy Bill Lucas Blues Band, a group that appeared in the 1970 Ann Arbor Blues Festival. He developed the ethnomusicology curriculum at Tufts University, where he taught from 1971–1986. Currently he is professor of music and director of the Ph.D. program in music at Brown University, and editor of *Ethnomusicology,* the journal of the Society for Ethnomusicology.

Preface

WHY STUDY MUSIC? There are many reasons, but perhaps the most important are pleasure and understanding. We have designed this book and its accompanying CDs and cassettes to introduce undergraduates to the study of music the world over. Although *Worlds of Music* contains musical notation, it may be used by students who do not read music. The only prerequisite is curiosity.

University courses in world music have increased dramatically since World War II, and the reasons are easy to comprehend. Most music departments now recognize that confining the study of music to the Western classics is ethnocentric. Students who love music are alive to *all* music. So are composers, and many use the world's musical resources in their newest works. This is an important feature of today's music, and the people who listen to it—now and in the future—will want to keep their musical horizons broad. Another reason for the interest in world music is the upsurge in ethnic awareness. As modern people try to locate themselves in a world that is changing with bewildering speed, they find music especially rewarding, for music is among the most tenacious cultural elements. Music symbolizes a people's way of life; it represents a distillation of cultural style. For many, music *is* a way of life.

The authors of this book are ethnomusicologists; and our field, *ethnomusicology,* is usually defined as the study of music in culture. Recently, some ethnomusicologists have defined the field as the study of music as culture, underlining the fact that music is a way of organizing human activity. By the term *culture* we do *not* mean "the elite arts," as it is sometimes used. Rather, we use the term as anthropologists do: culture is a people's total way of life. A people's culture is the sum total of their thoughts and actions, learned and transmitted through the centuries of adapting to the natural and human world. *Ethnomusicology is the study of music in the context of human life.*

I like to think of ethnomusicology simply as the study of people making music. People "make" music in two ways: they make or construct the *idea* of music, what it is (and is not) and what it does; and they make or produce the *sounds* that they call music. Although we experience music as something "out there" in the world, our response to music depends on the ideas we associate with that music, and those ideas come from the people (ourselves included) who carry our culture. We could not even pick out musical form and structure, how the parts of a piece of music work together to form a whole, if we did not depend on the idea that music must be organized rather than random, and if we did not learn to make music that way. Analyzing form and structure is characteristic of some cultures, including Western ones, but in other areas of the world people do not habitually break a thing down into parts for analytical purposes.

As students of music in culture, ethnomusicologists have every reason to investigate Western art music; that is, the tradition of Palestrina, Bach, Beethoven, Verdi, Stravinsky, and the like. But with some recent and notable exceptions, ethnomusicologists in North America have specialized in music outside this tradition. They know the Western classics well, but their interest embraces all music. Indeed, many have devoted years to performing music outside the Western mainstream. Further, because ethnomusicologists study more than the music itself (and some even deny that there is such a thing), they are not satisfied merely to analyze and compare musical forms, structures, melodies, rhythms, compositions, and genres. Instead, they borrow insights and methods from anthropology, sociology, literary criticism, linguistics, and history to understand music as human expression. In fact, until the 1950s, ethnomusicology courses in the United States were more likely to be found in anthropology departments than music departments, and some nineteenth-century founders of ethnomusicology were psychologists. Ethnomusicology is therefore interdisciplinary, combining elements of the arts, humanities, and social sciences. Because of its eclectic methods and worldwide scope, ethnomusicology is well suited to students seeking a liberal arts education.

The number of world music textbooks in print is very small, and most are theory and method books aimed at graduate students. The rest are world music surveys, but we think there are good reasons to avoid a survey course at the beginning level in particular. In its broad sweep a survey offers only a passing acquaintance with the music of many peoples. Too often a survey turns into a musical Cook's tour: if this is Tuesday, it must be India. The inevitable result is musical overkill; by the term's end students are so overloaded they can barely recognize different musical styles, let alone understand any one.

Instead of surveying the world of music, the best introduction, we think, explores in depth the music of a small number of representative human groups. This approach is not new; it adapts to ethnomusicology the case method in anthropology, the touchstone approach in literature, and the problems approach in history. Its object is not to pile up factual knowledge about various musical worlds, though certainly many facts will be learned. Rather, the point is to experience what it is like to be an ethnomusicologist puzzling out his or her way toward understanding an unfamiliar music. This process, we believe, is the best foundation for either future coursework (including surveys and seminars) or self-directed study and enjoyment of world music after college.

We decided on a small number of case studies because that is how we teach the introductory level world music course at our universities. We thought also that by writing about music in societies we know firsthand, we could write an authoritative book. Ethnomusicologists are a notoriously independent bunch, and the idea of adopting a textbook may strike some as a trifle confining. That is why we have tried to leave plenty of room for instructors to add examples and case studies of their own.

Each chapter, then, reflects our own choice of subject. It also reflects our different ways of approaching music, for we agree that music cannot be "caught" by one method only. Still, we organized the chapters on six guiding principles. First, we think a textbook in world music should go beyond merely avoiding elitism and ethnocentrism. As much as possible, an unfamiliar music should be understood at the outset in its own terms, that is, as the people who make the music understand it. Second, asking what the life of a musician is like in different societies, and answering in life histories and autobiographies, is essential if we are to know music as a human activity, not just a sequence of organized sound. Third, we single out the words of songs for special attention because they often convey the meaning and purpose of musical performances as the music-makers comprehend them. Fourth, we regard the musical examples not just as illustrations but as points of departure; therefore most of them can be heard on the cassettes accompanying this book. Fifth, student music-making projects—singing, building, and playing instruments—can, if properly directed and seriously approached, greatly increase appreciation of a musical style. Sixth, and most important, an introduction to world music should provide pleasure as well as knowledge.

The first edition of *Worlds of Music,* I wrote in the original Preface, contained enough basic material for a one-semester course. Most of us find it useful to assign some of the additional reading and listening suggested at the end of each case study, and some of us ask the students to keep a "listening journal" in which they write down their responses to the music. The second edition of *Worlds of Music* adds chapters on Japan, Indonesia, and Ecuador, and the cassettes have been increased in length to three hours. The music is now available on CDs. Some teachers supplement the book with case studies based on their own research areas. And so it is now possible to use *Worlds of Music* either in a two-semester world music sequence or, by selecting among case studies, in a one-semester introductory course.

We suggest that students begin with chapter 1, which introduces fundamental concepts about music in any culture. Chapter 10 guides the student through a fieldwork project. Because the project should begin well before the end of the term, we suggest that chapter 10 be read just after the first case study, and that students begin fieldwork immediately afterward. Many students say the field projects are the most valuable experiences they take away from this or any course, particularly when they must make sense of what they document in the field. The case studies, chapters 2 through 9, may be taken in any order.

Many colleges and universities have a one-semester introductory world music course, often called something like "Music of the World's Peoples." We have found that two to three weeks per case study is about right, so in a one-semester course the teacher should choose the four or five that best suit the course's pace and purpose. Some universities offer a two-semester introductory course in world music, usually divided on the basis of broad geographical areas. The second edition of *Worlds of Music* is appropriate as a core textbook for this kind of course as well, because it offers in-depth case studies of eight music-cultures.

If the first semester focuses on Europe and the Americas, for example, the teacher will choose the case studies in chapters 2, 4, 5, and 9; if the second semester focuses on Africa and Asia, the teacher will choose chapters 3, 6, 7, and 8. Each semester should then have enough time for a case study in the teacher's research area or elsewhere and for a student field project.

The most important change in the second edition is the three added chapters. Also, I have revised chapter 1, "The Music-Culture as a World of Music," and chapter 10, "Discovering and Documenting a World of Music," to reflect the most recent thinking in the field. Chapter 1 introduces a model, an organized set of questions, and a way of thinking that can be used to approach music in any culture. Chapter 10 leads to an original fieldwork project using the resources of the student's nearby world of music—family, neighborhood, community. The other chapters were individual assignments, and with the exception of chapter 3, each has undergone some revision. Jim Koetting, who wrote chapter 3, doubtless would have made minor changes in it for this edition, but he died in 1984 and we decided to let the chapter stand as a memorial. David Reck has condensed the two chapters on India into one. We are grateful to Bonnie C. Wade and James W. Kimball who read the book in its final stages and offered constructive suggestions. We appreciate the assistance of Maribeth Anderson Payne, editor at Schirmer Books, in seeing both editions of this project through production. We would be pleased to hear from our readers, and we may be reached by writing the publisher or any of us at our respective universities.

Jeff Todd Titon
General Editor

ONE

◆ ◆ ◆

The Music-Culture as a World of Music

MARK SLOBIN AND JEFF TODD TITON

THE MUSIC-CULTURE

So far as we know, every human society has music. Music is universal, but its meaning is not. A famous musician from the Orient was brought to a European symphony concert approximately one hundred fifty years ago. Although he was a virtuoso musician in his own country, he had never heard a performance of Western music. The story goes that after the concert he was asked how he liked it. "Very well," he replied. Not satisfied with this answer, his hosts asked (through an interpreter) what part he liked best. "The first part," he said. "Oh, you enjoyed the first movement?" "No, before that!"

To the stranger, the best part of the performance was the tuning-up period. It was music to him, and who was to say otherwise? His hosts. Music, then, though a universal phenomenon (scientists even send out music in space capsules, hoping to communicate with intelligent begins in distant solar systems), gets its meaning from culture, and different cultures interpret it differently. Recall from the Preface that by culture we mean the whole way of life of a people, learned and transmitted from one generation to the next. Because music and all the activities and beliefs associated with it are a part of culture, we used the term *music-culture* to refer to a group of people's total involvement with music. Accordingly, the European music-culture determines that the sound made by symphony musicians tuning up is not music.

We call music *music,* but not all music-cultures have a word for it. Writing about Rosa, the Yugoslav Macedonian village she lived in, Nahoma Sachs points out that "traditional Rosans have no general equivalent to the English 'music.' They divide the range of sound which might be termed music by Americans into two categories: *pesni,* songs, and *muzika,* instrumental music" (Sachs 1975:27). Of course, this distinction between songs and music is found in many parts of the world, even in the United States. Old-time Baptists in the South sometimes say, "We don't have music in our service," meaning they do not have instrumental music accompanying their singing. Other music-cultures have words for song types (lullaby, epic, historical song, etc.) but no overall word for music.

1

Partly because we have so broad a term as music in English, we can write a book like this.

Sound exists with or without people. Sound is a phenomenon of the world of nature. You probably remember the old puzzle, "If a tree falls in the forest and nobody hears it, does it make a sound?" We take the position that it does. In the West we would call that tree-falling sound noise, not music. Music and noise are ideas or concepts, something that people make out of sound. Our scientists tell us bird calls are for mating and marking territory and give them no significance outside the bird world. But for the Kaluli of Papua New Guinea, bird sounds are part of a song pattern that connects directly to the human world and involves feelings of sadness (Feld 1990). In sum, while sound exists as an independent phenomenon in the world, music is not an object "out there" and separate from us. Rather, music, like all other aspects of culture, is humanly constructed. That does not mean music is necessarily organized like anything else; it may have unusual, even unique, patterns. The ethnomusicologist John Blacking has defined music as "humanely organized sound" (Blacking 1973).

All of us are born into a world of sound and we learn from other people what sound is music and what sound is not. We may, of course, decide for ourselves; but the point is that people do decide what music is. Many years ago the avant-garde composer John Cage wrote a piece for typewriters. At its first concert performance the typists took their seats and started typing. The only sounds were the clicks of the keys, the tapping of the type, the movement of the carriages, and the bells signaling the end of each line. Many in the audience were perplexed: Was this music? a joke? or what? Would you consider it humanly organized sound? If nothing else, Cage's composition makes us realize that music is not something "given" but that it rests on an agreement among composer, performer, and listener.

AFFECT, PERFORMANCE, COMMUNITY, AND HISTORY: A MUSIC-CULTURE MODEL

We assume that all the readers of this book are curious about the music of the world's peoples and want to understand more about it. But confronting a new music can be daunting. Our first impulse might be simply to listen to it, to absorb it, to see whether we like it, whether it moves us. Our next impulse may be to let our bodies respond, to move to the music ourselves. But soon we ask questions about it: What is that instrument that sounds so lovely? How does one play it? Why are the people dancing? (Or are they dancing?) Why is someone crying? Why are the musicians in costume? What do the words mean? What kind of a life does the head musician lead? To formulate and begin to answer these questions in a comprehensive way we need to have some kind of systematic outline, or model, of any music-culture, or subculture, that tells us how it might work and what are likely to be its component parts.

We propose a music-culture model that is grounded or centered in music through performance (Titon 1988:7–10). To see how this model works out, take a familiar music-culture and recall a music event such as a concert, for example, that has moved you. At the center of the event is the music, sung and played by performers; the performers are surrounded by their audience, and the whole event takes place in its setting in time and space. We can represent this by a diagram of concentric circles (fig. 1–1). Now we transpose this diagram into four circles representing a music-culture model (fig. 1–2). At the center of the music (as you experience it) is its radiating power, its emotional impact, whatever makes you give assent, smile, nod your head, sway your shoulders, dance. We call that music's *affect,* its power to move, and place affect in the central circle of the model.

Performance brings music's power to move into being, and so we move from performers in figure 1–1 to *performance* in figure 1–2. Performance involves a great many things. In the first place, people mark performances, whether musical or otherwise, off from the flow of ordinary life: "Have you heard the story about . . ."; or "Now we're going to do a new song that one of the members of the band wrote while thinking about. . . ." When performance takes place, people know the difference. Sammy Davis, Jr., told an interviewer, "Once I get outside my house in the morning, I'm ON." We often mark endings of performances with applause. Second, performance has purpose. The performers intend to move (or not move) the audience, to sing and play well (or not well), to make money, to have fun, to learn, to advance a certain rite or ceremony; performance is evaluated partly on how well those intentions are fulfilled. Third, a performance is interpreted as it goes along, by the audience (who may cry out or applaud, or hiss a bad pun) and by the performers, who may smile when things are going well or wince when they make a mistake.

The most important thing to understand about performance is that it moves along on the basis of agreed-on rules and procedures. These rules enable the

Fig. 1–1. *Elements of a musical performance.*

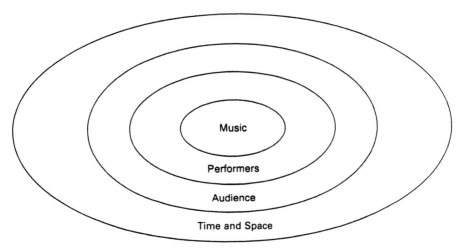

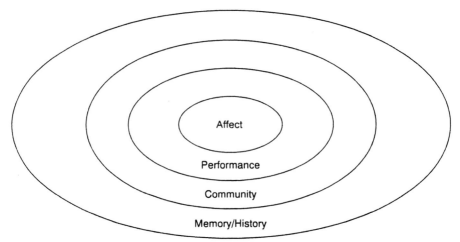

Fig. 1–2. *A music-culture model. (After Titon 1988:11.)*

musicians to play together and make sense to each other and to the audience. The performers do not discuss most of the rules; they have absorbed them and silently agreed to them. Starting at the same time, playing in the same key, playing in the same rhythmic framework, repeating the melody at the proper point—these are a few of the many rules that govern most of the musical performances that you have experienced. Even improvisation is governed by rules. In a heavy metal rock concert, for example, guitarists improvise melodic "breaks," but they cannot use all twelve tones of the chromatic scale; instead they almost always choose from the smaller number of tones represented by the blues scale (see chapter 4). Rules or accepted procedures govern the audience, too. Shouting is not only permitted but in some situations it is expected, along with other kinds of abandonment. What to wear, what to say—these, too, are patterned at any musical performance. Sometimes musicians try to break these rules or expectations, as in a ritual destruction of their instruments at the close of the concert. (And then that becomes an expectation.)

In our music-culture model, music in performance is understood as meaningfully organized sound that proceeds by rules. Finding out those rules or principles becomes the task of analysis. These rules include (but are not limited to) what is usually covered under musical analysis: mode, motif, melody, rhythm, meter, section, and so forth. Beyond that, we try to discover the rules covering ideas about music and behavior in relation to music, and the links between these rules or principles and the sound that a group of people calls music. You may resist the notion that music, which you think should be free to express emotion, is best thought of as governed by rules. We do not want to claim that musical performance is predetermined by rules, only that it proceeds by them. Music, in this view, is like a game or a conversation: without rules you could not have a game, and without agreement about what words are, what they mean, and how they are used, you could not hold a meaningful conversation. Nonetheless, just as meaningful conversations can express emotion, so can meaningful music, though not, of course, in exactly the same way. We claim, further, that if a listener does not understand the rules, he or she cannot understand the composer's or musician's intention, or the music's structure.

Audience occupied the third circle in figure 1–1; in our music-culture model we turn audience into the *community,* the group that carries the traditions and norms of performance. Performance is situated in community and is part and parcel of culture, for people bear the traditions that make up the culture. The community pays for and supports the music, whether directly with money or indirectly by allowing the performers to live as musicians. Community support usually influences the future direction of the music. In a complex society such as that of the United States, various communities support different kinds of music—classical, rock, jazz, gospel—and they do so in different ways. Classical music, for example, gets its strongest boost from middle-class people climbing the social and economic ladder. When music becomes a mass-media commodity, then packaging, marketing, and advertising are as crucial to the success of musicians as to perfume. How the community relates to the music-makers has a profound effect on the music. Among the folk music-cultures of preindustrial village societies, the performers are drawn from the community; everyone knows them well, and communication is face-to-face. At the other end of the spectrum is the postindustrial music-culture celebrity who guards his or her private life, performs from a raised platform, is a disembodied voice coming through a machine, and remains enigmatic to the audience. How the community relates to itself is another important aspect of performance. For example, do men, women, old people, and young people experience music differently? We will consider this issue later under Social Organization of Music.

Time and space, the fourth circle in figure 1–1, becomes *memory and history* in our music-culture model (figure 1–2). The community is situated in history and borne by memory, official and unofficial, whether remembered or recorded or written down. Musical affect, performances, and communities change over time and space; they have a history, and that history reflects changes in the rules governing music as well as the effect of music on human relationships. The development of radio, recordings, and television meant that music need not be heard in the performer's presence. This took the performer out of the community's face-to-face relationships and allowed people to listen to music without making it themselves. Today music is an almost constant background to many people's lives, but the musicians are largely absent. The music historian, too, alters the effect of music, for the historian's writing enters the stock of ideas about music. When white America became interested in blues music in the 1960s and began presenting blues concerts and festivals (see chapter 4), magazine and newspaper writers began asking blues singers questions about their music and its history. Knowing they would be asked these questions, the blues singers prepared their answers, sometimes reading and then repeating what writers had already said about blues.

Many times the subject of music is history itself. The Homeric poets sang about Odysseus; Yugoslavian *guslars* sang about the deeds of their heroes; European ballads tell stories of nobles and commoners; African griots sing tribal genealogies and history. Today, portable, inexpensive cassette tape recorders are revolutionizing community music history in the West, for they empower musicians and audience alike to record what they want to hear and listen to it again and again, and in this way they gain partial control over their history. When we study the history of a music-culture, or some aspect of it, we want to know not only what that history is, but who tells or writes that history and what is the historian's stake in it.

As you read through each of the case studies in the following chapters, you will want to bear this underlying music-culture model in mind. Because each of the case studies is centered in music and grounded in performance, you can use this model to understand how each chapter moves back and forth from affect to performance to community to memory and history. Musical analysis—that is, finding patterns in the sound by breaking the music into parts and determining how the parts function in the whole—is an important part of our procedure. Unlike the analyst who investigates Western classical music by looking at the composer's written score, we must usually deal with music that exists only in performance, without a notated set of instructions from a composer. The ethnomusicologist usually transcribes the music—that is, notates it—and then analyzes its structure. But it is impossible to understand structure fully without knowing the cultural "why" as well as the musical "what." A music-culture ultimately rests in the people themselves—their ideas, actions, and the sounds they produce (Merriam 1964:32–33).

If we think about the elements of a music-culture that our grounded model isolated (figure 1–2), we can see that they represent four interlocking components (table 1–1), and that we can transform them into a set of useful questions

Table 1–1. *The four components of a music culture.*

  I. Ideas about music
   A. Music and the belief system
   B. Aesthetics of music
   C. Contexts of music
   D. History of music
 II. Social organization of music
III. Repertories of music
   A. Style
   B. Genres
   C. Texts
   D. Composition
   E. Transmission
   F. Movement
IV. Material culture of music

---

that you can ask of any unfamiliar music-culture (or even a familiar one). As you read this book, and as you prepare for your field research project (chapter 10), see how each music-culture you encounter can be viewed through your particular answers to these broad, very abstract questions. Even now, while you read through the rest of this chapter, choose a music-culture you are familiar with (classical, jazz, new-wave rock, etc.) and see how it measures up to these questions.

COMPONENTS OF A MUSIC-CULTURE

I. Ideas about Music

A. *Music and the Belief System*

What is music (and what is not)? Is music human or divine (or both)? Is music good and useful for humankind? Is it potentially harmful? These questions reach into the music-culture's basic ideas of the nature of human society, art, and the universe. Cultures vary enormously in their answers to these questions, and the answers often are very subtle, even paradoxical; they are embodied in rituals that try to reconcile love and hate, life and death, the natural and the civilized. Even within one music-culture the answers may change with time: a medieval Christian would have trouble understanding one of today's jazz masses.

B. *Aesthetics of Music*

When is a song beautiful? When is it beautifully sung? What voice quality is pleasing, and what grates on the ear? How should a musician dress? How long should a performance last? Again, not all cultures agree on these aesthetic questions involving judgments of what is proper and what is beautiful. Some Americans find Chinese opera-singing strained and artificial, but likewise some Chinese think the European *bel canto* opera style is imprecise and unpleasant. Music cultures can be characterized by preferences in sound quality and performance practice, all of which are aesthetic discriminations.

C. *Contexts for Music*

When should music be performed? How often? On what occasions? Again, every music-culture answers these questions about musical surroundings differently (see illustration 1–1). In the modern world, where context can depend on just the flip of an on-off switch and a portable cassette player, it is hard to imagine the old days when all music came from face-to-face performance. Our great-grandparents had to sing or play, overhear music, or ask for it from someone near; they could not produce it on demand from the disembodied voice of a radio, television set, record player, tape recorder, or computer. How attentively

Jeff Todd Titon

Ill. 1–1. *Gospel singers at a pentecostal revival in the Southeastern United States. Guitars, banjos, and camp-meeting songs that would be out of place in some U.S. churches are appropriate in this context.*

you would have listened to a singer or a band a hundred years ago if you thought that this might be the only time in your life you would hear that music!

D. History of Music

Why is music so different among the world's peoples? What happens to music over time and space? Does it stay the same or change, and why? What did the music of the past sound like? Should it be preserved? What will the music of the future be? Some cultures institutionalize the past in museums and the future in world's fairs; they support specialists who (like ourselves) earn their living by talking and writing about music. Other cultures pass along knowledge of music history mainly by word of mouth down through the generations. Recordings, films, and videotapes now allow us to keep and re-hear musical performances much more exactly than our ancestors could—but only if we want to. One ethnomusicologist was making tapes as he learned to sing Native American music. His teacher advised him to erase the tapes and re-use them, but he decided to preserve his lessons.

Questions about music history may be asked inside or outside a particular music-culture. Most music-cultures have "historians" or music authorities, formally trained or not, whose curiosity about music leads them to think and talk about music in their own culture, ask questions, and remember answers. In some music-cultures, authority goes along with being a good musician; in other music-cultures, one need not be a good musician to be a respected historian. Historians usually are curious about music outside their own cultures as well, and they often develop theories to account for musical differences.

Of course, these four categories of ideas about music that we have just discussed—music and the belief system, aesthetics, contexts, and history—overlap. In most music-cultures, "good" music is tied to "beautiful" music and takes place in the right context. We separate them for convenience.

The individuals in a music-culture sometimes differ in their ideas about music. Ragtime, jazz, and rock 'n' roll were revolutionary when they were introduced. They met (and still meet) opposition from some Americans. This opposition is based on aesthetics (the music is thought to be loud, awful noise) and contexts (the music's associated lifestyles are thought to involve narcotics, free love, radical politics, and so forth). When smaller divisions exist within a music-culture, we recognize music subcultures, worlds within worlds of music. In fact, most music-cultures can be divided into several subcultures, some opposed to each other; classical versus rock 'n' roll, for example, or (from an earlier era) sacred hymns versus dance music and drinking songs. Sometimes the subcultures overlap: the performance of a hymn in a Minnesota church may involve region (the upper Midwest), ethnicity (German), and religion (Lutheranism)—all bases for musical subcultures. What musical subcultures do you identify with most strongly? What do you dislike? Are your preferences based on contexts, aesthetics, or the belief system?

II. Social Organization of Music

Social organization refers to how a group of people divides, arranges, or ranks itself. The sum total of musical ideas and performances is unevenly divided among the people in any music-culture. Some perform often, others hardly at all. Some make music for a living, while others are paid little or nothing. Because of age and gender, children, women, men, and old people sing different songs and experience music differently. Racial, ethnic, and work groups also sing their own special songs, and each group may be assigned its own musical role. All of these matters have to do with the social organization of the music-culture, and they are based on the music-culture's ideas about music, as described in section I above. We may ask, "What is it like [in such-and-such music-culture] to experience music as a teenage girl, a young male urban professional, a rural grandmother of German ethnic heritage living on a farm?" In each of the following chapters we follow the biography or autobiography of a musician partly because we are interested in how different individuals experience music and what part it plays in their lives.

Sometimes the division of musical behavior resembles the social divisions within the group and reinforces the usual activities of the culture. For example, when African pygmies sing as a group, they weave in their parts to build a complex, well-integrated whole. Researcher Alan Lomax points out that cooperative performances like these symbolize the pygmy stress on cooperative coordination in other spheres of life, such as daily work (Lomax 1976:41. See Turnbull 1962 for a vivid description of pygmy life and music).

On the other hand, music sometimes goes against the broad cultural grain, especially at festival time, or at important moments in the life cycle (initiations, weddings, funerals, etc.) Then, as we will see in chapter 5, people on the cultural fringe become important when they play music for these occasions. In fact, many music-cultures assign a low social status to musicians, yet also acknowledge their power and sometimes even see magic in their work. The two most important features of music's social organization are status and role: the prestige of the music-makers, and the different roles assigned people in the music-culture. Many of the musical situations in this book depend on these basic aspects of social organization.

III. Repertories of Music

A repertory is a stock of ready performances, and a music-culture's repertory is what most of us think as the "music itself." It consists of six basic parts: style, genres, texts, composition, transmission, and movement.

A. Style

This includes everything related to the organization of musical sound itself: pitch elements (scale, mode, melody, harmony, tuning systems), time elements (rhythms, meter), timbre elements (voice quality, instrumental tone color), and sound intensity (loudness and softness). All depend on the music-culture's aesthetics.

Together, style and aesthetics create a recognizable sound that a group understands as its own. We will learn in chapter 3 that the Kasena, a people living in the African state of Ghana, prefer their own music to that of their neighbors the Frafra who live down the road. They say the Frafra "have only *one* way to play, whereas we have many." Yet to most Americans Kasena and Frafra music sound alike. Are they alike? Not if each group can distinguish its music. The outsider studying Kasena music knows he is getting somewhere when he, too, is able to recognize the differences between Kasena and Frafra music and put that difference into words—or music.

B. Genres

Genres are the named, standard units of the repertory, such as "song" and its various subdivisions (e.g., lullaby, Christmas carol, wedding song) or the many types of instrumental music and dances (jig, reel, waltz, etc.). Most music-cultures have a great many genres, but their terms do not always correspond to terms in other music-cultures. Among the Yoruba in the African state of Nigeria, for example, powerful kings, chiefs, and nobles retain praise singers to sing praises to them (Olajubu 1978:685). The praise songs are called *oriki*. Although we can approximate an English name to describe them (praise songs), no equivalent genre exists today in Europe or America.

C. Texts

The words to a song are known as its text. Any song with words is an intersection of two very different and profound human communication systems: language and music. A song with words is a temporary weld of these two systems, and for convenience we can look at each by itself. Every text has its own history; sometimes a single text has several different associated melodies. On the other hand, a single melody can suffice for several texts. In blues music, for example, texts and melodies lead independent lives, coupling as the singer desires. The song itself (language and music together) is a recognizable, emotionally powerful unit in its own right. Anyone who has been abroad and suddenly hears a familiar homeland song knows just how powerful this impact can be.

D. Composition

How does music enter the repertory of a music-culture? Is music composed individually or by a group? Is it fixed, varied within certain preset limits, or improvised spontaneously in performance? Improvisation fascinates most ethnomusicologists, and we are no exceptions; chapters 3, 4, and 6 consider improvisation in African, African-American, and South Indian music. Perhaps at some deep level we prize improvisation not just because of the skills involved but because we think it exemplifies human freedom. Composition is also bound up with social organization: Does the music-culture have a special class of composers, or can anyone compose music? Composition is related to ideas about music: some music-cultures divide music into songs composed by humans and songs "given" to humans from deities, animals, and other nonhuman composers.

E. Transmission

How is much learned and transmitted from one person to the next, from one generation to the next? Does the music-culture rely on formal instruction, as in South India (chapter 6)? Is there a system of musical notation? Does a body of music theory underlie the process of formal instruction? How much is learned informally, by imitation? Does music change over time? If so, why and how?

Some music-cultures transmit music through a master-apprentice relationship that lasts for a lifetime (chapter 6). The master becomes a parent, teaching values and ethics as well as music. In these situations music truly becomes "a way of life," and the apprentice is "devoted" to the music his master represents. In other music-cultures (chapter 4, for example), there is no formal instruction, and the aspiring musician must glean from watching and listening, usually over a period of years. In these circumstances it is helpful to grow up in a musical family. When a repertory is transmitted chiefly by example and imitation and performed from memory, we say the music exists "in oral tradition." Music in oral tradition shows greater variation over time and space than music that is tied to a definitive, written musical score.

F. Movement

A whole range of physical activity accompanies music. Playing a musical instrument, alone or in a group, involves physical activity in producing the sound, but it also produces culturally specified movement inseparable from the music itself. That is, music quite literally moves people (dance), and the movement is an essential part of the performance. How odd it would be for a rock band to perform without moving in response to their music, in ways that let the audience know they were feeling it, was demonstrated by some of the new-wave rock bands. Groups like Devo projected the image of automatons. In one way or another, music connects with movement in the repertory of every culture.

IV. Material Culture of Music

Material culture refers to the tangible, material "things"—physical objects that can be seen, held, felt, used—that a culture produces. Examining a culture's tools and technology can tell us about the group's history and way of life. Similarly, research into the material culture of music can help us to understand the music-culture. The most vivid body of "things" in it, of course, are musical instruments. We cannot hear for ourselves the actual sound of any musical performance before the 1870s when the phonograph was invented, so we rely on instruments for important information about music-cultures in the remote past and their development. Here we have two kinds of evidence: instruments preserved more or less intact, such as Sumerian harps over 4,500 years old, and instruments pictured in art. Through the study of instruments, as well as paintings, written documents, and other sources, we can explore the movement of music from the Near East to China over a thousand years ago, or we can outline the spread of Near Eastern influence to Europe that resulted in the development of most of the instruments in the symphony orchestra.

We ask questions of today's music-cultures: Who makes instruments and how are they distributed? What is the relation between instrument makers and musicians? How are this generation's musical taste and style, rather than those of the old generation, reflected in the instruments it plays? Sometimes musical instruments become patriotic symbols of the culture's musical heritage. Examples are the Highland bagpipe of Scotland or the rebuilt ancient Celtic instruments of the peoples of Brittany and Ireland.

Sheet music, too, is material culture. Scholars once defined folk music-cultures as those in which people learn and sing music by ear rather than from print, but research shows mutual influence among oral and written sources during the past few centuries in Europe, Britain, and America. Printed versions limit variety because they tend to standardize any song, yet paradoxically they stimulate people to create new and different songs. Bertrand Bronson observed that printed ballad texts tend to fix people's memory of the words, but fail to curb their interest in melodic variation (Bronson 1969:61–62). Also, the ability to read music notation has a far-reaching effect on musicians and, when it becomes widespread, on the music-culture as a whole.

One more important part of music's material culture should be singled out: the impact of the electronic media—radio, record player, tape recorder, compact disc, television, and videocassette, with interactive computers that themselves can be programmed to represent music-cultures, talk, and sing at our command. This is all part of the "information revolution," a twentieth-century phenomenon as important as the industrial revolution was in the nineteenth. These electronic media are not just limited to modern nations; they have affected music-cultures all over the globe.

WORLDS OF MUSIC

Music-cultures, especially today, are dynamic rather than static; they are constantly changing in response to inside and outside pressures. It would be wrong to think of a music-culture as something isolated and stable, impenetrable and uninfluenced by the outside world. A conglomeration of music-cultures is taking place all over the world, a fact that sometimes makes it difficult to isolate traditional styles of music; but it would be wrong to assume that preelectronic music cultures were changeless. Speaking of Eastern Europe seventy years ago, Zoltán Kodály noted, "Folk tradition is not to be thought of as one uniform homogeneous whole. It varies fundamentally according to age, social and material conditions, education, district, and gender. Around 1910 a sharp enough difference existed between the song repertories of the three main ages of life. The middle-aged and elderly people in the village not only did not sing the songs of the young people, but generally did not know them. Still less did the young people know the songs of the older generation" (Kodály 1960:20).

In other words, culture contact and musical change and interchange did not begin with electronic media. American Indian Christian hymns, for example, resulted from missionary work that began when Europeans first came to the American continent (see chapter 4). The media have accelerated the pace of change and have influenced its direction in favor of urban, industrial music-cultures. These have ready access to the media and their music tends to drive rural and tribal music underground or out completely.

But music is a fluid, dynamic element of culture, and it changes to suit the expressive and emotional desires of humankind, the most changeable of the animals. Like all of expressive culture, music is a peculiarly human adaptation to life on planet earth. Each music-culture is a particular adaptation to particular circumstances. Ideas about music, social organization, repertories, and music's material culture vary from one music-culture to the next, but it would be foolish to say that one music-culture was "better" than another. Why? Because such a judgment is based on criteria from inside a single music-culture. To call another music-culture's music "primitive" imposes one's own standards on a group that does not recognize them. Such ethnocentrism has no place in the study of world music.

In the chapters that follow we explore several worlds, and worlds within worlds, of music. Although each world may seem strange at first, all are organized, purposeful, and coherent. Each world can be regarded as an ecological system, with the forces that combine to make up the music-culture (ideas, social organization, repertories, movement) in a dynamic equilibrium. A change in any part of the ecosystem affects the whole of it. In our study of world music we sometimes isolate parts of a music-culture and give the impression that this is the way they are—or that they have always been like this, and will continue to be so. At best, isolating parts of a music-culture for study is an oversimplification; at worst, an untruth. But given the limits of courses and textbooks, it is our only recourse.

REFERENCES CITED

Blacking, John
>   1973   *How Musical Is Man?* Seattle: Univ. of Washington Press.

Bronson, Bertrand
>   1969   "The Interdependence of Ballad Tunes and Texts," in *The Ballad as Song.* Berkeley: Univ. of California Press.

Feld, Steven
>   1990   *Sound and Sentiment: Birds, Weeping, Poetics and Song in Kaluili Expression.* 2nd ed. Philadelphia: Univ. of Pennsylvania Press.

Kodály, Zoltán
>   1960   *Folk Music of Hungary.* London: Barrie and Rockliff.

Lomax, Alan
>   1976   *Cantometrics: A Method in Musical Anthropology.* Berkeley: Univ. of California Extension Media Center.

Merriam, Alan P.
>   1964   *The Anthropology of Music.* Evanston, Ill.: Northwestern Univ. Press.

Olajubu, Chief Oludare
>   1978   "Yoruba Verbal Artists and Their Work." *Journal of American Folklore* 91:675–90.

Sachs, Nahoma
>   1975   "Music and Meaning: Musical Symbolism in a Macedonian Village." Ph.D. diss., Princeton Univ.

Titon, Jeff Todd
>   1988   *Powerhouse for God: Speech, Chant, and Song in an Appalachian Baptist Church.* Austin: Univ of Texas Press.

Turnbull, Colin
>   1962   *The Forest People.* New York: Clarion Books.

ADDITIONAL READING

Hamm, Charles, Bruno Nettl and Ronald Byrnside
  1975 *Contemporary Music and Music Cultures.* Englewood Cliffs, N. J.: Prentice-Hall.
Herndon, Marcia, and Norma McLeod
  1981 *Music as Culture.* 2nd ed. Darby, Pa.: Norwood Editions.
Hood, Mantle
  1982 *The Ethnomusicologist.* 2nd ed. Kent, Ohio: Kent State Univ. Press.
Ives, Edward D.
  1978 *Joe Scott: The Woodsman-Songmaker.* Urbana: Univ. of Illinois Press.
Keil, Charles
  1979 *Tiv Song: The Sociology of Art in a Classless Society.* Chicago: Univ. of Chicago Press.
Kingsbury, Henry
  1988 *Music, Talent, and Performance.* Philadelphia: Temple Univ. Press.
Lomax, Alan
  1968 *Folk Song Style and Culture.* Washington, D.C.: American Association for the Advancement of Science.
May, Elizabeth, ed.
  1981 *Musics of Many Cultures.* Berkeley: Univ. of California Press.
McAllester, David P.
  1949 *Peyote Music.* New York: Viking Fund Publications in Anthropology. no. 13.
———, ed.
  1971 *Readings in Ethnomusicology.* New York: Johnson Reprint Corp.
Merriam, Alan
  1967 *Ethnomusicology of the Flathead Indians.* Chicago: Aldine.
Nettl, Bruno
  1964 *Theory and Method in Ethnomusicology.* New York: Free Press.
———.
  1983 *The Study of Ethnomusicology: Twenty-Nine Issues and Concepts.* Urbana: Univ. of Illinois Press.
Pantaleoni, Hewitt
  1985 *On the Nature of Music.* Oneonta, N.Y.: Welkin Books.
Reck, David
  1977 *Music of the Whole Earth.* New York: Scribner's.
Seeger, Charles
  1977 *Studies in Musicology 1935–1975.* Berkeley: Univ. of California Press.
Slobin, Mark
  1976 *Music in the Culture of Northern Afghanistan.* Tucson: Univ. of Arizona Press.

T W O

◆ ◆ ◆

North America/ Native America

DAVID P. McALLESTER

American Indian music is unfamiliar to most non-Indian Americans.* Accordingly, the plan of this chapter is to present, first, a bit of overall perspective by contrasting three of the many different Indian musical styles. Second, we will look in detail at some of the many different kinds of music being performed here today in just one tribe, the Navajos. Here the musical life of the people will be related to their traditional culture and their present history. Only when we see music in its cultural setting can we begin to understand it.

THREE DIFFERENT STYLES

Sioux Grass Dance

The way to begin with music is to participate, either by listening or, better still, by performing. Let us start with the most "Indian" sound the American imagination can conceive of, a Sioux War Dance (ill. 2–1). Nowadays the Indians usually call it a Grass Dance, from the braids of grass the dancing warriors used to wear at their waists to symbolize slain enemies. It is also called the Omaha Dance after the Omaha Indians of the Western Plains who originated it.

Listen for a moment to the first recording (recorded selection 1; ex. 2–1) on the cassettes or CDs that accompany this book. When European scholars first heard this kind of sound on wax cylinder field recordings brought back to Berlin in the early 1900s they exclaimed, "Now at last we hear the music of the true savages!" For four hundred years European social philosophers had thought of American Indians as noble wild men unspoiled by civilization, and here was music that fitted the image.

*I am grateful to vigilant students for several corrections and improvements in this chapter; I would especially like to thank John Kelsey and Patrick Hutchinson. Mr. Hutchinson made a careful study of "Folsom Prison Blues," noting interesting textual and rhythmic elisions and complications not found in the original Johnny Cash recording. These are similar to the alterations noted by Robert Witmer in popular music performed by Blood Indians in Canada (1973:79–83).

Douglas Fulton. Courtesy of Gertrude Kurath

Ill. 2–1. *War dancers at a Michigan powwow.*

Nothing known to Europeans sounded like this piercing falsetto, swooping down for more than an octave in a "tumbling strain" that seems to come straight from the emotions. The pulsating voices with their sharp emphases, the driving drumbeat that seems to have its own separate meter, the heavy portamentos (slides) at the ends of phrases—what could better portray the warlike horsemen of the limitless American Plains? Another feature that astonished Europeans was the use of vocables (nonlexical or "meaningless" syllables) for the entire text of the song, as in the example we are listening to. Curt Sachs found this another reason for labeling this music *pathogenic* (arising from the emotions), as contrasted with *logogenic* music, in which meaningful words are the basis of the song (Sachs 1962:51–58). Sachs theorized that pathogenic music was what one would find in the early stages of social evolution. Perhaps his own ancestors sang like this when they were hunting wild horses across the plains of Europe and had not yet discovered agriculture.

Another supposed proof that American Indians belonged to an early stage of musical evolution was the surprising limitation in kinds of musical instruments they used. From north of Mexico to the Arctic the music was almost entirely vocal and the instruments were chiefly rattles and drums used only to accompany the voice. It should be pointed out, however, that the varieties of rattles and drums invented by North American Indians are legion. There are rattles made from gourds, tree bark, carved wood, deer hoofs, turtle shells, spider nests, and, recently, tin cans, just to name a few. There are frame drums and barrel drums of many sizes and shapes, and the water drum (described in detail on pp. 56–57) with its wet membrane is unique in the world. There are a few flutes and flageolets, and one-stringed fiddles played without vocal accompaniment, but these are rare. Instrumental ensembles in any way resembling an orchestra are unknown in traditional North American Indian music.

In Central and South America, on the other hand, the high native civilizations did have orchestras before the Europeans came to the Western Hemisphere. They readily added European instruments to their ensembles and blended their music with new ideas from Portugal and Spain. But only in the last thirty or forty years has this mingling of musics begun to happen on any large scale in native North American music. The vast majority of traditional songs are still accompanied only by the drum or rattle or sometimes both together.

To go back to evolutionary ideas for a moment, few scholars today find that a notion of "delayed evolution" explains the so-called simpler cultures of the world. In fact, they turn out to be not simple at all. A language, though it may never have been written down, may contain the most complex grammatical structures known to linguists. Folk music with no harmonies may contain melodic, modal, and rhythmic sophistication unattainable in harmonic music.

The chief joy of music comes from participating in it. Listen again to the Sioux Grass Dance song and see if you can sing along with it. You may think it is impossible, especially if you are a man and have never tried to sing in falsetto voice before. Until you get your courage up you might find it easier to try singing the song an octave lower than the Sioux singers. The transcription* (example 2–1) will help you with the words and melody.

If you cannot read notes, think of the transcription as a kind of graph tracing the line of the melody. Even with no musical training you can see patterns of movement from high to low and back up again. I have labeled the sections of the song that sound alike with the same letter of the alphabet to help the reader see where similar musical ideas are repeated. The overall structure of phrases in this song may be written as shown in figure 2–1.

The song starts with an A phrase, sung by a leader, but before he can finish it the other male singers break in with the same phrase repeated, and he joins them to sing it all the way through. I have indicated the first, uncompleted

---

*All musical transcriptions in this chapter are by David P. McAllester.

Ex. 2–1. *Sioux Grass Dance song. With the permission of Ray Boley.*

½A A B A₈ B A₈
½A A B A₈ B A₈
½A A B A₈ B A₈   B A₈

Fig. 2-1. *Phrase structure, Sioux Grass Dance song.*

phrases as ½A. Most of the melodic movement takes place in the B phrase. Here is where the melody drops a full octave below the tonal center established in the A phrase. In fact, the second half of B is almost an exact repeat of A an octave lower. I have indicated this pattern in example 2–1 by writing A with a lowered 8 (A₈) at the point where this transposed rendition begins. The song ends with a full repeat of A on the lower octave, labeled A₈. After this pattern has been sung through three times there is a pause and then B and A₈ are repeated one last time to end the song. Indian singers often call that last brief section the "tail" of the song, which is just what the European musical term *coda* means.

This song may be easy to understand in its overall structure, but it is not easy to sing. It goes fast, and it does not have a regular meter. Most of it is in triple, or three-beat, patterns, but every now and then the singers introduce a four-beat pattern. I have drawn brackets ⌐¬ over those spots so that the reader-listener-performer can see where they are. Notice that the melody makes the same downward dip at each of those spots where the meter breaks into four. Another difficulty in performing this song is that the song meter does not seem to coincide with that of the drum. It is very difficult to see how they relate to each other; to give some idea of the difference, I have written the approximate metronome reading of each. The best way to sing this is to "hang loose" and not try to count it out mechanically. Concentrate on the excitement that has made this kind of music the most popular native American style all over the country wherever there are Indian fairs, rodeos, and powwows. Like the Plains Indians' eagle-feather warbonnet and their stately, beautifully decorated tipis, the war dance is a symbol for "Indian." Though Indian singing styles differ from region to region, many non-Plains Indians, especially young people, have learned this style so well that they have been able to compete with Plains singers. There are non-Indians, also, who have risen to the challenge of this music and have won prizes for their singing, costumes, and dancing in powwow competitions. In singing this song, pay particular attention to the ornamentation: the sharp emphases, the pulsations, the glides. These are an important part of the special art of Plains singing.

The dancing that goes with this song style is based on a toe-heel movement first on one foot and and then on the other. An elaboration is shown below:

Foot:	left	right	right	left	left	right
Movement:	step toe-heel,	change toe-heel,	change toe-heel, etc.			

Each male dancer creates many personal variations and makes a solo display of his virtuosity. His body dips and bends but his head is very erect, sometimes nodding in time to the drumbeat and turning this way and that. His eyes are fixed on space and the expression is rapt and remote. Often he carries a decorated stick or other object in one hand, and during the dance he may manipulate it with all the subtlety a Japanese dancer uses with a fan. Every dancer must stop precisely on the last beat at the rhythmic break before the "tail." Then the dancing resumes with all its intensity for the last few moments and must stop exactly on the last beat of the song. One extra step disqualifies a dancer from the competition.

The movement and sound of the elaborate costume is an essential part of the Grass Dance and its music. Bells are often tied around the legs; today they are sleigh bells, often quite large, mounted on a leather strap. These resound with every step. Ribbons sway, feathers and porcupine-hair roaches quiver, beads and small mirrors gleam and flash. The costume is as elaborately ornamented as is the vocal style.

The women participate in the dance by moving around the periphery of the dance area using a subdued version of the dance step, or just walking. They wear shawls with very long fringes that sway in time to their movement. The women's voices enter the song an octave higher than the men's often on the B phrase when it starts down. In the song we are hearing they do not sing as a group until the second half of the A_8 phrase.

Zuni Lullaby

The next song (recorded selection 2, ex. 2–2) is chosen to provide a contrast with Plains singing and demonstrate that there is no single "Indian" musical style. It is a lullaby recorded in 1950 by an old grandmother, Lanaiditsa, on the Zuni Reservation in western New Mexico (ill. 2–2). You will have little difficulty

Ex. 2–2. Zuni lullaby. Lanaiditsa, Zuni, 1950.

Ill. 2–2. *Zuni mother and child, showing costume and hair style of the early twentieth century. Neg. No. 121630, photo: Coles/Bierwert. Courtesy Department of Library Services, American Museum of Natural History.*

Hm atseki	*my boy*
okshits'ana	*cottontail little*
pokets'ana	*jackrabbit little*
kochits'ana	*rat little*

1. *My boy, little cottontail,*
   Little jackrabbit, little jackrabbit;
2. *My boy, little cottontail,*
   Little rat, little boy, little boy;
3. *My boy, little jackrabbit,*
   Little cottontail, little cottontail;
4. *My boy, little jackrabbit,*
   Little cottontail, little rat, little rat.
5. *My boy, little jackrabbit,*
   Little cottontail, little rat, little rat (3 times)

Fig. 2–2. *Lyrics, Zuni lullaby.*

in following her and joining in with the song. The meter is rather free and the whole gentle song is on only two notes.

In this case the text is in translatable words instead of vocables (fig. 2–2), and you can see that the singer's feeling for the child is expressed in the repetition of diminutives: "Little boy, little cottontail, little jackrabbit, little rat." The words seem to be interchangeable in the first half of the song but then settle into the same sequence in the last three verses.

Repetition is a prominent feature in most Indian music in the United States, in the use of vocables, in the use of lexical texts where they occur, and in the melodic patterns. This is not because Indians are unable to create texts and music with a "fuller" content, in our sense, but because their aesthetic sense delights in repetitions and slight variations in these repetitions, variations that are sometimes too subtle for the ears of outsiders to detect (fig. 2–3). In Lanai-ditsa's song each textual phrase can be used with either musical phrase except for "my boy" which is always on an "A." She settles on "my little rat" for the ending of verse 4 and the three repeats of verse 5, which suggests that she finds it the most endearing of the diminutives.

The love of repetition that we have just been studying is present in Indian folk tales and other narratives and is very much a part of the way the Navajo singer, or medicine man, Frank Mitchell, tells the story of his life (see pp. 46–54).

Fig. 2–3. *Phrase structure, Zuni lullaby.*

```
        A  A   B  B
   A  A  A   B  B
      A  A   B  B
      A  A   B  B  B
   A  A  A   B  B  (three times)
```

Ex. 2–3. *Iroquois Quiver Dance song (note difference between the lyrics in fig. 2–4, as they would be spoken, and those here, as they appear in the song). With the permission of William N. Fenton.*

Iroquois Quiver Dance

Now let us listen to still another North American Indian musical style from across the country in the Eastern Woodlands. The next example on the cassette is an Iroquois Quiver Dance (recorded selection 3, ex. 2–3) or Warrior's Stomp Dance song. This was recorded in 1941 by Joshua Buck and Simeon Gibson at the Six Nations Reserve in Ohsweken, Ontario, but the song was made up years before that by Twenty Jacobs of Quaker Bridge, on the Allegheny Reservation in western New York.

The first thing striking the ear in example 2–3 is the "call and response" form. One singer utters a phrase of lexical text (the "call") and the other answers him with a vocable pattern: "yowe hi ye ye!" This alternation continues through the song. It is a pattern quite common in the Eastern Woodlands but rare elsewhere in North American traditional Indian singing. (Call-and-response singing can be heard in many world music cultures, as we shall see.) William Fenton's translation of the text (fig. 2–4) shows the jocular content found in these Stomp Dance songs.

'Tga na hóna' 'Ohswégen	yowe hi ye ye!
Filled is Ohsweken	
Dedjo dinyaakon' on	yowe hi ye ye!
With divorced women	
Wegah hano hiiyo	yowe hi ye ye!
With good looking ones	
We hoonon hiiyo	yowe hi ye ye!
Fine looking ones!	

Fig. 2–4. *Lyrics, Iroquois Quiver Dance song. With the permission of William N. Fenton.*

We hear voices in this Iroquois song that are relatively relaxed compared to the Plains singing. A characteristic Iroquois feature in singing style is the pulsations of the voice at the ends of phrases, indicated in the transcriptions by ♩♪ and ♩ ♩ . (In Plains singing, by contrast, pulsations occur all through the song.)

The Stomp Dance is a favorite recreational dance among Woodland Indians all through the eastern United States and Canada. Among the Iroquois it usually takes place in the longhouse, a meeting house with a stove at each end of the hall and benches along the sides. The participants form a line behind the leader. They imitate his "short jog step" (Fenton 1942:31) and any other turns and gyrations he may invent as they sing the responses to his calls. More and more of the audience joins the dance until the line is winding exuberantly all over the longhouse floor. Woodland tribes other than the Iroquois do not have longhouses and often do the Stomp Dance out-of-doors. They usually accompany their singers with a cowhorn rattle.

Making a "Cowhorn" Rattle

The adventure of music involves not only performance but also making the instruments to perform with. Following are steps for making a serviceable imitation of a cowhorn rattle (fig. 2–5). A section of cow's horn is not easy for most of us to obtain; a small fruit juice can, open at one end, will make a good substitute.

1. Any small metal can two or three inches tall and two to two-and-one-half inches in diameter will do. Make a plug for the open end of the can out of a disc of soft wood slightly wider than the diameter of the can. With a sharp knife or a file, bevel down one edge of the disc just enough so that it can be tightly wedged into the can.

2. Find a stick of hard wood, such as a straight tree branch about three-fourths of an inch in diameter; cut a one-foot length. A piece of birch dowel will do. Whittle away one end of the stick to make a tapering spindle about half an inch longer than the height of the can. At the base of the spindle leave a shelf as shown in the drawing.

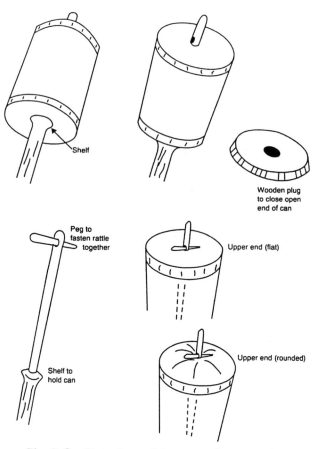

Fig. 2–5. *Steps in making a cowhorn rattle.*

3. Drill a hole in the wooden plug so that it will fit snugly over the spindle and seat itself, beveled side up, on the shelf. Punch a smaller hole in the bottom of the can and slide it, open end down, over the spindle until the rim of the can fits over the beveled edge of the plug. The end of the spindle should project a half-inch beyond the bottom of the can. Mark the spindle at the point where it emerges from the hole in the can. The mark should be as close to the bottom of the can as possible.

4. Remove the can and plug and fasten the plug in the open end of the can with furniture tacks with shiny brass heads. Drop fifteen or twenty BB shot or small pebbles into the hole in the bottom of the can to produce the rattling sound.

5. Drill a small hole in the spindle at the marked place and obtain a nail or peg that will fit tightly in the hole and project on both sides of the spindle. Fit the can back into place, plug-end down, and wedge the nail or peg through the hole in the spindle. This should hold the can firmly, supported by the shelf at the bottom end.

Extra Niceties

You could remove both ends of the can and have a wooden plug in each end. This would give you two rows of ornamental tacks, holding in the plugs. If you are good at woodworking you could turn the plug for the upper end on a lathe so that it is rounded, instead of being merely flat.

To make the can look like a cowhorn you could paint it dark brown with cream-colored streaks. See illustration 2–3 for how a cowhorn looks.

Notice in the illustration the different ways the handle can be carved to break the monotony of a straight stick. You can express your own creativity in how you do it.

How to Play the Rattle

This kind of rattle may be struck against the user's thigh or palm to produce a sharp impact. At the beginning of a song a tremolo effect is often produced by rapidly shaking the rattle, held high in the air.

MUSIC OF THE NAVAJO INDIANS

After this brief survey of three Native American musical styles, let us now take a deeper look into the musical life of still another Indian group, the Navajos of the Southwestern desert. By studying the relation of their music to their culture in some detail we can see how many different kinds of music there are in even one Indian community. When we consider the cultural context of the music we will see how closely music is integrated with Indian life. The autobiographical sketch of Frank Mitchell is included so as to give the reader a firsthand account, by a professional Navajo singer, of how he learned his music and what it meant in his life.

Ill. 2–3. *Iroquois cowhorn rattles, showing a variety of shapes and handles.*

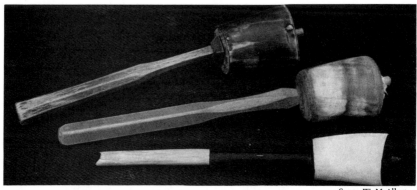

Susan W. McAllester

A Yeibichai Song
from the Nightway Ceremony

To begin again with sound, let us go first to one of the most exciting kinds of Navajo music, their Yeibichai songs. "Yei-bi-chai" (gods-their-grandfathers) refers to the grandfathers of the gods who come to dance at one of the major ceremonials, known as Nightway. The masked dancers who impersonate the gods bring supernatural power and blessing to help cure a sick person. Listen to recorded selection 4, example 2–4.

With its shouts, ornamentations, and falsetto voices, this song makes one think of the Plains Indians. Also similar to the Plains style is the tense energy of the singing. But the long introduction (phrases X, Y, and Z), sung almost entirely on the base note (the tonic) of the song, is strikingly different from the Indian songs we have heard before. Then the song leaps *up* an octave. In the first melodic phrase, A, the song comes swooping briskly down to the tonic again. The same descent is repeated (the second A) and then another acrobatic plunge takes place on B after two "false starts" that are very close to the first half of A. They could be called ½A and ½A. The song hovers on the tonic briefly (V and W) and then an interesting variation occurs—the second half of A is sung twice: (A½ + A½) followed by the *first,* also repeated (½A + ½A). The Navajos are noted for their bold experiments in artistic form. This is true in their silversmithing, their weaving, and their sand painting—here is an example from their music, too. The interweaving of motifs can be seen in the diagram of phrase patterns shown in figure 2–6.

It is helpful to look at an outline like the one below to see in visual representation the play of musical ideas, but it is far better to hear it, and singing is the best way of hearing. Listen again, now that you know the pattern of this complex and intriguing song, and try to sing it yourself while you are listening to Sandoval Begay and his group of Yeibichai singers. The text is entirely in vocables, but this song gives us a good illustration of how far from "meaningless" vocables can be. From the first yells it is clear to almost any Navajo that this is a Yeibichai song. The vocables serve to identify the kind of song. Moreover, in this song there is the identifying call of the gods themselves.

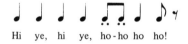

Hi ye, hi ye, ho - ho ho ho!

Though there are hundreds of different Yeibichai songs, they always contain this call of the Yei.

Yeibichai singers are organized in teams, often made up of men from one particular region or another. They create new songs or sing old favorites, each team singing a number of songs before the nightlong singing and dancing are over. The teams prepare costumes and masks and practice a dance of the gods that proceeds in two parallel lines with reel-like figures. They also have a clown who follows the dancers and makes everyone laugh with his antics: getting lost,

*Repeats from A, twice. High yell replaces "hiye" on first repeat; second repeat ends at "Fine."

Ex. 2–4. *Navajo Yeibichai song. With the permission of Willard Rhodes.*

```
X  Y  Z  A   A   ½A   ½A   B  V  W
         A½ A½ ½A    ½A   B  V
   Y' Z
   Y½    A   A   ½A   ½A   B  V  W
         A½ A½ ½A    ½A   B  V
   Y' Z
   Y½    A   A   ½A   ½A   B  V  W
         A½ A½ ½A    ½A   B  V
   Y' Z.
```

Fig. 2–6. Phrase structure, Navajo Yeibichai song.

bumbling into the audience, imitating the other dancers. The teams compete and the best combination of costumes, clowns, singing, and dancing receives a gift from the family giving the ceremony. The representation of the presence of the gods at the Nightway brings god-power to the ceremony and helps the sick person get well (see ill. 2–4).

This dance takes place on the last night of a nine-night ritual that includes such ceremonial practices as purification by sweating and vomiting, making prayer offerings for deities whose presence is invoked, and sand-painting rituals in which the one-sung-over sits on elaborate designs in colored sands and other dry pigments. The designs depict the deities; contact with these figures identifies the one-sung-over with the forces of nature they represent and provides their protective power. In the course of the ceremony hundreds of people may attend as spectators whose presence lends their support to the reenactment of the myth upon which the ceremony is based. The one-sung-over takes the role of the mythic hero and the songs, sand paintings, prayers and other ritual acts recount the story of how this protagonist's trials and adventures brought the Nightway ceremony from the supernatural world for the use of humankind. Besides the Yeibichai songs there are hundreds of chanted songs with full, elaborate texts (see pp. 43–46 below).

Such a ritual drama as Nightway is as complex as a production of a Wagnerian opera. The organization and performance of the whole event is directed by the singer or ceremonial practitioner who must memorize every detail. Such men and women are among the intellectual leaders of the Navajo communities. The life story on pp. 46–54 is a rare glimpse into the mind of such a person.

Most readers find the Yeibichai song difficult to learn. The shifts in emphasis, the many variations, and the difficult vocal style demand hours of training before one can do it well. But there are many other kinds of Navajo music. Let us now listen to another song (recorded selection 5) from the largest—200 thousand people—and one of the most progressive Indian tribes in the United States.

Folsom Prison Blues

Of course you can join in this song right away. If you are not familiar with country-and-western music, this is "Folsom Prison Blues," originally by Johnny

Neg. no. 2A 3634. Courtesy American Museum of Natural History (Photo: Boltin)

Ill. 2–4. *Ceremonial practitioner making a sandpainting of a Lightning Deity in flint armor.*

Cash. It is played and sung by the Fenders, an all-Navajo country band from Thoreau, New Mexico (ill. 2–5). This song is here to make sure the reader knows that country music is a great favorite with Indian people, especially in the West, just as it is with a vast part of the general American public. There are some thirty or more country-and-western bands on the Navajo reservation alone. Several of them, like the Fenders, the Sundowners, and the Undecided Takers, have issued records that are bought by thousands of Indians. Equally popular are non-Indian country singers such as Tanya Tucker and Don Williams. The cowboy image is appealing to most westerners, including many Indians, who identify with the open life and the excitement of the roundup and the rodeo. The Fenders' liner notes begin:

> The five Fenders are genuine cowboys . . . as much at home on the back of a bucking rodeo bronc as behind the wild guitar at a good old rodeo

Ill. 2–5. *Album cover of The Fenders, an early Navajo country and western group.*

dance. These boys believe that to be a No. 1, all-around cowboy, you must be able to play the guitar and sing just as well as you ride, rope and bull-dog.

The Navajo Way of Life

Who are these Navajos we are listening to, and where and how do they live? As mentioned before, they are our largest Indian tribe. Descended from Althabascan-speaking nomadic hunters who came into the Southwest as recently as six or seven hundred years ago, they now live in scattered communities ranging from extended family groups to small towns on a reservation of some 25 thousand square miles (larger than West Virginia) spread over parts of New Mexico, Arizona, and Utah (see fig. 2–7). The total census of the Navajos is uncertain, since several thousand of them live off the reservation in such cities as Chicago, Los Angeles, and San Diego. The reason for their move is largely economic. Their population has outgrown the support afforded by the reservation.

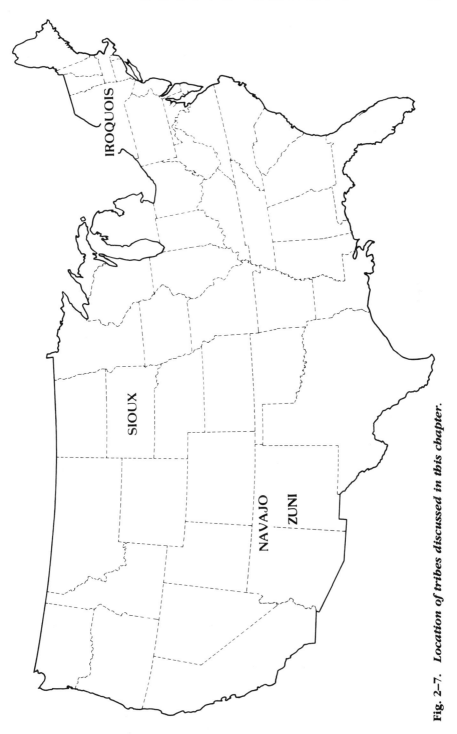

Fig. 2–7. *Location of tribes discussed in this chapter.*

On the reservation the Navajos' livelihood is based to a small but culturally significant degree on farming, raising sheep and other stock, weaving, and silversmithing (see ill. 2–6). The major part of their $90 million annual income comes from coal, uranium, oil, natural gas, and lumber. Much of their educational and health funds derive from the Department of the Interior, some of it in fulfillment of the 1868 treaty that marked the end of hostilities between the Navajos and the United States Army. Personal incomes range from the comfortable salaries of tribal administrative and service jobs to the precarious subsistence of marginal farmers. Many Navajos are supported on various kinds of tribal or governmental relief.

Though much of traditional Navajo culture remains intact, the People (Dinéh), as the Navajos call themselves, also welcome new ideas and change. Their scholarship funds enable hundreds of young people to attend colleges and universities around the country, including their own Navajo Community College on the reservation. A battery of attorneys and a Natural Resources Committee keep watch on the mining leases and lumber operations that produce most of their income. They also operate motels, restaurants, banks, and shopping centers, and they encourage small industries to establish themselves on the reservation. Some Navajos jet to administrative and development conferences in Washington, D.C.; others speak no English and herd sheep on horseback or on foot miles from the nearest paved road.

The men dress in western style and some of the women still wear skirts and

Ill. 2–6.   *Navajos still travel on horseback in many parts of the reservation.*

Neg. no. 335258. Courtesy American Museum of Natural History (Photo: M. Raney)

blouses copied from the dresses worn by United States Army officers' wives in the 1860s, during the imprisonment of the Navajos at Fort Sumner, New Mexico. The skirts have shortened in recent years and Navajo taste has always demanded the addition of buttons, rings, bracelets, necklaces, and heavy belts of silver set with turquoise. The men wear this jewelry, too, sometimes with the added adornment of silver hatbands. Young people, male and female, are more and more seen in the blue jean attire of other young people anywhere in the country. In country communities men and women sometimes wear bright wool blankets from the Pendleton mills in Oregon over their other clothes as an overcoat in cold weather. The garment is now so identified with traditional Navajo costume that it is regularly worn by the protagonist in ceremonials. The Navajos' own famous rugs are woven for cash income; most of them go to the local store, sometimes still called a trading post, to pay for food and other supplies. Some of these rugs are so finely woven and designed that they have brought $20,000 and more in the world market for fine arts (see ill. 2–7).

Navajo houses range from the modern stucco ranch houses and trailer homes of tribal officials, administrative staff, and school personnel to smaller one-room houses of every description. Many of the old-style circular log hogans (Navajo *hooghan,* place-home) can still be seen. Navajo ceremony requires a circular floor plan, and many adaptations of this well-loved and symbolically important shape are designed into new kinds of structures. The Tribal Council Building in Window Rock, Arizona, is a round sandstone structure with Indian murals on the walls and is large enough to accommodate 74 council members from all parts of the reservation. The Cultural Center at the Navajo Community College at Tsaile, Arizona, is six stories of concrete, steel, and glass, but it is octagonal, with a domed roof. Inside, at the heart of the building, is a replica of a traditional hogan with a dirt floor and a smoke hole that goes up four stories through a shaft to the open sky. It is there as a religious symbol and a meditation room. School buildings, chapter houses, information centers, and arts and crafts outlets exhibit other variations in size and design on the circular shape, which is symbolic of the shape of the earth itself, and on the domed roof, which is symbolic of both mountaintops and the vault of the sky.

Traditional Popular Music

With the sketch given above of Navajo life as a background, let us return to their music. The most popular musics on the reservation now are probably rock 'n' roll, country and western, and country gospel. Together they constitute the predominant music heard on the Navajo broadcasts made by radio stations in Gallup, Farmington, Holbrook, and other cities surrounding the reservation; they are heard at teenage dances at schools, civic centers, and rodeos. Though the Navajo standard of living is comparatively low for the United States, the People are nevertheless enough of a buying public so that much advertising is directed toward them in the Navajo language. The music they are offered is based on requests that come by mail to the radio stations from the reservation.

Neg. no. 14471. Courtesy American Museum of Natural History (Photo: P. E. Goddard)

Ill. 2–7. *Hand-weaving is a source of income to many Navajo women. This scene, from the 1920s, is still common today.*

Besides rock 'n' roll and country music, many radio requests are for Squaw Dance songs from the public part of the Enemyway ceremonial. The Circle Dance and other dance songs, and the Sway songs and Gift songs of Enemyway are all known, collectively, as "Squaw Dance songs." These are the hit tunes of traditional Navajo life. Compared to the Yeibichai songs, Squaw Dance songs are easy to sing, but still to an outsider they can contain some surprises. Many of these are sung entirely on vocables, but the Circle Dance song "Shizhané" (recorded selection 6; ex. 2–5) contains words that can be translated as well. If you play this song a few times and follow the words and music provided here, you should be able to get into the swing of this lively melody. Since you do not have to worry about producing the high falsetto sounds of the Yeibichai song, you can concentrate on other fine points.

Pay attention to the sharp little emphases marked with >. See if you can reproduce the nasal tone the Navajos like in their singing. Every phrase ends with

♪ ⁷ ♩. ♩.

he,   nai ya

This is characteristic of Circle Dance songs, as is the triple meter:

etc. (McAllester 1954:52). Notice how the A phrases introduce the melodic elements that are more fully developed in B and then even more so in C. The whole structure, too long to include in full on the cassette, is given in figure 2–8.

The translatable portion of the text, in the C phrases, is like a nugget in the middle of the song, framed by a vocable chorus before and after it. This is a favorite principle of design in other Navajo arts as well as music. It is the dynamic symmetry discussed by Witherspoon (1977:170–174) and illustrated in weaving and silver jewelry designs. The brief, humorous text (figs. 2–9, 2–10) is, like many another in Navajo song, intended to make the girls laugh and pay attention to the singers. Though the dance is part of a sacred ceremony it is also a courtship situation and a social dance as well.

It helps in the enjoyment of the song to linger for a moment on the choices of expression that make the words so witty. The song begins with fatuous self-congratulation. But then we learn both from the form "yah" after "house" and from the neuter static form of sizí, "she who is standing," that the girl is really propped against the house. The suggestion is that she has had too much to drink and therefore is unable to be actively searching for (running after) the singer at all, even though he claims she is. The irony of the situation is combined with a jesting implication that women drink too much and chase after young men. Since it is actually the men who do most of the drinking and chasing after the opposite sex, the song is all the funnier. Kiyah sizíní also carries the meaning, "prostitute." As in all clever poetry, the zest is in the subtle shades of meaning.

Fig. 2–8. *Phrase structure, "Shizhané."*

X   A A B B

     A A B B C C

     A A B B

The text as it is sung:
Shizhane'e, shizhane'e, kiya sizini shika nootaał,
'aweya he nai ya.

Free translation: I'm in luck, I'm in luck!
She's leaning up against the store front,
Looking everywhere for me!

As the Navajo is spoken, with literal translation:

Shizané	me-good luck
kíyah	house-under/against
sizíní	standing-the one who
shíká	me-for/after (as in running after one)
nóotááł	searching for (3rd person)

Fig. 2–9. *Lyrics, "Shizhané." With the permission of Albert Sandoval Jr. and Ray Winnie.*

The Enemyway Ceremony

Religion is one of the keys to culture. We will understand the Navajos better if we take a closer look at the Enemyway ceremony in which "Shizhané" is used. In Navajo life this is one of the most frequently performed rites in their traditional religion. Like Nightway, discussed above, it is a curing ritual. In this case the sickness is brought on by the ghosts of outsiders who have died. Enemyway is often performed for a returned Navajo member of the United States Armed Forces, or others who have been away from home among strangers for a long time. Often a Navajo who has been in a hospital and returns home cured, in our sense, has an Enemyway performed because of the inevitable exposure to the spirits of the many non-Navajos who have died in such a place (see ill. 2–8).

The ceremony involves two groups of participants, the "home camp," and the "stick receiver's camp." The latter participants represent the enemy and carry a stick decorated with symbols of the warrior deity, Enemy Slayer, and of his mother, Changing Woman, who is the principal Navajo deity. The decorated stick is brought from the home camp along with gifts of many yards of brightly colored yarn. The first night of the ceremony consists of singing and dancing at

Fig. 2–10. *Note on pronunciation in Navajo.*

The ' indicates a glottal stop, as in "oh-oh!" ('o-'o).

ł   is like the Welsh ll in Flloyd, unvoiced with the breath coming out on either side of the tongue.

aa   indicates a long "a"   likewise: oo and other vowels

ą   indicates a nasal "a"   likewise: o and other vowels

é   indicates a high "e:"   Navajo has speech tones like Chinese.

ée   indicates a long "e" falling from high to low in tone

Vowels have "Continental values."

Courtesy Andy Tsihnahjinnie

Ill. 2–8.   *Scene by famed Navaho painter, Andy Tsihnahjinnie, shows drumming, singing, and dancing at the public part of an Enemyway ceremony.*

the stick receiver's camp. This kind of dancing is the only time in traditional Navajo life that men and girls dance together. It was, and is, a time for fun and courtship. Before the dancing starts there is a concert of "Sway songs," in which the courtship theme may be expressed (fig. 2–11). A majority of the Sway songs, however, have texts entirely of vocables.

After an hour or so the singing shifts to dance songs and the girls appear, looking for partners. It is always "ladies' choice," a reflection, perhaps, of the powerful position women have in Navajo society. They own the household; the children belong to the mother's clan, not the father's; and when a couple marry it is traditional for the husband to move in with his wife's family.

In the dance the girls are likely to act bashful, but they find partners and the couples dance along together following other couples in a large circle. The step is simply a light stepping along with a bounce on each step. When a girl is ready to change partners she lets the man know by demanding a token payment. Even some Navajos do not know that this is a symbol of the war booty brought back by Enemy Slayer from a mythical war and given away to Navajo girls in the story in celebration of the victory. The song texts of the dance songs often poke fun at the girls and sometimes refer to these payments (fig. 2–12). After a few hours of dancing, a Signal song (McAllester 1954:27) indicates that the singing is to go back to Sway songs. The dancing stops and the Sway songs may go on for the rest of the night. Again, the symbolism is of war; the group of singers is divided into

> Heye yeye ya,
>> Lonesome as I am,
>> Lonesome as I am, ha-i na,
>> Lonesome as I am,
>> Lonesome as I am, ha,
>> Lonesome as I am, na'a- ne hana . . . .

Fig. 2–11. *Lyrics, Navajo Sway song. David P. McAllester,* Enemy Way Music, *pp. 29, 37. Papers of the Peabody Museum of Archaeology and Ethnology, vol. 41, no. 3. Copyright © 1954 by the President and Fellows of Harvard College.*

two halves representing the home camp and the enemy, and the singers compete in vigor, repertory, and highness of pitch.

They stop at dawn, but after a rest and breakfast a new kind of singing, a serenade of Gift songs, takes place. The home camp people sing outside the main hogan in the stick receiver's camp, and in exchange small gifts like oranges and boxes of Cracker Jacks are thrown to the singers through the smoke hole. Larger gifts such as expensive blankets are brought out and handed to responsible members of the singing group; these presents will be reciprocated later in the ceremony. Most of the Gift songs are old and have text entirely in vocables, but a few of the newer ones have words concerning the hoped-for gifts (fig. 2–13).

The gifts, like the payments during the dancing, represent war booty. The trip of the home party can be seen as a raid into enemy country and the gifts as the booty they take home with them. But reconciliation is symbolized at the same time, since the stick receiver's camp provides supper and camping facilities, and since the meal and gifts will be returned in a similar exchange on the third morning.

After the breakfast and gift singing on the second day, the stick receiver's party prepare to move toward the home camp. Most of the home camp people leave early, but one of their number remains as an official guide to lead the stick receiver to a good camping place a few miles from the home camp. They time

Fig. 2–12. *Lyrics, Navajo Enemyway Dance song. David P. McAllester,* Enemy Way Music, *p. 45. Papers of the Peabody Museum of Archaeology and Ethnology, vol. 41, no. 3. Copyright © 1954 by the President and Fellows of Harvard College.*

> He-ne, yane, yana-,
>> Yala'e-le- yado'eya 'ana he,
>> Yala'e-le- yado'eya ne . . . .
>
> Your daughter, at night,
>> Walking around, yado'eya yana hana,
>> Tomorrow, money,
>> Lots of it, there will be, yana hana,
>
> Yala'e-le- yado'eya na'ana,
> Yala'e-le- yado'eya na'ana he . . . .

Heye yeye yana,
    Your skirts, how many? yi-na,
    To the store I'm going, 'e hyana heye yeye ya,
    To Los Nores I'm going, 'e hya 'ena hya na . . . .

'e-ye yeye yana,
    Goats, I came for them, yo'o'o 'ene hanena,
    Goats, I came for them yo'o'o 'ene hahe,
    Yo'o'o 'ena heye yeye yana. . . .

Fig. 2–13. *Navajo Enemyway Gift song. David P. McAllester,* **Enemy Way Music,** *p. 48, songs 52, 53. Papers of the Peabody Museum of Archaeology and Ethnology, vol. 41, no. 3. Copyright © 1954 by the President and Fellows of Harvard College.*

their arrival to take place at about sundown, and another night of singing and dancing follows at this new camp.

Early the next morning the war symbolism of the ceremony is sharply emphasized with a sham battle. The stick receiver's people ride into the home camp with yells and rifle shots, raising a lot of dust and committing small depredations such as pulling down clotheslines. After four such charges they retire to a new campsite a few hundred yards away and a procession from the home camp brings them a sumptuous breakfast. After the meal, the return gift singing takes place at the hogan of the one-sung-over.

Now comes further, heavy war drama. In a secret indoor ritual the afflicted person is given power and protection by sacred chanting and is dressed for battle. At the climax of the ceremony he goes forth and shoots at a trophy of the enemy, thus ritually killing the ghost. The songs used in the preparation of the warrior include long derisive descriptions of the enemy and praise of Navajo warriors (Haile 1938:276–284). If the person being sung over is a woman, a male proxy takes her place when it comes to shooting the enemy ghost.

In the late afternoon a Circle Dance is performed at the stick receiver's new camp. Men join hands in a circle the two halves of which represent the two camps. It is now that songs like "Shizhané" (ex. 2–5) are sung. The two sides of the circle take turns singing in a competition to see who can sing the best songs most beautifully. As the songs alternate, so does the direction in which the Circle Dance moves. Most of the songs have no translatable words and those that do are not overtly about war, but the presence of the two competing sides is a reminder of conflict, and it is thought that every drumbeat accompanying the songs drives the enemy ghosts farther into the ground. After awhile a girl carrying the stick and several other women may enter the circle and walk around following the direction of the dancing men. The symbols of Changing Woman and her warrior son incised on the sacred stick are further reminders of the meaning of the dance.

After the Circle Dance, another dramatic event takes place: the secret war name of the afflicted person is revealed. Members of the stick receiver's camp walk over to the home camp singing as they go. Four times on the way, they stop

Ex. 2–5. *"Shizhané." Navajo Circle Dance song. With the permission of Albert Sandoval Jr. and Ray Winnie.*

and shout out the identity of the enemy. Then the stick receiver sits down in front of the ceremonial hogan and sings four songs that mention the name of the enemy and that of the one-sung-over. In traditional Navajo life it is impolite to address anyone by name and, in particular, by his or her war name. Polite address is by a kinship term, real or fictitious. Examples of war names are She Went Among War Parties, or He Ran Through Warriors (Reichard 1928:98–99).

The songs describe battle with the enemy and refer to the anguish of the enemy survivors. The death of the enemy ghost is mentioned. Then, after a serenade of Sway songs, the stick receiver's party move back to the dance ground at their camp, and the last night of the ceremony begins with a further selection of Sway songs. After an hour or so the singing changes to dance songs and dancing and, as on the previous two nights, may go on for several hours. Again the Signal song indicates the end of dancing and the rest of the night is spent in Sway song competition between the two camps.

At dawn the ceremony ends with a brief blessing ritual conducted while facing the rising sun. The stick receiver's party departs and the afflicted person, now protected by the many symbolic ways in which the ghost has been eliminated, spends a period of four days in rest and quiet while the effect of the ceremony becomes established over the entire household.

The "Classical" Music of the Navajos

We have listened, so far, to examples of the public or popular music in two Navajo ceremonials, and a new kind of popular music, Navajo country-and-western. But we have not considered the music at the core of Navajo traditional religious philosophy, the great ceremonial chants. These are the long series of songs that accompany the ritual procedures such as we have described for the Nightway (the purifications, prayer offerings, and sand-painting procedures) and for Enemyway (preparation of the drum and decorated stick, dressing the one-sung-over and giving him or her power and protection). Illustration 2–9 shows yet another ceremonial chant, the Mountainway.

These chants are "classic" in that they have a tradition going back for generations, no one knows how many; they have enormous scope—one chant may contain over five hundred songs and the texts comprise many thousands of lines of religious poetry; they contain in their prayers and songs, and in the related myths the meaning the Navajos find in the natural and supernatural worlds.

The performance of the chants may be brief or extended depending on the needs of the one-sung-over, the person to be cured. Excerpts of a few hours may be sufficient, or an extended version of as much as nine nights may be needed. To understand why, we need to consider the Navajo concept of illness.

The disease theory of the Euro-American world is recognized by the Navajos and they gladly take advantage of hospitals, surgery, and antibiotics. But, in addition, they see bad dreams, poor appetite, depression, and injuries from accidents as resulting from disharmony with the world of nature. This view is somewhat like our own in the realm of psychiatry and psychosomatic medicine,

Ill. 2–9. *Navajo fire dance from the Mountainway ceremony. The dancers represent fire deities who have come to help a sick person recover.*

Neg. no. 127657. Courtesy American Museum of Natural History.

but the Navajos go still farther. They see the power of animals, birds, and insects, and also of earth, water, wind, and sky, not just in a sentimental way but as active potencies that have a direct influence on human life. All of these forces may speak directly to human beings and may teach them the songs, prayers, and ritual acts that make up the ceremonials. At the center of this relationship with the natural world is the concept of *hózhǫ́ǫ́* (beauty, blessedness, harmony), which must be maintained, and which, if lost, can be restored by means of ritual. The prayers invoke this state over and over at their conclusions (fig. 2–14).

The ceremonial chants, some fifty of them, dramatize the Navajo creation story, an interlocking network of myths as long and complex as Greek mythology or the Vedas of India. No one person knows the entire story, but the tradition lives in the remarkable memories of several hundred ceremonial practitioners, men and women called "singers" (hatáálí) in Navajo. They direct the dance, art, and theater, chant the music, and recite the prayers that constitute these extraordinary achievements of the human spirit. They learn in the oral tradition, as apprentices, over many years. Some of these practitioners are now teaching religion at such culturally oriented schools as the Rough Rock Demonstration School, near Chinle, Arizona, and the Navajo Community College at Tsaile, Arizona. One such practitioner has dictated his life story, a narrative of over three hundred pages. Excerpts from this remarkable account are presented here, pp. 46–54.

No complete recording of a ceremonial is available on commercial discs or tapes and there are very few commercial recordings of even one of the thousands of songs that make up this great literature of religious music. The main reason is that most singers feel these matters are too sacred to be made public. Often the concern is expressed that an uninitiated person might use one of these songs improperly, through ignorance, and cause great harm to the community, or worse yet, rob the song of its potency. Though the singers who recorded the next song (recorded selection 7) did not share this belief, we respect the feelings of those who do and therefore present only a fragment of the song and give the text only in translation here.

The song form is characteristic of ceremonial music (see fig. 2–15). There is an introduction on the tonic after which a chorus in vocables begins. The melody may be restricted, as in this case, to only three or four notes, or it may move about with a range of an octave or more. In any case, the interest of the

Fig. 2–14. *Concluding phrase of Navajo prayer.*

> *Hózhǫ́ǫ́ nahasdlį́į́',*
> *Hózhǫ́ǫ́ nahasdlį́į́',*
> *Hózhǫ́ǫ́ nahasdlį́į́',*
> *Hózhǫ́ǫ́ nahasdlį́į́'!*

> *Conditions of harmony have been restored,*
> *Conditions of harmony have been restored,*
> *Conditions of harmony have been restored,*
> *Conditions of harmony have been restored!*

'Eye neye yaŋa,
'Eya wane yaneye ne-ya
'Eya wane yane yene yaŋa 'eyo weneya . . . .

I have been searching everywhere,
    Over the earth,
    That is what I was told to do,
I have been searching everywhere,
    Over the earth.

I have been searching everywhere,
    Over the mountains,
    That is what I was told to do,
I have been searching everywhere,
    Over the mountains.

I have been searching everywhere,
    Under the sun,
    That is what I was told to do,
I have been searching everywhere,
    Under the sun.

I have been searching everywhere,
    For the fire,
    That is what I was told to do,
I have been searching everywhere,
    For the fire.

I have been searching everywhere,
    With water,
    That is what I was told to do,
I have been searching everywhere,
    With water.

'Eya wane yaneye ne-ya,
'Eya wane yaneye na-yaŋa 'eyo weneya . . . .

Fig. 2–15. *Lyrics, Navajo Shootingway song.*

music is in the many subtle repetitions of a highly repetitive form. A section of the chorus is usually repeated at the end of each verse in a kind of burden, adding still further to the feeling of repetition.

Shootingway is a ceremonial that reenacts that part of the creation myth in which a hero, Holy Young Man, goes in search of supernatural power. Before his adventures are over he has lived among snake people, fish people, buffalo people, and has been carried up into the sky by thunder people. In the sky he was taught the Shootingway ceremonial by the Sun so that this knowledge might be brought back to earth for the protection of humankind. The ceremony has many purposes, among them being the restoration of harmony between people and snakes, water and lightning. A person suffering from snakebite might be taken to the hospital for treatment and then, later, might undergo Shootingway in order to end the bad relations with the snake people that led to the snakebite in the first place.

The Shootingway song tells about Holy Young Man's journey to the snake country. He is singing to the Sun, whom he met when he was in the mountains, and he tells about a fire that he has seen glimmering in the distance at night when he was camping. Each day he tried to find the fire and this is what led him at last into the snake country. He married four beautiful snake wives and thus became related to these powerful creatures. During his stay among them he was given their power to take back to earth. Today, when someone is having trouble with the snake people the restoration of harmony can be achieved by the ceremonial reenactment of this episode in Shootingway.

Before the song begins a fire has been kindled in the ceremonial hogan and a symbolic representation of the snake country prepared. To the east, south, west, and north of the fire images of snakes are laid out in colored pigments on the ground. There is a black, zigzag snake about three feet long facing the fire from the east and a blue one of the same shape facing the fire from the south. On the west is a straight white snake and on the north a pink one, also straight, and sprinkled with bits of glittering mica. As the song goes on, the one-sung-over, in the role of Holy Young Man, walks around the fire stepping over the snakes, thus acting out the journey into the snake country. The heat of the fire causes all the participants in the ceremony to sweat profusely in a rite of purification, and a series of other acts also drive out evil and further identify the one-sung-over with the protagonist in the myth. To conclude this part of the ritual the singer cools off everybody in the hogan by sprinkling them liberally with water shaken from a bundle of eagle feathers. This is the water mentioned in the last verse of the song.

Even this brief account of a fraction of one of the great ceremonials is enough to give the reader an idea of how the music functions in support of an impressive drama. Shootingway is one of the ways the Navajos remind themselves of the sources of their means of dealing with the supernatural. The ceremony depicts the Navajo view of themselves in relation to the natural world about them.

The beauty of the music, the poetry, the sand paintings, and the myths that lie behind all of these has attracted the attention of scholars worldwide since the 1890s. Some representative examples of the many books written about Navajo myths and ceremonies are listed in the bibliography: Matthews 1894, Kluckhohn and Wyman 1940, Haile 1947, Reichard 1950, Witherspoon 1977, Wyman 1983, and Farella 1984.

The Life Story of a
Navajo Ceremonial Practitioner

Frank Mitchell (Oltai Tsoh: "Big Schoolboy") was born near Wheatfields, Arizona, in 1881 (see ill. 2–10). In the course of his eventful life he was a sheepherder, railroad worker, cook, handyman-interpreter, wagon freighter,

Mable Bosch

Ill. 2–10. *Frank Mitchell, Navajo Blessingway singer, Chinle, Arizona, 1957.*

headman, tribal council member, and tribal judge. In his early maturity he learned Blessingway, one of the most important of the Navajo ceremonies, from his father-in-law. How this affected his whole life is told in his autobiography.

There is no other full autobiography of a Navajo singer. In the excerpts presented here, a number of aspects of Navajo life and music are illustrated:

Repetitive, narrative style: Repetition has been mentioned above as a significant element in the form of Navajo music, narrative, and the other arts.

Importance of women: In the opening we are given a glimpse of a matrilocal, matrilineal family. Traditional Navajo families live in the mother's household and the children belong to the mother's clan. Women own their own property. It is not surprising that the principal deity is Changing Woman.

Traveling about: The old nomadic life-style of the Navajos has not entirely disappeared. Frank's childhood memories show how it was to follow the livestock a hundred years ago.

Navajo practicality: Frank became a singer for practical rather than spiritual reasons. The spiritual dimension of his calling can be seen only between the lines.

The value of Navajo songs: This is stated not in aesthetic terms but in terms of healing the sick, bringing prosperity, and enabling the possessor of certain songs to become a leader in the community.

Speech and leadership: "Chief" in Navajo means "one who speaks." The voices of humans and all other creatures are the culminating point of sacred descriptions in prayers and songs. In Navajo thought, wind is the ultimate power and the voice is the wind made articulate.

Navajo humor: It is important to remember that Indians, too, have their witty songs and funny stories. Frank was the beloved jokester of his large family. He was known for his ability to keep up the spirits of the participants in a long ceremonial with his ready supply of jokes and funny comments.

Frank Mitchell died in the hospital at Ganado, Arizona, in 1968, a few weeks after he dictated his last paragraphs of the life story that he wanted to leave as a legacy to his children and grandchildren.

> I was just a small boy when I began to remember things. We happened to be living at a place called Tsaile; that is where I first began to remember things. I remember that I had a grandmother and my mother had some sisters besides herself. In those days a family like that used to stay close together. We moved around together; when we moved from one place to another, we always went in groups.
>
> In those days the men who were singers and performed ceremonies were the only ones who went around and treated the sick. That is what they were occupied with. I had an uncle on my father's side who was very harsh. He would scold us all of the time. One time there was someone sick in the family and they were performing a ceremony. While that was going on we were told not to sleep. Whenever we fell asleep, they would wake us and make us stay awake. Finally I got so sleepy that I could not stay awake any more. I was sitting next to this uncle of mine who was pretty harsh, and I guess that I fell asleep and just rolled over right beside him. My uncle jumped up, grabbed me by the hair on the side of my head, and yanked me up, putting me back down in a sitting position. I could see he was pretty angry. Of course I did not look straight at him; I just glanced sideways over there every now and then to watch him. After that I did not go to sleep again; I just stayed awake for the rest of the ceremony until it was over. Then we were told, "Now you can go to sleep." That was something I remember very plainly because of course I

was old enough to remember things then. . . . [All excerpts reprinted with permission from Frisbie and McAllester 1978:28–29]

The People traveled mostly on horseback; when we moved with the sheep we used horses to carry our belongings. We, being children, of course had to go along. Whenever the family started moving like that we children would sit in back of the rider. We were small and fell asleep sometimes, so they used to take anything they could find and tie us around the waist to the rider so we would not fall off. That is the way we moved around, tied to the riders so we could sleep sitting on those horses. The main reason for moving around like that was to look for new grazing ground and water for the sheep and horses. [29–30]

The leaders who went around recruiting children for school talked to the People about what the advantages would be in the future if they would put their children in school. The People would get angry and say, "No, absolutely not! I'm not going to give up my child; while I'm still alive I'm not going to turn my child over to those foreigners. Outsiders are not going to take my child away while I am still living." That's what they used to say. They would sometimes get out a butcher knife and toss it in front of those doing the recruiting and say, "Well, go ahead, cut my throat first; you'll have to do that before you can take my child." [57]

At school we just went by the bell. It was a big bell like the one they have there by the cattleguard at the Franciscan church here in Chinle. At a certain hour we would go to bed. Every time that bell rang, it meant that we had to get in line, or go to bed, or get up and get ready for breakfast, or dinner, or supper. . . . [63]

After awhile I thought I had had enough of school life so I took the first chance I got when I heard of some work that was available down on the railroad. The reason that I did not stay at school was because another boy, a schoolmate of mine, and I planned together to work on the railroad in the west somewhere. We planned this secretly, skipped out from school and went down on the railroad. The Navajos were already working on the railroad then, the railroad that was coming out of California, around Needles, and all down this way. So without telling my folks or his where we were going, we sneaked off. . . . [68–69]

Everybody at home started to get suspicious about where we were and my late uncle, my mother's brother whom we called Old Man Short Hair, inquired around and learned that it was likely we were with the railroad crew somewhere in the west. So he went in to Gallup and asked to work on the railroad. Of course he really did not want a job; he just wanted to look for us. . . . After my uncle overtook us and worked with us for a while, the railroad moved our crew back toward Flagstaff to a place called Seligman, Arizona, at the other side of Ash Fork. They had a railroad camp there where we all worked for a while. Then we were told, "You'll have to move now, go back to your country. There is no more work here. . . ." [80–81]

[Editor's note: Because Frank knows a little English he finds various jobs at trading posts, a mission, and a sawmill. He marries, obtains a wagon from the government, and becomes a freighter, hauling supplies from Gallup, New Mexico, to Chinle.]

Later on I came back over here because my wife's parents were getting pretty old and sick. I gave up hauling freight and started tending their farm and livestock. My father-in-law was a well-to-do man: he had cattle and sheep and horses and I just started taking care of them for him. Also, I knew that he was a Blessingway singer and I went out with him whenever he performed this ceremony. I noticed that the songs I learned from He Who Seeks War were the same as the ones my father-in-law was singing.

Before I began to learn these things, way back before that, I did not even think about life as being an important thing. I did not try to remember things or keep track of what happened at certain times. Nothing seemed to matter to me, I just didn't care about anything, so long as I kept on living. But then when I began to learn the Blessingway it changed my whole life. I began really thinking about ceremonies. I had heard singing before that but now I began to take it more seriously because I began to realize what life was and the kind of hardships we have to go through. Before I started learning Blessingway, the older people used to tell me that I should think about life more seriously. "If you don't know any songs you have nothing to go by. If a child grows up in a family like that he doesn't know where he is going or what he is doing." That is what the older people told me, that I should have something to live by. . . . I used to go out with my father-in-law, Man Who Shouts, whenever he was asked to perform the Blessingway. I went wherever he did. At first I just watched and then finally I had learned practically everything he was doing and before I knew it I was helping him with the ceremony. Finally I reached the point where I had learned it well enough so that I had a ceremony of my own. . . . [192–193]

[My father-in-law said to me] "If you are a singer, if you remember your ceremonies really well even if you get old, even if you get blind and deaf, you'll still remember everything by heart, how each part of the ceremony is performed." He said to me, "Even though you are so old you can't ride a horse or you can't even see anymore, people will still have a use for you until old age finally finishes you off."

So that is why I chose that way of life. And I believe it now: it is true that even as old as I am now, unable to get around too much, people still come to have my ceremony done over them. I have it inside my head so well that I remember everything and even though I can't get around they come in a wagon or a car for me and take me over to where the ceremony is needed and then bring me back. So I think my father-in-law was right. If I had decided to be a farmer at that time I probably wouldn't have lasted very long. [193–194]

It is a custom with the People that, for instance, some family, even though everything may be going all right and nothing is wrong, still may say, "Well, let's have a Blessingway to freshen things up, to renew ourselves again." So they do. Or sometimes they might have acquired some valuable goods, if they have been off trading or something, and have brought them home. Then the things that they brought in from other places, well, it is on their minds that, "That's what we're blessed with in this family." They might feel they need the Blessingway because you do not wait until some misfortune happens before you have it. That is the reason it is called the peaceful way, the healing way, the blessing way. There is no specific time … it depends on the family. If they feel they should have it, then they do it, just an ordinary Blessingway.

Of course if you are able to have that ceremony, if you have the means to put it on, well, then you should do it. But if you have not, then in that case you just keep putting it off until you are able to bear the cost. . . .

Blessingway is used for everything that is good for a person, or for the people. It has no use other than that. For instance, when a woman is pregnant she has the Blessingway in order to have a good delivery with no trouble. It is also done so that she and her child may have a happy life. In case of bad dreams it is a kind of warning that there are some misfortunes ahead of you; in order to avoid that you have Blessingway so that you will have happiness instead. Or if you are worried about something, your family will want to get you back, to get that out of your mind, out of your system, so that you may have a good life. It is the same for any other things that could cause you to worry, to feel uneasy about yourself. That is the sort of thing it is used for. As for the prayers, you say, "Beauty shall be in front of me, beauty shall be in the back, beauty shall be below me, above me, all around me." On top of that you say about yourself, "I am everlasting, I may have an everlasting life with beauty." You end your prayers that way. . . . [218–219]

I remember all that I know about the Blessingway because I had those years of study to get it all in my head. And from my experience of learning I understand that it is not just my ability that makes it possible. I believe that there is a spirit that really is answering my prayers, because all these years I would not have been able to learn so much if I did not have such help. I could not do it by myself, so there must be something beyond human power helping me. . . . [237–238]

In Navajo religion there are prayers for certain purposes. I found out from my own father that in Blessingway there was a song for headmen, and I learned that from him. I think that this is another reason why things came easily for me when I was talking to the People. It may be one reason that I was recognized for being a talker and a leader among the People, why I became well known as a headman and even eventually ended up in the Tribal Council. . . . [241]

There are lots of songs that go with being a headman or leader. They start out from the beginning, way back with the first people. The story starts with how it was planned at first and how the first people decided who were to be the chiefs. After these chiefs were elected, the songs go along describing how they were dressed. They tell about all of the things they were wearing, their shoes, leggings, sash and skirts, belts, wristlets and beads, their head plumes and everything up to the last thing, that which is put in their mouths from which their speeches are known. That last thing is like the power to speak; it was put into their mouths so they could have the wisdom to say wise things and so the People could understand them. There are enough of those songs to sing them all night without sleeping. The songs are used in a series, but they are not just to be sung any place. You can only use them when someone is going to be a chief, a good leader; they can have the songs done for them. There are so many songs in that series that you could almost have a Blessingway done with them; there are just about as many songs involved in that as there are in the Blessingway itself. From the start to the end of that, the whole thing is like a Blessingway. The story of the songs are just like Blessingway right from the beginning: how the earth was first formed, how the mountains came up. The songs go on like that. It would probably take a little longer to do than the regular Blessingway; it is just like Blessingway when you do that except that the ceremony is mostly just singing. Almost all of what takes place is the singing of the Chief songs. . . . [244]

Once I was placed there as one of the councilmen, I began to be asked to do different things. One of the things that there was a lot of talk about during this time was education and the need for building schools on the reservation. We also talked about hospitals and preventing outsiders from moving in with different things like industrial plants. We did a lot of work and I concerned myself with all those things. . . . [256] We talked about that a lot on the Council, and we decided to ask for the schools and also hospitals and all of those things from Washington.

Several of us were then appointed to go to Washington to ask that these things be granted. I went over there with several other men. We went before those people and asked for a school and a hospital and other things. Henry Taliman, the tribal chairman, Howard Gorman, the vice-chairman, and Red Moustache's brother were some of the others who went over there, too. We were asked to fly there but most of the delegates were afraid of going in an airplane, so we went on the train. While we were there we were given sight-seeing tours around Washington. I got to see the White House, Arlington Cemetery, the Unknown Soldier's Tomb, and other places. One of the delegates got tired when we were near the Washington Monument. He wanted to rest but he could not find a place to sit down. So he took off his moccasins and laid down on the grass in front of the Monument. He was wearing half-socks like the ones I used to knit for myself. This man went to sleep and while he was sleeping a crowd gathered around looking at him. When he woke up he asked me, "What are all of these people standing around here looking at me for?" I said, "My younger brother, they are waiting for you to get up to see what kind of a creature you are. They are wondering whether or not when you get up you will crawl on all fours, like a bear." He replied, "You bear, you would say that." [257–258]

While I, myself, stand for the good of the People, right now I am just watching these things. I cannot step in there and try to do some of the things I used to do because I am getting pretty well along in years. So I just sit by and watch. I think about the future; of course I may never get to see it, but I just wonder how things will be in so many years, what improvements there will be for the benefit of the People. I wish I were young again, so I could see more of these things as time goes on. But those are just wishes and of course I do not expect to see those things. . . . [310–311]

In the early days, the old people were our teachers. They said that as long as we observed the rules laid down for us by the Holy People, everything was going to go along smoothly. But they said it would not last forever. Sooner or later we were going to start breaking the rules. Then that would lead us to ruin. It is like a seed of any kind, like corn, or beans, or anything that you put in the ground. You plant it, and it sprouts and bears fruit and grows to a certain extent. When it matures you harvest what it has produced; the stalks and leaves wither because their use is past. But you still have the seeds to continue planting and arriving at a new life. That is what the older people taught us. If you did not observe these things you are bound to ruin yourself. . . . [311]

When you get put into a position of leadership, that teaches you to have some respect. Even if you have been irresponsible in the past, you now have to behave and lead a good life as an example to your people. [315]

There are still lots of people coming around here wanting me to do Blessingway for them, but sometimes now because of my physical condition I have to refuse. When they come to ask, it just depends on how I feel. If I think that I can stand it, then I accept. . . . But a lot of the time now I'm not able to sing Blessingway. I can't stand the strain of being in a sitting position for that long, and my voice also gets tired. I especially feel the strain in the wintertime. The nights are long then, and performing that Blessingway is very strenuous even though we wait to start the all-night singing until pretty well on into the night. Of course in the summertime the nights are short. I will do Blessingway again when I get well and when I think that I am able to do it.

As you know, last fall I had my sacred bundle renewed and, of course, a Blessingway was used for that. But even though I had that and all of the other ceremonials I've been telling you about, right now my ailments are still hanging on. I still think that we have not done the complete cure. The doctors do not seem to be able to tell me what the matter is, either. I went over to the Ganado hospital and they thoroughly examined my body. They could not find anything anywhere that could be causing my troubles. Finally they decided to take some tissue out of my stomach, just a small piece. I was not really operated on then. The doctor just said that there was no equipment there at Ganado to analyze what they had taken out of me, and that he would send it to Denver to find out what it was. They gave me some medicine and told me to go home. . . . [321–322]

While I was over at the Ganado hospital, and even before I went there, I had a lot of dreams and most of them were about dead people, those who had already passed away, even women. Those things were beginning to bother me; I was worrying about them. So I decided to have another ceremony. I also wanted to see if I could get some relief from the pains that I was still feeling a lot of the time. So I went and asked Black Sheep from Black Mountain to come over here and perform some of his small ceremonies for me to see if those could straighten out my dreams and give me some relief from those pains. He came down here and did some Ghostway rituals for me. He said prayers, cut prayersticks, bathed me and painted me with the blackening and reddening ceremonies. You can do those things to find out what effect they will have. If you feel a bit better after those, then you can go ahead and have the big ceremonial. After he did that I don't remember having any more dreams. I just forgot all about them. Before those things were done, as soon as I woke up, I would begin to think about what I had been dreaming about, but since then I do not do that any more. I still dream, but I do not remember what those dreams are about. I have felt a little better since Black Sheep performed all of those things for me, and right now I am thinking about calling him back again for a big, regular five-night Ghostway. Then, maybe I will go back to the hospital again. . . . [323]

The Native American Church

In their comparatively recent history the Navajos have felt the call of two highly organized religious movements from outside their traditional culture. One is the Native American Church, an Indian movement with roots in ancient Mexico and recent development in Oklahoma. This religion established itself firmly in the United States in the nineteenth century and thereafter developed different perspectives and music from that which can still be seen among the Tarahumare and Huichol Indians of Mexico. It found its way into the Navajo country in the 1930s. By the 1950s it had grown in this one tribe to a membership estimated at twenty thousand.

This music is strikingly different from traditional Navajo music. Let us listen to a hymn from the Native American Church and then consider the role of this music in contemporary Navajo life (recorded selection 8, ex. 2–6).

What first arrests the attention is the quiet, introspective quality of the singing in this simple melody. Members of the Native American Church speak of their

Ex. 2–6. *Navajo Peyote song. With permission of Willard Rhodes.*

music as prayer. Although the text has no translatable words, the repetitive simplicity of vocables and music expresses a rapt, inward feeling. According to one theory, Native American Church hymns are derived from Christian hymnody. The quiet slow movement and the unadorned voice, so unlike the usual boisterous, emphatic, out-of-doors delivery in Indian singing, seem to suggest this interpretation. On the other hand, there are many more features that are all Indian: the rhythmic limitation to only two note values, ♪ ♩ (a specialty of Navajo and Apache music), the descending melodic direction, the rattle and drum accompaniment, the pure melody without harmony, the use of vocables. These features are present in Native American Church music in many different tribes all across the continent to such a marked extent that a distinct, pan-tribal "peyote style" can be identified (McAllester 1949:12; 80–82). In the present song, every phrase ends on "he ne yo," anticipating the "he ne yo we" of the last phrase. This ending, always sung entirely on the tonic, is as characteristic of Native American Church music as "amen" is to Christian hymns and prayers.

True to its Oklahoma origin, the Native American Church ideally holds its meetings in a large Plains Indian tipi. This is often erected on Saturday evening for the all-night meeting and then taken away to be stored until the next weekend. Such mobility enables the meeting to move to wherever members want a service. There are also more permanent tipis standing on quiet lots in such Navajo towns as Window Rock and Lukachukai, where an established congregation meets regularly. Meetings are sometimes held in hogans since they, too, are circular and have an earth floor where the sacred fire and altar can be built.

The Indians of the Native American Church use a water drum and a rattle to accompany their singing. The drum is made of a small, old fashioned, three-legged iron pot with a wet, almost rubbery, buckskin drumhead stretched over the opening. The pot is half full of water which is splashed over the inside of the drumhead from time to time by giving the drum a tossing motion. This act serves to keep the drumhead moist and flexible while in use. The player kneels, holding the drum on the ground tipped toward his drumming hand. He controls the tone with pressure on the drumhead from the thumb of his holding hand. He strikes the membrane rapidly and rather heavily with a smooth, hard, slightly decorated drumstick. It is supposed that the water inside the pot has something to do with the strong resonance of this and other kinds of water drums, but no physical studies have yet been made to test the theory.

The peyote rattle is made with a small gourd mounted on a handle-stick in much the same way as the cowhorn rattle of the Iroquois (see pp. 25–27). There is no carved shelf on the handle, however; the stick merely fits very snugly into the gourd plug so that it is wedged tight. The distal end of the stick protrudes two or three inches beyond the gourd and a tuft of dyed horsehair is attached. This is often red to symbolize the red flower of the peyote cactus. Many Native American Church members hold a beautifully decorated feather fan during the service, and use it to waft toward themselves the fragrant incense of cedar needles when these are put into the fire. The feathers of the fan are mounted in separate movable leather sleeves, like the feathers of the Plains warbonnet. This allows the user to manipulate the fan in such a way that each feather seems to have a quivering life of its own.

The ritual consists of long prayers, many groups of four songs each (sung in turn by members of the meetings), a special water break at midnight, and fellowship breakfast in the morning. At intervals, under the direction of the leader of the meetings, a Cedar Chief builds up the fire, puts cedar incense on the coals, and passes the cigarettes to make the sacred smoke that accompanies the prayers. He also passes small pieces of a cactus called *peyote* (from the Aztec *peyotl* "wooly," describing the fine white hairs that grow in tufts on the cactus). When eaten, peyote produces a sense of well-being and, sometimes, visions in vivid color. The peyote is eaten as a sacrament since Father Peyote is one of the deities of the religion. The Native American Church is sometimes called the Peyote Church.

A crescent-shaped earthen altar six or seven feet long lies west of the fire and a large peyote cactus plant, symbolic of Father Peyote, is placed at the midpoint of the crescent. Prayers may be directed to Father Peyote and some members can hear him responding to their pleas for help in meeting the difficulties of life. The intense feeling of dedication and piety at Peyote Meetings is expressed through prayers and testimonies, often with tears running down the cheeks of the speaker. Prayers include appeals to Jesus and God, as well as to Father Peyote. Peyotists consider that the Native American Church is hospitable to all other religions and includes their ideas in its philosophy and beliefs. Prayers are made for friends and family members who are ill or otherwise in need of help. Leaders of the Church, of the Navajo tribe, and of the country at large are also included in the prayers.

The Water Drum

The water drum is widespread in North and South America. It is the only drum used in traditional Navajo and Apache music. The Navajos make theirs on a clay pot eight or ten inches high and use an unusual drumstick made of a twig bent around and tied in a loop at the distal end. The Apaches use the same kind of drumstick but make the drum of a large iron pot. The buckskin drumhead is stretched over an opening two or two-and-a-half feet across and several of the singers beat the drum at the same time. A deep booming sound is produced in contrast to the softer thump of the Navajo drum (see ill. 2–11)

The Iroquois and the Chippewas in the Eastern Woodlands make water drums using a hollowed-out log or a wooden keg. They do not have the looped drumstick but use a straight stick somewhat carved or, as in the case of the medicine drum of the Menomini, a somewhat elaborate curved stick. Eastern Woodland water drums range from five or six inches to two feet or more in height and from five or six inches across the drumhead to as much as fourteen inches or more.

The peyote drum seems to be an elaboration on the pot drum of the Navajos

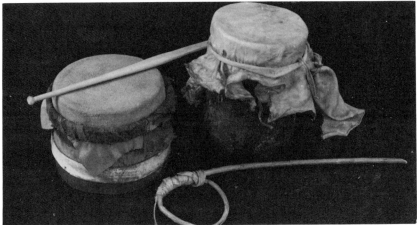

Susan W. McAllester

Ill. 2–11. *Two kinds of water-drum. On the left is an Iroquois drum made from a short section of hollowed-out log. On the right is a Navajo pottery water-drum, used only in the Enemyway ceremony.*

and Apaches. Nowadays the old-fashioned pot is hard to find and members of the Native American Church can buy a specially manufactured aluminum replica that is much lighter to handle and gives the same sound. The Church has also developed its own kinds of jewelry and costume and a genre of Indian painting depicting peyote meetings and peyote visions.

Since the water drum is so widespread in North and South America it would be an interesting project for students of Native American music to make one. The peyote drum is difficult to assemble. It is also so intensely symbolic to members of the Native American Church that it might be in questionable taste for a nonmember to attempt to make this particular kind of water drum. However, the traditional Iroquois, Navajo, and Apache water drums are used for social dancing and so do not have the same religious feelings associated with them.

Figure 2–16 contains the instructions for making a simple water–drum. Iron pots or wooden kegs are hard to find, but a number ten tin can makes a good substitute. Buckskin is also difficult to obtain, but a chamois skin from an auto supply store or a piece of rubber from an inner tube can be used instead. Indians sometimes make such an alternative drum themselves if they cannot obtain the traditional materials.

Navajo Hymn Music

Sharing the popularity of peyote hymns among the requests that come in at the rate of several hundred a week at such radio stations as WGLF in Gallup, New Mexico, are Christian hymns. The many Christian missions on the reservation are appreciated for their ministry by the Navajos who have joined them. The hospitals, schools, and other services associated with the missions are a boon

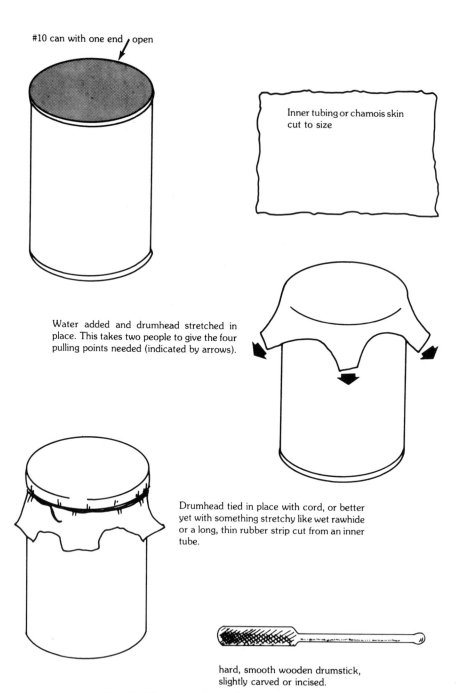

#10 can with one end open

Inner tubing or chamois skin cut to size

Water added and drumhead stretched in place. This takes two people to give the four pulling points needed (indicated by arrows).

Drumhead tied in place with cord, or better yet with something stretchy like wet rawhide or a long, thin rubber strip cut from an inner tube.

hard, smooth wooden drumstick, slightly carved or incised.

Fig. 2–16. *Steps in making a water drum.*

not only to church members but also to the hundreds of other Navajos who take advantage of them.

Navajo listeners make requests for particular hymns on the occasion of a birthday in the family, the anniversary of a death, or some other signal family event. When the request and the hymn are broadcast, the occasion is made known to hundreds of listeners. The hymns may be performed by nationally known gospel singers, but Navajo gospel singers as well have made records, and requests are likely to focus on these. One such group is the Chinle Galileans, a Navajo country gospel group. Their lyrics are in English and their music is the familiar country combination of electric guitar and percussion (recorded selection 9, ex. 2–7).

The interesting thing about this music is that it has so few features that could be called traditionally Indian. Like the Fenders (pp. 30–32) the Galileans have adopted a new style of music wholeheartedly. The clues that the performers are Navajos are in the English words with a Navajo accent and, in the case of the Fenders, in certain melodic and rhythmic short-cuts, compared with the Anglo original. This is what appeals to Navajo listeners and makes them feel that the performing groups are some of "their own."

New Composers in Traditional Modes

Among the new kinds of Navajo music is a genre of recently composed songs based, musically, on Enemyway style (usually Sway songs or Dance songs) but not intended for use in that ceremony. The texts are in Navajo since the songs are intended for Navajo listeners, but they contain social commentary in a dif-

Ex. 2–7. *"Clinging to a Saving Hand." With the permission of Roland Dixon.*

ferent vein from that in the popular songs of Enemyway. The new message is one of protest. A good illustration would be the treatment of the use of alcohol in the old songs and the new. The first example in this contrast is a Skip Dance song from Enemyway (fig. 2–17), probably dating from the 1920s.

"Navajo Inn" is a recent song by Lena Tsoisdia, a social service worker at Window Rock, the headquarters of the Navajo tribal government. The title takes its name from a drive-in liquor store that used to do a thriving business a few miles from Window Rock. The store was just across the reservation boundary and was thus outside the jurisdiction of the tribal prohibition laws. The lyrics refer to the Inn and speak despairingly of women finding their husbands, unconscious, behind "the tall fence."

Ruth Roessel, a prominent Navajo educator, has composed a song about the "Long Walk," when the Navajos were defeated and rounded up by Kit Carson and his troops in 1864 and forcibly removed to a large concentration camp at Ft. Sumner, New Mexico. The hardships of the march, which preceded four years of captivity, are recounted here (fig. 2–18).

The two examples here have not been recorded on commercial discs but several Navajo composers of new songs in styles based on Enemyway popular songs have published their work on popular discs. Kay Bennett (Kaibah) has produced three records on her own label. Danny Whitefeather Begay, Cindy Yazzie, and Roger McCabe have released "My Beautiful Land" on the Canyon Records label with fifteen popular songs in this new genre. "Los Angeles Sweetheart" by Danny Whitefeather Begay will give an idea of how those songs go (fig. 2–19). It is in the Skip Dance style as indicated by the formula

he ye,   ya - na

In this record many of the songs are nostalgic, about Navajos who have left the reservation to find work and wish they could go home again. Others are "flirting songs" referring to the courtship situation at a Squaw Dance. The mingling of the new experience in big cities and the traditional dance scene at an Enemyway

Fig. 2–17. *Lyrics, Navajo Enemyway Skip Dance song.*

'E- ne- ya,

My younger brother,
My whiskey, have some! Naŋa he, ne-ye,

My younger brother,
My whiskey, have some! Naŋa, he, ne-ye,

Your whiskey is all gone, ne,
My whiskey, there's still some, wo,

He yo-o-wo-wo, he yo-o-wo-wo,
Heya, we, heyana, he, nai-ya.

Long, long ago, our people,
Our grandfathers, our grandmothers,
Walking that long distance,
There was no food, there was no water,
But they were walking a long distance,
But they were walking a long distance!

At Fort Sumner, it was when they got there
They were treated badly,
They were treated badly.

"I wish I were still back in my own home,
I wish I were still back in my own home!
We shall never forget this,
The walk that we are taking now.
We shall never forget this,
The walk that we are taking now.
Even then, we still like our own land,
Even then, we still like our own land!"

Fig. 2–18.   *Lyrics, "The Long Walk." With the permission of Ruth Roessel.*

ceremonial is reflected in the record's cover design, which combines the four sacred mountains, automobiles, hogans, and skyscrapers.

Our last example of Navajo music is a new development stemming from the Mormon sect of Christianity and portraying ideas both musically and in words that express the new Indians at the end of the twentieth century in the United States. The song is "Proud Earth," which can be heard on the accompanying cassette (recorded selection 10). The composer is Arliene Nofchissey Williams, a Navajo, who wrote the song while she was a student at Brigham Young University. The words (fig. 2–20) reflect the Mormon respect for Indian culture and

Fig. 2–19.   *Lyrics, "Los Angeles Sweetheart." With the permission of Ray Boley.*

Heye, yaŋa, heye, yaŋa,

Awe 'a-no 'aweya'a heye, yaŋa,
Awe 'a-no 'aweya'a heye, yaŋa,

Hene ya'o wowo 'awe ya'a heye, yaŋa,
Hene ya'o wowo 'awe ya'a heye, yaŋa,

Oh, that girl, oh, that girl,
To a place called "L.A." that's where she went,
She went, aweya'a heye, yaŋa,
To a place called "L.A.," that's where she went,
She went, aweya'a heye, yaŋa,
"All kinds of jobs for you," she wrote,
But she had another man, 'ano 'aweya'a heye, yaŋa,

Hene ya'o wowo 'awe ya'a heye, yaŋa,
Hene ya'o wowo 'awe ya'a heye, yaŋa.

Proud Earth (The Song of The People)

The beat of my heart is kept live in my drum,
And my plight echoes in the canyons, the meadows, the plains,
And my laughter runs free with the deer,
And my tears fall with the rain,
But my soul knows no pain.

I am one with nature,
Mother Earth is at my feet,
And my God is up above me,
And I'll sing the song of my People.

Come with me, take my hand, come alive with my chant (heya, heya)
For my life already knows wisdom, balance and beauty.
Let your heart be free from fear (heya, heya)
And your joy meet with mine,
For the peace we can find.

We are one with nature,
Mother Earth is at our feet,
And our God is up above us,
And we'll sing the song, the song of the people (heya, heya),
And we'll sing the song, the song of the people.

Fig. 2–20. *Lyrics, "Proud Earth." With permission of Arliene Nofchissey Williams.*

the Indian closeness to nature. At the same time the song reflects the aspiration of the Latter Day Saints to unify the Indian people under one God. Musically, there are Indian elements such as the use of a steady, repetitive drumbeat and vocables, as well as European-American elements such as a string orchestra, harmonies, interpretive dynamics, and a text in English. The use of the voice of the late Chief Dan George, an Indian film star, as narrator adds to the richness of the production. The song is a "hit" on the Navajo reservation and elsewhere among Indian people. It is frequently requested in broadcasts beamed to Indians in the Southwest. It was produced in Nashville with all the musical technology that the name implies, and at the same time it is an Indian message record, telling the world what Indians feel they have to contribute to world culture from their mythopoeic philosophy of nature.

We have ranged over the music of several generations and several religions in an effort to find clues to the thought of just one Indian tribe. Even so we have barely touched on the complexities of this rich and rapidly changing culture. One of the most powerful messages that reaches the outsider is that Indian traditional culture is still vital and growing in its own ways even while Native American people are adopting new ideas and technology from the Euro-American culture around them. This fact is clearly reflected in the many different kinds of music that coexist on the Navajo reservation and in thousands of Navajo homes in Chicago, Los Angeles, San Francisco, and innumerable other locations away from the reservation.

To varying degrees this picture of Navajo music exemplifies what is happening to other Indian communities around the country. The different Indian cultures are embarked on an adventure in which the larger populace around them must inevitably share. Many Indian elements have already become part of the culture that is called "American." Some of these have been superficial: an Indian word such as "squash" or "moose," or a bit of local legend. Other contributions have had enormous economic import, such as the corn and potatoes that feed much of the world. There is now evidence that some of the music and the other Indian arts, and the religious and philosophical ideas that lie beneath them, are becoming accessible to an increasingly sympathetic American public. No culture remains static and the Indians will continue to contribute to other world cultures, which are themselves in the process of change.

REFERENCES CITED

Densmore, Frances
    1910   *Chippewa Music.* Washington, D.C.: Bureau of American Ethnology Bulletin 45.

Farella, John R.
    1984   *The Main Stalk, A Synthesis of Navajo Philosophy.* Tucson: Univ. of Arizona Press.

The Fenders
    1966   *Second Time 'Round.* Thoreau, N. Mex. 12" LP recording.

Fenton, William
    1942   *Songs from the Iroquois Longhouse.* Washington, D.C.: Smithsonian Institution Publication 369.

———
    N.d.   *Songs from the Iroquois Longhouse.* Library of Congress AFS L6.

Frisbie, Charlotte J., and David P. McAllester.
    1978   *Navajo Blessingway Singer: Frank Mitchell 1881–1967.* Tucson: Univ. of Arizona Press.

Gill, Sam D.
    1981   *Sacred Words, A Study of Navajo Religion and Prayer.* Westport, Conn., and London: Greenwood Press.

Haile, Fr. Berard
    1938   *Origin Legend of the Navajo Enemy Way.* New Haven: Yale Univ. Press.

———
    1947   *Prayerstick Cutting in a Five Night Ceremonial of the Male Branch of Shootingway.* Chicago: Univ. of Chicago Press.

Kluckhohn, Clyde, and Dorothea Leighton
    1938   *The Navajo.* Cambridge: Harvard Univ. Press.

Kluckhorn, Clyde, and Leland C. Wyman.
    1940   *An Introduction to Navajo Chant Practice.* Menasha, Wis.: Memoirs of the American Anthropological Association, No. 53.

Kurath, Gertrude P.

    1966   *Michigan Indian Festivals.* Ann Arbor, Mich.: Ann Arbor Publishers.

Matthews, Washington.

    1894   "Songs of Sequence of the Navajos," *Journal of American Folk-Lore* 7:185–94.

McAllester, David P.

    1949   *Peyote Music.* New York: Viking Fund Publications in Anthropology, no. 13.

————

    1954   *Enemy Way Music.* Papers of the Peabody Museum of Archaeology and Ethnology, vol. 41, no. 5. Cambridge, Mass.: Harvard Univ. Press.

My Beautiful Land and Other Navajo Songs.

    N.d.   Canyon Records ARP 6078 (Phoenix, Ariz.). Danny Whitefeather Begay, Cindy Yazzi, and Roger McCabe.

Navajo Country Gospel.

    N.d.   The Chinle Galileans. LPS 9039 (Chinle, Ariz.) Larry Emerson, Jerry Tom, Roland Dixon, Donnie Tsosie, Lee Begaye, Emerson Luther.

Proud Earth.

    N.d.   Salt City Records SC-60 (Provo, Utah). Chief Dan George, Arliene Nofchissey Williams, Rick Brosseau.

Reichard, Gladys A.

    1928   *Social Life of the Navajo Indians.* New York: Columbia Univ. Press.

————

    1950   *Navajo Religion.* New York: Bollingen Foundation.

Rhodes, Willard, ed.

    N.d.   *Navajo: Folk Music of the United States.* Washington, D.C.: Library of Congress, Division of Music, Archive of American Folk Song AFS L41.

————

    N.d.   *Puget Sound: Folk Music of the United States.* Washington, D.C.: Library of Congress, Division of Music, Archive of American Folk Song AAFS L34. With 36-page booklet on Northwest Coast culture (Erna Gunther) and music (Willard Rhodes).

Sachs, Curt

    1962   *The Wellsprings of Music.* The Hague: Martinus Nijhof.

Sioux Favorites

    N.d.   Canyon Records ARP 6059 (Phoenix, Ariz.).

Songs from the Navajo Nation

    N.d.   Recorded by Kay Bennet (Kaibah). Produced by K. C. Bennet. (Gallup, N. Mex.)

Witherspoon, Gary

    1977   *Language and Art in the Navajo Universe.* Ann Arbor: Univ. of Michigan Press.

Witmer, Robert

    1973   "Recent Change in the Musical Culture of the Blood Indians of Alberta, Canada." *Yearbook for Inter-American Musical Research,* 9:64–94.

Wyman, Leland C.

    1983   *Southwest Indian Drypainting.* Albuquerque: Univ. of New Mexico Press.

ADDITIONAL READING

Bailey, Garrick, and Roberta Glenn Bailey
    1986   *A History of the Navajos, the Reservation Years.* Santa Fe, N. Mex.: School of American Research Press.
Deloria, Vine Jr.
    1969   *Custer Died for Your Sins: An Indian Manifesto.* London: Collier-Macmillan Ltd.
Dyk, Walter
    1966   *Son of Old Man Hat.* Lincoln: Univ. of Nebraska Press.
Goodman, James B.
    1986   *The Navajo Atlas, Environments, Resources, People, and the History of the Diné Bikeyah.* Norman: Univ. of Oklahoma.
Hadley, Linda
    1986   *Hózhǫ́ǫ́jí Hané' (Blessingway).* Rough Rock, Ariz.: Rough Rock Demonstration School. (in English and Navajo)
Neihardt, John G.
    1961   *Black Elk Speaks.* Lincoln: Univ. of Nebraska Press.
Underhill, Ruth M.
    1953   *Red Man's America.* Chicago: Chicago Univ. Press.

ADDITIONAL LISTENING

Anilth, Wilson, and Hanson Ashley
    1981   *Navajo Peyote Ceremonial Songs, vol. I.* Indian House 1541 (Taos, N. Mex.).
Boniface Bonnie Singers
    1968   *Navajo Sway Songs.* Indian House 1581 (Taos, N. Mex.).
Boulton, Laura
    1957   *Indian Music of the Southwest.* Folkways Records, FW 8850 (New York). With 11-page booklet.
Burch, Sharon
    1989   *Yazzie Girl.* Canyon Records 534 (Phoenix, Ariz.).
Four Corner Yeibichai
    1988   Canyon Records 7152 (Phoenix, Ariz.).
Iroquois Social Dance Songs
    1969   Iroqrafts QC 727 (Ohsweken, Ontario, Canada). 3 vols.
Isaacs, Tony
    1968   *Night and Daylight Yeibichai.* Indian House IH 1502 (Taos, N. Mex.).
Rhodes, Willard
    1949   Music of the Sioux and the Navajo. Folkways Records FE 4401 (New York). With 6-page pamphlet.
Smith Family Gospel Singers
    1987   *Touching Jesus, vol. II.* Canyon Records, 620 (Phoenix, Ariz.)
XIT
    1972   *Plight of the Red Man.* Motown Record Corp. R536L (Detroit). Protest songs

in Rock style; XIT is acronym for "Crossing of Indian Tribes," in reference to the pan-tribal makeup of the group.

MAJOR SOURCES FOR RECORDINGS

Canyon Records and Indian Arts, 4143 North Sixteenth Street, Phoenix, Ariz. 85016, phone: (602) 266–4823. This is the major distributor of native American recordings. It stocks not only the large inventory under its own label but keeps in print many of the recordings of smaller distributors, some of which have otherwise gone out of business. It carries recordings of traditional music and also newer genres such as Indian rock, gospel, and country and western.

Indian House, Box 472, Taos, N. Mex. 87571, phone: (505) 776–2953. This company specializes in traditional Indian music and typically devotes an entire tape to one genre such as Taos Round Dance songs, or Navajo Yeibichai songs. The abundant examples and the excellent notes make these tapes valuable for scholars as well as other interested listeners.

Library of Congress. Archive of Folk Culture, Motion Picture, Broadcast, and Recorded Sound Division, Library of Congress, Washington, D.C. 20540, phone: (202) 707–7833. This collection includes the Willard Rhodes recordings of Native American music: excellent recordings and notes from all across the country.

Smithsonian/Folkways. The Folkways Collection, Smithsonian Institution, Washington, D.C. 20560, phone: (202) 287-3262. The inventory of the Ethnic Folkways Records and Service Corp., formerly of New York City, has been preserved at the Smithsonian Institution and new recordings on a joint label are being produced. Their holdings include many early recordings of native American music.

T H R E E

◆ ◆ ◆

Africa/Ghana

JAMES T. KOETTING

THE WESTERN POINT OF VIEW

Africa used to be called the "Dark Continent"—dark, perhaps, because of the skin color of most of its inhabitants, but mostly because the outside world knew very little about the geography and peoples of this vast land mass, particularly in the area south of the Sahara Desert. Today the Sahara serves as a division between northern and southern (or black) Africa, and it is the latter that we will explore musically in this chapter. The ethnomusicologist Mantle Hood often pointed out to his students that to study any music it is necessary to deal with it on its own terms. Since most of us are European-oriented Westerners, our perceptions of African music may tell us little about how that music is perceived by those who perform and consume it in Africa. Our own music—its sounds and contexts—has been shaping our hearing and aesthetic standards from almost the time we were born. We can assume that most African music will be quite different from what we are used to hearing. We can assume further that our own musical culture will predispose us to certain biases with regard to African music. This predisposition means that from a European frame of reference certain African sounds will intrigue and delight while others may sound like little more than disorganized noise at first. The same kinds of things happen when Africans hear our music. So in what follows, be prepared to confront musical biases, and be prepared to deal with the unknown.

We will be dealing with the unknown in more than the sense of just our own lack of knowledge. The fact is that few non-Africans even today understand African music in any more than a superficial way. And few Africans write about their own music (a most notable exception being J. H. Kwabena Nketia, who has written prolifically on the subject). Although they value music both as art and life, Africans are not obsessed with talking about their music. They simply make it and use it.

It is not difficult to gain a superficial knowledge of African music. It is easy enough to count and describe the musical instruments, electronically analyze melodic intervals, or more or less describe the goings on at a performance. It is even easy to notate fairly accurately most African music. The difficulties rise when we try to pry beneath the surface to understand its inner workings, what makes African music "tick." Historically, Europeans have not been adept at finding out, and at least part of the problem was their urge to generalize about African music from an unrelentingly European frame of reference. That is, they often failed to deal with African music on its own terms.

Any attempt to make generalizations about music in sub-Saharan Africa is dangerous and is bound to be unsatisfying. Too many different ethnic groups having different social, political, and musical systems live in this vast area. A Senegalese praise singer (*griot*) hears little in common between his music and, say, that of the Ba'Benzélé pygmies. It is not uncommon for the people of one African village to say that the people in the next village "make only noise" instead of music. They say that because, although they understand their own music perfectly well, the music of the next village uses different rules and has different aesthetic standards that they do not understand. When we are unfamiliar with a musical system, its music is apt to sound "all the same" to us, and it is this very natural reflex that gives rise to the urge in Western writers to generalize about African music. Of course, the reflex works both ways. In his last book, *The Wellsprings of Music,* Curt Sachs, one of the fathers of ethnomusicology, tells the story of a musician from the Middle East who had been studying music in Germany for eleven years. The musician confessed to Sachs that even after all that time he still could not tell the difference between symphonies of Haydn and those of Mahler (Sachs 1962:139).

The point is that just as Western musics can sound pretty much the same to non-Western listeners, so non-African listeners may have difficulty in making fine distinctions among a variety of African musics. This happens because, generally speaking, the various forms of Western musical expression have more in common with one another than any of them has with any African music. But although it is difficult to generalize about African music when dealing with it in terms of itself, it may be helpful to look at African music from a Western vantage point as a way of beginning to deal with our music-culture's biases—be they positive or negative, correct or incorrect—as they relate to African music. What follows are some generalizations about African music from the Western point of view.

Function

As is often said, a high proportion of African music is functional and is not performed outside of its intended context. People do not sing rowing songs just for pleasure outside of the context of rowing a boat; music for religious rites is heard only when those rites are being performed; dance music is played only at dances; and so on. This is noteworthy mostly when contrasted to our own uses of similar types of music. In our culture one need not be "drivin' steel" to sing the song "John Henry"; much religious music is performed in concert situations having nothing to do with religious services; and dance music may be performed "for your listening pleasure" in contexts where no dancing takes place.

Percussion

To some Westerners "African music" conjures up visions of drums and nonmelodic percussion instruments being played with wild abandon. In terms of sheer numbers, the variety of drums and other percussion instruments found in Africa is staggering. There are hand drums, stick drums, talking drums, frame drums, drum chimes (drums tuned to specific pitches and played like a xylophone), water drums (see chapter 2, pp. 56–57), slit gongs (usually called "drums" even though they have no stretched membrane), bells, iron gongs, rattles, percussion sticks, drums that are squeezed, drums that are scraped—the list of categories and subcategories and the variety of playing techniques seem almost endless. We Westerners make note of this bewildering variety probably because our own music tends not to feature a wide variety of percussion instruments, but we must also realize that in Africa the human voice is one of the prime musical instruments; that other melodic instruments including harps, zithers, fiddles, xylophones, flutes, trumpets, and others abound; and that as important as rhythm is in African music, we cannot afford to neglect melodic, harmonic, and other aspects of the music.

Rhythm

Part of our fixation on African rhythm stems from the fact that much of our own music, by comparison, tends to be rather simple and straightforward rhythmically. In most Western music a single underlying rhythmic pattern (the meter) accounts for all of the simultaneously sounding parts. We usually have little trouble knowing where to tap our feet in our music. Much African music, on the other hand, seems almost to negate the concept of meter as we know it when, for example, various apparently conflicting rhythms are woven into one another to sound a complex web of interlocking and crossing patterns. African rhythms *are* complex, but they may seem all the more so in relation to most Western rhythmic concepts.

Innate Musicality

It has been thought and said that Africans are born with musical talent. Because music is so important in the lives of many Africans and because so much music is performed in Africa, we are apt to think that all Africans are musicians. The impression is reinforced when we look at ourselves and find that we have become largely a society of musical spectators. Music is important to us, but most of us can be considered consumers rather than producers of music. We have records, television, concerts, and radio to fulfill many of our musical needs. Then, too, we tend to compartmentalize the arts and to distinguish between artist and audience. In most situations where music is performed in our culture it is not difficult to distinguish the audience from the performers, but such is often not the case in Africa. Alban Ayipaga, a Kasena semiprofessional musician from northern Ghana, says that when his flute and drum ensemble is performing, "anybody can take part." This is true, but Kasena musicians recognize that not all people are equally capable of taking part in the music. Some can sing along with the drummers, but relatively few can drum and even fewer can play the flute along with the ensemble. It is fairly common in Africa for there to be an ensemble of expert musicians surrounded by others who join in by clapping, singing, playing rattles, or somehow adding to the totality of musical sound. Performances often take place in an open area (that is, not on a stage) and so the lines between the performing nucleus and the additional performers, active onlookers, and passive onlookers may be difficult to draw from our point of view.

Notation and Improvisation

Africans do not traditionally write down (notate) their music as a way of preserving or teaching it. Rather, music is learned by rote and preserved by memory. In the past, this custom led Westerners to believe that the music was not organized, that it was composed "on the spot"; or, if some parts seemed to be set, others were thought largely improvisatory. While an understanding of variation and improvisation techniques is indeed important if one is to gain a deeper understanding of the structure and aesthetics of African music, it is also necessary to realize that these techniques are almost always related to strict rules of musical grammar that guide musicians, dancers, and listeners. In some African music there is no improvisation or even variation of any kind (the *akadinda* piece to be discussed later is an example of this). In other forms (such as the Kasena *jongo* example to follow) variation is the norm. In generalizing about African music we must keep in mind that just because composers and arrangers do not traditionally notate their music we would be wrong to assume that the product is disorganized. It is better to begin with the assumption that strict rules—rules often quite different from those guiding our own music—are in operation.

When foreign peoples came to sub-Saharan Africa to trade, explore, enslave, Christianize, Islamize, and colonize, some of them made attempts to understand Africans and their cultures on more than just a superficial level. Some early reports—such as the work of Robert S. Rattray in Ghana (Rattray 1923, 1927)—exhibit keen insight and understanding, but for the most part, the outside world continued, and in some cases still continues, to think of sub-Saharan Africa as a savage, primitive, and forbidding place in need of cultural, economic, and social modernization. After more than a century of moderately intense contact with Africa great gaps remain in our knowledge of its peoples and their cultures. If this judgment is less true of certain fields of inquiry, it is still quite true of ethnomusicology.

Before we leave the subject of Africa's contact with the outside world, it should be pointed out that there is a distinction to be made between "African music" on the one hand and "music in Africa" on the other. The former we might call "traditional music"; the latter includes traditional music but also encompasses syncretic (mixed) and foreign musics that are regularly performed in much of Africa. The long period of contact among Europe, Islamic cultures, the America's, and sub-Saharan Africa, as well as the meeting and mixing of indigenous cultures within the continent itself, present problems in any discussion of music in Africa. From our position in present time it is difficult to trace the history and development of most African musics. Especially, it is difficult to tell exactly where mixing has taken place. We will not attempt to deal with the problem here except as it relates to a particular kind of West African town music called "highlife."

MUSIC FROM GHANA (AND UGANDA)

In this chapter we can begin an exploration of sub-Saharan African music, not by attempting an overview (the musical scope of Africa is far too broad to permit that) or by describing a typical African music (the range of expression is too wide). Rather, we will be looking at some few musical types, the people who perform them, and where, why, and how they do it. Most of the examples come from Ghana in West Africa, where I lived and worked for two years. One example comes from Uganda, where I had the good fortune to work as a graduate student with Professor Klaus Wachsmann. A more or less intimate view of these few musics will, it is hoped quite simply, stimulate you to explore further the marvels of African musics and cultures.

Kasena Jongo

To begin, listen to recorded selection 11 on the CD or cassette. The music and the dance that goes with it are called *jongo,* and here it is being played by five fine musicians from Mayoro, a small village in the Kasena area of uppermost Ghana (ill. 3–1). The song is "Sara Muru, Gwa Ba Na" ("A Thousand Dancers, Four Drummers"—the drummers are praising themselves for being able to provide music for so many people). The melody is played by three three-hole flutes called *wui* (singular, *wua*), accompanied by two hourglass-shaped drums called *gungwe* (singular, *gungonga*).

The music is just one part of a dynamic situation involving dancers and some reason for people's getting together. People do *jongo* when they are happy: perhaps at a party after the millet harvest, at a wedding, or during the last stage of a funeral celebration for an old person when his or her spirit is finally sent to heaven, which is a happy occasion. Let us take as an example a wedding party. People come to the appointed place and formally greet the elders, any important people (such as a chief), and the bride and groom. The guests and functionaries eat, drink, and talk, but there is no music yet except, perhaps, for a group of small children who begin to sing for their own pleasure. Not all the guests at the

James T. Koetting
Ill. 3–1. *Kasena musicians and jongo dancer at a funeral celebration.*

wedding enjoy dancing, or are good at it; but for many, the dance to follow the formal wedding proceedings will be the highlight of the celebration, and those people, young and old alike, eagerly await the arrival of the musicians.

Some music can be heard in the distance. The musicians have formed a group outside the living compound and are approaching it playing a special kind of music for walking, the same kind of music they would use to honor a chief or other important person as he is led from one place to another. When the musicians arrive at the dancing area they might play some special nondance music (called *len yoro*) to warm themselves up and get the guests' juices going. After that they might switch to music for one of the dances just for men (*nagila* or *pe zara*). The women are eager; they want to dance, too.

Soon the musicians switch to *jongo,* and now the women may dance. In *jongo,* groups of people do not dance together. Instead, someone who wishes to dance waits at the edge of the cleared space reserved for dancing and, when he or she "catches" the music, jumps into the ring dancing to be observed (and judged) by the onlookers. If a dancer is good (or, sometimes, just very young, very old, or very pretty) people run into the ring and stick coins on the dancer's forehead. It is customary for this money to be turned over to the musicians, and it often constitutes their main form of payment. When the music is exciting it encourages the people to dance, and when a particularly good dancer jumps into the ring, the musicians respond by playing with more animation.

"Sara Muru, Gwa Ba Na" is just one of many *jongo* songs to be sung and played during the dance, and just a portion of that is on the cassette, but even in that small portion perhaps you can hear the growing excitement, animation, and variation of the music. A good Kasena flute and drum ensemble can keep the music and dancers at fever pitch by playing without stopping yet constantly changing tunes and varying them endlessly. Let us look a bit more closely at the music.

The music is certainly happy, but you might be a little bit confused by what you hear. In this case the tune is not sung (although it might be sung by the drummers), and the melody itself is divided up among the three flutes. This particular *jongo* tune is short (just one measure or twelve fast pulses long) but it is repeated and varied over and over again.

Giving an accurate example of this kind of African melody in musical notation presents some problems. First of all, the musicians do not think in terms of specific pitches and rhythms as notes on a page; they learn the music by rote. Second, the standard Western staff notation as we know it is best suited to display pitches of our equal-tempered system; and the pitches you are hearing are not in this system. And third, no two Kasena flute sets (even two sets owned by the same musicians) are tuned alike, so the same tune played on different sets may sound quite different, sometimes like a different tune altogether. (This variation does not imply a lack of skill in instrument-making—our Western bias might lead us to that conclusion—but rather it reveals an approach to melody and harmony that is free of the confines of a standardized pitch, tempered-scale tuning system.) The notational problems are not insoluble, but the solution would require pages of explanation and a notation system that, for our purposes, might confuse more than it helps. With these points in mind (and the fact that you have the "real" music to listen to on the cassette for comparison) I shall use standard Western staff notation for the sake of simplicity and readability.

Example 3–1 notates a basic form of the "Sara Muru" tune as it might be sung by the drummers. The short melody could be sung straight through or divided in half, one person or group singing "sara muru" with the rest answering "gwa ba na." If a melody is divided up in this way it is called "call and response," a kind of musical organization used in much African music.

The flutes also divide up the melody into a call and response pattern when playing a simple version of it. Since each of the flutes has just three finger holes (and sometimes just two if a player chooses to plug the bottom hole), the number of pitches available on any one flute is limited. However, the flutes are of different sizes so the pitch range of many melodies can be covered. When a melody requires, the flutes play in a form called "hocket," a dovetailing of melodic pitches in a form more complex than simple call and response. The highest flute (*wubala*) usually plays the first part of the tune, and it is answered by the two lower flutes (*wusanga* and *wunia*). In the recording the drums begin, the lower flutes enter on their part (the second half of the melody), and finally the highest flute joins them with the first part of the melody. Example 3–2

Ex. 3–1. *Jongo melody, "Sara Muru Gwa Ba Na."*

Sa - ra mu - ru,   gwa   ba   na

shows what the first two cycles of the tune look like. (The text has been included under the flute parts just so you can compare the flute melody with the vocal example that came before it.)

You can see that there are differences between the two versions (or realizations) of the melody. In most African music this is to be expected. Variation is a basic concept in African music. Melodies are not written down, and often it cannot be said that any one version is more correct than any other. You can even see a slight difference between the two notated cycles of flute melody, but both are clearly related to the tune (see ill. 3–2).

"Sara Muru" is a very short song. Just repeating and slightly varying it over and over during a performance (which might include something like 175 cycles of the tune) would soon become boring to the musicians and dancers. In the style of flute playing associated with the village of Mayoro (where these musicians come from) the high flute is given great freedom to vary his part, sometimes to the point where it has nothing to do with the basic tune. Notice that in this recording the high flute moves away from the melody but always returns to it. The artistry of this music (and of this *wubala* player named Donga) is that with just a few pitches and a very short tune, the variations are almost limitless.

Kasena musicians say that their drumming is easier than the flute playing. A flute ensemble might know more than a hundred tunes—some long, some short, some simple, and some complex—that they could play for *jongo* dance, but the drummers are required to play just a single set of rhythm patterns to go with all the tunes, although they may vary those patterns somewhat. Still, the drumming seems to be far from simple. In our example just two drums are playing. These are hourglass-shaped drums, each having two drumheads held together by leather thongs. The drum is held between the arm and rib cage, and when the leather thongs are squeezed the drumheads tighten and the pitch rises. The Kasena call this kind of drum *gungonga*. When they are played in pairs, one is pitched slightly lower than the other, and they are given names similar to the pitched flutes; the high drum is then called *gungongbala,* the lower one *gungongnia.* Similar drums (but, of course, with different names) are also used by the Yoruba, Builsa, Hausa, Dagomba, and other West African peoples. Some of these other peoples make more use of the pitch-changing potential of this type of drum than do the Kasena. You can hear some highs and lows in the recording, but the most usual Kasena technique is to squeeze the drum

Ex. 3–2. *Jongo melody, "Sara Muru Gwa Ba Na," as divided by flutes.*

(Sa - ra   mu-ru)   (Sa - ra   mu-ru)

(gwa   ba   na)   (gwa   ba   na)

James T. Koetting

Ill. 3–2. *Kasena flute players.*

slightly, releasing the pressure as soon as the head is struck; the resultant sound is of a falling pitch every time the drum is struck.

To show what these drums are playing for "Sara Mura," we can use a series of boxes, each one representing an eighth note (♪). Empty boxes mean that no sound is initiated in that unit of time. Still, you may find it difficult to follow the drumming from the notation in example 3–3. One reason is that the two drums are so close in pitch that it is often difficult to distinguish one from the other as they play interlocking patterns. The patterns notated are those generally heard once the music is underway. To hear what these combined rhythms sound like, try drumming or clapping them with someone else.

| Gungongbala | ● | | ● | | ● | | ● | ● | | ● | | ●● |
| Gungongnia | ●● | | | | ●● | | | ● | | ●● | | ●● |

Ex. 3–3.   *Drums, "Sara Muru Gwa Ba Na."*

Drums other than the *gungonga* and other percussion instruments may be used to accompany *jongo*. Sometimes it is a pair of large calabash drums (*kori*) with goatskin heads that are beaten with the hands (ill. 3–3). At other times it is a larger set of cylindrical drums (called *gullu*) with two heads laced together

Ill. 3–3.   *Kori drums.*

James T. Koetting

that are played with either two sticks or a stick and a hand (ill. 3–4). In casual situations the men might simply drum on small calabash bowls that they hold between their knees; when not being used as musical instruments, these bowls are hung up in the house for use in the kitchen.

There is more to musical instruments in Africa than just how they look and how they are played. Many people in Africa, including the Kasena, understand that material objects have spirits or souls, that is, they are more than just material objects. Anthropologists have called this understanding "animism." When a Kasena craftsman makes a calabash drum, for example, he does not just cut the calabash, attach the head, and begin to play. Certain things must be done for the spirit of the drum to insure that the drum will "speak" properly. The drum maker goes to the house of a woman known to be a gossip and picks up some pebbles from her yard (but he does this surreptitiously; he does not want the woman to know he thinks she is a gossip). These pebbles are put inside the drum so that it too will be talkative. Other things are put inside as well: the skin of a certain frog that can expand its neck skin a great deal (so that the drum skin will remain supple), a bit of lion skin (so that the drum will roar), and, in modern days, some pieces of zinc roofing material (these are put in just to rattle). When the drum is finished, all these things jiggle around inside as it is played. They make up part of the sound of the drum, but they are also a part of the drum's spirit.

The Kasena are not the only Africans who, from our point of view, "adulterate" musical instruments to make them rattle. The Asante of Ghana may sew a metal noise maker on a drum head that rattles when the drum is struck; some xylophone-type instruments have gourd resonators in which holes are drilled

Ill. 3–4. *Gullu drums.*

James T. Koetting

and covered with a thin membrane that buzzes when the key above it is struck (ill. 3–5); buzzing devices may be added to the keys of a *sansa* or the bridge of a chordophone; even the rattle of bracelets or other accouterments worn by musicians or dancers is considered to add favorably to the sound of music. Jeff Titon reports that he has known blues guitarists in the United States to put rattlesnake rattles inside their instruments in order to make them sound better, and Appalachian fiddlers have been known to do this as well.

The Kasena are only one of Ghana's peoples. If you ask a Kasena what he thinks of the music of his neighbors (the Frafra, Builsa, Nankani, Mamprusi, and others) or the music of other Ghanaian groups living further to the south (the Dagomba, Asante, Ewe, Fanti, or Ga, for example) he will most likely say that he

Ill. 3–5. *Xylophone with gourd resonators. The spots on the gourds are holes covered with membranes that buzz when the keys are struck.*

James T. Koetting

"understands" (an equivalent of "likes") his own Kasena music. He may point out that the Frafra (who live just down the road from the Kasena, play almost the exact same musical instruments, and also dance *jongo*) have "only one way to play, whereas we have many." That is another way of saying "all their music sounds alike to me." Of course, Frafra music does not sound "all alike" to the Frafra, and, in fact, the Frafra might say the same thing about Kasena music that the Kasena say about theirs. The Kasena and Frafra are culturally related in many ways, and from an outsider's point of view, the two musics also are related. However, to the Kasena and Frafra the two musics may have little in common. I point out this discrepancy to emphasize that there can be no single description, no one set of rules or unified aesthetic standards that can account for sub-Saharan African music as a whole. In many cases, and the Kasena are a prime example of this, such rules and aesthetic standards are confined to quite small geographic areas or ethnic units. There are many musics in Africa. Sometimes, as with languages, musics of two peoples may be so similar as to be mutually intelligible. Often, however, they are not.

A Personal History and View of Kasena Music by a Kasena Musician

William Alban Ayipaga Connelly is a traditional musician in the Kasena-Nankani region of Ghana (see ill. 3–6). An instructor in a public school, he is also considered to be the best musician in the Vonania *wui* (flute) and *kori* (calabash drums) ensemble. While I was working in Ghana, Alban was my close friend, a valued assistant and invaluable teacher. We spoke together often, and this is what he told me one day when I asked him to speak about his life as a musician. The tape-recorded interview took place on August 8, 1973, in Navrongo, Upper Region Ghana.

> CONNELLY: I came from Vonania, and in Vonania you have three sections. You have the head place which is a subchief in the village; that is Wosania. My section is called Telangania. The other one is Namolania. Vonania in general first generated from one place. There is one rock in Navrongo town called "Vona." We came from that place. Even now, we the people from Vonania do not go to Vona. We believe that if you go there you will see your great grandfathers, or perhaps you will see some things that are not to be seen, and you may come home and die, so we don't go there.
>
> We [Vonania] are related to Bonia, Korania, and Bundunia. In these four villages we have no intermarriage at all. However beautiful your daughter is, someone within these four villages will not marry her. And we do things in common. Now that the four sections have grown larger than before, they have separate celebrations, but formerly, if a headman died at Bonia, the four

James T. Koetting

Ill. 3–6. *William Alban Aypaga Connelly.*

villages would go there to take part in war dances. And if someone died at Vonania, the other three too will come. Likewise Korania and Bundunia. We used to perform our funerals the same, especially the headmen's funerals, but we are now many people, so many that we found that it would be boring for us to be traveling from village to village to do these things.

In Telangania my father is the second man to the headman there. If there is any celebration within the Telangania section and something is killed, our house must take the lion's share, because it is believed that our great-grandfather, who first settled at that place, had a younger brother, and the younger brother had so many children, but Telanga himself had only one son, and that was our father who was Telanga's only son. But the other people [with whom meat from a kill must be shared] in the section, they are about three, so anything that is killed we shall take half and give half to the three. So my father is of importance, in Telangania especially.

The thing which made me interested in music was when I was a small boy I heard my uncles playing these drums, so I started to learn how to play the drums. We have *kori* drums and *yongo wui* [large flutes played in pairs] in our house. Long ago Vonania too had a *yongo* group, but it died out about forty years ago. But formerly, Vonania in general used to dance *yongo* too, and the *wui* are in my house. So with these *kori* in my house and the *wui,* I took interest in our local music, and I learned how to play it. At present I can play *kori* (the *kornia* [a lower-pitched drum] and *korbala* [a higher-pitched drum], I can play the three flutes, I can play the *yongo wui,* I can play the tomtom [*gungonga,* an hourglass-shaped drum]. And any instruments our locals use here, I should think I can play them well.

KOETTING: Which instruments were taught to you by your uncles?

CONNELLY: They taught me how to play the *kori.*

KOETTING: And how did you learn to play *wui?*

CONNELLY: Anytime there was a dance or an old man died, and then after the old people or the adults played their *jongo* and they were tired, then the young boys too would get the whistles [*wui*] to learn from that. So as they rest the young boys would start to learn. If they made a mistake, those who were perfect in it would correct them, "You should do this and not that." So I learned how to play these things when I was small.

KOETTING: How old were you then?

CONNELLY: Then I was five to six years old. Even before I went to school I was able to play *kori* very well and the whistles too. And in the school I happened to join the school band and I played a flute [Western flute]. That was the then St. Mary's Catholic Primary School. From there I entered St. Mary's Middle School, which was formerly called the Junior Seminary in Navrongo. At that time it was the only middle school in the Upper Region.

KOETTING: The *only* one?

CONNELLY: The only one. I can say there were a few [others], but they were meant for local council schools, but this one was meant for Catholics, so people from Jirapa, Wa, Bawku, Bolgatanga attended this middle school. Both the primary and middle schools were the first schools in the Upper Region here, Navrongo. The Catholic missionaries started the schools here.

I was in middle school form one in 1953. In '57, [Ghana's] independence year, I passed out from middle form four, and I taught as a pupil teacher at Bawku Benduri in '58. In 1959 I went for Certification B teacher's training course. In '60 I finished the course, and I was sent to Chiana to teach there. I taught at Chiana for one year, and then came to Korania for one year. From Korania I went to Vonania for two years. I was promoted to head teacher and sent to Zuarungu Early Primary. I taught there for four years. From Zuarungu I went to Tongo; I taught there for two years. From Tongo I came back to Navrongo District and taught at Kologo Primary. From Kologo Primary I came to Wuru Primary near the town [Navrongo]. From Wuru I came to Saboro. From Saboro I came to Ada Primary, and then last year [1973] I was sent to Basina Primary.

KOETTING: Why were you moved so often?

CONNELLY: At that time there weren't enough trained teachers; there were only pupil teachers, so they tried to have a trained teacher at each school to help the pupil teachers. So any place they found that there was no trained teacher, and you like to go to the place, you were sent there.

KOETTING: And what about housing and moving the family?

CONNELLY: When I was at Chiana I had no wife. I married my wife in 1964; that was at the time I was at Zuarungu, so I was there with only my wife. My parents were in my village here, Vonania.

KOETTING: When you were a student in primary and middle school what kinds of traditional music events did you participate in?

CONNELLY: We have so many types of people in our school here, people from Bawku, Bolgatanga, etc. So every Saturday we had "Saturday Entertainment," and this was done by districts. A Saturday would come and the Navrongo boys would entertain the whole school. Another Saturday the Frafras would entertain; another Saturday the Builsas; another Saturday the Dagartis, another Saturday the Kusasis [these are different ethnic groups]. So I used to take part. I even taught some of my friends how to play the *kori* and then the *wui;* when in middle school I was then perfect in them. And then I learned to play the *gullu* [drums] in my father's uncle's house. When I was young my grandmother took me there, so I learned how to play *gullu* there in my father's uncle's house, that is Gongunia. In school I polished it up because we had *gullu* there for practice. So I practiced and I became perfect there.

KOETTING: Was it only after you came back to Vonania to live that you began to play with the group you play with now?

CONNELLY: No. When I was still in school I was not a boarder; I was a day boy. Only on Saturday Entertainments I used to go there to entertain myself and go home because my house is not far from the school. We had our group formed even before I went to middle school. I was playing *kornia,* and another boy was playing the *korbala.* Every Easter and Christmas we used to go out and play to the market and get some money and then come to share. That was way back in '52 and until 1960, when my uncles retired in playing because of old age. Then our group took over. So now, if there is any celebration in our section or in the town, instead of our uncles or brothers to play, we rather play.

KOETTING: Does your group have a leader?

CONNELLY: Yes. I should have been the leader of our group, but because I am a government employee I am always going to work, so I have handed everything over to my uncle, who is the same age as me. He is always in the house, so if there is any celebration or we want to do any drumming and dancing, he will go around and tell the people and then get all the drums prepared and the whistles—wash them, clean them with oil—and make everything set for the entertainment. [There follows a description of how musical instruments are maintained, which is excluded here.]

KOETTING: You mentioned that the younger musicians, including yourself, took over from the older ones. Did this happen all at once?

CONNELLY: No, not all at once. It happened . . . say when they are going to play *jongo,* we (the younger people) would start it. We would start practicing the *jongo* and then [the older musicians would] come to take over. If we were going to an in-law's funeral, we would move out with the drums, play until we got to the place, then our brothers would take the instruments to play. We started like that, not all at once.

KOETTING: Did the older group dissolve—stop playing all at once—or did one man leave, then another?

CONNELLY: Oh, still we mix. When we go to dance, those, our brothers, still join us even today. They still join us to play for their own interest. Any place we are going, they go with us and they will go and take part with the drumming for their own interest; not that we cannot do it well.

KOETTING: How about the next generation, the boys younger than you?

CONNELLY: Those younger than we people, we have given them a set of whistles, and they have started training now; they have started learning how to use them. After harvest they always get their own drums and they start to play. So, in about five to six years they will also be fine. Even some of them join us today too. Say at present if there is something important in the house and they want me and I'm not there, a working day if I am in the place [school], there are some young boys who will take my place. But the music will not be the same as if the real group were playing. But when we are playing, *anybody* can take part.

KOETTING: How long does it take to become perfect in *wui?* Say in your case, how long did it take?

CONNELLY: I was in primary school when I joined my brothers as an expert musician. A time came that one of them left for the South, and I was in primary school when I was asked to take part in the drumming on a Christmas day blowing the whistles through the town. So it didn't take me a long time to learn.

KOETTING: Do musicians always learn from relatives—brothers and uncles?

CONNELLY: Anyone who is interested in the music may join a group, not just those with fathers and brothers who are musicians.

KOETTING: What do people say about those who have musical talent? Is there anything special about them?

CONNELLY: No. If you have interest in the music you will pick it up. I should think it only lies in the interest of the individual. Some choose to learn *kora* [singular of *kori*], others *sinyegule* (basket rattles), *wui,* or tomtom, it depends on individual interest.

KOETTING: Do you believe there is such a thing as talent?

CONNELLY: Some people say that, that there is such a thing as talent, but I don't believe it. I've never been to someone for *juju* (magic) to take part in playing this thing or to learn certain things, but I do it well. And there are some people who believe that there is some medicine at Wuru or Gia that, if you take it, you will be perfect at singing, but I don't believe it.

KOETTING: How many children do you have?

CONNELLY: I have three children now. I should have had four now, but I lost one last year.

KOETTING: How old are they?

CONNELLY: The first one is about seven years, and the second one who died should have been five and a half. Then the last two: one is three and the other one is one year and four months.

KOETTING: What are they, males or females?

CONNELLY: They are all females. I am sorry. [There follows some small talk which is excluded here.]

KOETTING: Is there anything you would like to add?

CONNELLY: Yes. I am interested in the Western music too, but only I can't get the means to learn. I'm interested in playing a guitar, then a flute or a trumpet if I can get to learn, but where to get these things to learn is a problem.

KOETTING: There is no one in Navrongo who—

CONNELLY: No.

KOETTING: What about the band at St. Mary's School?

CONNELLY: The band is spoiled long since, so no band again here.

KOETTING: What would you do if you learned Western music?

CONNELLY: I'd like to be a musician, that's why I'd like to learn it.

KOETTING: But you are a musician.

CONNELLY: I am a local musician; I want to be a general one. If I can teach it or play it, whether my local music or any band, a general band somewhere, I would like it in that way.

KOETTING: What do you think about doing local music in the schools?

CONNELLY: I tried teaching our local music last year when I went to Basina School. I bought some whistles. There was no one to help me teach these children the music, and no one to help financially too. I couldn't get the things all at once. So I bought some calabashes to make *kori* for them, and I have got the whistles too. So if I get all this done I will start a local music group in the school there.

KOETTING: Are the children interested?

CONNELLY: They are *very* interested, only the school is a mixed school. You have some "coasters" (the people who come from the south, we call them "coasters"), Ashantis, Fantis, Ewes, Builsas, all sorts of people in town. Because the school is in the town [Navrongo] all the workers send their children there. So most of these town schools are mixed schools; we have all tribes there. But if I'm able to get the drums, the whistles, the *gungonga,* and the *sinyegule,* I will start a drumming group there.

When I left Ghana in 1975, Alban was in training on government scholarship to become an art specialist in the schools. The training school was located on the outskirts of Navrongo, and he continued performing with the Vonania flute and drum ensemble. Let us now look at a music of another of Ghana's peoples, the Asante.

Asante Kete

The Asante (or Ashanti) people live about four hundred miles south of the Kasena in Ghana. They are a much larger group than the Kasena and play quite different kinds of music. Generally speaking, we know more about the Asante than we do about the Kasena. The Asante live closer to the coast, which has always been the West African area having the most contact with Europeans. Asante armies gave the English a great deal of trouble when England tried to subjugate them. They were a force to contend with, and they gained the respect and fear of the English. One result of this was that the English tried to know their enemy (and later ally) and studied and wrote much about the Asante. As you can imagine, little of the writing dealt with musical matters, but such sources certainly help us to put Asante music in perspective.

Unlike the Kasena, who have been called a chiefless society, the Asante have an elaborate social organization, and a hierarchy of chiefs leading from the king of Asante (the *Asantehene*—"hene" means "chief") down through paramount chiefs (chiefs in charge of several towns or villages), village chiefs, clan chiefs, and so on. Even a music ensemble has a chief, so it is important when one is using the term *chief* to know what level of chief it is.

The Asantehene and his paramount chiefs were once very powerful, and even today, although Ghana has a central government, these chiefs are recognized by the government, and they have certain powers and rights. One of the traditional rights they had and continue to have is that of maintaining special groups of musicians, music ensembles not allowed to common people. Such ensembles, comprising both the musical instruments and the music they play, are symbols of royalty and power. One of these ensembles is called *kete* ('keh-tay). *Kete* is a royal ensemble whose ownership is restricted to the king of Asante and paramount chiefs. The ensemble performs at a variety of royal (and sometimes nonroyal) functions at the command of the king or paramount chief.

In the old days the chiefs and the king in particular supported a great many retainers that lived at or near the palaces. The basic responsibility of the royal musicians was to provide music for the chief, the royal clan, or for whomever the chief wished it. Things are a little different now. The king and chiefs can no longer afford to maintain large numbers of retainers, but royal music, since it is so important to the position of the chief, is still actively supported. Some *kete* musicians, for example, may work at regular jobs nowhere near the palace or even in another town, but they are still expected to perform at the command of the chief. As a result, these days the chief may have to run an announcement in the classified section of several newspapers to get the musicians together: "Will all *kete* musicians of the Asantehene please report to the palace at 8:00 A.M. on the 21st of November to perform for ..."

Kete music is mainly for drums, and I include it here to demonstrate the beautiful complexity and precision found in so much African drumming. In recorded selection 12 on the accompanying CD or cassette, the lead drummer (called the "master drummer") was Kwasi Badu, a royal musician, but the rest of the drummers were students at UCLA, where Badu taught for several years. The reason for using this particular recording is that it clearly demonstrates how simple individual drum rhythms are piled up to make a complex whole; the recording also proves that performing this music, if at a somewhat simple level, is not beyond the abilities of non-Africans.

The general structure of the drumming style of which kete is a part has been very well explained by Professor J. H. Kwabena Nketia, an ethnomusicologist and the director of the University of Ghana's Institute of African Studies (see, for example, Nketia 1963). Nketia explains that in most Akan drum ensembles— Akan is the language of the Asante and several related groups—a basic rhythm, called the "timeline," is the essential rhythmic underpinning of the music. It is like a base drum in a marching band; the musicians listen to it stay together, and its part seldom changes (see ill. 3–7). Then there are one or more instruments that play simple rhythm patterns that fit in with and are intended to go mainly with the timeline. At the next level is usually one drum that plays rhythms that fit with the master drum, and finally comes the master drum itself; the master

James T. Koetting

Ill. 3–7. *Royal drums of the Akan people being carried in procession.*

drummer is the ultimate leader of the ensemble, who plays the most complex and varied rhythms. Keep in mind that this is just a general format that may, to a greater or lesser extent, fit many African drum ensembles (see ill. 3–8). Before dealing specifically with *kete* it is again necessary to discuss some problems of notation.

Just as was the case with the Kasena flute music, there are difficulties in trying to represent *kete* drumming in notation. The problem is not that the spatial relationships between strokes on the instruments are not clear, for they almost always are. Nor is it that the rhythm patterns are too complex or too random to

James T. Koetting

Ill. 3–8. *Instruments of kete ensemble. L-R: two torowas, dawuro, apen-temma, master drum (kwadum), donno, aburukuwa II, aburukuwa I.*

notate; the rhythm patterns, taken individually, are nearly always quite simple, and they fit together in specific ways. The problem lies in displaying these patterns in a way that demonstrates how they fit together from the Asante point of view rather than our European one, and still rendering them readable. It is not an easy problem to solve, but it must be addressed lest we oversimplify and conceptually westernize this music, and in the process neglect or obscure what is uniquely Asante in it.

Some simple facts about much African music in general and *kete* in particular will serve to point up the problems of notating (and therefore understanding) it.

1. African drummers in my experience do not tap their feet; they do not necessarily think in terms of controlling underlying pulses (like the beats of a measure) to time their playing, but the music *is* nevertheless strictly timed.

2. Each of the simultaneously sounding rhythm patterns being played across the ensemble normally has a conceptualized specific beginning point, but the beginning points of the patterns of various instruments may not coincide. Using the same measure lines for all parts, as in a score, destroys the individuality of each part; using different measure lines for each part destroys the unity of the whole.

3. It seems that one of the important aspects of much African rhythm is its metric ambiguity. Duple (two-beat) and triple (three-beat) time seem to be mixed together, sometimes one coming to the fore and sometimes the other, depending upon what our ears fix on at the moment. If it is indeed the intent of the music to be metrically ambiguous, how could this be shown in notation?

4. In addition to the duple-triple problem, a single rhythm pattern may sound different depending on its context. For example, the most common timeline pattern used in *kete* is the same as that used in another kind of Asante music called *adowa,* but usually—it depends somewhat on the specific *kete* or *adowa* piece being played—the effect when comparing *kete* and *adowa* is of hearing two different timeline patterns with different beginning points and different

internal structures. This effect is due to the influence on our ears of the master drum and the supporting patterns that go with it. It is another kind of ambiguity or duality that is difficult to render in notation.

A great deal of time and effort could fruitfully be spent investigating these problems. If we understood them better we would be a long way toward comprehending African rhythmic structure. But there are still many gaps in our knowledge and disagreement among scholars as to how to interpret (and therefore notate) African rhythms. A thorough examination of this topic has no place in an introductory book, but you should at least be aware of the problems and keep an open mind as you listen and look at the examples. The notated examples included here are accurate in terms of the durational aspects of individual patterns and the relationship between patterns. I have, however, taken some liberties with their conceptualization (organization) in the interests of clarity.

The *kete* timeline pattern serves to illustrate one of the problems involved with notating African rhythm. This pattern would be taught orally; a student would learn to say, "*sang si sang sang si sang si*" as a series of heavy accents (*sang*), light accents (*si*), and spaces, and the resultant pattern could be notated as shown in example 3–4. When you listen to the recording, it is this pattern that the master drum plays to bring in the gong timeline; however, the gong plays only the *sangs*, as is common. Your own ears may hear (and Western musical thinking in general suggests) the last notated *sang* as a more logical beginning point of the timeline, particularly when the timeline is heard in context of the full ensemble. Thus, notating the timeline as starting from the last *sang* also makes sense. Keep this in mind as we discuss and you listen to the other rhythm patterns of *kete*.

Listen again to the beginning of the example of *kete* (no. 12 on the cassette). This recording was done particularly to show how the various levels or parts fit together; the musicians greatly stagger their entrances. In a real performance of *kete* the master drummer would give the signal to begin, and all the instruments would enter as soon as they were ready; the entire starting-up process might take just one or two cycles of the gong. The order of entrances on the recording, notated from the first stroke each instrument plays, is as follows:

1. The master drummer begins by giving the musicians a signal to ready themselves to play. He does this by saying (in drum language) *"ago?"* ("Is anybody home?"). The master drum then plays the timeline pattern to bring in the gong (/ indicates a light stroke):

2. The gong (*dawuro*) enters on the timeline (but leaving out the light strokes).

3. The rattle (*torowa*) joins the gong on the timeline.

sang			si	sang			sang		si	sang		si	

Ex. 3–4. *Kete timeline.*

4. The next two instruments to enter have the same name (*aburukuwa*) and both are basic supporting instruments. The first (which will be referred to as "*aburukuwa* I") is a high-pitched drum played with two thin sticks:

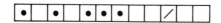

The second is smaller but lower in pitch and is played with heavier sticks:

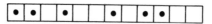

5. The last instrument to enter is a hand drum (*apentemma*), and this instrument in *kete* is an intermediate supporting instrument. That is, its pattern is intended to fit more with those of the master drum than do the patterns of the other instruments:

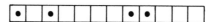

With the entrance of the hand drum, the master drum begins to play the specific set of patterns that go with the *kete* piece "Atine," and the music is in full swing. The patterns above have been notated from the conceptual beginning of each. To see how these patterns interact, we will now rearrange the *dawuro* (gong) pattern so that it begins on its last stroke (which is the strongest pulse heard across the ensemble and the pulse you probably hear as a logical beginning of ensemble patterns) and we will rearrange the other patterns—including a typical one of the master drum—to conform to it below in score fashion (ex. 3–5). Notice that all of the instruments play on the strong first notated pulse and that this is followed by a rest across the ensemble. Listen for this to help orient your ear. Asterisks in the *dawuro, torowa, aburukuwa* II, and master drum patterns indicate the conceptual beginnings of those patterns.

"Atine" is one of about fifteen *kete* pieces. Actually, "Atine" is itself a medley of *kete* pieces that are traditionally joined together in a performance. Just the first section of "Atine" (a piece called "Akatape") is included in the recorded example, but as a performance continues, the master drummer plays a certain signal that changes pieces in the "Atine" medley. These signals affect mostly the

Ex. 3–5. *Kete, "Atine," drum pattern.*

Dawuro	•				•*		•		•				
Torowa	•				•*		•		•				
Aburukuwa I	•		•		•	•	•			/			
Aburukuwa II	•		•			•		•	•			•*	
Apentemma	•		•					•	•				
Master drum	•			•	•		•			•*	•		

apentemma player, who must change his patterns according to the piece. The other instruments do not change patterns as long as "Atine" is being played, and because they play the same patterns throughout, the difference between "Atine" pieces is quite subtle.

The most interesting thing about the master drum's piece-changing signal, however, is that the master drummer may play it and then *not* change pieces. A rule for "Atine" is that the master drummer may signal for a change of pieces and then not change, but he cannot change pieces without playing the signal. By playing the signal, the master drummer is, in effect, saying to the *apentemma* player, "Listen carefully, I *may* change pieces." If he does change, the *apentemma* player must, as soon as he knows what the new piece is, select the proper pattern to go with it; if the piece does not change after the signal is given, he would, of course, continue on his previous *apentemma* pattern. The master drum-changing signal is notated in example 3–6. Listen for it in the recording and notice that after it is played, the pieces does not change; the master drummer returns to patterns he has already played, and the *apentemma* pattern remains the same.

The kind of structure we see in *kete*—relative short, simple, and repeated rhythms piled on top of one another—is typical of most Asante drumming and of other kinds of African music as well, so the lessons we can learn from studying it closely are important. When non-Africans hear this kind of music for the first time they might think that it is mostly improvised, that the drummers (or other musicians) get together and play whatever they feel like playing. A listener might even think that it is not organized at all. A simple analysis of this music, however, reveals that it is indeed highly organized. And watching, listening to, and learning from African musicians confirms this evidence. In *kete*, the rhythm patterns must be played accurately, and they must fit together in precise (and predetermined) ways or the music is wrong. Although the gong plays a basic pattern to which all the musicians and dancers listen, the ultimate responsibility for the musical precision of the group is in the hands of the master drummer. If anyone goes astray, the master drummer will know it immediately and he will do something to correct the situation. The master drum controls the tempo and signals the beginnings and endings of pieces (see ill. 3–9).

A good master drummer has a vast store of musical knowledge. He must know the proper patterns to play for each piece, and he must be able to join them together in an interesting way so that the music does not sound mechanical. He must know what pieces to play, depending on the situation. If, for example, the ensemble is playing "Atine" at a gathering and the paramount chief (or king) gets up from his stool and begins walking, the master drummer should switch

Ex. 3–6. *Master drum changing signal, "Atine."*

(The first line may be played 1, 2, or 3 times before going on to line two.)

James T. Koetting

Ill. 3–9. A kete master drummer.

the ensemble to a piece that is suitable for processions. Kwabena Nketia says that in *kete* the piece "Apente" (which is also part of "Atine") might be used in that situation; he says that the "general rhythmic character [of "Apente"] is embodied in the interpretive formula: ɔhene nam, ɔmpɛ ntɛm (the chief walks; he is not in a hurry)" (Nketia 1974:129–130). This piece is appropriate because it advises the chief to walk carefully; should the chief stumble, it would be a bad omen.

How does a master drummer learn his art? It is a long process that may begin as soon as an infant (often the son of a drummer) shows any sign that he has musical talent. Such a child may be given toy drums to play with. As he grows older he will be taught the simple supporting patterns and the proper ways to hold the drumsticks; he will learn how to strike the drum properly. Since musical notation is used nowhere in sub-Saharan Africa, the drummers have others ways of remembering their patterns. A common mnemonic device is the use of verbal phrases or nonsense syllables that go with certain patterns (such as the "Apente" phrase given above and the *sang* and *si* pattern for the *kete* gong rhythm). Only after a drummer has learned to perform well on all of the supporting instruments is he capable of dealing properly with the master drum.

Apart from the musical knowledge required to play the drums properly, a drummer must also have a good deal of physical strength. Often the drummers are required to play for long continuous stretches of time, and doing this can be exhausting. I have seen musicians "work out" on their instruments with the sole purpose of building their endurance. While teaching at the University of Ghana, I witnessed a vivid example of this discipline involving not a drummer but a xylophone player, Joseph, who had been brought from Nandom in northern Ghana to work at the Institute of African Studies at Legon. I remember hearing Joseph playing his xylophone on a particularly hot day. The music was coming not from the relative cool spot in a grove where Joseph usually practiced but from a small, nearly airless room where the xylophones are stored. I went into the room and saw Joseph attacking his instrument with uncommon vehemence; sweat was literally rolling from his body. It appeared crazy for him to be doing this on such a day and in such a place. Joseph did not acknowledge me when I entered the room, and he continued playing for another ten or fifteen minutes as I watched and listened. When he finally stopped I asked him if he had gone mad. He said no, it was just that he had been hired to play for an upcoming funeral celebration that might last all night. At home, he said, he often played for these long affairs, but here in the South he seldom did. His playing at the Institute did not require long continuous hours of playing, and it was therefore necessary for him to get into shape for the funeral. He explained that his patrons and the guests at the funeral celebration would expect the music to last all night and that they would think ill of him if he could not provide it. Joseph felt that by working out in this small room in the heat of the day he would be able to gauge his readiness for the funeral performance.

The two musics from Ghana that we have looked at thus far are different from one another, but they they also share some common traits. The musics of both the Kasena flute and drum ensemble and the Asante *kete* drums are based on short repetitive patterns that may be varied. In both cases the patterns of individual instruments interlock to produce a composite sound in such a way that no one instrument by itself quite makes African musical sense. In other words, the relationship between the various instruments in these ensembles is more intimate than that existing between, say, a melody and its harmony. Even though the high flute in the Kasena ensemble and the *kete* master drum are considered to be the most important instruments in each ensemble, both are just one component part of an intricate whole.

How to Perform African Cross-Rhythm

Africans learn music by doing music, and we, too, can benefit from trying to perform it. Certain kinds of information and understanding can come only from getting involved in the *doing,* even if that can only be at a rudimentary level. Try to perform some of the notated examples in this and later sections, but try to do it in an African rather than a Western frame of reference. Understanding one basic concept of African structure will help you: very often rhythmic and melodic patterns of several players are intimately related, often so intimately that a single musician has difficulty performing his part all by itself outside the context of the ensemble. Let us look at this concept as it might work rhythmically. Try clapping (or drumming) the following pattern over and over in a repeated sequence.

This pattern makes sense to us as a rhythmic whole; it is a complete idea or phrase. It is also a pattern heard very often in African music, but there it would very likely be performed by two players, as shown in example 3–7.

When Western musicians look at the two patterns below they call the rhythm "two against three," a "cross-rhythm," or "polymeter," and in so doing they point up the *difference* between the two patterns. Now, it is true that *physically* the first player produces three pulses against the second player's two pulses, but *mentally* the players are not thinking of two pulses versus three, they are thinking of and relating to the sound of the complete pattern (♩ ♫ ♩). The difference is subtle but extremely important to an understanding of much African rhythm. It has nothing to do with the actual sound that is produced by the two players, but a great deal to do with how they conceptualize it.

Clap the complete pattern by yourself, then try the two-player pattern by tapping one pattern with your left hand and the other with your right hand. When you make the switch from clapping to tapping the trick is not to change your conception of the sound produced; continue to hear it as a single line, a single rhythm. Finally, clap with someone else, each of you taking one of the player's parts, and, again, relate to the total sound and not just the part you are producing. With practice you will find that the two of you are operating as one. When that happens you are producing African music.

We now turn to a music from Uganda in East Africa that demonstrates this same principle in a somewhat different way.

Baganda Akadinda

Can you imagine a musical composition that lasts a mere two seconds and in which the notes fly by at a speed of approximately twelve per second? Such is

Ex. 3–7. *Two-against-three cross-rhythm.*

| player 1 |
| player 2 |

the case in Baganda *akadinda* music (recorded selection 13). The *akadinda* is a xylophone played by the Baganda people of Uganda. It is one of several types of regional xylophones, and the particular one we will be discussing has seventeen keys and is played by three men. Like Asante *kete*, *akadinda* xylophone music is essentially intended for royalty. *Akadinda* musicians were in the employ of the *Kabaka* (or king) of Buganda, a powerful state in Uganda until 1966, when the *Kabaka* was overthrown and that office abolished. Because there is no longer a *Kabaka* of Buganda this music is seldom heard today, although—largely through the efforts of Klaus Wachsmann, an ethnomusicologist who was curator of the Uganda Museum at Kampala from 1948 to 1957—some of this fine music has been preserved on recordings, and *akadinda* players remained in the employ of the museum. We also know much about this music from the research of Gerhard Kubic and Lois Anderson (Kubic 1969; Anderson 1968).

The *akadinda* is classified as a free-key xylophone, as the keys are not attached to any frame or resonating chamber. When there is to be a performance the keys are taken out and simply laid across two banana-tree stalks. Thin twigs are then stuck into the stalks between each key to keep them more or less in place. Two players sit on one side of the instrument facing the third player on the other side. Each hits the *akadinda* with two wooden mallets.

Before discussing how the *akadinda* is played and how tunes are structured, it is necessary to say something about the tuning system used for this musical instrument. *Akadinda* tuning divides the octave into five nearly equal intervals (whereas the Western or European octave is divided into twelve equal half-steps, the chromatic scale). This means that the smallest interval on the *akadinda* is equal to approximately 2.4 half-steps of the Western chromatic scale. It is, in other words, about as different from the tuning system we are used to as it can be. Theoretically, at least, an equidistant five-tone (or pentatonic) scale should sound quite foreign to our ears. However, when you listen to the music it is likely that the tuning will not disturb you; it may not sound as "out of tune" as you think it should. What happens is that our ears, so used to the Western tempered scale, tend automatically to adjust these intervals to sound like the ones we expect to hear. In addition, most Western music is arranged around a tonal center defined by a specific series of whole- and half-steps (normally a major or some kind of minor scale). Our musical conditioning, it seems, requires a tonic pitch or home base so that we can put a melody into perspective, but it can be difficult for sensitive Western ears to perceive a tonic in any scale made up of approximately equidistant intervals. I point this out only because you may find that the tonal center seems to change from one hearing to the next; your ear may adjust to the intervals one way one time and another way the next. Figure 3–1 illustrates the approximate difference between Western chromatic intervals and the *akadinda*'s nearly equidistant pentatonic scale. I hasten to add that it has never been proven that *akadinda* makers attempt to achieve absolute equidistance in tuning their instruments. In a thoroughgoing article on xylophone music in Buganda, Gerhard Kubic reports that while some instruments

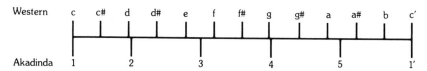

Fig. 3–1. *Western chromatic intervals compared with akadinda intervals.*

come very close to equidistance others are far enough off so that equidistance as an ideal tuning is questionable (Kubic 1969:70).

Because most of the *akadinda* intervals fall in the "cracks" of the Western system, it is less than helpful to use Western staff notation to render the melodies. Instead, we will simply assign the numbers one through five to the pitches of the *akadinda* octave. This convention (called "cipher notation") is commonly used in notating the music of fixed-pitch instrument such as xylophones.

The example of *akadinda* music on the accompanying cassette was recorded by Klaus Wachsmann in 1949, when recording technology was not what it is today. The sound quality and speed regulation fall short of perfection, but the playing is expert. The piece is "Kawuta Yeggalidde" ("Kawuta Has Shut Himself Up"); a transcription of it appears in the aforementioned article by Gerhard Kubic.

I am particularly fascinated by the structure of *akadinda* music. The music is put together in a strict hocket form. It is the same general approach to melody construction that we saw with the Kasena flutes—several parts fitting together to make up a melody—but the technique is different. The seventeen-key *akadinda* is usually played by three musicians who divide the music into two basic parts called the *okunaga* and *okwawula*. The *okunaga* part is more important melodically and it is usually longer than the *okwawula*. The player who sits alone on one side of the instrument plays the *okunaga* part with two sticks in parallel octaves: 2 1 2 1 2 1 2 $\underline{5}$ (the line under $\underline{5}$ indicates that the part goes from 2 down to 5 rather than up to it). It is the *okunaga* part that you hear alone at the very beginning of the recording. The next part to enter is one-half of the *okwawula* part played in octaves by the left-hand sticks of the other two players, who sit across from the *okunaga* player: 2 3 1 $\underline{5}$| 2 3 1 $\underline{5}$. As soon as this part is established in relation to the *okunaga,* these two players add the right-hand pattern of the *okwawula* part: 4 5 4 4 | 4 5 4 4. The whole thing, when it gets going, is a steady-pulsed rhythmic round; between each note of the *okunaga* comes first the left- then right-hand strokes of the *okwawula,* as shown in example 3–8.

What is being produced on the xylophone, then, is a rapid-fire string of twenty-four notes played with machine-like precision. (When I was learning to play this instrument, my teachers might say after a good performance, "Ah, it

Ex. 3–8. *Akadinda music, "Kawuta Yeggalidde."*

okunaga	2		1		2		1		2		1		2		5		
okwawula LH)		2		3		1		5		2		3		1		5	
okwawula RH)			4		5		4		4		4		5		4		4

sounded like a machine.") At a speed of approximately twelve notes per second, the total melodic material of the piece lasts just two seconds. Of course, the short piece is repeated over and over, but none of the parts is altered in any way. There is no improvisation in *akadinda* music.

This static, repeated sequence of pitches, however, does not tell the whole story of *akadinda* melodic construction. The melody of "Kawuta Yeggalidde" is not made up of all of the twenty-four notes; nor is the melody just one of the parts (with the other two being considered accompaniment). Rather, the actual melody is described as a resultant, something arising out of the combination of the two (or three, depending on how you look at it) parts.

Kubic describes in detail the *akadinda* composition process, although the actual tune for "Kawuta Yeggalidde" is not included (Kubic 1969:49–54). He points out that *akadinda* melodies are set to vocal tunes. The *okunaga* part is composed first and its equally spaced notes should fall on pitches of the vocal melody. If, for example, the vocal melody to be set were "When Johnny Comes Marching Home," the *okunaga* part might be the evenly spaced notes (indicated by arrows) in example 3–9. Then, some of the *okwawula* pitches would pick up the other melody notes. Other *okwawula* pitches would be left over and act as a kind of linear harmony. The process is often more complicated than this, however, since *okwawula* parts are sometimes standardized to the extent that in all likelihood they would disagree with at least some melody pitches. Another problem in understanding the exact relationship between *akadinda* and vocal tunes exists since, in many cases, the original vocal tune is no longer known.

There are many kinds of xylophones in Africa, most of them centered in West, Central, or East Africa, and the musics played by them are as varied as the instruments themselves. By contrast with the *akadinda,* a single instrument played by three men in a hocket format, we might mention the *timbila* xylophone orchestras of the Chopi people of Mozambique. Here xylophones of various sizes (with resonators) are joined together in large orchestras. Instead of playing in hocket, these instruments (the equivalents of soprano, alto, tenor, and bass voices) play melody and counter melodies (Tracey 1948). At the other extreme, simple xylophones consisting of nothing more than free keys laid across the outstretched legs of the player may still be found in some parts of Africa. Nketia (1974:81–84) and Marcuse (1975:22–27) survey African xylophone types; the *akadinda* is just one of many.

Music of Work

As I pointed out earlier, much of African music is intimately tied to a specific context or function; that is, it does not exist as a pure art form in itself, but must

Ex. 3–9. *Hypothetical arrangement for okunaga, "When Johnny Comes Marching Home."*

be seen as inextricably related to essentially nonmusical activities such as religious rites, rowing, hoeing, funerals, royal occasions, and so forth. As the *Kasena* musicians would say when referring to special music performed at the funerals of important men, "We don't play this music by heart," meaning, "We don't play this music for pleasure anytime we feel like it." This special *Kasena* music is never heard outside the context of these funerals.

The idea of context-specific music in Africa is often used to point up a difference between African and European musics. It is claimed that they emphasize such music whereas we, thinking of music as an art form capable of standing on its own, do not. In truth, however, much African music is considered by Africans to be art in and of itself, and, of course, Americans have music that is specifically related to certain contexts. Some people sing in the shower, and most of these shower Carusos would not dream of performing in any other context. "Easy listening" music (sometimes called "beautiful music") that floods the FM waves is intended to provide a non-attention-getting background for eating, doing housework, shopping, doing office work, and so forth. We are not supposed to *listen* to it; people would not go to a concert hall to hear it.

Nevertheless, the fact remains that a considerable portion of music in Africa is intended to be performed in specific contexts, and this fact holds less true in our own country. And when, as is sometimes the case in Africa, a music is heard *only* in relation to a specific context or function, it may be difficult to separate the music part of the performance from the sounds or actions of the activity with which the music is associated. Such is the case in our next example.

Listen now to recorded selection 14 on the CD or cassette. It sounds like music and, of course, it is; but the men performing it do not quite think of it that way. These men are working, not putting on a musical show; people pass by the work place paying little attention to the "music." (I used to go often to watch and listen to them, and they gave the impression that they thought I was somewhat odd for doing so.) The four men making the sounds you hear are workers canceling letters at the University of Ghana post office. Each letter must be canceled by hand, a boring task that these men make more palatable by setting the work to music. Twice a day the letters that must be canceled are laid out in two files, one on either side of a divided table. Two men sit across from one another at the table, and each has a hand-canceling machine (like the price markers you may have seen in supermarkers), an ink pad, and a stack of letters. The work part of the process is simple: a letter is slipped from the stack with the left hand, and the right hand inks the marker and stamps the letter—a repetitive task by anyone's standards but one made for setting to music since it is rhythmic (or can be made so) and it produces audible sound.

This is what you are hearing: the two men seated at the table slap a letter rhythmically several times to bring it from the file to the position on the table where it is to be canceled (this act makes a light-sounding thud). The marker is inked one or more times (the lowest, most resonant sound you hear) and then stamped on the letter (the high-pitched mechanized sound you hear). As you can hear, the rhythm produced is not a simple one-two-three (bring forward the letter—ink the marker—stamp the letter). Rather, musical sensitivities take over. Several slaps on the letter to bring it down, repeated thuds of the marker in the ink pad and multiple cancelations of single letters are done for rhythmic interest. Such repetition slows down the work, but also makes it much more interesting for the workers.

The other sounds you hear have nothing to do with the work itself. A third man has a pair of scissors that he clicks—not cutting anything, but adding to the rhythm. The scissors go "click, click, click, rest" (♩ ♩ ♩ 𝅘𝅥𝅮) a basic rhythm used in popular dance music. The fourth worker simply whistles along. He and any of the other three workers who care to join him whistle popular tunes or church music that fits the rhythm.

These post office workers provide us with a modern example of work music in Africa, but there are many traditional forms of it. Drummers may be sent to the fields to provide rhythm for workers harvesting or weeding crops; men pulling a fishing net might sing to coordinate their efforts; women using poles to beat down the dirt floor of a house might sing and stomp in rhythm. Sometimes the music is intended to help the workers work together, make the task go faster, or keep the work steady; it always makes the work more fun.

Brass Band Highlife

When white men first looked at sub-Saharan Africa they believed they were seeing peoples living in much the same way as their ancestors had for millennia. Some assumed that by studying African music they could gain some understanding of what man's earliest music was like. In fact, we can only guess about man's earliest music, and there is no particular reason to think it sounded anything like what can be heard in Africa today.

Through the centuries in Africa—before and after foreign contact—it can be assumed that African music was changing. When African peoples met in wars, trading, and migrations they exchanged more than blows, commodities, and greetings; they exchanged music and musical instruments as well. And later, when white and black cultures clashed and mingled in Africa and the New World, certain musically mixed forms were created. It is possible, then, to discuss music in sub-Saharan (black) Africa on several different levels:

1. The music of an African ethnic group that has been influenced by nothing outside of that ethnic group. It is unlikely that any such music exists in Africa today, but the idea is useful as a constant.

2. Music in Africa that results from change, mixing, and innovation in Africa and not influenced by any culture outside of Africa.

3. African music that exhibits traits of both African and non-African musics. This is often referred to as syncretic music.

4. Music created and/or performed in Africa that comes wholly from outside Africa.

The categories above are neat, but in real life they are not so easy to employ. For example, we might label African music at the first two levels as "traditional." That term, however, is not easy to define, and it must be used warily. When we think of tradition usually something old and relatively unchanging comes to mind, but how old is old, and how much and what kinds of change will cause something to be removed from the realm of the traditional to that of the nontraditional in our minds? Since cultures are seldom static the line between the traditional and nontraditional, if it is to be drawn, must be drawn according to an arbitrary set of parameters. We might say that the music discussed in the previous sections could be described as traditional and, at the other extreme, that a performance of a Beethoven symphony by the Ghana National Symphony Orchestra is nontraditional music in Africa. Let us turn to one example from what is a fairly broad middle ground consisting of forms that are to a greater or lesser extent syncretic (combined).

Listen to recorded selection 15 on the CD or cassette. This is a uniquely Ghanaian blend of European and African musics that the Ghanaians call "highlife." Its general sonority should be more familiar to you than the previous African examples since the main musical instruments being used (trumpets, trombones, alto and baritone horns, tuba, and snare and bass drums) are not native to Africa but were imported there from Europe and the Americas. These instruments were imported originally to form bands to play marches and other types of European band music. Such bands with Ghanaian musicians often were attached to military and police organizations, and some were even introduced in schools. These European-type bands still exist in Ghana, but others, such as the Nyakrom Brass Band on the cassette, have formed in small southern communities to play, among other things, "highlife."

Highlife (a reference to the fancy dress balls and generally good living enjoyed by the British in Ghana and those educated Ghanaians who imitated them) is a happy music with a carefree dance. The dance is usually done by couples— another European element, since couple-dancing (male with female) is rare in "traditional" Africa. This particular recording was made at a Vandal's Day celebration at the University of Ghana, a day when students let loose in fun. The students hired the band first to parade around the campus with them and then to play for a dance (ill. 3–10).

As you listen to the music perhaps you are reminded of an ill-trained, somewhat raucous junior high school band in the United States. True, the intonation seems to be "off," the playing techniques are not so refined, and the musicians do not seem to be quite together. But wait. What criteria are we using to evaluate this performance? The Nyakrom Brass Band is one of the finest in Ghana. Just because these men are playing European instruments does not necessarily mean that they must play them in a European tuning system with European techniques and in European forms and structures. Although this music has some European elements (the harmonic structure and a prevailing 4/4 metric pulse), African elements are strongly present as well.

We can determine some of the African elements in this brass band music by

James T. Koetting

Ill. 3–10. *The Nyakrom Brass Band in procession at a Vandal's Day celebration at the University of Ghana.*

comparing it to the previous African examples we heard. First of all, although this piece is melodic and harmonic, the main emphasis seems to be on the rhythm. The percussion section of the Nyakrom Brass Band is larger and more varied than one would expect to find in a European band. Hand drums (in this case, *congas*) are added, as are several types of gongs. If you listen carefully you can hear a small gong playing the following timeline-like pattern: 𝄞 In highlife music this pattern is usually present (compare to the scissor clicks in the post office example). This short pattern is, in fact, the timeline of an Akan dance music called *sikyi* (pronounced "seechee"), but whereas in *sikyi* the timeline may stand in various relationships to *sikyi* tunes (just as the *kete* time-line seems to shift from piece to piece), in highlife it is always on the "ands" of two, three, and four:

$$\text{1} \quad \text{2} \quad + \quad \text{3} \quad + \quad \text{4} \quad +$$

That is why it can be said that highlife is in 4/4 time when making that judgment about other forms of African music is problematic even when they are clearly made up of four-pulse groups.

The emphasis on rhythm is brought out further in the way that some of the horns are played. Notice that the middle brass (alto horns and trombone) often sound what are essentially rhythmic rather than melodic or harmonic patterns; they play rhythm patterns on a single note, functioning more like tuned drums than anything else. And listen to the bass drum, one of my favorite instruments in this band. The basic job of a bass drum in an American or European marching band is audibly to keep the beat, a steady boom, boom, boom. That idea is just not interesting enough for African rhythmic sensitivities; so the drummer varies his pattern to fit with certain melodic phrases. In fact, the overall rhythmic complexity and togetherness of this brass band's performance are quite impressive.

The "problem" of the band's intonation is more difficult to pinpoint. In the first place, many of the brass instruments are quite old and in poor repair (leaks, spit valves missing, tuning slides frozen, etc). In short, it is impossible to play them together in European tuning (see ill. 3–11). In addition, however, it must be pointed out that tuning systems in southern Ghana do not generally require

Ill. 3–11. *Many brass band instruments have seen better days, but new instruments are costly.*

James T. Koetting

the precision characteristic of Western European tempered tuning. We saw this phenomenon in relation to the tuning of Kasena flutes, and the same holds true here. Without more information it is difficult to make a blanket statement, but it would be better to assume that this brass band is not out of tune from the Ghanaian point of view.

The playing of highlife in Ghana is not restricted just to brass bands. Choral groups (called "singing bands"), accompanied by one or two drums and perhaps a harmonium, perform it; ensembles made up of just drums and a single acoustic guitar play it; dance bands, rock bands, and, on occasion, even string orchestras play it. Even though many of the musical instruments and elements of music used in highlife are European, in the hands of Ghanaian musicians the music is truly African. And in the minds of some it is even considered to be a traditional form.

Conclusion

We have studied just six examples of sub-Saharan African music, hardly enough to draw many conclusions. Although the examples shared some common features, such as relatively complex rhythmic structure, each of the six was unique; and it would not be difficult to find a hundred other examples equally unique. In a way, that is the story of African music and musicians. Musical creativity in Africa seems nearly boundless, the musical palette almost as multihued as one could imagine.

REFERENCES CITED

Anderson, Lois
  1968   *The Miko Modal System of Kiganda Xylophone Music.* 2 vols. Ph.D. diss., Univ. of California, Los Angeles.

Kubic, Gerhard
  1969   "Composition Techniques in Kiganda Xylophone Music." *African Music* 4 (no. 3):22–72.

Marcuse, Sibyl
  1975   *A Survey of Musical Instruments.* New York: Harper & Row.

Nketia, J. H. Kwabena
  1963   *Drumming in Akan Communities of Ghana.* Edinburgh: Thomas Nelson.

———.
  1974   *The Music of Africa.* New York: W. W. Norton.

Rattray, Robert S.
  1923   *Ashanti.* London: Oxford Univ. Press.

———.
  1927   *Religion and Art in Ashanti.* London: Oxford Univ. Press.

Sachs, Curt
  [1962]   1965. *The Wellsprings of Music.* Reprint. New York: McGraw-Hill.

Tracey, Hugh
   1948 *Chopi Musicians: Their Music, Poetry, and Instruments.* London: Oxford Univ. Press.

ADDITIONAL READING

Bebey, Francis
   1975 *African Music, A People's Art.* Translated by Josephine Bennett. Westport, Conn.: Lawrence Hill.

Berliner, Paul
   1978 *The Soul of Mbira.* Berkeley: Univ. of California Press.

Chernoff, John Miller
   1981 *African Rhythm and African Sensibility.* Chicago: Univ. of Chicago Press, Phoenix Books.

Jones, A. M.
   1959 *Studies in African Music.* 2 vols. London: Oxford Univ. Press.

Merriam, Alan P.
   1958 "African Music." In *Continuity and Change in African Cultures.* ed. William R. Bascom and Melville J. Herskovits. Chicago: Univ. of Chicago Press.

Wachsmann, Klaus, ed.
   1971 *Essays on Music and History in Africa.* Evanston: Northwestern Univ. Press.

ADDITIONAL LISTENING

Although many excellent recordings of African music have been produced, the number of these readily available in the United States is not large. The recordings listed here are excellent and available.

Africa: Drum, Chant and Instrumental Music
   1976 Recorded in Niger, Mali, and Upper Volta by Stephen Jay. Nonesuch Explorer Series H-72073. Jacket notes by Stephen Jay.

Africa East and West
   1969 Produced by the Institute of Ethnomusicology, UCLA, for African Arts Study Kit Series I. Edited by Mantle Hood. Includes music of Ghana and several other areas. I. E. Records IER-6751.

Africa/Shona Mbira Music
   1977 Recorded in Mondoro and Highfields, Rhodesia, by Paul Berliner. Nonesuch Explorer Series H-72077. Cover notes by Paul Berliner.

Alhaji Bai Konte: Kora Melodies from the Republic of the Gambia, West Africa
   1973 Recorded by Marc D. Pevar. Rounder Records 5001. Notes by Marc and Susan Pevar.

Drums of West Africa: Ritual Music of Ghana
   1977? Recording and Notes by Richard Hill. Lyrichord LLST 7303.

Unesco Collection—An Anthology of African Music.
Edited for the International Music Council by the International Institute for Comparative Music Studies and Documentation in collaboration with the Royal Museum of Central Africa, Tervuren. Produced by Barenreiter-Musicaphon. This collection contains several excellent recordings available separately. Of particular interest are those of the Ba-Benzélé Pygmies and the Hausa of Nigeria.

F O U R

◆ ◆ ◆

North America/Black America

JEFF TODD TITON

Music of work, music of worship, music of play: the traditional music of black people in the United States has a rich and glorious heritage, embracing generations of the black experience. Neither African nor European, it is fully a black American music, changing through the centuries to give voice to changes in black people's ideas of themselves. Yet despite the changes, it retains its black American identity, with a stylistic core of ecstasy and improvisation that transforms the regularity of everyday life into the freedom of expressive artistry. Spirituals, the blues, jazz—to Europeans, these unusual sounds are considered America's greatest (some would say her only) contribution to the international musical world. Of course, modern black music does not sound unusual to Americans, and that is because in this century the black style transformed popular music in America—the music of the theater, movies, radio, and television. Today, country music, rock, rap, reggae, and, tellingly, advertising jingles owe a great debt to the black sound. Locate some old 78 rpm records from around the turn of the century; perhaps someone in the neighborhood has a few in the attic or you may find some in your college or local public library. The music on these old records will sound stilted, square, extravagantly dramatic, unnatural, jerky— not because of the recording process, but because of the influence of grand opera singing and marching band instrumental styles of the period. But in the 1920s, aptly called the Jazz Age, Bessie Smith and other black jazz and blues singers revolutionized the craft of singing popular music. Their approach was close to the rhythm and tone of ordinary talk, and this natural way of singing caught on. American popular music was never the same again.

MUSIC OF WORSHIP

The easiest way to get acquainted with a music-culture in the United States is to survey its popular music on the radio. Most American cities have one or two radio stations programming black music. Listen for a couple of weeks and you will hear mostly contemporary music: soul, funk, reggae, rap, whatever, with

106

occasional sidetrips into the blues and jazz. But on Sundays the standard fare is recorded religious music, along with remote broadcasts of worship services from black churches in the city and surrounding suburbs. These live church broadcasts showcase a broad spectrum of black religious music: modern gospel quartets, powerful massed choirs, and soloists whose vocal acrobatics far exceed those of their pop music counterparts. Congregational singing is also heard on these broadcasts: camp-meeting choruses, particularly among Pentecostals, and hymns, particularly among Baptists. Listen now to a hymn (recorded selection 16) sung by a black Baptist congregation in Detroit. It is the first verse of the familiar Christian hymn, "Amazing Grace," but the performance style is unfamiliar to most people outside the black church. A deacon leads the hymn. Since the microphone was placed next to him during the recording, his voice is heard above the rest. He opens the hymn by singing the first line by himself: "Amazing grace how sweet it sounds." The congregation then joins him, and very slowly they repeat the words, sliding the melody around each syllable of the text: "Amazing grace how sweet it sounds." Next, the deacon sings the second line by himself: "That saved a wretch like me"; then the congregation joins him to repeat it, slowly and melismatically (that is, with three or more notes per syllable of text): "That saved a wretch like me." The same procedure finishes the verse.

That one verse is all there is to the performance. The singers do not use hymnbooks; they have memorized the basic tune and the words. Notice that the congregation, singing with the deacon, do not all come in at the same time; some lag behind the others a fraction, singing as they feel it. It is a beautiful and quite intricate performance; try singing along. The transcription of the first two lines (ex. 4–1) may be helpful, but after listening a few times you may be able to sing it, even without reading the transcription; after all, the people in the congregation learned it by ear.*

Next, look at the lyrics to "Amazing Grace" (fig. 4–1). This way of organizing the singing in church, in which a leader sings a line and then repeats it with the congregation, is called *lining out.* Lining out psalms and, later, hymns was a standard practice in colonial America. Black slaves and freedmen worshiped with whites and picked up the practice from their example. Today lining out survives in a great many black Baptist churches, whereas it has all but disappeared from white churches.

This version of "Amazing Grace" has many typical characteristics of black music in the United States. The words are sung in English, and they fall into stanzas as most English folk songs do. But the style of the performance is black

---

* Notation in this chapter employs an arrow above a notehead to indicate a pitch slightly higher (or lower, depending on the direction of the arrow) than notated but insufficiently high or low to be notated by the neighboring chromatic step. A solid line between successive noteheads indicates a vocal glide. Time value of grace notes should be subtracted from the previous note. An "x" on a staff space of line indicates the approximate pitch of an unstable, half-spoken syllable. A fermata above a notehead indicates a pitch held slightly longer than notated; an inverted fermata indicates a pitch held slightly shorter than notated. This additional notation is an attempt to make the Western staff-scale notation system more responsive to world music styles.

Ex. 4–1. *Transcription, "Amazing Grace," as sung at the New Bethel Baptist Church, Detroit, Michigan, June, 1978. Collected and transcribed by Jeff Titon.*

Fig. 4–1. *Lyrics to verse 1, "Amazing Grace," as lining-out hymn.*

Deacon (solo):

                                       DEACON AND CONGREGATION (CHORUS):

Amazing grace how sweet the sound

                                       AMAZING GRACE HOW SWEET THE SOUND

That saved a wretch like me

                                       THAT SAVED A WRETCH LIKE ME

I once was lost but now am found

                                       I ONCE WAS LOST BUT NOW AM FOUND

Was blind but now I see.

                                       WAS BLIND BUT NOW I SEE.

African. The singers sway freely to the music, dancing it with their bodies. As we saw in chapter 3, the leader–chorus call-and-response is the predominant African group vocal organization. The singing tone quality alternates between buttery smooth and raspy coarse. Intonation is slurry around the third, fifth, and seventh degrees of the scales. The tune is playful, ebbing and eddying like the ocean tide.

These attributes of traditional black American music can be understood more clearly if this version of "Amazing Grace" is contrasted with a white, Anglo-American version of the same hymn from the southern Appalachian mountains (recorded selection 17 on the cassette). The white song leader stands erect like the soldier of the Cross he is, chest out, eyes front, unmoving save for his hand, which marks the regular and clearly audible beat. Leader and congregation sing together instead of in call-and-response alternation. The choral texture is polyphonic instead of heterophonic. The song leader's tone quality is unvaryingly coarse, giving an impression of energetic seriousness rather than playful ecstasy. His tune is stately, measured, and decorated. The transcription (ex. 4–2) of the first two lines compares his singing to the tune as it is printed in the church hymnbook (ex. 4–3). His variations are deliberate, and they differ slightly from one another in each of the four verses that make up the performance. But they are restrained in comparison to the melodic decoration sung by the black deacon. A few more hearings of this Anglo-American example reveal subtleties such as the upward catch on the release of certain tones, as, for instance, at the end of the word *grace* in the very first line. Try imitating the Anglo-American

Ex. 4–2. *Transcription, "Amazing Grace," as sung at the Fellowship Independent Baptist Church, Stanley, Virginia, August, 1977. Collected and transcribed by Jeff Titon. The transcription follows the melody as sung by the songleader. Printed in the lower staff for comparison is the melody as written in the church hymnal. (See also ex. 4–3.)*

Amazing Grace

John Newton   Wm. Walker

Ex. 4–3. *"Amazing Grace."* Source: **Church Hymnal (Cleveland, Tenn.:** *Tennessee Music and Printing Co., 1951).*

version as well as the African-American version; both are much-admired examples of their kind. Your efforts to sing will increase your understanding of the musical styles—and your pleasure in the musical experience.

Our radio survey of black music reveals a vital church music culture. Suppose we enter the black church and observe it firsthand (see ill. 4–1). It is a Baptist church with a large sanctuary, seating perhaps fifteen hundred on this warm Sunday morning. The men are dressed in blue or black vested suits, with black socks and shoes. A few of the younger men are conspicuous in tan, baby-blue, or burgundy colored suits with matching shoes. The women wear dark suits or dresses, and many have on fashionable hats; all of them wear stockings and dress shoes. Choir members have green robes over their formal attire. To keep a

Jeff Todd Titon

Ill. 4–1. A young deacon chants an improvised prayer. The microphone connects with the church's public address system. Detroit, Michigan, 1978.

breeze, they swish fans supplied by the funeral homes that have printed their advertisements on them.

When we hear "Amazing Grace," we have come in on the deacons' devotional, an early part of the worship service consisting of old-time congregational hymn singing, Scripture reading, and a chanted prayer (fig. 4–2; ex. 4–4) offered by a deacon while the rest hum and moan a wordless hymn in the background. The praying deacon improvises his chanted prayer—the words and tune—which begins as speech and then gradually turns to a chant with a definite tonal center, moving at the close in a regular meter; the congregation punctuates the deacon's

Fig. 4–2. Text, closing section of prayer.

> *Oh Lord. [Congregation: Yes!]*
> *Have mercy today, Father. [Yes!]*
> *You know where we at. [Yes!]*
> *You know our hearts. [Yes!]*
> 5 *You know our hearts' desire. [Yes!]*
> *Please Jesus! [Yes!]*
> *Please Jesus! [Yes!]*
> *Go with us today. [Yes!]*
> *I know you know me. [Yes!]*
> 10 *You know all about me. [Yes!]*
> *Now Lord. [Now Lord!]*
> *Now Jesus. [Now!]*
> *When we can't pray no more [Yes!]*
> *over here [Yes!]*
> *(Spoken): give us a home somewhere in thy kingdom.*

Ex. 4–4. *Closing section of chanted prayer, by deacon and congregation of Little Rock Baptist Church, Detroit, Michigan, October, 1977. Collected and transcribed by Jeff Titon. The congregation's response [Yes!] is in brackets; the transcription follows the melody (lines 3–10) as chanted by the deacon, who improvises the words and tunes as the Spirit moves him.*

phrases with shouts of "Yes," "Now," and so forth, which are intoned on the tonal center (C in the musical example).

The deacons lead the devotional from the altar area, and after the devotional is through, the activity shifts to the pulpit where announcements are made, offerings are taken up, and responsive reading is led. Interspersed are modern gospel songs, sung by soloists and the high-spirited youth choir, accompanied by piano and organ. The preacher begins his sermon in a speaking voice, but after about fifteen minutes he shifts into a hoarse musical chant (fig. 4–3; ex. 4–5), all the while improvising and carrying on his message (ill. 4–2). As they did for the praying deacon, the congregation punctuates the preacher's phrases with shouts of "Well," "Yes," and so forth, on the tonal center. Sometimes the preacher fits his chant into a regular meter for brief periods, lasting from perhaps ten seconds to a minute. But more often the chanted phrases are irregular. Still, compared to phrases in ordinary conversation, they are relatively uniform and, when punctuated by the congregation, they give the *impression* of regularity. Speaking to me of the rhythm of his chanted preaching, Reverend C. L. Franklin of Detroit told me, "It's not something I can beat my foot to. But I can *feel* it. It's in me." It is also in the members of the congregation who sway back and forth with each phrase.

Eventually the sermon closes and an invitational song follows, led by a soloist from the choir (ill. 4–3). Three or four people heed the invitation and come forward to join the church. A final offering is taken up, the preacher gives the benediction, and the choir comes down from the choir stand, locks arms in the altar area facing the pulpit, and joins the congregation in singing "Amen."

Altogether, song and chant have taken up at least half the running time of the

Nicodemus was a ruler.
He was a
rich man.
You know everybody loves money.
5 Everybody loves to look, be looked upon.
Everybody loves to be called somebody.
Ah I imagine Nicodemus was ah in that category.
And ah he heard about God.
I don't know where he heard about him back but he heard of
10 something about God.
What he was doing.
And ah
he
made it up in his
15 mind
that he was going to see God.
And ahh he made
an appointment with him.
And ahh the Scripture says that it was at night.
20 It's all right
in the midnight
to make appointment with him.
It's all right
to make appointment with him
25 if it is at noon day.
You should make appointment with him.
I made appointment with him one day
and ahh
I told him my situation.
30 Oh lord.
And everything went all right.
Mmm
hallelujah.
And Nicodemus said,
35 he said, "I know
that no man can do these things
except God be with him."
You know God says
in the
40 Scripture here,
he say you can do all things.
"You can do all things in my name
if you'll vow in me
and I'll abide in you."
45 You should get in Christ.
You should get in touch with God.
Learn a little more about him.
And when you've found Christ
just wrap around him and
50 and everything will be all right.

Fig 4–3. *Text, excerpt from chanted sermon.*

It's   all   right _____   in   the   mid - night

to make ap - point - ment with him.   It's   all   right _

to make ap-point-ment with him   if   it   is   at   noon day.

Ex. 4–5. *Excerpt from chanted portion of sermon, St. Mark's Baptist Church, Minneapolis, Minnesota, August, 1968. Collected and transcribed by Jeff Titon. In reading the words, pause about ½ second at the end of each measured line. This tune transcription of lines 20–25 follows the melody as chanted by the preacher who improvises the words and tune as the Spirit moves him.*

worship service: the old-style singing of the deacons' devotional, the traditional chant of the prayer and sermon, and the modern gospel songs. The music is literally moving; it activates the Holy Spirit, which sends some people into shouts of ecstasy, swoons, shakes, holy dance, and trance (ill. 4–4). If they get so carried away that they are in danger of fainting or injuring themselves, they are restrained by their neighbors until members of the nurses' guild can reach them and administer aid. In this setting, music is a very powerful activity—and the church is prepared for its effects.

Ill. 4–2. *Reverend C. L. Franklin, pastor, New Bethel Baptist Church, Detroit, Michigan, chanting ("whooping") as he delivers the sermon's climax, 1978.*

Jeff Todd Titon

Jeff Todd Titon

Ill. 4–3. *Temple of Faith Choir, Detroit, Michigan, 1978.*

Ill. 4–4. *Religious music quickens the Holy Spirit and sends a woman into trance. Detroit, Michigan, 1977.*

Jeff Todd Titon

Much of the music of black Christian worship in the United States is traditional. We have seen that the lining-out tradition dates from colonial America, and many of the hymns sung are the same vintage. The black spiritual was a later development, born of the integrated camp-meeting revivals in the late eighteenth and early nineteenth centuries. Today they can be heard in their most traditional form as the "choruses"—one verse repeated several times—in Pentecostal services, while in Baptist and Methodist services they are featured in carefully arranged, multi-versed versions sung by trained choirs in a tradition that hearkens back to the Fisk Jubilee Singers of the late nineteenth century (ex. 4–6). The style of these chanted prayers and sermons is at least as old as the early nineteenth century, and probably older, though of course the deacons and preachers improvise the content. A great deal of scholarship has been devoted to the origins and meaning of the black spiritual (see, for example, Lovell 1972) but much research on the older hymns, modern gospel songs, chanted prayers, and sermons remains to be done.

MUSIC OF WORK

A work song, as the name suggests, is a song workers sing to help them carry on. The song helps by taking their minds of the monotonous and tiring bending, swinging, hauling, driving, carrying, chopping, poling, loading, digging, pulling, cutting, breaking and lifting (ill. 4–5). A work song also paces the work. If the job requires teamwork, work song rhythms coordinate the movements of the workers (ill. 4–6).

Work songs were widely reported among black slaves in the West Indies in the eighteenth century, and in the United States in the nineteenth. Most scholars believe black work songs must have been present in the American Colonies even though the documentary evidence is thin. While it is conceivable that black American work songs were influenced by British work songs (sea shanties and the like), the widespread, ancient, and continuing African work song tradition is the most probable source (see pp. 97–99).

Work music is hard to find in the United States today. Where people once sang, machines now whine; the jackhammer has replaced the pickax. The once-vital black American work song tradition is dying.

But in an earlier America, black people sang work songs as they farmed and as they built the canals, railroads, and highways that became the transportation networks of the growing nation. In his autobiography, *My Bondage and My Freedom* (1855), ex-slave Frederick Douglass wrote: "Slaves are generally expected to sing as well as to work. A silent slave is not liked by masters or overseers. 'Make a noise,' 'make a noise' and *'bear a hand,'* are the words constantly addressed to the slaves when there is silence amongst them. This may account for the almost constant singing heard in the southern states." After Emancipation, the singing continued whenever black people were engaged in heavy work: clearing and grading the land; laying railroad track; loading barges and poling them along the rivers; build-

Ex. 4–6. *"Swing Low, Sweet Chariot." Source: G. D. Pike,* **The [Fisk] Jubilee Singers** *(Boston: Lee and Shephard, 1873), p. 166.*

Walker Evans. Courtesy of the Library of Congress

Ill. 4–5. *Farmer plowing field, Tupelo, Mississippi, 1936.*

ing levees against river flooding; felling trees. And the inevitable farm work: digging ditches, cutting timber, building fences, plowing, planting, chopping out weeds, and reaping and loading the harvest.

The words and tunes of these work songs fit the nature of the work. People working by themselves or at their own pace in a group sang songs that were slow and without a pronounced beat; tunes were hummed or words were fit in

Ill. 4–6. *Workers lining track, Alabama, 1956.*

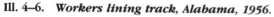

Frederic Ramsey, Jr.

as the singer wished, passing the time. As a farm boy, Leonard "Baby Doo" Caston learned to sing work songs by copying the practice of older farmhands (ex. 4–7). Not surprisingly, the words of these songs show that the singers wanted to be elsewhere, away from work. In group labor that required teamwork and a steady pace, people sang songs with a pronounced beat, which coordinated their movements. About thirty years ago a rowing work song, "Michael, Row the Boat Ashore," was recorded by a group of white singers who had probably never come any closer to the work than crewing on the Connecticut River; but their version became a best-selling record on the popular music charts. The song was first reported in the 1867 collection of *Slave Songs in the United States* (ex. 4–8). The words to work songs are open ended; that is, the song leader can improvise new lines ("Michael, row the boat ashore," or "O you mind your boastin' talk,") and repeat old ones until his stock is exhausted and his voice gives out, while the rest of the workers merely sing the responsorial burden ("Hallelujah!") after each line, in a call-and-response pattern.

What makes a good song leader? What is the purpose of work songs? Collecting work songs in 1947 inside the Mississippi State Penitentiary at Parchman, Alan Lomax asked these questions of the black inmates whose singing he recorded:

LOMAX: Do you think it makes work easier when you sing?
INMATE: Yessir.

Ex. 4–7. *Solo worksong, sung by Leonard "Baby Doo" Caston, Minneapolis, Minnesota, May, 1971. Collected and transcribed by Jeff Titon. SOURCE: Titon 1974a.*

[Other stanzas:] *I'm going up the country baby and I can't take you.*
There's nothing up the country that a monkey woman can do.

Hey—captain don't you know my name?
I'm the same old fellow who stole your watch and chain.

I'm going away baby to wear you off my mind.
You keep me worried and bothered all the time.

Michael Row the Boat Ashore

1. Mi - chael   row   de boat   a - shore.   Hal - le - lu -
[Cho.]

jah! 2. Mi-chael   boat   a gos - pel   boat. Hal - le - lu - jah!
[Cho.]

3. *I wonder where my mudder deh (there).*
4. *See my mudder on de rock gwine home.*
5. *On de rock gwine home in Jesus' name.*
6. *Michael boat a music boat.*
7. *Gabriel blow de trumpet horn.*
8. *O you mind your boastin' talk.*
9. *Boastin' talk will sink your soul.*
10. *Brudder, lend a helpin' hand.*
11. *Sister, help for trim dat boat.*
12. *Jordan stream is wide and deep.*
13. *Jesus stand on t' oder side.*
14. *I wonder if my maussa deh.*
15. *My fader gone to unknown land.*
16. *O de Lord he plant his garden deh.*
17. *He raise de fruit for you to eat.*
18. *He dat eat shall neber die.*
19. *When de riber overflow*
20. *O poor sinner, how you land?*
21. *Riber run and darkness comin'.*
22. *Sinner row to save your soul.*

Ex. 4–8. Worksong, "Michael Row the Boat Ashore." SOURCE: *Slave Songs of the United States, compiled by William Francis Allen, Charles Pickard Ware, and Lucy McKim Garrison (New York: A. Simpson & Co., 1867), pp. 23–24.*

LOMAX: Do you think you can do more or do you think you can slack off when you sing?

INMATE: Nosir, what makes it go so better—when you're singing, you forget, you see, and the time just pass on 'way; but if you get your mind devoted on one something, it look like it will be hard for you to make it, see—make a day—the day be longer, look like.... So to keep his mind from being devoted on just one thing, why, he'll just practically take up singing, see ...

LOMAX: What's the most important thing about a good leader ... does he have a real good voice or a strong voice or what?

INMATE: Well ... now it wouldn't just exactly make any difference about the

> dependability of his voice or nothing like that, boss; but it would, it
> take the man with the most experience to my understanding to
> make the best leader in anything. You see, if you'd bring a brand
> new man here, if he had a voice where he would sing just like Peter
> could preach, and he didn't know what to sing about, well, he
> wouldn't do no good, see, but here's a fellow, he, maybe he ain't
> got no voice for singing, but he's been cooperating with the peoples
> so long and been on the job so long till he know just exactly how it
> should go, and if he can just mostly talk it, why, and you understand
> how to work, well it would go good with you—it don't make any
> difference about the voice . . .
>
> LOMAX: You mean he has to know the timing?
>
> INMATE: Yessir . . . that's what it takes, the time, that's all it is. You can just
> whistle and, if you know the time and can stay in time with the axes,
> you can whistle and do, cut just as good as you can if you were
> singing . . . but you have to be done experienced. [Lomax 1976].*

The aesthetic standards of the black work song call for a good sense of the beat
and the ability to time it to the work at hand. A sweet-sounding voice that is
always in tune may be desirable in other situations but it is not important in the
work song tradition.

In some southern prisons black inmates sang work songs (recorded selection
18; ex. 4–9). This song, "Rosie," is used to regulate the axe-blows when felling
large trees. Sometimes as many as ten men circle the tree and chop, five pulling
their axes out just before the other five all strike at once. Axes are swinging
through the air at all times, back and forth; the work is dangerous and the timing
is crucial. Without work songs, the white and Latin inmates chopped two to a
tree. With work songs, the black inmates chopped four, six, eight, or ten to a
tree. The work goes faster and better, and the singing group feels pride and
solidarity in its accomplishment. In the words of Bruce Jackson, an experienced
collector of prison work songs, "The songs [may] change the nature of the work
by putting the work into the worker's framework rather than the guards'. By
incorporating the work with their song, by, in effect, coopting something they
are forced to do anyway, they make it *theirs* in a way it otherwise is not" (Jackson
1972:30).

MUSIC OF PLAY

Having begun our acquaintance with black American music through brief examinations of the music of work and worship, it is time now to turn to the music
of entertainment, or play. True, there is an element of play in the performance
of religious songs and work songs in the black tradition. Churchgoers admire
the beautiful performance of a verbally adept preacher as he plays with the

---

* ©Alan Lomax. Used by permission.

Rosie

M. K.

Well _____   Ro   -   sie   O   Lord,   gal.

ah _____   Ro   -   sie _____   O   Lord,   gal.

Ex. 4–9. *Worksong, "Rosie." Sung by inmates of Mississippi State Penitentiary, Parchman, Mississippi, 1947. Collected by Alan Lomax; transcribed by Mieczyslaw Kolinski.* Source: *Courlander 1963. Reprinted courtesy of Columbia University Press.*

resources of language and gesture, and they clap their approval as a solo singer sustains a climactic pitch or goes through intricately improvised melodic variations with great feeling; work songs introduce a playful, distancing attitude toward the labor at hand. But although religious songs and work songs contain elements of play, their purpose is worship and work. In contrast, music of play plays for its own sake, for entertainment, for pleasure, even when its effect is educational, cathartic, or ecstatic.

We have heard the music of play in our radio survey which led us to observe the music of worship in the church. If we walk through the black neighborhood outside the church after the service is over, we find ourselves surrounded by the music of play. Teenagers walk down the street carrying boom box radios and cassette players that throb with the latest R&B and rap hits. Young children skip rope on the side streets, jump-rope rhymes and chanting taunts at one another. Jukeboxes can be heard in the bars and barbecue joints that line both sides of the main street. When night falls, some of the bars have live entertainment—a local band that plays the blues, and in a fancy nightspot a nationally known jazz combo. Downtown in the city auditorium a soul music revue is scheduled, while in the public gardens a concert of classical music offers the premiere performance of an atonal composition by a black composer who teaches at the city university.

Blues

The local band that plays the blues will provide us with a detailed case study of blues music, which will be our subject for the rest of this chapter. The blues is a familiar music, but its very familiarity presents problems. Chief among them is the misconception that blues is a subset of jazz, that it was a historical phenomenon, a contributing stream that flowed, some time after Bessie Smith died, into the river of jazz. Nothing could be farther from the truth. Blues is best understood as a feeling—"the blues"—and as a specific musical form, whereas jazz is best thought of as a technique, as a *way* of forming. Jazz musicians applied their technique to the blues form, but blues did not lose its identity. Muddy Waters (ill. 4–7), Albert King, B. B. King, Albert Collins, and Robert Cray, who rose to national prominence as blues singers, came from a vital tradition. Until the 1950s, when desegregation and the Civil Rights Movement changed African-American social and economic conditions, the blues music-culture, with its

Ill. 4–7. *Muddy Waters (McKinley Morganfield), studio photo, Chicago, Illinois, early 1950s.*

singers, country juke joints, barrelhouses, city rent-parties, street singing, bar scenes, nightclubs, lounges, recordings, and record industry, was a significant part of the black music culture in the United States. Since then, although diminished in scope, and despite predictions of its impending demise—predictions that have come regularly for the past sixty years—it continues to flourish. It undergoes periodic revivals, and its audience now is worldwide. Blues singers and their bands regularly tour Britain and Europe, and some live there permanently. Not long ago Johnny Copeland and his blues band played throughout Africa, sponsored by the U.S. State Department.

Blues and the Truth

The best entry into the blues is through the words of the songs. It is hard to talk at length about words in songs, and harder still to talk about music. As Charles Seeger, one of the founders of the Society of Ethnomusicology, reminds us, it would be more logical to "music" about music than to talk about it (Seeger 1977:16). And in the blues music culture, when the setting is informal, that is just what happens when one singer responds to another by singing verses of his own. Another common response to blues is dancing. Dancers and listeners as a rule have no interest in an articulate body of blues criticism. Speaking of oral literature as a whole, Dennis Tedlock points up the paradox with gentle irony: "Members of primary oral cultures generally limit themselves to brief remarks about performances when they say anything at all, and such remarks are quickly forgotten. There is no such thing as an oral performance of the great critical discourse of the past" (Tedlock 1977:516).

The most common response to blues music is a feeling in the gut, dancing to the beat, nodding assent, a vocalized "that's right, you got it, that's the truth"—not unlike the black Christian's response to a sermon or a gospel song. A good, "deep" blues song leaves you feeling that you have heard the truth, and there is not much more that needs saying. But the words to blues songs are tough. They can stand up to inquiry, to analysis. Since the words pass from one singer to another as a coin goes from hand to hand, they become finely honed and proverbial in their expression: economical, truthful. Response to the words of the songs can be talked about in words. Moreover, blues lyrics have a legitimate claim as serious literature. As Cleanth Brooks, R. W. B. Lewis, and Robert Penn Warren have written—and it would be hard to find a more distinguished trio of literary critics—"In the world of music the recognition of blues as art is well established. But waiving their value as musical art, we may assert that they represent a body of poetic art unique and powerful. . . . No body of folk poetry in America—except, perhaps, the black spirituals—can touch it, and much of the poetry recognized as 'literature,' white or black, seems tepid beside it" (Brooks, Lewis, and Warren 1973:II, 2759).

We began by taking an extended look at a single blues performance (recorded selection 19), "Poor Boy Blues," by the Lazy Bill Lucas Blues Band (ill.

4–8). Bill Lucas is the vocalist; he accompanies himself on electric guitar, and he is joined by two other accompanists, one on acoustic guitar and the other on drums. The recording was made in Minneapolis, Minnesota, in 1970. Listen to it now, paying particular attention to the lyrics (fig. 4–4).

Ill. 4–8. *Lazy Bill Lucas, Minneapolis, Minnesota, 1968.*

Poor Boy Blues

1. *I'm just a poor boy; people, I can't even write my name.*
   I'm just a poor boy; people, I can't even write my name.
   Every letter in the alphabet to me they look the same.

2. *Mother died when I was a baby; father I never seen.*
   Mother died when I was a baby; father I never seen.
   When I think how dumb I am, you know it makes me want to scream.

3. *Ever since I was the age around eleven or twelve,*
   Ever since I was the age around eleven or twelve,
   I just been a poor boy; ain't caught nothing but hell.

4. *When I was a child Santa Claus never left one toy.*
   When I was a child Santa Claus never left one toy.
   If you have any mercy, please have mercy on poor boy.

Fig. 4–4.   *Text, "Poor Boy Blues."*

Response to the Lyrics of "Poor Boy Blues"

I did not choose "Poor Boy Blues" because the words were outstanding; they are typical. For me, some of it is good, some not; some of it works, some does not. "I'm just a poor boy; people, I can't even write my name" produces an automatic response to sympathy for the poor boy, but it is not a very deep response. I am sorry for the poor boy's illiteracy, but, heck, everyone has problems. When the line repeats I am anxious to hear how the stanza will close. "Every letter in the alphabet to me they look the same" brings to my mind's eye a picture of a strange alphabet in which all letters look alike or, rather, in which the differences in their shape have no meaning. The image is clear, it works, and it involves me. This poor boy may be illiterate but he is perceptive. And not only the image itself succeeds; the delay of the most important word in the line, *same,* until the end, and the impact of its rhyme with *name* convinces me I am hearing the truth. Blues singer Eddie "Son" House told me this about how he put his blues stanzas together: "I had enough sense to try to make 'em, rhyme 'em so they'd have have *hits* to 'em with a meaning, some sense to 'em, you know" (Titon 1977:52) (ill. 4–9). The inevitable rightness of the rhyme—you expect it and it rewards you—hits harder than an unrhymed close, particularly because the end rhyme always falls, in blues, on an accented syllable.

I do not respond to "Mother died when I was a baby"; I resist a statement that sounds sentimental. This is not because I think of myself as some kind of tough guy, but because I want the sentiment to be earned. I much prefer the statement at the close of the line: "father I never seen." The effect is in the contrast between the mother who died and the father who might as well be dead. In the image of the father who has never been seen is the mystery of not knowing one's parents. It is not just missing love; for all we know the poor boy was raised by loving grandparents. But a child takes after parents, inherits the biology, so to speak; without knowing your parents you do not fully know yourself. That is the real terror of the poor boy's life. "When I think how dumb I am, you know it makes

Jeff Todd Titon

Ill. 4–9. *Eddie "Son" House, Minneapolis, Minnesota, 1971.*

me want to scream" is a cliché; the rhyme is forced. Okay, scream. Nor do I respond to the third stanza when I hear it; but when I think about it, it seems curious that the poor boy says he began to catch hell from age eleven or twelve. I guess he was catching it all along, but did not fully realize it until then. That is a nice point, but a little too subtle to register during a performance. I would have to sing it several times myself to appreciate that aspect of it.

The final stanza takes great risk with sentimentality, calling up Christmas memories, but it succeeds by a matter-of-fact tone—"When I was a child Santa Claus never left one toy"—that dispels the scene's stickiness. Santa Claus never left a toy for anyone, but a child who believes in Santa can enjoy an innocent world where presents reward good little boys and girls. If he could not believe in Santa, I wonder if he ever had any part of the innocent happiness people seem to need early, and in large doses, if they are going to live creative lives. Or it could have been the other way around: he believed in Santa, but Santa, never bringing him a toy, simply did not believe in him.

The song now leads up to it final line, a plea for mercy. "You" are addressed directly: if you have any mercy, show it to the poor boy. Will you? If you heard this from a blind street-singer would you put some coins in his cup? Would you be more likely to show mercy to the poor boy than to someone down on his luck who just walks up and asks for spare change? The song will strike some people as sentimental, calling up an easy emotion that is just as quickly forgotten as it is evoked. T. S. Eliot, in a widely influential argument, said that in a work of literature any powerful emotion must have an "objective correlative"; that is, it must be demonstrated by the work itself that there is good reason for the emotion (Eliot 1920). Has "Poor Boy Blues" given you good reason for mercy? Have you been told the truth or were you played for a sucker?

Autobiography and the Blues

The effect of "Poor Boy Blues" on a disinterested listener can take us only so far, because we have been considering the words in a broad, English-speaking context. What do the words mean to someone in the blues music culture? What do they mean to Lazy Bill Lucas? As "Poor Boy Blues" is sung in the first person, does the "I" speak for Lucas? What, in short, is the relation of the song and the singer?

More than any other subject, the correspondence between the words to blues songs and the lives of the singers has fascinated people who write about the blues. The blues singer's image as wandering minstrel, blind bard, and untutored genius is idealized, but, according to Samuel Charters, "There is no more romantic figure in popular music than the bluesman, with everything the term involves. And it isn't a false romanticism" (Charters 1977:112). The result is that most books on blues are organized biographically. Some writers have gone so far as to derive the facts of an otherwise obscure blues singer's life and personality from the lyrics of his recorded songs. Published life stories of blues singers in their own words, on the other hand, are few (see, for example, Brunoghe 1964; Titon 1974a). If these first-person life stories are read properly, they can be understood as far more reliable expressions of the blues singer's own personality than his song lyrics are, since the lyrics often are borrowed from tradition. But whatever the impulse, most people assume that the lyrics of a blues song do speak for the singer; Paul Oliver wrote, for example, "One of the characteristics of the blues is that it is highly personalized—blues singers nearly always sing about themselves" (Oliver 1974:30). If that is true, then "Poor Boy Blues" should be a reflection of the life and thoughts of Lazy Bill Lucas.

I was a close friend of Bill Lucas's for six years, playing guitar in his blues band for two of them. During the course of our friendship I tape recorded his recollections of his life for publication first in *Blues Unlimited* (Titon 1969), a British blues research journal, and later in the accompanying notes to his first

American LP (Titon 1974b). Let us look, then, at parts of Lucas's life history and see if "Poor Boy Blues" speaks for him.

The Life History of Bill Lucas, Blues Singer*

I was born in Wynne, Arkansas, on May 29, 1918. I never heard my mother say the exact *time* I was born: she was so upset at the time I guess she wouldn't remember. I have two sisters and three brothers; I was third from my baby sister, the third youngest.

Ever since I can remember, I had trouble with my eyesight. Doctors tell me it's the nerves. I can see shapes, I can tell colors, and I know light and dark, but it's hard to focus, and no glasses can help me. An operation might cure it, but there's a chance it could leave me completely blind, and I don't want to take that gamble.

My father was a farmer out in the country from Wynne. He was a sharecropper, farming on the halvers.† In 1922 we moved to Short Bend, Arkansas, but my father wanted to get where there were better living conditions. A lot of his neighbors and friends had come up to Missouri and told him how good it was up there.

About every two or three years we moved from one farm to another. Some places you had good crops, according to the kind of land you had. Some places we had real sandy land, and that wasn't good; but in the places that were swampy, that black land, that was good. You know when you're sharecropping cotton and corn you look for the best location and the best living conditions. And you could move; you didn't have a lease on the place.

So my family moved to Advance, Missouri, in 1924. We moved by night but that doesn't mean we had to slip away. They loaded all our stuff in a wagon and we caught the ten o'clock train. That was my first train ride; I loved the train then. Advance was about twenty-five miles west of the river; it wasn't on the highway, just on the railroad. It was a little town of 500; it consisted of two grocery stores and a post office which doubled over into a saloon. We never did go to town much except on Saturdays. In the summertime we'd go in about every week to carry our vegetables to sell in a wagon: watermelons and cabbage and stuff.

My father wanted to own his own farm, but that was impossible. That was a dream. He didn't have enough money to buy it and there weren't any loans like there are nowadays. We owned cattle, we owned pigs. We had about thirteen milk cows, and we had leghorn chickens that gave us bushels of eggs. We were better off than our neighbors because we would sometimes swap our eggs for something we didn't have. We were blessed with eggs and chickens and milk. We were blessed. I tried to, but I never did learn how to milk. I wasn't too much use on the farm. I did a lot of babysitting but not too much else.

There weren't many guitars around, but in 1930 my daddy got me a

* ©1974 by William Lucas and Jeff Titon. A fuller version accompanies Titon 1974b.
† A sharecropping arrangement in which the landlord supplied the tenant with a shack, tools, seed, work animals, feed, fuel wood, and half the fertilizer in exchange for half the tenant's crop and labor.

guitar. I remember so well, just like it was yesterday, he traded a pig for it. Money was scarce down there; we didn't have any money. The boy wanted $7 for it. We didn't have money but we had plenty of pigs. Our neighbors had some boys that played guitar, but they never did take pains and show me how to do it. I would just watch 'em and listen. I learned from sounds. And after they were gone, then I would try to make the guitar sound like I heard them make it sound. It was easier to play single notes than chords. Right now till today I don't use but two fingers to play guitar; I don't play guitar like other people. I wanted the guitar because I liked the noise and it sounded pretty.

After I got it and come progressing on it, a tune or two here or there, my dad and mama both decided that would be a good way for me to make my living. I knew all the time I wanted to make a career out of it, but after I came progressing on it, well they wanted me to make a career out of it too. But they said I had to be old enough and big enough to take care of it, not to be breaking strings and busting it all up.

My father got me a piano in 1932 for a Christmas present. That was the happiest Christmas I ever had. He didn't trade pigs for that; he paid money for it. Got it at our neighborhood drugstore. It was an upright. It had been a player piano but all the guts had been taken out of it. Well, at the time I knew how to play organ, one of those pump organs. I had played a pump organ we had at home that came about the same time as the guitar. A woman, she was moving, she was breaking up housekeeping, and she gave us the organ. I had two pedals on it and you'd do like riding a bicycle. So it didn't take me long to learn how to bang out a few tunes on the piano.

I didn't know what chords I was making. We got a little scale book that would go behind the keyboard of the piano and tell you all the chords. It was a beginner's book, in big letters. I could see that. You know, a beginner's book *is* in big letters. And I wanted to learn music, but after I got that far, well, the rest of the music books were so small that I couldn't see the print. And that's why I didn't learn to read music.

I did learn to read the alphabet at home. My parents taught me, and so did the other kids. I used to go to school, but it was just to be with the other kids, and sometimes the kids would teach me. I was just apt; I could pick things up. I had a lot of mother-wit.

So I bumped around on the piano until 1936, when we left the country and came to Cape Girardeau, Missouri. I had to leave my piano; we didn't have room for it. I almost cried. That was when I started playing the guitar on street corners. My dad had day work; that was the idea of him moving to the city, trying to better his living conditions. I forget what he went to work as: I think he worked in a coal yard. We stayed at my sister's house; one of my oldest sisters was married. But we had to go back to Commerce, Missouri. My dad couldn't make it in Cape Girardeau so we went to Commerce. I don't know what he thought he was going to do there because that was a little hick town, wasn't but about 300 in population there. He didn't farm there; I vaguely can remember what we did now.

At that time I didn't know too much about blues. We had a radio station down there but they all played big band stuff and country-and-western music. But we didn't call it country-and-western music back then; we called it hillbilly music. Well, hillbilly music was popular there and so I played hillbilly music on the guitar and sang songs like "She'll be Coming Round the Mountain" and "It Ain't Gonna Rain No More" and "Wabash Cannonball." The only time I heard any blues was when we'd go to restaurants where a juke box was and they'd have blues records. And my daddy had a windup phonograph, and we had a few blues records at home by Peetie Wheatstraw and Scrapper Blackwell and Curtis Jones— the old pieces, you know. So I learned a little bit about blues pieces off the records I'd hear around home. I heard Bessie Smith and Daddy Stovepipe and Blind Lemon Jefferson.

At that time I didn't have any knowledge of music. I liked any of it. I even liked those hillbilly songs. And when I heard the blues I liked the blues, but I just liked the music, period. And when I played out on street corners, I'd be playing for white folks mostly, and that was the music they seemed to like better, the hillbilly music. So I played it because I'd been listening to it all the time on the radio and so it wasn't very hard for me to play. The blues didn't *strike* me until I heard Big Bill Broonzy; that's when I wanted to play blues guitar like him.

We lost our mother in 1939. We buried her in Commerce, and we left Commerce after she died. My dad, he went to St. Louis in 1940, still trying to find better living conditions. Later that year he brought me to St. Louis, and that's where I met Big Joe Williams. At that time he wasn't playing in bars or taverns; he was just playing on the street. So he let me join him, and I counted it an honor to be playing with Big Joe Williams because I had heard his blues records while I was still down South. And so we played blues in the street.

But I didn't stay in St. Louis long. My dad and I came to Chicago the day after New Year's in 1941. Sonny Boy Williamson was the first musician I met with up there. I met him over on Maxwell Street, where they had all their merchandise out on the street, and you could buy anything you wanted on a Sunday, just like you could on a Monday. They had groceries, clothes, hardware, appliances, right out on the street, where people could come to look for bargains. That was a good place to play until the cops made us cut it out. I played a lot with Sonny Boy.* Little suburban places around Chicago like Battle Creek, and South Bend. We were playing one-nighters in taverns and parties. Sonny Boy would book himself, and I went around with him. There wasn't much money in it; Sonny Boy paid my expenses and a place to stay with his friends. He was known all up around there. He played with me when he couldn't get nobody else. I didn't have a name at the time.† But I had sense enough to play in time and change cords when he changed; it wasn't but three changes anyhow. We didn't play nothing but the funky blues. He just needed somebody to keep time, back him up on guitar.

Big Bill Broonzy was my idol for guitar, and I'd go sit in on his shows. He'd let me play on the stand between times; I'd play his same songs. Bill

---

* Harmonica player John Lee Williamson (d. 1948).
† He means the name Bill Lucas was unknown to the blues audiences.

knew I couldn't do it as well as he did, so he wasn't mad. In fact he appreciated me for liking his style. I also liked T-Bone Walker, but he made so many chord changes! I was unfortunate to learn changes; I never did know but three changes on the guitar.

I used to play with Little Walter* on the street, too, in the black section, where they wanted the blues. I quit playing that hillbilly music when I left St. Louis. In St. Louis I was getting on the blues right smart after I met up with Big Joe Williams. But white folks in Chicago or here in Minneapolis don't like hillbilly music. They tell you right away. "What you think I am? A hillbilly?"

I started in my professional career in 1946 when I joined the union. We all joined the union together, me and Willie Mabon and Earl Dranes, two guitars and a piano. We took our first job in 1946 on December 20, in the Tuxedo Lounge, 3119 Indiana, in Chicago. They paid union scale, but scale wasn't much then. The leader didn't get but $12 a night, the sidemen $10. We worked from 9 P.M. until 4 A.M. It was a real nice club. These after-hours clubs always had good crowds because after 2 o'clock everybody would come in. We had a two-week engagement there, and I thought it was real good money. But then we were kicked back out on the street.

Little Walter and I used to play along with Johnny Young at a place called the Purple Cat. 1947. That's where he gave me the name "lazy" at. We'd been there so long Little Walter thought I should go up and turn on the amps, but I never did go up and do that thing, so that's why he started calling me "lazy" Bill, and the name stuck.

In 1948 I started in playing with Homesick James, and sometimes also with Little Hudson. I started out Little Hudson on playing. When I first met him in Chicago around 1945 or 1946 he wasn't playing. Of course he had a guitar, but he wasn't *doing* nothing. I started him and encouraged him and so he'd come and sit in with me and Sonny Boy or me and Willie Mabon or whoever I'd be playing with. He just started like that. And when he got good he was respected. He had a right smart amount of prestige about him, Hudson did. I switched to playing piano in 1950 because they had more guitar players than piano players. But of course I'd been playing piano all along—just not professionally, that's all. Little Hudson needed a piano player for his Red Devils trio. Our first job was at a place called the Plantation, on 31st Street, on the south side of Chicago.

I don't know where he got the idea of name from, but the drummer had a red devil with pitchforks on the head of his brass drum. And he played in church, too! Would you believe they had to cover up the head of the drum with newspapers? He'd cover the devil up when he'd go to church.

I had a trio, Lazy Bill and the Blue Rhythm, for about three or four months in 1954 (ill. 4–10). We were supposed to do four records a year for Chance, but Art Sheridan went out of business and we never heard about it again. We did one record. Well, I didn't keep my group together long. You know it's kind of hard on a small musician to keep a group together in Chicago very long because they run out of work, and when

---

* Walter Jacobs, generally acknowledged as the finest blues harmonica player after World War II.

Courtesy of Jo Jo Williams

Ill. 4–10. *Lazy Bill and the Blue Rhythm, studio photo, Chicago, Illinois, 1954. L-R: Lazy Bill Lucas, James Bannister, "Miss Hi-Fi," Jo Jo Williams.*

they don't get work to do, they get with other guys. And there were so many musicians in Chicago that some of 'em were underbidding one another. They'd take a job what I was getting $12 for, they'd take it for $8.

I was doing anything, working with anybody, just so I could make a dime. On a record session, any engagement at all. For awhile I was working with a disc jockey on a radio station. He was broadcasting from a dry cleaners and he wanted live music on his broadcast. I did it for the publicity; I didn't get any money for that. Work got so far apart. Every time I'd run out of an engagement, it would be a long time before another one came through. And so Mojo and Jo Jo,* they had come up here to Minneapolis. They had been working at the Key Club, and they decided they needed a piano player. I wasn't doing anything in Chicago; I was glad to come up here. I had no idea I was doing to stay up here, but I ended up here with a houseful of furniture.

Lazy Bill Lucas and "Poor Boy Blues"

Bill Lucas's account of his life ends in Minneapolis in 1964. The following year I began my graduate studies at the University of Minnesota and met him at a university concert. By that time he had two audiences: the black people on the

---

* George "Mojo" Buford, harmonica player, and Joseph "Jo Jo" Williams, bass player.

North Side of the city who still liked the blues, and the white people in the university community. The 1960s was the period of the so-called "blues revival" (Groom 1971) during which thousands of blues records from the past four decades were reissued on LPs, dozens of older singers believed dead were "rediscovered" and recorded, and hundreds of younger singers, Bill Lucas among them, found new audiences at university concerts and coffee houses and festivals. The revival, which attracted a predominantly young, white audience, peaked in the great 1969 and 1970 Ann Arbor (Michigan) Blues Festivals, where the best of three generations of blues singers and blues bands performed for people who had traveled thousands of miles to pitch their tents and attend these three-day events. Bill Lucas was one of the featured performers at the 1970 festival. For his performance he received $400 plus expenses, the most money he ever made for a single job in his musical career.

In the 1960s and 1970s Bill Lucas could not support himself from his musical earnings. A monthly check (roughly a hundred times the minimum hourly wage) from government welfare for the blind supplemented his income. Blues music was in low demand; even now, most of Minneapolis's black community under the age of fifty prefer the current black popular music, while others like jazz or classical music. Some even make a point of disliking blues, either because they are fundamentalist Christians who associate blues with sin, or because they view blues as the expression of a resignation that is out of touch with modern attitudes toward human rights. Nor was there sufficient work in the university community for Bill. He sang in clubs, bars, and at concerts, but the work was unsteady. When I was in his band (1969–1971) our most dependable job was a six-month engagement for two nights each week in the "Grotto Room" of a pizza restaurant. Classified by the musicians' union as a low-level operation, it paid the minimum union scale for an evening's work from nine to one: $23 for Bill, $18 for sidemen (about $60 and $50, respectively, in today's money). On December 11, 1982 Bill Lucas died. A benefit concert to pay his funeral expenses raised nearly two thousand dollars.

His life history not only gives facts about his life but expresses an attitude toward it, and both may be compared with the words of "Poor Boy Blues" to see whether the song speaks personally for Bill Lucas. Some of the facts of the poor boy's life correspond but others do not. I asked him whether the line about all the letters in the alphabet looking the same held any special meaning for him, and he said it did. Unless letters or numbers were printed very large and thick he could not make them out. On the other hand, unlike the poor boy in the song who never saw his father, Lucas and his father were very close. Moreover, his experiences of Christmas were happy, and one year he received a piano. What about the attitudes expressed in the song and in the life history? Neither show self-pity. Bill did not have an illustrious career as a blues singer; he scuffled with hard times and took almost any job that was available. Yet he was proud of his accomplishments. "I just sing the funky blues," he said, "and people either like it or they don't."

"Poor Boy Blues" cannot therefore be understood to speak directly for Bill

Lucas's personal experience, but it does speak generally for it, as it speaks for tens of thousands of people who have been forced by circumstances into hard times. Thus, in their broad cultural reach, the words of blues songs tell the truth.

Learning the Blues

One question that bears on the relation between Lazy Bill Lucas and "Poor Boy Blues" is the authorship of the song. In fact, Lucas did not compose it; it was put together by St. Louis Jimmy Oden and recorded by him in 1942. Lucas learned the song from the record. Learning someone else's song does not, of course, rule out the possibility that the song speaks for the new singer, for he may be attracted to it precisely because the lyrics suit his experiences and feelings.

Almost all blues singers learn songs by imitation, whether in person or from records. There is no such thing as formal lessons. In his life history, Lucas tells how he listened to neighbors play guitar and how he tried to make it sound like they did. After he developed a rudimentary playing technique, he was able to fit accompaniments behind new songs which he learned from others or made up himself. Unquestionably the best way to come to know a song is to make it your own by performing it. Listen once again to "Poor Boy Blues" (recorded selection 19), and concentrate first on the instrumental accompaniment. The guitarists

and drummer keep a triple rhythm behind Lucas's singing. When Lucas pauses, the guitar responds with a sequence of single-note triplets (ex. 4–10). This triplet rhythm is a common way of dividing the beat in slow blues songs. When accented monotonously, as in many rock 'n' roll tunes from the 1950s, it becomes a cliché. Music students familiar with dotted rhythms (from marches and the like) should resist the temptation to hear this as a dotted rhythm. Recordings of white musicians before World War II attempting to play blues and jazz very often do not flow or "swing" because the musicians are locked into dotted rhythms.

Now listen to the rhythm of Lucas's vocal, and try to feel both rhythms, vocal and accompaniment, at the same time. You might find this attempt difficult. The reason is that Lucas very seldom sings squarely on the beat. The transcription of his melody (ex. 4–11) is an oversimplification for the sake of readability, but even here we see a great deal of syncopation, in seemingly delayed entrances or anticipations of the beat. Lucas is not having a hard time *finding* the beat; on the contrary, he deliberately avoids it.

Ex. 4–10.   *Rhythmic outline, "Poor Boy Blues."*

Poor Boy Blues

Lazy Bill Lucas

Ex. 4–11. *"Poor Boy Blues," stanza 3, sung by Lazy Bill Lucas, Minneapolis, Minnesota, May, 1970. Collected and transcribed by Jeff Titon.*

The musical brilliance of "Poor Boy Blues" rests on the difference between vocal and instrumental rhythms. Accents contrast; at times each part has its own meter. The reason is this: while the accompanying instruments stay in triple meter, Lucas sings in alternating duple and triple. In other words, passages of two-against-three polymeter (especially apparent at the outset of measures 1, 5, and 9 in ex. 4–11) alternate with passages of three-against-three single meter. I have written example 4–11 in 4/4 to bring out the contrast. One feels that Lucas initiates each vocal phrase in triple meter, then quickly shifts to duple, hurrying his phrasing in imitation of speech rhythm.

In chapter 3 we saw that two-against-three polymeter characterizes black African music. Here we see a connection between African and black American music: rhythmic complexity and polymeter. But our example from the blues is not just an instance of continuous polymeter, as in Africa. Rather, blues music (and jazz, and reggae) *shifts* into and out of polymeter, playfully teasing the boundary. When these shifts occur rapidly, the boundary between single meter and polymeter breaks down. The result is a new sense of time: the graceful forward propulsion we hear as "swing" that makes us feel like moving our whole body in response.

To sing "Poor Boy Blues" a Lucas does, begin by simply *saying* the words to get a feel for the speech rhythms. If you read music, use the transcription (ex. 4–11) as a guide, but always follow the recording. Listen to the way he slides up

Ex. 4–12. *The blues scale (key of G for convenience).*

to the high G in measures 2, 6, and 10, indicated on the transcription by a solid line just before the note heads. Then hear how he releases "poor" (measure 9) and slides directly afterwards into "boy." This sliding and gliding is another type of musical "play," this time with the pitch, not the beat. Finally, listen to him attack the word "twelve" (measures 3 and 7) just ahead of the bar-line rather than as written.

Lucas sings "Poor Boy Blues" in a musical scale I have called the blues scale (Titon 1971). This scale (ex. 4–12) is uniquely African American, though about fifty years ago it penetrated American pop music. It typifies blues, jazz, spirituals, gospel tunes, and other black American music. It differs significantly from the usual Western diatonic major and minor scales, and it does not correspond to any of the medieval European church modes. The blues scale's special features are the flatted seventh and the presence of *both* the major and minor third. (Another special feature, seemingly a later development, is the flatted fifth.) A typical use of this double third, sometimes termed the "blue note" by the jazz writers, is shown in measure 8 of example 4–11: Lucas enters on the minor third and proceeds directly to the major third. This is yet another example of "playing" with the pitch in black American music.

If you are a guitarist, it will be easy to chord along with the record, reading the chord diagrams in figure 4–5. The transcription shows where the chords begin. Lucas plays "Poor Boy Blues" in the key of G. With the exception of his G and G^7 chords, he employs standard first-position fingering. He prefers the dominant to the dominant seventh (here D instead of D^7) on guitar, but the opposite when he plays piano.* Most of his single-note runs are made in the first position, but sometimes he moves up the guitar neck on the first two strings to play the highest notes. If you learn to pick out the accompaniment from the record by ear, you will be learning blues guitar in one of the traditional, time-honored ways.

Composing the Blues

Besides learning blues songs from other singers and from records, blues singers make up their own songs. Sometimes they think a song out in advance; sometimes they improvise it during performance. Often a performance is a combination of planning and improvisation. The blues song's first composition unit is the line. If you sing the blues most of your life, blues lines will run through your mind like proverbs, which many indeed are: for instance, "You'll never miss your water till your well runs dry." A male singer might rhyme it with a line like,

---

*Lucas accompanies himself on piano in another version of "Poor Boy Blues" on *Lazy Bill Lucas,* Philo LP 1007.

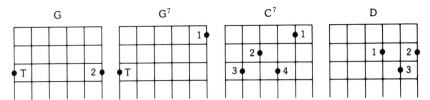

Fig. 4–5. **Guitar chord positions, "Poor Boy Blues."**

"Never miss your woman till she say good-bye" (a female singer's rhyme: "Never miss your good man till he say good-bye"). The singer has just composed his stanza:

> You'll never miss your water till you well runs dry,
> No, you'll never miss your water till your well runs dry,
> I never missed my baby till she said good-bye.

It is unusual for a blues singer to "compose" self-consciously. Instead, lines and stanzas seem to "just come," sometimes in a rush but more often one at a time and widely spaced. Blues singer Booker White called the songs he made up "sky songs": "I have an imaginary mind to do things like that. Didn't have nary a word written down. I just reached up and got 'em" (Evans 1971:253). Another blues singer, Robert Pete Williams, described how his songs came to him: "The atmosphere, the wind blowing carries music along. I don't know it if affects you or not, but it's a sounding that's in the air, you see? And I don't know where it comes from—it could come from the airplanes, or the moaning of automobiles, but anyhow it leaves an air current in the air, you see? That gets in the wind, makes a sounding, you know? And that sounding works up to be a blues" (Wilson 1966:21). Statements like these show the universal aspect of the blues and the singer as an interpreter of the natural world. The sounding airplane, the moaning automobile trace a human pattern in the surrounding atmosphere that "affects" only the gifted interpreter, the translator, the blues singer. When the singer turns it into a song for all to hear, the universal truth is apparent.

If the blues singer plans his stanzas in advance, he memorizes them, sometimes writing them down. As we have seen, the stanzas may or may not speak directly for the personal experience of the singer. St. Louis Jimmy, author of "Poor Boy Blues," said this about another of his songs, "Goin' Down Slow": "My blues came mostly from women. . . . 'Goin' Down Slow' started from a girl, in St. Louis—it wasn't me—I've never been sick a day in my life, but I seen her in the condition she was in—pregnant, tryin' to lose a kid, see. And she looked like she was goin' down slow. And I made that remark to my sister and it came in my mind and I started to writin' it. . . . I looked at other people's troubles and I writes from that, and I writes from my own troubles" (Oliver 1965: 101–102).

Songs that blues singers memorize usually stick to one idea or event. A memorized song, Lucas's "Poor Boy Blues" has four stanzas on the circumstances leading to the poor boy's cry for mercy. But the words in an improvised song seldom show the unity of time, circumstances, or feeling evident in a memorized song. After all, unless you have had lots of practice, it is hard enough to improvise rhymed stanzas, let alone keep to a single subject (compare McLeod and Herndon 1981:59 on improvised Maltese song duels). So an improvising singer usually throws in some memorized, traditional stanzas along with stanzas he puts together on the spot.

A Blues Song in the Making

Today, some blues songs are improvised in performance but most are memorized beforehand. This memorization is a later trend in the history of the blues, and results from the impact of commercial blues records (they began in the 1920s) on singers born after about 1910. Singers who wanted to make records studied them and got the idea that a song ought to last about three minutes and stick to one theme—as most recorded blues songs did. So they composed and memorized their songs, and they memorized other singers' songs. Of course, they could not avoid learning traditional stanzas and building a mental storehouse, but more and more they sang from memory instead of improvising. Today the influence of records is overpowering, so singers very seldom change lyrics when learning other people's songs and, like rock bands trying to "cover" hit records, they copy the instruments too. In short, most blues singers today think a blues song should have a fixed, not variable, text.

But a few older blues singers continue making up their own songs, improvising in performance and seldom singing a song the same way twice. Improvisation is of great interest because it helps us understand how the mind works. In improvisation the creative mind is on display. One older singer who improvised was Big Joe Williams, the man Lazy Bill Lucas sang the blues with on the streets of St. Louis in 1940 (ill. 4–11). In his songs we will take a closer look at improvisation, but first let us review his fascinating musical career.

Big Joe Williams was born on October 16, 1903, on a farm near Knoxford Swamp, just outside of the town of Crawford, Mississippi.* He made his first musical instrument when he was a young teenager. It was a one-stringed instrument called a "diddly-bow." "I made it from baling wire," he said. "Like I'd go to your house and take two spools, and I'd put one spool down at the bottom of the wall, one at the top, and when I want to make different tones . . . I'd take a bottleneck, or even a whole bottle." The diddly-bow was a common instrument among black people in Mississippi, and it has been reported elsewhere (Evans 1970). The string is played by plucking one end and stopping the other end by sliding a bottle (or another smooth object) along its length. The distance of the string from the plucked end to where the object rests determines the pitch. It is easy to make and play the diddly-bow, and directions for doing it are given on pp. 150–154 of this chapter.

---

* Biographical information on Big Joe Williams comes from Leo W. Bruin, "Malvina My Sweet Woman: The Life Story of Big Joe Williams," booklet accompanying *Big Joe Williams,* Oldie Blues LP OL 2804 (Holland).

Jeff Todd Titon

Ill. 4–11. *Big Joe Williams at the Smithsonian Festival of American Folklife, Washington, D.C., 1976.*

Still in his early teens, Big Joe Williams left his home and family and began a life on the road that continued for more than sixty-five years. Traveling through Alabama, he worked in the turpentine camps; in Mississippi, he worked on the levee camps; but soon he had acquired enough skill to pursue a full-time musician's career, traveling throughout the South and singing at house-rent parties in the cities, open-air or juke-joint Saturday night bootleg whiskey dances out in the country, in the lumber camps, barrelhouses, and wherever else people wanted good music and good times. Mississippi was his home base in the latter part of the 1920s, where he sang with the outstanding bluesmen of the period, including Charley Patton, father of the Mississippi Delta blues, his partner, Eddie "Son" House, and later, House's pupil, the legendary Robert Johnson. Songs, stanzas, and instrumental techniques passed from one singer to another in the folk tradition of the down home blues, a tradition and a style quite different from the blues of the same period sung by women like Ida Cox, Ma Rainey, Clara Smith, Ethel Waters, and Bessie Smith. These blues queens were stage show actresses, pop singers who took pride in their ability to sing the latest songs penned by a New York-based black Tin Pan Alley. Backed by jazz bands, their blues was quite sophisticated compared to the rough insistence of the down home vocal and guitar or barrelhouse piano sound.

From 1930 until 1949 Big Joe Williams lived and worked in St. Louis, making frequent trips south to Memphis and the Mississippi Delta, and north to Chicago. During this period he recorded several dozen commercial 78s, which RCA Victor sold on its Bluebird label. But musical styles and musical taste were changing, and the people came to prefer the urbane sounds of B.B. King and T-Bone Walker. He found it harder to support himself in the 1950s, while his record output dwindled and the jobs in clubs were fewer and farther between. He traveled more often, finding work in country juke-joints where they still liked the old-fashioned sound. In the 1960s, he became a central part of the blues revival in Chicago, singing and playing the blues at folk music clubs on Chicago's North Side, and recording several LPs for the Chicago-based Delmark label. But despite his new association with the promoters of the blues revival, he took to the road from time to time, traveling south to his old audiences. Fiercely independent, he never stayed long in one place. His fame spread to white audiences through the recordings he made for Delmark and Folkways, through numerous appearances at colleges and folk festivals, and three European tours with the American Folk Blues Festival, in 1963, 1968, and 1972. As age overtook him, he moved back to his home town of Crawford, Mississippi, but he had an active musical career at home and abroad until he died in 1982.

Throughout his more than sixty-year blues career, Big Joe Williams was a prolific blues composer. His best-known song is "Baby Please Don't Go," which dates from 1921 (fig. 4–6). Even in his seventies, Williams continued to compose songs. At the 1976 Smithsonian Institution Festival of American Folklife, he was proud to perform his latest composition, "Watergate Blues." I recorded him singing it three times on three successive days, and I was not surprised to find that each version was different from the others.

If you look at the differences in these three versions (figs. 4–7a,b,c) you will begin to understand how the improvising blues singer composes at the moment of performance. Read them now (and pay particular attention to the stanzas that begin with the rooster addressing then hen). The first thing you notice is the

Fig. 4–6. *Lyrics, "Baby Please Don't Go."*

Baby please don't go,
Baby please don't go,
Baby please don't go back to New Orleans 'cause I love you so.

Turn your lamp down low,
Turn your lamp down low,
Turn your lamp down low, crying all night long, baby please don't go.

1. *Yes I went to the gas station this morning,*
    trying to get my gas ticket straight.
    He said, "No, Big Joe, you can't get but three gallons of gas
    because of this Watergate."
    Every time I'm telling you, I can't see a thing but Watergate.
    Well I'll be so glad, so glad, when President Ford gets everything straight.

2. *Well the rooster told the hen,*
    "I want all the hens to go out and lay."
    She said, "No: Watergate is in my house, boy,
    and I ain't gonna do what you say."
    Every time I reach for the newspaper I can't see a thing but Watergate.
    Well I'll be so glad, so glad, when President Ford gets everything straight.

3. *I want everybody*
    to leave President Nixon alone.
    Let him leave the hospital in California
    go back to his old home.
    Well oh, can't hear a thing but Watergate.
    I'll be so glad, so glad, when President Ford gets everything straight.

4. *I got a handful of nickels,*
    a pocketful of dimes,
    potful of water, good children,
    all the time.
    Oh yeah, can't hear a thing but Watergate.
    Be so glad when President Ford get everything straight.

Fig. 4–7a.   *"Watergate Blues," version 1. July 3, 1976.*

stanza form. It differs from the typical three-line blue stanza of "Poor Boy Blues." In "Poor Boy Blues" Bill Lucas sang a line, then more or less repeated it, and closed the stanza with a rhyming punch line. Most blues stanzas fall into this three-line pattern, particularly traditional stanzas. But some, like "Watergate Blues," fall into a different line pattern consisting of a quatrain (four lines rhymed abcb) and a rhymed two-line refrain that follows to close out each stanza. The contrast between the three-line stanza and the quatrain-refrain stanza can easily be shown in a diagram, for the quatrain fits into the first four measures (bars) of the twelve-bar blues strophe, while the refrain fits into the last eight bars of the twelve-bar blues strophe (fig. 4–8). The quatrain-refrain pattern became popular after World War II. It usually offers story vignettes in the quatrain to prove the truth of the repeated refrain. In "Watergate Blues" the quatrains show why the Watergate affair is such a nuisance.

The stanza form, whether three-line or quatrain-refrain, is of course preset, and so it acts as a mold into which the improvising singer pours his words. Just *any* words will not do, because the refrain has to repeat, lines must rhyme, and the whole thing has to make sense. The quatrain-refrain form is a little more difficult to improvise in because the quatrain lines are so short and come so fast. Now let us look at Big Joe Williams's improvisations in the three versions of "Watergate Blues." You might think it would be easiest just to improvise in the

1. *Yes I went out to the gas station this morning,*
    tried to get my gas ticket straight.
    Said, "No, I can't guarantee but three gallons of gas.
    Remember the Watergate."
    Oh, every time I look at my tv, can't hear a thing but Watergate.
    Well, I'll be so glad, so glad, when President Ford get every doggone thing
        straight.

2. *Well the rooster told the hen,*
    "I want you to go and lay."
    Say, "Watergate my home and I
    don't play still."
    Every time I look at my tv, can't hear a thing but Watergate.
    Well, I'll be so glad when President Ford, lord, get everything straight.

3. *I got a handful of nickels boys and*
    pocketful of dimes,
    houseful of children all
    all are mine.
    They was a-crying, "Can't hear a thing but Watergate."
    I'll be so glad when President Ford gets every doggone thing straight.

Fig. 4–7b. *"Watergate Blues," version 2. July 4, 1976.*

quatrain and memorize the refrain; but if we compare the refrains Williams sings, we find differences, so it seems he has not memorized them. The general idea is the same—that is, the idea that everywhere the singer looks he cannot avoid news of Watergate. But the exact expression of that idea varies, as Williams substitutes the radio, television, and newspaper one for the other.

Now behind this apparently simple technique of substitution lies part of the explanation of the blues singer's ability to improvise. Let us remember how hard this is, compared, say, to a kind of improvisation we are familiar with because we do it all the time: namely, conversation. In conversation we can stop and think, but a blues singer has to keep going, and he also has to rhyme. So to help himself, the blues singer relies *partly* on memory. What he has memorized are words that go together and the patterns of their togetherness. By combining and manipulating and substituting these word groups he puts together his lines and stanzas spontaneously. It is important to realize that his improvisation does not proceed word by word—that would be too hard—but word group by word group.

Suppose we call each of these word groups a *preform* (Titon 1978). A preform is something roughly pre-sized and shaped that is brought back from storage and given its final form just before use. These blues word groups are preforms stored in the memory, then retrieved and given a final shape—verb tense, for instance, or gender—just before singing. We need an illustration, and the stanzas in which Big Joe Williams begins, "I got a handful of nickels" will do (fig. 4–9). In each version, lines 1 plus 2 make up a preform, roughly stored and then sung almost identically. They end in "dimes," which has the long *i* plus the nasal near the close to set up the rhyme. Now in each version lines 3 plus 4 also make up

1. *Yes I went out to the bus station this morning,*
   trying to get my ticket straight.
   Said, "You can't get but three gallons of gas boy you
   'cause you know this Watergate."
   And every time I pick up my paper I can't hear a thing but Watergate.
   Yes I'll be so glad when President Ford get every doggone thing straight.

2. *Well the rooster told the hen now,*
   "Want the hens all go lay."
   Said, "No; I'm not home, I can't lay no more,
   'cause I got nothing but Watergate."
   Whoa whoa lord I can't see a thing, yes nothing but Watergate.
   Yes I'll be so glad, so glad when President Ford get every doggone thing
      straight.

3. *Well I want everybody*
   to leave President Nixon alone.
   Let him out the hospital in California
   and go back to his next home.
   Well, I say I can't hear a thing but Watergate.
   Every time I pick up my paper I read about nothing but Watergate.

4. *Well the rooster told the hen now,*
   "I'll be like a old crow.
   See, I got Watergate in my house and I can't
   live there no more."
   Every time I listen at the television can't see a thing but Watergate.

Fig. 4–7c.   *"Watergate Blues," version 3. July 5, 1976.*

preforms, but they are different preforms. So Williams found two different pre-forms, one in each version, for lines 3 plus 4, each ending the stanza sensibly and with a different but proper long *i* plus nasal rhyme. This is how the impro-vising blues singer builds up his lines and stanzas from preforms at the moment of singing.

If preforms always worked perfectly we would never know for sure that they (rather than straight memorization, or word-by-word improvising) were the key to improvisation in blues. But because they sometimes fail we can see them in process. In other words, we need to look at failed improvisations as well as successful ones to confirm that improvisation proceeds by preforms.

Consider the four quatrains in the three versions of "Watergate Blues" that begin, "Well the rooster told the hen." In three of them Williams follows this line with "I want the hens to go out and lay" or some rough variant. Each is sensible and effective, and together they suggest preforms. But the failure in stanza 2, version 2, confirms it. "Watergate my home and I don't play still" neither rhymes nor make sense. What happened? Williams sang "play," showing he had a good rhyme; he just failed to recall a good preform, like "'Ain't gonna do what you say." Probably his mind got stuck on a preform involving "play."

Is it possible that Williams memorized several slightly different quatrains? This tactic would have been terribly inefficient. If he wanted to sing from memory, he

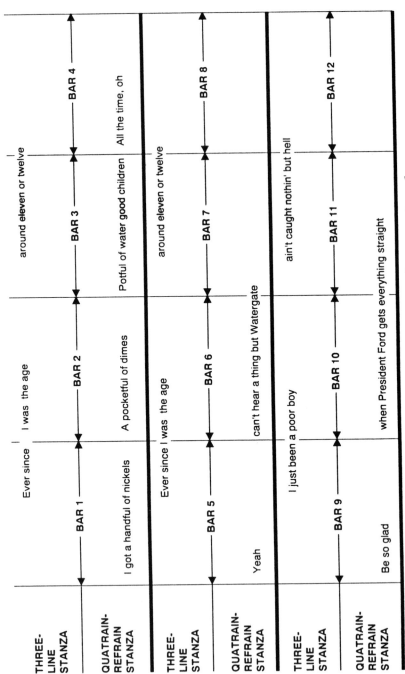

Fig. 4–8.   *Two twelve-bar blues stanza forms compared.*

Version 1 [Preforms 1 & 2]	Line	Version 2 [Preforms 1 & 3]
Preform 1 { I got a handful of nickels,	(1)	I got a handful of nickels, boys, } **Preform 1**
A pocketful of dimes,	(2)	Pocketful of dimes,
Preform 2 { Potful of water, good children	(3)	Houseful of children all } **Preform 3**
All the time.	(4)	All are mine.

Fig. 4–9. *Two stanzas built from preforms compared.*

would memorize a single quatrain. No, I think the preform theory best fits the evidence. The idea is the same at the root of these rooster-hen quatrains: the hen cannot or will not lay because Watergate upsets her. Now if Williams had memorized, the same idea would come out in the same quatrain every time, or at least many times. On the other hand, if Williams's memory failed he would pause—come to a dead halt, or garble. But—and this is crucial—Williams expresses the same idea wonderfully well in a variety of ways. He even varies his rhymes ("say" and "Water*gate*" rhymed with "lay"). Williams improvises, and the preform theory shows us how.

"Watergate Blues" is an unusual topical song, blending the nuisance of the winter 1973–1974 gas shortage with the Watergate burglary. But the idea that the media spent too much time on Watergate was shared by many Americans who simply wanted to be done with it; and it appealed, also, to the audience at the Festival of American Folklife when Williams sang it not far from the Watergate building itself. The creative artist who continues to create in old age, whether a Big Joe Williams or a Pablo Casals, is always awe-inspiring. Perhaps the lesson is that creative artistry does not depend so much on youth and strength as on vision, and that vision may be sustained, and sustaining, into old age.

How to Make and Play a One-Stringed Diddly-Bow

The musical bow, a single string stretched on a frame of some kind, like a hunting bow, is a widespread tribal musical instrument. Related to it is the one-stringed diddly-bow, a traditional black American instrument. Many blues singers who grew up on Southern farms—such as Big Joe Williams—recall it as their first musical instrument. One-String Sam accompanied himself on a small, portable diddly-bow as he sang "I Need $100" in Detroit in the early 1950s (recorded selection 20; fig. 4–10). I cannot make out the lyrics of stanza 2 with much confidence.

Despite its simple construction and playing technique, the diddly-bow produces a very satisfactory blues sound. It will be easy to build and learn to play it even if you have never built an instrument before. Follow illustration 4–12, showing Compton Jones, or make the variant shown in fig. 4–11. A list of building materials and a construction diagram for a portable diddly-bow are shown in this figure. The wood can be obtained free from the scrap pile of a sawmill or lumberyard. For a couple of dollars, any musical instrument store should be able to supply you with a single guitar machine head, some hard plastic bridge and nut material, and a steel string. Try to get a banjo string with a "loop end" that will fit easily over the wood screw at the bridge end of the instrument (see fig. 4–11).

1. *You know I talked with mother this morning,*
   mother talked with the judge.
   I could hear her, eavesdropping, you know I
   understood their words.
       She said, "I need $100.
       You know I—.
       You know I need $100
       just to go my baby's bond."

2. *You know me and my little girl got up this morning.*
   She said she wanted to freeze to death.
   Told her in the icebox to look in, baby I
   freeze my ice myself.
       I just need $100.
       I say I need—.
       You know I need $100
       just to go my baby's bond.

3. *You know I left your mother standing, baby,*
   In her doorway crying.
   Come begging and pleading don't
   mistreat your little girl of mine.
       I said, "Mother-in-law I need $100.
       All I need's—.
       All I need $100
       just to go my baby's bond."

4. *You know my houselady come telling about*
   want to talk for an hour,
   want to go to the Red Cross people you know
   want a sack of Red Cross flour.
       I told her all I need's $100.
       All I need's —.
       Baby if I had $100
       I could go and go my baby's bond.

Fig. 4–10.   *Lyrics, "I Need $100."*

Saw a notch for the nut near one end of the piece of wood, then cut the wood back to the end. Glue a piece of scrap wood to the bottom of the cutaway. Drill a hole for the string anchor pole and attach the machine head to the scrap wood bottom. Make sure that the top of the string anchor pole is lower than the top of the nut (fig. 4–12).

Glue the nut flush against the notch so that the top of the nut is about ⅛ inch higher than the stringboard. Saw a notch for the bridge near the other end of the stringboard, and glue in the bridge so that it is about ¼ inch higher than the stringboard. Insert a small wood screw between the bridge and the short end of the stringboard, leaving about ¹⁄₁₆ inch clearance between the board and the head of the screw to fit the string loop on. Glue two pieces of scrap wood underneath the stringboard to serve as a table rest. Attach the loop end of the

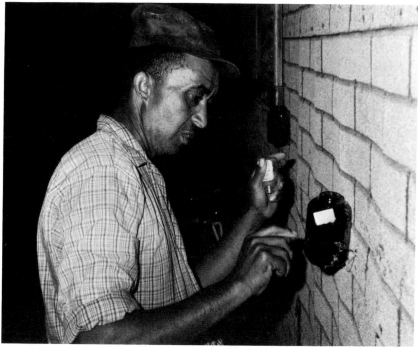

Cheryl T. Evans

Ill. 4–12.   *Compton Jones plays the diddly-bow, near Senatobia, Mississippi, 1971.*

banjo string over the wood screw, then push the other end through the machine head anchor pole, taking up most of the slack. Knot the string around the anchor pole and turn the machine head knob, tightening the string until when you pluck it, it produces the same pitch as the tonic (here, the lowest and most frequently played tone) on One-String Sam's accompaniment for "I Need $100." Check the pitch against the record.

Fig. 4–11.   *How to make a portable, one-stringed diddly-bow.*

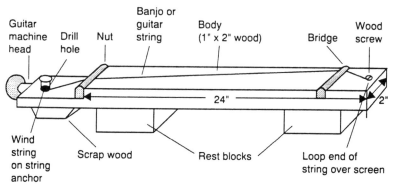

Side View:

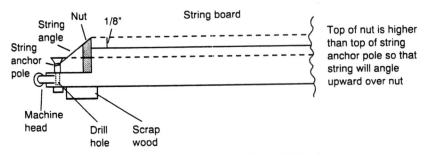

Fig. 4–12. *Close-up, nut end of diddly-bow.*

Play your diddly-bow by plucking the string near the bridge with the thumb of one hand while sliding a smooth device such as a bottleneck, lipstick case, piece of copper tubing, pipe tool, or pocket knife atop the string with the other hand. For the moment, ignore the sliding aspect and concentrate on the hand that does the plucking. Leave the other hand out of it entirely. Now hold the diddly-bow with the heel of your plucking hand falling just between the wood screw and the bridge; slight pressure will prevent the instrument from moving on the table. Turn your hand counterclockwise and make a half-fist with your fingers loosely tucked so that your thumb is parallel to the string and can pluck the string comfortably in a motion always away from your body.

The rhythm that One-String Sam uses in "I Need $100" is the same triplet rhythm that Bill Lucas used in "Poor Boy Blues": CHUNG, k'CHUNG, k'CHUNG, k'CHUNG, and so on. In musical notation:

$$\frac{12}{8} \quad \overset{\ulcorner3\urcorner}{\flat} \overset{\ulcorner3\urcorner}{\flat} \overset{\ulcorner3\urcorner}{\flat} \overset{\ulcorner3\urcorner}{\flat} \quad \textit{etc.}$$

The simplicity of the instrument allows us to invent a diddly-bow notation—similar to the box notation in chapter 3—that shows how to play "I Need $100" or any other song. In the diddly-bow notation each triplet beat will be marked with a box:

The basic rhythm for "I Need $100" comes out like this:

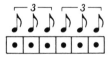

CHUNG   k' CHUNG   k' CHUNG

With your thumb plucking away from your body, play the diddly-bow in that rhythm for awhile until it is comfortable. If your hand gets cramped, stop and shake it out. Keep it loose; move the whole thumb as a unit, not just the upper part above the knuckle. Come back to it every so often, and by the end of a day it will have become second nature.

That is about all there is to the right-hand part (or left-hand part, if you are left-handed) of "I Need $100." The other hand's part is even simpler; in fact, most of the time it does nothing at all while you pluck the tonic as you have just been practicing. At other times it slides a bottleneck or other smooth device along the top of the string to make the whining, zinging sounds you hear on the record.

Traditionally, the diddly-bow is played with a bottleneck slide. Any hard object that can be held easily in your hand will serve, but glass makes the best sound. Find a bottle with a cylindrical neck (fig. 4–13). Glass cutters are available at hardware stores and specialty shops, and they give a sure, neat cut. Another way to part the neck from the bottle uses simpler materials but it is not foolproof. You will need a bowl of ice water, a candle, and a piece of string about 4 inches long. Light the candle and wait until some molten wax forms around the wick-well. Dip the string through the molten wax, covering it thoroughly. Before the wax on the string hardens, tie the string around the bottleneck where you want the break to occur. Then hold the bottleneck over the candle, lighting the waxed string so its burns evenly all around. While it is still burning, plunge the bottle, neck first, into the ice water. Most of the time the neck will break off. Carefully file any jagged edges smooth. Alternately, use a glass medicine bottle whole, without cutting off the neck.

Hold the medicine bottle or bottleneck comfortably in your hand so you can rest it and slide it gently but firmly up and down the string of the diddly-bow from the nut to the area where your other hand plucks the string. If you press too hard, the string will touch the fingerboard and the sound of the plucked string will be muffled. If you don't press at all, the bottle will jiggle and rattle when the string is plucked. Gentle pressure gives a clear, ringing tone.

Practice sliding the glass on the diddly-bow. Make certain you have a good grip on the side so you can take it off the string when playing the tonic and can put in on the string at various locations. Pluck the string as you slide. Now, find the various simple pitch intervals with the slide on the string (fig. 4–14). The octave will be sounded when the slide is about halfway between the nut and

Fig. 4–13. *Choosing the right bottle.*

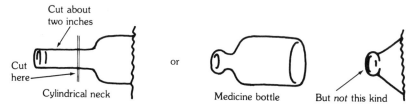

Cut about two inches

Cut here

Cylindrical neck

or

Medicine bottle

But *not* this kind

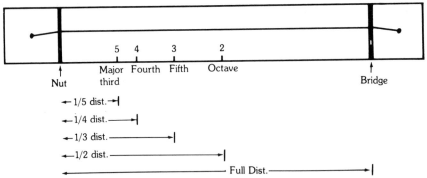

Fig. 4–14. *Marking intervals on the diddly-bow.*

bridge. With a pen or pencil, mark this point on the stringboard with the number 2 (for one-half the distance to the bridge). The perfect fifth will be sounded when the slide is one-third of the distance between the nut and bridge. Mark this point on the stringboard with a 3. The perfect fourth will be sounded when the slide is one-fourth the distance between the nut and bridge. Mark this point on the stringboard with a 4. The major third will be sounded when the slide is one-fifth the distance between the nut and bridge. Mark this point with a 5. These will be your reference points for the intervals used in "I Need $100," and of course they will come in handy as well when you want to play other songs.

The marks you have just made on your stringboard will easily be incorporated in our diddly-bow notation to indicate where to place the slide. A dot (zero) inside the notation box indicates that the slide is off the string; this is the tonic. Now each of the numbers on the stringboard can be put inside notation boxes to tell you where to place the slide as you pluck the string with the other hand. Try this:

♪	♩	♪	♩
●	4	5	●

This four-tone sequence is one of Sam's typical moves in "I Need $100." He plucks the tonic for a count of one triplet, then puts on the slide at 4, plucks the string, and holds the tone for a count of two triplets. Next he moves the slide on the string back to 5—actually, slightly to the nut side of 5, because he uses a neutral rather than a major interval of a third—and plucks the string for a count of one triplet. Finally, he takes the slide off and plucks the tonic for a count of two triplets. Listen to the record and pick out the spots where he plays this sequence.

When you have mastered this four-tone sequence, you are well on your way to Sam's accompaniment for "I Need $100." The accompaniment Sam uses in the first stanza is written out in box notation in example 4–13. The jagged lines after 3 and 2 indicate a vibrato, which Sam makes by wiggling the slide back and forth

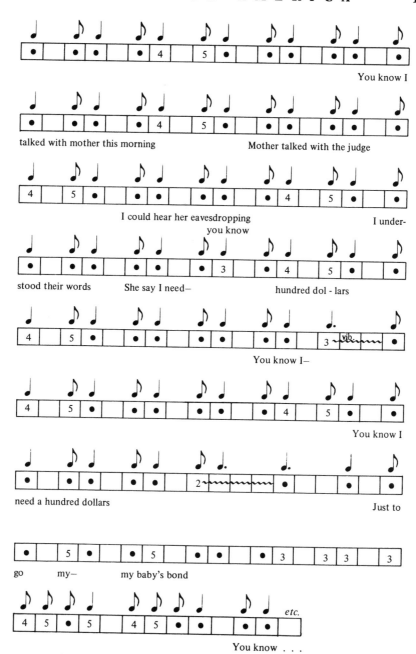

Ex. 4–13.   *Diddly-bow accompaniment for "I Need $100," as played by One-String Sam (recorded selection 20). Transcribed by Jeff Titon.*

quickly on the string in the general area of the stringboard mark. Put the record on and play along with One-String Sam.

Social Context and the Meaning of the Blues

The blues songs we have taken a close look at, "Poor Boy Blues," "Watergate Blues," and "I Need $100," are typical and can bring us toward a definition of blues as a song form. Textually, blues songs consist of a series of rhymed three-lined or quatrain-refrain stanzas, each sung to more or less the same tune. Blues tunes usually consist of twelve-measure (bar) strophes, and they employ a special scale, the blues scale (ex. 4–12). They are rhythmically complex, employing syncopation and, at times, conflicting rhythms between singing and instruments. Many other attributes of blues songs—melodic shape, for instance, or the typical raspy timbre—are beyond the scope of an introduction but may be followed up elsewhere (see Titon 1977). But in one resect "Poor Boy Blues" and "Watergate Blues" are *not* typical: the subject of their lyrics. Most blues lyrics are about lovers, and they fall into a pattern arising from black American life.

The blues grew and developed when most black Americans lived as share-croppers on Southern cotton farms, from late in the nineteenth century until just before World War II, when farm mechanization began to displace the black workers and factory work at high wages in the northern cities attracted them. Down home, young men and women did not marry early; they were needed on the farm. If a young woman became pregnant, she had her baby and brought the child into the household with her parents. She did not lose status in the community and later, she often married the father of her child. When a woman did marry young, her partner usually was middle-aged and needed a woman to work and care for his children from a prior marriage. It was good to have plenty of children; when they came of age to work more hands could go into the cotton and corn fields. Adoption was common; when families broke up, children were farmed out among relatives.

Sociologists and anthropologists, some of them (like Charles Johnson) black, studied this sharecropping culture in the 1920s and 1930s. Interested in patterns of love, marriage, and divorce, the field-workers found that partners separated because one could not live with the other's laziness, violence, or adultery. These reasons added up to "mistreatment," the very word they used. A woman was reported as saying her current lover was "nice all right, but I ain't thinking about marrying. Soon as you marry a man he starts mistreating you, and I ain't going to be mistreated no more" (Johnson 1966:83). Blues songs reflected these attitudes; mistreatment was the most common subject. Once the subject was established, people began to expect mistreatment as the appropriate subject for blues songs, and although many blues were composed about other subjects, the majority had to do with lovers and mistreatment. After World War II the sharecropping culture was less important; the action now took place in the cities where most had gone: Atlanta, New York, Washington, Detroit, Memphis, St. Louis, Chicago, Dallas, Houston, Los Angeles, Oakland. But black family patterns persisted among the lower classes in the urban ghettos, and so did the blues.

Blues lyrics about mistreatment fall into a pattern. The singer casts himself or herself in the role of mistreated victim, introduces an antagonist (usually a mistreating lover) provides incidents that detail the circumstances of the mistreatment, and draws up a bill of indictment. Then, with the listener's tacit approval, the victim becomes the judge, and the drama turns on the verdict: will he or she accept the mistreatment, try to reform the mistreater, or leave? Resigned acceptance and attempted reform resolve a minority of blues songs. Most often the victim, declaring independence, steps out of the victim's role with an ironic parting shot and leaves. "Dog Me Around," as sung by Howlin' Wolf is typical in this regard (fig. 4–15; ill. 4–13).

In stanza 1 the singer complains of mistreatment, saying his lover treats him like a dog. "Dog me around" is black American vernacular. We learn in stanza 2 that the singer may also be guilty; "If I treat you right" implies mistreatment on both sides of the relationship. (Stanza 2 could be interpreted as dialogue spoken by the singer's mistreating lover; but without an obvious clue, like, "She said," point of view seldom shifts in blues lyrics.) The singer resolves the drama in stanza 3 when he declares he will leave his lover. "Just tell 'em I walked outdoors" is an understatement that shows how little the affair means to him.

Blues music in black culture helps lovers understand each other and, since the themes are traditional and community-shared, blues songs give listeners community approval for separation in response to mistreatment. The listener who recognizes his or her situation in the lyrics of a blues song is given a nice definition of that situation and shown just what might be done in response. At a Saturday night party, or at home alone, a mistreated lover finds consolation in the blues (ill. 4–14).

The Blues Today

The great variety of settings and styles of the blues today reveals something of the history of its development and the resiliency of its form. Chameleon-like, it

Fig 4–15. *Lyrics, "Dog Me Around," by Howlin' Wolf (Chester Burnett).*
Copyright © 1974, Modern Music Publishing Co., Inc. Used by permission.

Dog Me Around*

1. *How many more years have I got to let you dog me around?*
   How many more years have I got to let you dog me around?
   I'd just as soon rather be dead, sleeping way down in the ground.

2. *If I treat you right you wouldn't believe what I've said.*
   If I treat you right you wouldn't believe what I've said.
   You think I'm halfway crazy; you think I ought to let you have your way.

3. *I'm going upstairs, I'm going to bring back down my clothes.*
   I'm going upstairs, I'm going to bring back down my clothes.
   If anybody asks about me, just tell 'em I walked outdoors.

Ill. 4–13. *Howlin' Wolf (Chester Burnett), Ann Arbor Blues Festival, Ann Arbor, Michigan, 1969.*

can alter its appearance to suit changing conditions of the blues music-culture. But despite varied techniques and instrumentation it has not changed its basic substance: the blues scale, the twelve-measure form with its characteristic tonic-subdominant-dominant seventh harmonic support, the three-line or quatrain-refrain stanza, and the rhythm crossing between vocal and accompaniment. The timbre, number, and arrangement of the accompanying instruments has changed the most, and with it the sound and feeling of the music: precise and sophisticated, as in the blues performances of Jimmy Rushing with the Count Basie orchestra late in the 1930s; powerfully hard-driving, as in the immensely popular recordings of such 1940s blues shouters as Wynonie Harris, Tiny Bradshaw, and Joe Turner, who were pretty much responsible for the *blues* in *rhythm 'n' blues;*

Frederic Ramsey, Jr.

Ill. 4–14. *Dancing at a juke joint, Alabama, 1957.*

or funky and down home, as in the Memphis-, Detroit-, and Chicago-based blues of such singers as Elmore James, Muddy Waters, Howlin' Wolf, and Jimmy Reed, who captured a large share of a declining blues market in the 1950s.

Combining jazz-band precision with the force of rhythm and blues (R & B), and featuring a stingingly modern amplified lead guitar, T-Bone Walker's extremely successful 1940s sound had a host of imitators, including Lowell Fulson and most notably B. B. King, to say nothing of generations of British and American rockers. Meanwhile in the house parties and juke joints of the rural South, especially in Texas, Arkansas, and Mississippi, solo singer-guitarists, sometimes with a friend sitting in on guitar or harmonica, continue to sing and play the blues for friends and neighbors. Outside this professional and semiprofessional blues music-culture are countless black blues singers and musicians who no longer perform regularly but who, without a great deal of persuasion, sing on occasion for family and friends.

Today's most active blues music-culture is located in Chicago, a city with a history of great hospitality to the blues (see ill. 4–15). Dozens of blues clubs may also be found in such cities as Houston, St. Louis, Memphis, Oakland-San Francisco, and Detroit. Well-known blues singers like B.B. King and Albert Collins tour nationally and, sponsored by the U.S. Department of State, as goodwill ambassadors abroad. *Living Blues* (Center for the Study of Southern Culture, Univ. of Miss., University, MS 38677) publishes in each issue a list of blues clubs, scheduled singers and bands, and dates, along with radio programs, films, and other events in cities throughout the United States and Canada.

To hear a recorded example of the modern blues sound, listen to "Sweet Home Chicago" by The Fieldstones, a Memphis-based blues band (recorded selection 21; ill. 4–16).

Jeff Todd Titon

Ill. 4–15.   *Cicero Blake, vocalist, performing with Mighty Joe Young's Blues Band at Eddie Shaw's Club, Chicago, Illinois, 1977.*

The Fieldstones consist of Wordie Perkins and Willie Roy Sanders, electric guitars; Lois Brown, electric bass; Bobby Carnes, electric organ; and Joe Hicks, vocal and drums. David Evans, who produced their album (*The Fieldstones: Memphis Blues Today:* High Water LP 1001) and wrote the jacket notes, describes their music as sounding "as low down and funky as the most primitive cotton

Ill. 4–16.   *The Fieldstones.*

patch blues and at the same time as polished and contemporary as the latest hit on the radio." Much of this polish results from the band's aesthetic preference for a clean, crisp sound: they keep the drumheads very tight and the electric guitars amplified with only a minimum of distortion. And at the same time, the band is steeped in tradition. Their repertoire includes blues songs like "Saddle Up My Pony" and "Dirt Road" that are more than sixty years old, and the guitarists play with their fingers instead of a pick, favoring the key of E like so many traditional Mississippi Delta blues guitarists.

"Sweet Home Chicago" is a blues classic (fig. 4–16). First recorded by the legendary Delta bluesman Robert Johnson in 1936, it is a staple in the blues repertory and it has been recorded by several prominent rock bands. Robert Johnson probably did not compose the song; most likely he drew on versions by Roosevelt Sykes and James "Kokomo" Arnold current in oral tradition at the time of his recording. But he did originate its most distinctive feature: the walking bass line.

To be sure, "walking the basses" was a definitive characteristic of the boogie-woogie, barrelhouse piano style favored by blues pianists in the 1920s and

Fig. 4–16. *Lyrics, "Sweet Home Chicago." Transcribed by Jeff Titon.*

Sweet Home Chicago

1. *Come on, baby don't you want to go;*
   Oh come on, baby don't you want to go
   Back to the same old place, sweet home Chicago.

2. *Come on, baby don't you want to go;*
   Oh come on, baby don't you want to go
   Back to the same old place, sweet home Chicago.

3.   *One and one is two,*
   Two and two is four,
   Way you love me little girl, you'll
   Never know, crying "Hey,
        baby don't you want to go
   Back to the same old place, sweet home Chicago."
   [Spoken:] All right, let's go to the windy city, you all.

4. *Come on, baby don't you want to go;*
   Oh come on, baby don't you want to go
   Back to the same old place, sweet home Chicago.

5.   *Two and two is four,*
   Four and two is six,
   Way you left me little girl you left me in a
   Heck of a fix, crying "Hey,
        baby don't you want to go
   Back to the same old place, sweet home Chicago;
   Back to the same old place, sweet home Chicago;
   Back to the same old place, sweet home Chicago."

1930s. But Johnson took the idea of the walking bass and adapted a new version of it on the guitar, emphasizing the seventh-chord (ex. 4–14); and this small but significant innovation was copied by a host of guitarists and, later, bass players. In the 1950s it became a familiar sound in rhythm 'n' blues and rock 'n' roll. Johnson is also interesting to the blues historian because of his rhythmic innovations and the magnificent poetry of his lyrics, but this is not the place to discuss him. (His original recordings may be heard on the Columbia CD C2K 46222, *Robert Johnson: The Complete Recordings*.)

This walking bass figures prominently in the instrumental introduction to The Fieldstones' version of "Sweet Home Chicago," where it may be heard in the electric bass and second guitar. The bass, guitars, and drums establish a strong triplet rhythm (see the discussion of "Poor Boy Blues" and ex. 4–10 above). And, like Lazy Bill Lucas in "Poor Boy Blues," Joe Hicks sings in a duple meter, playfully lagging behind the beat, setting up some intriguing two-against-three polyrhythms in contrast to the instrumental accompaniment. It is almost as if he floats the lyrics atop the pulsating music. To really feel the syncopation, try singing along.

Today the young blues singer with one of the largest followings is Robert Cray. Born in Columbus, Georgia in 1953, Cray grew up listening to soul music—the Stax/Volt sound of the 1960s, as well as to Ray Charles, Sam Cooke, and, perhaps the most important influence on his singing, Bobby Bland. In 1969 he heard blues guitarist Albert Collins and modeled his guitar-playing after him. Forming a band in 1974, he recorded his first album in 1978, *Who's Been Talkin'*, released in 1980. Several albums followed in which Cray fused a new sound, a mixture of blues, funk, and soul, that was very much is own. Most of his songs do not follow the 12-bar blues form, but a few do, and we listen to one of them now, "The Score" (recorded selection 22).

Cray begins "The Score" playing his electric guitar, then he sings a verse, responding on guitar in the silences after he sings each line. The rest of the band (piano, electric bass, drums) joins Cray in the second verse. You will hear a walking bass line like that in "Sweet Home Chicago" (recorded selection 21). Cray's guitar breaks after the verse become more adventurous. The lyrics draw up a familiar blues indictment: the singer's lover is cheating on him, and he says she must leave for good (fig. 4–17). The first verse is in AB form, the second is quatrain-refrain, and the third doubles the quatrain before the refrain. Even here, in a song that follows standard blues patterns rather closely, Cray chooses to extend the boundaries of the blues verse form.

Accompaniment to "The Score" is in an underlying $^{12}/_8$ meter, and the drummer plays the triplets. Like Bill Lucas (ex. 4–11), Cray plays with the beat when he sings, seldom attacking his syllables on the beat (ex. 4–15). Particularly around the third beat of each measure, Cray avoids accenting the downbeat. The rhythm of measure 10, for example, is far more complex than notated. Like Lucas, he has moved into duple rhythm here while the band continues in triple. Melodically, the flatted third and seventh are prominent.

1. Well all right baby,
    I guess I know the score.

    You better get to packin';
    I don't want you 'round here any more.
2. You come home lookin funky,
    Your clothes all in a mess;
    And your stone [storm?] it wasn't fittin'
    Any better than your dress.

    Well all right baby,
    I guess I know the score.

    You better get to gettin';
    I don't want you 'round here any more.
3. You came in one time too many,
    Lyin' out both sides of your mouth;
    You said you was at your mother's
    But I really got my doubts.

    I see you at the Rainbow
    Hangin' out with Red;
    And if I get my hands on you, baby,
    You're gonna wish that you were dead.

    Well all right baby,
    I guess I know the score.

    You better get to movin';
    I don't want you 'round here any more.

Fig. 4–17. Lyrics, "The Score." Transcribed by Jeff Titon.

Ex. 4–14. Outline of "walking bass" on guitar, after Robert Johnson, in key of C for convenience (Johnson usually played in E).

You come home lookin' funky, your clothes all in a mess, and your stone it wasn't fittin' any better than your dress. Well all right ba — by — now I know the score ——. Well you bet - ter get to gettin'; I don't want to see you 'round here any more ——.

Ex. 4–15. *Transcription of "The Score."* © *1980 Joliet Music Administered by BUG. Used by permission.*

A FEW FINAL WORDS

Although most of Robert Cray's songs do not follow standard blues forms, he thinks of himself as a blues singer and he is being promoted as one. Is he? (And who is to say?) We pause to reflect on what happens once a musical genre has been recorded, written about, studied, defined: some of that interpretive activity is carried back to performers, and now people expect the music to conform to those definitions. Record producers, promoters, writers, and lately, scholars, few of them raised in the blues music-subculture, are partly responsible for codifying the rules of the genre. They brought about expectations that struck at the fluidity of the genre, hobbled its emergent qualities, and created a complex situation involving attitudes toward race and a stake in whatever money was to be made. How, once standardized, can blues music change and grow, yet still remain blues? Must singers stay with the old forms, changing only their contents—new wine in old bottles, new lyrics, new instrumentation, in old settings? Must festival promoters choose blues singers on the basis of how well they conform to the genre? Should a "folklore police" enforce the rules?

To pose the questions this way is to answer them: "No." In the 1960s, blues, a music that had lost its great popularity among black Americans, captured the hearts of a new audience, young white Americans and Europeans, particularly those who saw in the blues a revolt against stifling middle-class values. In the 1970s the blues revival ebbed as many grew tired of the same old sound. Now, in the early 1990s, we are in the midst of a new blues revival as a new generation of African Americans honors blues as roots music, and others discover the music for the first time. Just a few years ago I was in Chicago and heard a woman blues singer with a very powerful voice singing in a club, backed by a four-piece band. It turned out she had studied voice in preparation for the opera, then decided she would have a better career singing blues. Do these historical, economic, and audience changes mean we should abandon our music-culture model (chapter 1) in the face of real-world complications? No, but we need to keep in mind that it *is* a model, an ideal. Music-cultures respond to economic, artistic, and interpretive pressures from without as well as within; music-cultures are not isolated entities. Music-cultures have histories that reveal that response to these pressures, and "catching" or defining a music at any given time comes at the expense of the long view. Finally, students of world music face the same problem that confronts other observers: the need to account for their own effects on what they observe.

Music of work, music of worship, and music of play: in this chapter, two brief examinations of work songs and religious music and an in-depth case study of the blues have introduced black music in the United States, its historical background, the part it plays in people's lives, and a perspective from which it can be approached. Instead of blues, many other contemporary black musics—jazz, for example, or rap or soul music—could have served equally for our case study. I have appended a short list of further reading and listening, but the next logical step is fieldwork (chapter 10).

REFERENCES CITED

Brooks, Cleanth, R. W. B. Lewis, and Robert Penn Warren
    1973   *American Literature: The Makers and the Making.* 2 vols. New York: St. Martin's Press.
Brunoghe, Yannick, ed.
    1964   *Big Bill Blues.* New York: Oak Publications.
Charters, Samuel
    1977   *The Legacy of the Blues.* New York: Da Capo.
Courlander, Harold
    1963   *Negro Folk Music U.S.A.* New York: Columbia Univ. Press.
Eliot, T. S.
    [1920] 1964   "Hamlet and His Problems." In *The Sacred Wood.* Reprint. New York: Barnes & Noble.
Evans, David
    1970   "Afro-American One-Stringed Instruments." *Western Folklore* 29:229–45.
———
    1971   "Booker White." In *Nothing But the Blues,* edited by Mike Leadbitter. London: Hanover Books.
Groom, Bob
    1971   *The Blues Revival.* London: Studio Vista.

Jackson, Bruce
  1972   *Wake Up Dead Man: Afro-American Worksongs from Texas State Prisons.*
         Cambridge, Mass.: Harvard Univ. Press.
Johnson, Charles S.
  [1934] 1966 *Shadow of the Plantation.* Reprint. Chicago: Univ. of Chicago Press.
Lomax, Alan
  1976   Brochure notes to *Negro Prison Songs from the Mississippi State Penitentiary.*
         Reissue of Tradition LP 1020 (see "Additional Listening"). Vogue Records
         (U.K.) VJD 515.
Lovell, John, Jr.
  1972   *Black Song: The Forge and the Flame.* New York: Macmillan, 1972.
Lucas, William ("Lazy Bill")
  1974   *Lazy Bill Lucas.* Philo LP 1007 (North Ferrisburg, Vt.).
McLeod, Norma, and Marcia Herndon
  1981   *Music as Culture.* 2nd ed. Darby, Pa.: Norwood Editions.
Oliver, Paul
  1965   *Conversation with the Blues.* London: Cassell.

  ———

  [1972] 1974   *The Story of the Blues.* Reprint. Radnor, Pa.: Chilton Books.
Seeger, Charles
  1977   *Studies in Musicology, 1935–1975.* Berkeley: Univ. of California Press.
Tedlock, Dennis
  1977   "Toward an Oral Poetics." *New Literary History* 8.
Titon, Jeff Todd
  1969   "Calling All Cows." *Blues Unlimited,* nos. 60–63.

  ———

  1971   "Ethnomusicology of Downhome Blues Phonograph Records, 1926–1930."
         Ph.D. diss., Univ. of Minnesota.
  ———, ed.
  1974a *From Blues to Pop: The Autobiography of Leonard "Baby Doo" Caston.* Los
         Angeles: John Edwards Memorial Foundation.

  ———

  1974b *Early Downhome Blues: A Musical and Cultural Analysis.* Urbana: Univ. of
         Illinois Press.

  ———

  1978   "Every Day I Have the Blues: Improvisation and Daily Life." *Southern Folk-
         lore Quarterly* 42.
Wilson, Al
  1966   "Robert Pete Williams, His Life and Music." *Little Sandy Review* 2 (no. 1).

ADDITIONAL READING

Albertson, Chris
1972   *Bessie.* New York: Stein and Day. [Biography of Bessie Smith.]

Baldwin, James

> 1965   *Go Tell It on the Mountain.* New York: Dell. [Novel centering on black religious experience.]

Barlow, William

> 1989   *Looking Up at Down.* Philadelphia: Temple Univ. Press.

Bruynoghe, Yannick

> 1964   *Big Bill Blues.* New York: Oak Publications. [Blues singer Big Bill Broonzy's life history.]

Evans, David

> 1982   *Big Road Blues.* Berkeley: Univ. of California Press.

Fahey, John

> 1970   *Charley Patton.* London: Studio Vista. [Life and music of important Mississippi blues singer.]

Ferris, William

> 1978   *Blues from the Delta.* New York: Doubleday.

George, Nelson

> 1988   *The Death of Rhythm & Blues.* New York: E. P. Dutton

Grissom, Mary Allen

> [1930] 1969   *The Negro Sings a New Heaven.* Reprint. New York: Dover Books.

Jackson, Bruce.

> 1972   *Wake Up Dead Man.* Cambridge, Mass.: Harvard Univ. Press. [Work songs.]

Jones, LeRoi

> 1963   *Blues People.* New York: William Morrow.

Keil, Charles

> 1966   *Urban Blues.* Chicago: Univ. of Chicago Press.

Leib, Sandra

> 1981   *Mother of the Blues.* Amherst: Univ. of Massachusetts Press. [About Ma Rainey.]

Oster, Harry

> 1969   *Living Country Blues.* Hatboro, Pa.: Folklore Associates.

Palmer, Robert

> 1981   *Deep Blues.* New York: Viking Press.

Ramsey, Frederic, Jr.

> 1960   *Been Here and Gone.* New Brunswick, N.J.: Rutgers Univ. Press. [Folk music.]

Sandberg, Larry, and Dick Weissman

> 1976   *The Folk Music Sourcebook.* New York: Knopf. [Annotated discography includes recordings of black music.]

Shaw, Arnold

> 1978   *Honkers and Shouters.* New York: Collier Brooks. [Rhythm 'n' blues.]

Titon, Jeff Todd

> 1990   *Downhome Blues Lyrics.* 2nd ed. Urbana: Univ. of Illinois Press. [Anthology of post–WWII lyrics.]

Williams, Melvin D

> 1974   *Community in a Black Pentecostal Church.* Pittsburgh: Univ. of Pittsburgh Press.

ADDITIONAL LISTENING

B. B. King Live at the Regal. ABCS509.
Bessie Smith: the World's Greatest Blues Singer. Columbia GP 33.
Let's Get Loose: Folk and Popular Blues Styles. New World NW 290
McKinley Morganfield aka Muddy Waters. Chess 2CH 60006.

Negro Blues and Hollers. Library of Congress AFS L59.
Negro Church Music. Atlantic SD-1351.
Negro Prison Songs. Tradition 1920.
Negro Religious Songs and Services. Library of Congress AFS L10.
One-String Blues. Takoma B 1023. [Diddly-bow.]
Really! The Country Blues. Origin Jazz Library OJL-2.
Religious Music: Congregational and Ceremonial. Library of Congress LBC 1.
Roots of the Blues. New World NW 252.

F I V E

◆ ◆ ◆

Europe/Peasant Music-Cultures of Eastern Europe

MARK SLOBIN

TWO SONGS ABOUT THE RAIN

This chapter will introduce you to Eastern Europe, a region that many Americans are tied to by heritage. We will learn about the old peasant way of life that prevailed when Eastern Europeans left for America in the late nineteenth and early twentieth centuries, and how that tradition has continued into the present. We start with a song (fig. 5–1) sung by Rumanian children in a traditional village; the song is called "Paparuda" and is addressed to the rain.

You can hear the song by listening to recorded selection 23 on the accompanying cassette. As you listen to it and look at the words, you may recall the American song shown in figure 5–2.

The rain songs are similar in two ways—the singers (children) and the subject (the force of Nature is addressed); but there are also many sharp differences between them.

We can start with the differences in the words. The American song is a straightforward command chanted by the child who cannot go out and play. It has no special metaphors or figures of speech, just as no special costume or equipment is necessary to perform the song. In addition, the text is sung solo, and even includes the child's name. Though addressed to the rain, it is meant for the

Fig. 5–1. *"Paparuda."*

Paparuda, ruda (come, little rain, come!), come out and water us with your full buckets over the whole crowd. When you come with the hose, let it flow like water; when you come with the plough, let it run like butter; when you come with the sieve, let it be a barn-full. Give me the keys, old woman, that I may open the doors and let the rain come down. Come, little rain, come!

167

Rain, rain, go away, little (name of singer) wants to play;
Rain, rain, go away, come again some other day.

Fig. 5–2.   *"Rain, Rain, Go Away."*

singer. At least there is no social context for the tune; it does not speak for a *group*. Notice also that no special meaning attaches to the rain other than that it gets in the way of fun.

The words of the Rumanian song differ in all the ways just mentioned. They seek the rain's bounty instead of demanding better weather for playtime. From the mention of rain, the text shifts to the image of the plough and butter, calling upon the fertility of the earth and the beasts. Instead of denying the course of the seasons, the song impatiently begs Nature to continue to round from winter to spring: it seeks to continue, rather than stop, action. The song rings with particular urgency because it is sung during times of drought. In short, the group performance emphasizes a real social context for the song.

In the whole context of the Rumanian song, no detail seems accidental. The children wear skirts made from flowers that are symbols of spring, and they carry sieves that are a survival of the rain symbol of ancient Greek gods. The children themselves are probably unaware that these symbols have lasted for centuries. The very presence of the children might stand for the rising generation, associated with the forces of growth (vs. death). Growth is invoked when the adults sprinkle the singing, dancing children with water. The "old woman" mentioned who controls the keys to the rain is probably related to the effigy of a hag carried and burned by children in other parts of Eastern Europe as part of a spring ritual: she stands for winter and must die. Thus, a local village musical performance is connected to a network of *regional* beliefs and musical performances.

The entire performance of "Paparuda" can be interpreted as a magical ritual, with the children acting as ambassadors to the forces of nature. We will have more to say about rituals shortly. For now, what seemed to be a "simple" song can be seen for what it really is—a complicated cultural package involving props, social organization, and text, supported by deeply held beliefs. Perhaps it is not so surprising that during the severe drought in the western United States of 1976–1977 American Indian rainmakers were called upon to try to reassert the old ties of magic and music with nature, while at the same time in England, ancient Druidic rites were revived to break the dry spell.

What of the musical differences between the two rain songs? Sing the American song first; it needs no special rehearsing since there is just one melody line—an easy one to pick up as it has just two notes. Now try singing the Rumanian song. First, you must divide your group into two parts: one chants the unchanging "hai, ploitsa, hai" line while the others have text (do it on a syllable like "la"). The singers with text also have different notes to think about; there are six here, as opposed to only two in the American song. Just because music comes from a technologically simpler environment, does not mean that it must be musically simpler.

PEASANT CULTURE

To understand the Eastern European peasant's environment, we first need to know what peasant culture is. Only then will we be ready to look at the music itself. Eric Wolf, who has studied peasant culture thoroughly, locates the peasant midway in a range of people who grow crops, somewhere between the primitive cultivator at one end of the spectrum and the modern farmer on the other (see ill. 5–1). All "play the game with nature," as he puts it, but each has a different stake in this life-and-death game and each uses different rules. (Wolf 1969:3–5).

Primitive cultivators tend their crop and share the harvest with kinfolk in a more or less egalitarian group or tribe. Peasants, on the other hand, occupy the bottom of a hierarchy that includes landlords who extract rent, middlemen who purchase the crop, and overlords who tax the surplus. Peasantry emerged in Neolithic times, about ten thousand years ago, when agriculture became so efficient that a ruling class emerged and took a portion of the surplus food raised by the peasants. This upper class consisted of administrators, soldiers, priests, and eventually, skilled craftsmen and artists, including musicians. These privileged people created an urban, court-centered culture away from the peasant majority. You will read about the court music of India, for example, in the next chapter.

As the head of his household, the peasant must try to support his extended family (wife and children plus assorted relatives), but they all are part of a subject class (see ill. 5–2). The modern farmer, on the other hand, is a sort of agricultural businessman who operates in a complex market economy. In today's industrialized world, landowning farmers may be better off than the working poor of the cities if they can learn to exploit up-to-date technology,

Ill. 5–1. *Working the land: Eastern Europe peasants in the Polesie region, Ukraine, 1930's.*

Courtesy of Obrebski Collection, Archives of the University of Massachusetts at Amherst

Courtesy of Obrebski Collection, Archives of the University of Massachusetts at Amherst

Ill. 5–2. *An Eastern European peasant family, 1930s. As household head, the peasant had to organize and maintain a large, extended family unit such as the one pictured.*

marketing, and credit to create what we call "agribusiness," a far cry from the peasant whose musical life we will be examining shortly. In the modern world, peasantry has diminished everywhere. Still, in large areas of Central and South America, the Middle East, and Southern, Southeastern, and Northern Asia, peasant life survives. In Europe, our present focus, there are peasants still, or at least the memory of peasant folkways and life-styles is still alive, particularly in East-

Ill. 5–3. *View of an Eastern European peasant village. Polesie region, Ukraine, 1930s.*

Courtesy of Obrebski Collection, Archives of the University of Massachusetts at Amherst

ern Europe (see ill. 5–3). In Western Europe, advanced capitalist support systems have changed the rules of the game, while in Eastern Europe socialism later introduced modifications, but here the older peasant may still be seen as a household head tied by strong bonds of kinship and mutual support to a locale where his forefathers are buried, trying to raise crops with little control over and great dependence on nature and an imposed marketing system. At the end of the chapter we will see how the peasant's life and music-culture (and those of his children and grandchildren) have changed in modern times. But first we will consider the more traditional layers of the Eastern European peasant music-culture. Of course, we can only touch on a few colorful samples of the old peasant life, for we do not mean this chapter as a comprehensive text on the region.

Much of the music we will examine here was collected before World War II. Before that enormously devastating and tragic period, peasantry had resisted significant modernization throughout Eastern Europe. After the destruction and governmental reorganization of the region following the war (which cost some twenty-five million lives in the Soviet Union alone), urbanization increased and new, popular forms of music gained ground. For this reason, some of the descriptions you will read are in the past tense; however, much of this music has survived either in original or reconstructed form. The governments of all the Eastern European countries take great pride in their national past and encourage the documentation and preservation of peasant music and arts.

MUSIC OF THE OLDER GENERATIONS: RITUAL MUSIC

A ritual is a formal practice or custom. The formality of rituals sets them off from everyday life, and the accompanying music is an important part of this formality. Ritual lies close to the heart of the peasant's expressive connection to nature and the forces of the universe. It is often hard for Americans to understand the importance of ritual music, since there is so little of it in American life. But think for a moment that even the most "far-out" modern weddings include *some* kind of music, and that every sports event demands the playing of "The Star-Spangled Banner."

Peasants have two major types of ritual events, related to the two great overlapping cycles of peasant life. One is "calendric," tied to the yearly recurring round of occasions, while the second is linked to the individual's own life cycle, from birth and entrance into his or her society through the passage of another world at death. The calendric cycle was traditionally divided into rituals related to nature and agriculture, and rituals connected to the circle of religious or national celebrations. These latter rituals are determined by culture, not nature, but the two categories often merge on a given day, such as St. John's Day, widely celebrated across most of Europe, which "happens" to fall on Midsummer Night's Eve, the longest day of the year (June 23). The church claims that this significant natural event belongs to a major religious figure, St. John. In recent decades new red-letter days have been arbitrarily set for official celebration of great victories, the founding of a city or nation or the establishment of a new form of government—such as November 7 in Russia, marking the victory of socialist power in 1917.

Looking at a festival calendar for any European people in a particular generation, we see a patchwork of solemn or joyous celebration representing pagan agricultural and Christian theological (e.g., Christmas) events, some purely local (a town's patron saint), others commemorations of local or national events. We note also extra-calendric ceremonies associated with times of trouble, such as epidemics, invasions, or droughts. We began this chapter with a Rumanian agricultural ritual, a song for a time of disaster. This ritual occurs also in parts of Yugoslavia and Bulgaria.

The songs and rites of the life cycle form an equally broad collection of music and ceremony. We will limit our discussion of ritual music to the organization and music of just two traditional ritual categories, the wedding and the lament, largely in two areas of Eastern Europe: Russia and Rumania.

The Wedding

In peasant society, the wedding is crucial not only for the couple but also for the entire extended network of kinfolk on both sides (see ill. 5–4). It also represents an important moment in the life of a whole village, since any wedding makes an alliance between two rival, potentially conflicting households. Here, ritual is exceptionally elaborate, involving large expenditures of money

Ill. 5–4.   *An Eastern European wedding: the bride and groom. Polesie region, Ukraine, 1930s.*

Courtesy of Obrebski Collection, Archives of the University of Massachusetts at Amherst

and goods over the course of several days and many events (see ills. 5–5, 5–6). As Hungarian researchers have observed: "Weddings rank foremost among popular customs; they are a veritable accumulation of ceremonies containing mythical, religious-ritual, legal, economic, musical, and mimic elements. In some places they became almost festive plays with their chief and supporting characters, supernumeraries, fixed scene, time, music, dances, and audience" (CMPH 1956:III/B,689).

Our example for the older style of wedding comes from the White Sea region of Russia, a remote and inhospitable corner of Eastern Europe near the Arctic Circle that, because of its isolation, is a treasure house of older folklore and music. Only the older people know all the songs and customs; even way out in the village of Varzuga the young folks have new and different ways.

Let us start with a wedding song, "Na Solnechnom Vskhode, na Ugreve" ("At dawn, at the warming") (recorded selection 24; fig. 5–3).

As in our Rumanian rain song, the words here are symbolic in very standardized, well-understood ways. Often in Russian folk song, natural landscapes are described before the important human characters take center stage. Natural objects signify the humans; here the "curly birch tree" stands for the maiden, while the nightingale is her suitor. As the song progresses it becomes clear that the words refer to the forthcoming union between Annushka and Ivan, the two families being Aleksandrovich and Mikhailovich. Using the imagery of fairy tales, the song tells of Ivan-nightingale's flight to the parental high tower of Anna, who has not yet braided her hair in the married woman's knot. It ends by announcing that Anna must belong to Ivan and become the slave of his father and mother.

Ill. 5–5. *An Eastern European wedding: musicians about to start the wedding procession. Polesie region, Ukraine, 1930s.*

Courtesy of Obrebski Collection, Archives of the University of Massachusetts at Amherst

Courtesy of Obrebski Collection, Archives of the University of Massachusetts at Amherst

Ill. 5–6.   *An Eastern European wedding: procession through the village street. Polesie region.*

Fig. 5–3.   *"Na Solnechnom Vskbode."*

At dawn, at the warming
A bushy white birch-tree stands.
Past that white bushy birch-tree
Goes no road, no path,
No broad way, no footpath, no passageway.
Gray geese fly, but do not honk;
White swans fly, but do not cry.
Just one young nightingale sings.
He flies to the father's courtyard,
To the mother's high tower;
He gives Annushka heartache,
Makes it known to Mikhailovna
That Annechka shouldn't be living at her father's,
Sitting in the high tower,
Nor combing her unruly head,
Nor plaiting her blonde braid,
Nor twining a ribbon into her braid,
Nor wearing a red-gold belt,
But that Anna should be with Ivan
To be (his) father's slave,
To be mother's daughter-in-law,
To be Ivan's bride.
So hail to Ivan and Anna!
Let's congratulate Alexandrovich and Mikhailovna!

Notice that Anna's becoming Ivan's bride is actually listed last in the song after her subordination to the in-laws. Ritual wedding songs emphasize this unfortunate outcome of marriage. No wonder the younger generation, who marry for love, not because of prearranged family alliances, have forgotten some of these songs and related customs, like the bride's lament. In some parts of Eastern Europe a bride is not considered to have carried out her role properly if she fails to weep, wail, and bemoan her fate. Bridal laments are very similar in structure, and sometimes in imagery, to the death lament to be discussed below. In the Eastern European Jewish tradition, a bride and groom fast before the wedding, as if it were the holiest day of the liturgical year, Yom Kippur (the Day of Atonement), and the customs are full of references to death, tying together all of the most solemn expressive aspects of traditional ritual at the wedding.

Let us now look at the music of "Na Solnechnom Vskhode" (ex. 5–1). It is structurally similar to the Rumanian rain song in having more than one part. Here we have a leader who begins the song, followed by the chorus chiming in. This leader–chorus or call-and-response format is typical of many Eastern European genres, particularly among the eastern Slavic peoples (Russians, Ukrainians, Belorussians). But the piece gets one stage more complicated by having

Ex. 5–1. *Russian wedding song, "Na Solnechnom Vskhode."* Source: Balashov and Krasovskaia 1969:83.

the chorus briefly split into two lines of music, creating polyphony (many-part music). The eastern Slavs are very fond of singing polyphonically, though not in the classical harmony of a Bach chorale or opera chorus. Notice the fairly expressionless voice quality; try to imitate it. This feature seems to go along with the circular, nonstop quality of the singing: there are no clear line breaks. This detached manner of singing underlines and expresses the ritual nature of the song. It is as if the singers are saying: it's not ourselves in particular, but the village as a whole, indeed, the tradition, that is singing. Just as in many parts of the world (including parts of Eastern Europe) ritual dance and action are done under the cover of masks, so singers may sometimes seem to put an anonymous mask on their voices when singing ritual songs.

Finally, the scale structure of our wedding song is worth a closer look. If we write out all the notes the song uses in order from lowest to highest, we find the short scale transcribed in example 5–2, this scale is used not just in these wedding songs of Varzuga village, but in a huge number of old songs in the Russian tradition that related to rituals of the summer season. This scale, as used in the wedding song, represents the intersection of the yearly cycle and the individual life cycle.

The Varzuga wedding is quite complex, consisting of eleven different stages with numerous small substages and ceremonies, most of which have their own set of songs. But the customs and songs may differ just down the road in nearby villages; how much more, then, across the vast expanse of Russia! Individual variety is the lifeblood of folk music, whether from person to person or village to village.

To help you follow the Varzuga wedding, we have included a diagram (fig. 5–4) of the standard peasant hut of the region. A list of the cast of characters in the wedding follow; thereafter, we will describe the basic stages of the ritual.

Principals in the Varzuga Wedding

bride and her parents
groom and his parents
godparents
matchmaker
main organizer and master of ceremonies
professional female lamenter
best man, groom's helpers
bride's helpers

Ex. 5–2.   *Scale of "Na Solnechnom Vskhode."*

Numbers on hut diagram below:

1. Beam beyond which matchmaker cannot pass without permission.
2. "Great" corner, with icons, where chief guests sit.
3. Side room where bride is dressed.
4. Where bride weeps during "handshaking" (may be removed for guests).
5. Where bride meets guests.
6. Where bride receives gifts and unplaits hair.
7. Blind corner in which couple sits to avoid evil eye.
8. Route of groom's procession in and out.

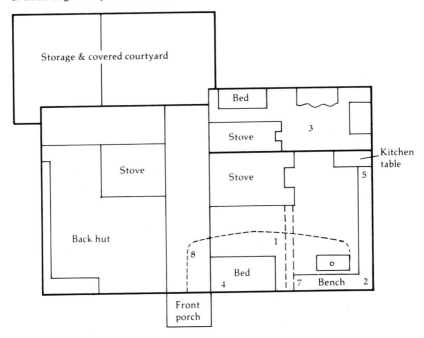

Diagram of Hut with Locations of Key Wedding Activities

Fig. 5–4. *Russian peasant wedding: scene of action.*

bridesmaid–cooks

assorted kinfolk on both sides, many with special titles

Stages of the Varzuga Wedding

1. *Matchmaking.* This is the domain of the matchmaker, who steps into the hut, but not beyond the doorway beam (1 in fig. 5–4). Given permission to advance, he is offered tea, whereupon he proposes a match, using stylized phrases. If the family rejects the match, the matchmaker's head is smeared with flour. This professional hazard probably insures the matchmaker's careful choice of prospective bride and groom.

2. *Handshaking.* Now the pact, including the important financial matter of dowry (paid by bride's father to groom's family), is concluded with a hand-

shake, and official festivities begin. The lamp by the family icon (holy paint-ing) is lit. If the bride dislikes the match she may try to put out the lamp to show her disapproval; this is the only act of rebellion she is allowed. She then begins to weep and bemoan her fate, standing at a designated spot (4). Older women pour in to watch the bride's lament.

3. *Girl friends' visits.*   The next day is full of song as the maiden's girl friends gather at her hut to lend moral support. Sewing clothes for the trousseau, the girls (all aged about fifteen) sing a song cycle about the forthcoming mar-riage. The song we examined first, "Na solnechnom vskhode," is a "girl friends' visit" song. This period may continue for as long as two weeks.

4. *Bathing.*   The day before the wedding the chief bridesmaid–cook and her assistants begin the enormous task of cooking and baking. Meanwhile, the public bath has been heating (indoor plumbing was unknown in traditional peasant life) and the bride is led there by her girl friends. At the door she sings a special lament on an improvised text, repeated after the bath. Thus in addition to the standardized, traditional numbers the wedding repertoire also includes individualized songs in which the participant can express her per-sonal feelings.

5. *Gifts and unbraiding.*   After the bath the bride puts on a new outfit and sits in a special place (6). The male and female helpers organize the events. First, female kinfolk and girl friends bid farewell and bring presents. The professional lamenter (a woman) helps the bride wail and sings songs spe-cific to each type of guest—godparents, siblings, and so forth. Finally, a sister unbraids the girl's maiden plaits, later to be redone into the married woman's knot under a kerchief. Transformations are physically as well as emotionally marked in peasant life.

6. *Greeting.*   Seated in a special place (5) the girl receives non-kin guests. Villagers flock to the porch to look in and listen to the songs.

7. *Blessing.*   A formal blessing of the maiden by her parents must take place before the groom and his party arrive. It is a solemn and emotional moment.

8. *Groom's arrival.*   Greeted by torch-bearing bride's relatives, the groom's party enters, following a prescribed route (8). Everyone is seated in a fixed order; wedding protocol is always strict. Bride and bridegroom are now called "prince" and "princess"; relatives are "lords" and "ladies." Choral songs are sung until the bride, who in the meantime has left, is led back in by her father. She carries a tray with small vodka glasses, which she offers in prede-termined order with fixed greetings to the groom's kinfolk. She is taken out to the side room (3) to be dressed. Many songs have been sung, all in a similar style, unifying the event musically. Great care is taken throughout to avoid the "evil eye." This is a powerful force recognized by people in many parts of the world, and is often associated with bad people who can put a "hex" on someone. Should marital troubles arise later, it may be blamed on careless-ness at the wedding.

9. *Church ceremony.*   Only now does the couple, accompanied by the main

participants (but excluding the parents) link up with organized religion. Proceeding to the village church, they are led in hymns by the village priest, representative of the Orthodox Church, who completes a brief ceremony. 10. *Viewing and banquet table.* Now the action shifts to the groom's house. The bride's hair is rearranged. The bride and groom are finally fed. Now the bride's kinfolk arrive and sit in prescribed order. Full-scale feasting and singing commence. A chorus sings different songs for each type of guest—parents, relatives, friends, bachelors, old folks—a service for which the chorus receives payment. Cries of *"gor'ko, gor'ko!"* ("bitter") are heard, requiring a drink each time. Eventually the guests join the singing, and dancing begins for everyone but the bride. As the party breaks up, the couple accompany the bride's parents halfway home on a specially decorated reindeer, since this is Arctic country.

11. *Final feats.* The next morning, the first of her married life, the bride arises early and helps her mother-in-law bake. They make pancakes for a dinner held for all the kinfolk. Now the couple sits in the host's place at the table. The bride's kin then invites everyone to one last feast, where fresh, hot pancakes are also served. Final gifts are exchanged and the wedding ends, completing weeks of elaborate and expensive preparation and days of carefully observed ritual. If all goes well, family feuds have been avoided, individual pride expressed, and a proper marriage begun.

In recent times much of this White Sea ritual has waned as modern ways reach even into the far North. Girls choose their own husbands and wail less. Many smaller details of food preparation and minor ceremony have vanished. Yet the songs remain, standing now as the clearest embodiment of the ritual. Once again we see music's lasting power to bind the village to the occasion.

Many aspects of the North Russian wedding complex do not occur in other regions of Eastern Europe. For example, the bride's lament is far from universal. Yet many of the basic concepts are quite widespread. Songs bewailing the bride's lot were indispensable among the Jews, but were performed by the *badkhn*, the professional master of ceremonies, rather than by the bride. A similar tradition exists among Rumanian peasants; figure 5–5 shows part of the text of a bridal lament performed in the 1950s by a professional peasant wedding entertainer. Changing hairdos (symbolic of the change from an unmarried to a married state), the need to leave parents, and nature imagery are all characteristics of this Rumanian song which link it—though not by direct borrowing—to the songs of the Arctic village of Varzuga, underscoring cultural similarities across the region.

Musically "Cintecul Miresii" (recorded selection 25) provides us with a strong contrast to the austerity of the Russian North. Here tradition has assigned the gifted professional, rather than the amateur girl's group, the job of expressing a communal sentiment, and he employs a flexible, poignant melodic line, backed by expressive flourishes of the violin and the steady beat of the lute, to set the ladies weeping at the bride's fate. We shall see later how this fits in with the mu-

Even today [in the 1950s], Rumanian peasant weddings may last for several days, and the celebrations are punctuated by ritual moments embellished with music and dances, some of magical origin. . . . the most important wedding song, "Cintecul Miresii" (The Song of the Bride) is sung as the bride bids farewell to her parents and their home and her former way of life. The moment is solemn, the song poignant, and the bride often weeps bitterly when it is sung. [1963:n.p.]

"Oh, my child, you have your parents, alas! why never are you getting married? You'll find it hard to forget your parents' love, for the love of a husband is like the leaf of a dry pear tree. When you put yourself in his shade you'll be bitterly sorry, for the love of a husband is like the leaf of a dry pear tree or an old fence post! Little bride, little bride! ask your godfather not to decorate you with garlands but to leave your hair simply plaited by your mother and sister. Till now you've been with the young girls, tomorrow you'll be with the married women, and the day after with the old women, and on Wednesdays with your aunts, ay! on Wednesdays with your aunts."

Fig. 5–5. *Lyrics to "Cintecul Miresii," A Rumanian wedding song.*

sician's role and image in general. Notice the strongly falling shape of the melody, starting from a high, throbbing pitch in both voice and violin versions and gradually descending. This probably indicates an influence in Rumania of nearby Middle Eastern, particularly Turkish, song style. Though cultural intent and symbolism may unify a region as large as Eastern Europe, musically the many subregional and local styles reflect the historical ties of one or another ethnic group or locale. A Turkish influence would be far less likely up near Varzuga's Arctic Circle.

The Lament

Like the intensely communal ritual of the wedding, which allows for response from both groups and individuals, the shock of death traditionally also involves both personal and social expression of emotion. We will consider various types of songs of mourning, or laments. Finding and recording death laments is extremely difficult; as Zoltán Kodály notes for Hungary: "They [laments] are difficult to witness, because their existence is denied, and nothing will persuade people to perform before strangers. It is useless for the collector to attend funerals, for as soon as he is noticed, the mourning ceremonies are omitted, even where they are normally practiced" (Kodály 1971:85). This reluctance to display strong personal emotion in public is based on genuine deep feeling. When a peasant woman has at last been persuaded to sing a lament in front of the tape recorder, she breaks down and sobs regularly, often at the end of each musical line, because the singing rouses powerful emotions and brings to her mind the original reason for singing the lament—the death of a loved one.

The first song we will take up is a communal lament, sung by peasant women in Rumania (recorded selection 26). These group songs punctuate the funeral at specified times. They are somewhat impersonal; first, because they are sung for everyone's funeral; second, because professional mourners, not relatives of the deceased, sing the songs; the third, because the texts usually avoid specific reference to the person being buried.

The lament's collective nature is underlined by other features. It addresses the local beliefs about death and expresses the peasant view of man, religion, and fate. This Rumanian communal lament speaks of the dead person's long journey "from the land of pity to the pitiless land," and mentions such customs as planting a decorated pine tree at the head of a grave. Reinforcement of local belief is part of the function of a publicly sung communal song. The intensely social nature of the funeral and surrounding ritual has been noticed in Hungary, where the ceremony is one "at which not only hidden traits of the deceased and of his relatives come to light, but the entire population is exposed to critical observation. The occasion throws into sharp relief the community life of the whole village. Those present or absent will be weighed and judged according to their behavior" (CMPH 1966:V,99). A person's passing from the world, like his or her emergence into adult life through marriage, is a matter of not just personal, but communal importance in peasant culture.

Musically, we find reflection of the collective nature of this type of lament in the social organization of the singing. Though Rumanian songs are largely solo (as opposed to the polyphony we noticed in Russia), this lament is performed antiphonally, that is, by alternating groups, as if to emphasize the fact that group cooperation is required for the feeling of ritual solidarity. It is interesting that the two groups overlap, with one drawing out its last pitch to serve as a supporting drone, or constant, unchanging pitch, for the second group. Perhaps this musical support system parallels the emotional support of the community. Figure 5–6 gives a rough scheme of the musical structure; the cross-hatching indicates places where the two groups of singers come together. Try to listen for the small differences that occur when different groups sing the same line, or when the same line repeats; these variable features, which people do not learn from a printed page, are the heart of folk music.

The individual lament differs radically from the group lament. First, it is not sung by outsiders to represent communal response but by members of the immediate family, usually women. Assigning musical roles by gender, which in chapter 1 we noted as a characteristic of many music-cultures, is often quite clear in the lament. Second, the private songs of loss make specific reference to the

Fig. 5–6. *Communal Rumanian lament.*

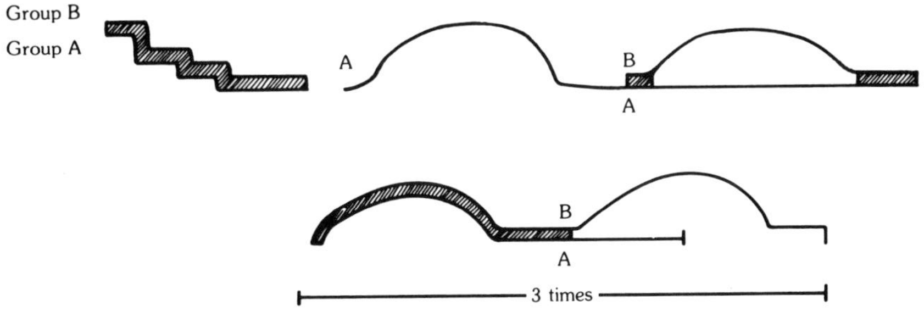

dead person and seem to be intensely personal calls by the bereaved to the deceased. This quality is apparent in the text (fig. 5–7) of a Rumanian woman's lament for her eight-year-old brother. She addresses her brother directly, and mentions other details of the family's life. The reference to going "behind the cross" might relate to the Orthodox Church belief that the other world lies behind the paintings and the cross of the church.

Notice as you listen to this solo lament (recorded selection 27) how compactly it is organized into short lines, which seem like outbursts of emotion, reinforced by the sob-like breaks at the end of each line. This is typical of the older lament style. The texts are partially or completely improvised by the singer; that is, she (or he) makes them up on the spur of the moment. Here we see a strong contrast to the fixed wordings and melodic structure of the communal lament; the individual is allowed to pour out grief through less restricted channels. As one Hungarian woman has said, "You can't guess what a relative of yours will say when she casts herself down on the coffin. When my little daughter died I could not have told you what I was going to put into the lament or what I would sing all the time over her dead body until I stood up to sing. You don't think it out, you just speak as it comes to your lips" (CMPH 1966:V,94). However, there are time-tested formulas of text and tune that act as traditional guidelines for this highly personal expression of emotion. Hungarian scholars find similar phrases and images cropping up in all the laments of a single village. Musically, certain repetitive phrases and endings are likely to recur. Alexandru and Lloyd note that the Rumanian mourner's fellow villagers "listen critically and do not hesitate to comment on how well she sings" (notes to Columbia KL 5799), just as Kodály says that Hungarians "watch the performance carefully and discuss it afterwards: 'she wailed beautifully,' 'she hasn't even mourned for him,' etc." (Kodály 1971:85). This statement reveals that even in the shadow of death and grief a community makes aesthetic evaluations, something we identified in chapter 1 as a key aspect of a music-culture. It also shows how the group wants to keep even individual, improvised singing within the bounds of acceptable innovation, just as all individual behavior in the village is channeled within the bounds of tradition. In general, peasant music is a combination of group conservatism and individual expression. The former lends stability, while the latter introduces change.

Long after the funeral the appeal to the dead embodied in the individual lament can be continued. In Jewish tradition, as well as for some Hungarian

Fig. 5–7. *Lyrics, solo Rumanian lament.*

My darling, my little brother, now we two are parted.
You've gone behind the cross, you've gone behind the
cross and hidden behind the door.
Someone has called you away to our mother because she loved you.
You wouldn't stay with father and you've broken his heart.
Just as he was counting himself lucky to have you, my little
mother led you away beside her.

peasants, it was possible traditionally for a woman to ease her emotional burdens by addressing a long improvised song in lament style to a departed relative, often singing directly at grave side, for years after the relative's death. These songs might comment on current family problems, "updating" the deceased's spirit. In peasant life, the other world is fairly concrete, to be taken seriously, and numerous rituals seem to pacify the souls of the dead to keep them from returning to their old homes and causing trouble among the living.

Powerfully expressive genres like the lament can adapt to new individual and group needs. Russian folklorists noted the great decline of lament singing in the 1930s, but were surprised to see its vigorous revival in the face of the agony of World War II. A striking case of this rebirth of the lament took place in the village of Tonezh, in Belorussia. In 1942 German SS troops massacred 260 villagers in reprisal for raids by anti-Nazi guerillas. The sole survivor, Tat'iana Borovskaia, along with villagers who earlier had fled to the forest, created a new communal lament as they buried the dead. This song became the centerpiece of Tonezh's annual commemoration of the catastrophe, held in the village square at least through the 1960s. Another type of revived lament of the period was the song mourning recruits into the army, a variety of song thought to have vanished after World War I.

Before leaving the gloomy subject of laments, we should point out that peasants have a sense of humor as well. In Hungary parodies of laments are often sung by children as part of play-funerals, and also by adults at feasts (such as weddings) or on holidays. At carnival time a bass fiddle might be buried to the accompaniment of ridiculous laments; typical lyrics are shown in figure 5–8.

TWO PROJECTS INVOLVING RITUAL

Find a family ritual and re-create it. All around us, not just among ethnic groups, we Americans are involved in ritual activities. Some of these are as old as our culture, while others are more recent. One interesting thing about rituals is that once they are established, they become so much a part of our mental landscape that they seem ancient. For example, the custom of singing "The Star Spangled Banner" at sports events began only around World War II, but it seems

Fig. 5–8. *Lyrics, Hungarian parody laments.*

I am mourning, I am lamenting you —
Though I don't feel my heart is aching:
I only feel my feet are cold!

You should have waited until the geese were killed
So you could have had a good dish of giblets!

The day before yesterday my goose died;
Yesterday it was my pig that died —
Now it's his turn!

like an age-old custom. The object is to locate an American ritual, study it, then find a way to re-create it in class, perhaps assigning parts. Consider, for instance, Thanksgiving: after all, it is probably our most widely observed ritual. Everyone seems to do something for Thanksgiving, and often much the same things; they will immediately spring to your mind upon reading this passage. But there is a lot of variation, too: Who organizes? Who cooks? Is there music? Is it a time of family harmony or arguments about roles, responsibilities, and relationships? Is it held at home or outside? There is a core sense of shared understanding at the center of every ritual, but at the edges there is a great deal of individual, family, or group variation.

Of course, Thanksgiving is just a sample of American ritual; there are many other events. Weddings would be an excellent subject, since we have just spent some time studying their intricate organization in peasant culture. Like Thanksgiving, there is a core idea of what needs to happen at a wedding to make it a proper ritual; then, even more than Thanksgiving, we find terrific fluctuation based on personal and family taste. Often there is a great deal of conflict, since the lack of a strict program, such as we saw in the Russian wedding, means that disagreement and argument over the content of the ritual can easily spring up. If you know of an impending wedding, or have been through one recently as family member or friend, try to document it and bring the ritual to class, including the music. Bar mitzvahs, christenings, and confirmations are similarly good targets of research and presentation.

Create a ritual and perform it.   This is a project that calls for plenty of imagination and creative work, and might well be done as a team. Rituals mark particular times of life and/or the year, or historical events, and new ones occur all the time. There is no reason you cannot join in this process by creating your own ritual. Here are the basic ground rules:

a. Pick the commemorative reason for the ritual. This can include quite a variety of possibilities, ranging from marking an important person's birth- or death-day, an event in the history of your group or the nation, or a life-cycle occasion. Even the time, place, and context of the class itself can function as a ritual, where all has been prepared for that very moment and celebrated for its own sake.

b. Identify the components of your ritual. These should include some music-making (vocal and/or instrumental), which must be appropriate to the event. There is a whole field of other components to include: dress, movement, decor (color schemes might be useful), lighting, ritual objects.

c. Establish the coherence of the ritual. No matter what elements you choose as building blocks, the overall shape of the ritual must be nicely organized aesthetically and be clear to the participants and the audience. There is no room for mystification here. What is true of ritual in general is that everyone has a good idea of what is going on, even if some participants may be more knowlededge or have access to secret information. Rituals must be communal and so must be well understood by everyone; yours should not be an exception to this general rule.

d. Allow time for response. Part of the communal nature of ritual is group confirmation of the process. Response is crucial here: one does not arbitrarily stage a ritual, then disappear. The actors usually stay in the village and are guided by participant and audience feedback. Even if outside professionals perform, they must meet audience standards or face the prospect of not being rehired. Year after year and generation after generation, a ritual must continue to meet the expectations and satisfy the feelings of the group. Otherwise it will go by the board, as rituals tend to do if enough disapproval or apathy is registered. The Puritans' habit of locking offenders into the stocks for public disapproval is an example of an outmoded ritual. A more recent example is the modification or elimination of fraternity hazing.

Part of the point of the two projects just outlined is to get you to think beyond just a purely "musical" understanding of world music. In many languages, what we call music is often not distinguished from other activities, like dance and ritual. Music is just one track in a multichanneled activity called performance. It is important that you try to observe, or put together for yourself, the way music is nested within often elaborate sets of activities that coincide at a given time and place. In a sense, all music making is ritual, involving place, time, dress, symbolic behavior, and roles. Finding or creating a ritual is a way of becoming aware of that face and of taking part in the process yourself.

MUSIC OF THE OLDER GENERATIONS
NOT TIED TO SPECIFIC OCCASIONS

Up to now we have looked at music tied to specific occasions in the life of the individual or the village. As deeply felt and important as these ritual songs are, they represent only half of the music making. The other sphere of song includes songs suitable for varied occasions (see ill. 5–7). Some of these songs cluster around certain contexts; the lullaby, for example, though not part of ritual, is appropriate only for certain singers, audiences, times, and places.

We will consider the two major types of nonritual song: narrative and lyric. Narrative songs, as the title suggests, are those that tell stories, such as epics (tales of heroes and history) or ballads (shorter story songs). Lyric songs, which concentrate more on emotions than on storytelling, embrace many topics, the best-known being romantic love, both happy and unhappy. The unhappy aspect is predominant in Eastern Europe, as in the neighboring peasant music-cultures of the Middle East where marriages were arranged and where assaults on a girl's virginity or a wife's honor provoked bloodshed. But lyric songs also touch on countless other themes, such as the beauties of nature, the horrors of war, the difficulties of emigration of America, the sufferings of prisoners, or the pangs of poverty.

Ill. 5–7. *Eastern European peasant girls at work indoors. Activities like weaving were important for folksinging. Polesie region, Ukraine, 1930s.*

Narrative Songs

From this genre we will examine a song from northwestern Russia (Pskov region). "Akh Vy Gory" (ex. 5–3) is a song of the type peasants call "drawn-out" or "protracted" song (*protiazhnaia pesnia*). This type of song is often marked by some features apparent in the musical notation for example 5–3. First, the tempo is slow (the metronome mark of ♩ = 56–58 means less than one beat per second; compare that with your heart beat). Second, the rhythm is free, rather than fixed; that is, the flow of time is unbounded rather than divided up into a clear beat you could tap your foot to (indicated in ex. 5–3 by the frequent

Ex. 5–3. *Russian ballad, "Akb Vy Gory." Source: Kotikova 1966.*

ial,   da, oi   sto   -   ial syr - ze - lio...   sto-ial syr - ze -

lio...   syr   ze - lio - (a)-nyi to   dub.

Ex. 5–3. *(Continued)*

changes in time signature). Third, the melody is highly ornamented and melismatic. Look at single syllables such as the *go* of measure 3 or the *byo* of
measure 5, set to several smoothly flowing notes; at each repetition of the
musical line (marked A, B, etc.) the melody changes slightly as the singer creates
highly expressive and fluid musical contours for the text. You can see how the
text is broken up; the single word *vorobyovskie* (referring to mountains of
Vorobyov) is extended over several measures and two musical lines, sung as
"Vo-ro-bye . . . vo-ro-bye . . . Vo-ro-bye-(a-o)-vskie, Vo-ro-bye-vski-e," a technique
(melisma) that helps explain the peasant's term "drawn-out" song.

The text (fig. 5–9) begins in the typical Russian way that we noticed earlier—
with a six-line description of nature. Only after this long panorama, which moves
in on its subject like a zoom lens, does the active narrative begin. The human
story unfolds (lines 7ff.) in a dialogue between the eagle and the crow. This
short narrative song seems like an episode from a long heroic epic, like the *Iliad*
of Homer, in which we view the fallen hero after the fateful battle. The description of three attendant mourning bird-women recalls the women's lament, while

Fig. 5–9. *Lyrics, "Akh Vy Gory."*

O you mountains, my mountains, O Vorobyov mountains
These mountains gave birth to nothing
But the Yani (? a stream) with its steep banks.
Near the banks stood a moist green oak tree;
On the oak sat a young eagle.
In its claws it held a black crow.

He (the eagle) did not attack him but kept asking:
"Where have you flown, black crow?"
"I flew to foreign places, I saw strange wonders.
There lay a white soldier's body.
And no one recognized him.
Three swallows recognized this body.
The first recognized him: his dear mother.
And the second swallow: his dear sister.
And the third swallow: his young wife.
The dear mother cried as a river flows.
The dear sister cried as a stream flows.
And the young wife cried like the dew falls."

the identification of the women as birds reminds us of the wedding song we examined. Notice the order of the women, and the progressively smaller share of grief from mother to sister to wife (river–stream–dew). This reflects the traditional hierarchy of age before youth and kin before stranger, and is quite opposite to the more romantic, modern focus one could imagine, which would stress the wife first. "Akh Vy Gory" is a cousin of the well-known English ballad, "The Two Ravens," which has a similar basic plot outline involving a spectator-bird and a fallen knight. The English song, however, centers on the fallen hero's hawk, hound, and lady, leaving out the mother and sister, perhaps, reflecting a different social emphasis in the two cultures. However, the similarity between the English and Russian versions illustrates that the ballad (a narrative song consisting of short verses, with the same melody for each verse) is one of the most widespread and characteristic genres of folk music across all of Europe, east and west.

Lyric Songs

Scholars use the notion of "lyric song" very broadly, including many topics and types. We will look at two very different lyric songs, one from Yugoslavia and one from Poland.

In the Republic of Bosnia and Hercegovina, Yugoslavia, the ethnomusicologist Ankica Petrovic has collected and described a remarkable vocal genre called *ganga*. These songs are sung by a small group of either men or women (never mixed) who are from the same village and who know each other very well. Often, *ganga* singers meet at an early age and continue singing together for decades, fine-tuning their sensitivity to each other's sound and skills. Should a woman from a nearby village marry into another village, it might be very hard for her to find singing partners even if her style is quite close to the local way of singing; her new fellow singers will immediately notice even the slightest shade of differences in the nuances of their *ganga*.

Ganga sounds very strange on first listening for two reasons: the insistence on very close intervals, which tend to grate on the ear, and the practice of accompanying the lead singer by intense backup sounds the local people call "chopping" or "sobbing." Example 5–4 (recorded selection 28) is a women's *ganga* that will give you a sense of the style; listen to it several times until the strangeness wears off. Of course, to experience *ganga* properly, you should be singing it. Singers are very aware of the acoustic quality they are producing, so *ganga* is not easy to record. When Petrovic took a group of women into the studio, the sound engineers tried to put a microphone on each singer separately to clarify the sound, but the women refused. They must perform their songs in a tight semicircle, touching shoulders, so they can listen properly to each other and create the right mood. This technique confused the engineers but not the women. They told the technicians exactly where to place the microphone for best sound quality.

Petrovic delved deeply into many sides of the singers' aesthetic, their feelings

Ex. 5–4. *Transcription of a Ganga song.*

about their music. She found a direct correlation between musical features and this aesthetic:

> The melodic range and intervals in this polyphonic singing reflect mutual human relationships within the framework of small interacting communities, while the importance of individual personality is emphasized by individual improvisation. At the end of the *ganga*, when songs finish on two different tones a major second apart, it is as if different individuals are given the same rights in the community. (1977:335)

When *ganga* is sung right, it has a powerful effect on its performers and listeners:

> Good performances can move them to tears and "shudders," but with a sense of happiness; and they arouse feelings of love and sexual passion among younger people, as well as strong feelings of regional identity among both young and old alike. (1977:331)

This comes as close as any available description to spelling out the intensity the term *lyric song* can encompass. The song text of example 5–4 is typical of two aspects of *ganga*: reference to the singers' village (underscoring the localism of the genre) and a commentary on love:

> *Podvelesh, My Dearest Place*
> 1. *Podvelesh, my dearest place,*
>   *A paradise for boys and girls.*
> 2. *My dear, my beloved, you are my*
>   *flower—*
>   *If I don't happen to like someone else.*
> 3. *Love lasts for years, my dear.*
>   *How long will ours?*

Musically, "Podvelesh" features the *ganga* style of a lead singer who projects the song text alone, then is joined by two singers in the "chopping" style. For purposes of easy reading, the tiny differences between singers 2 and 3 have been left out as they are hard to hear and follow. You cannot really write down the music of *ganga* just by listening to a tape; you might not be able to tell even how many singers there are since the pitches are so close together and the resulting sound quality is so dense.

To show a lighter side of love and flirtation, let us look at a Polish song (ex. 5–5; fig. 5–10). It is more Western European in flavor and should be easy for you to pick up; try singing it on a syllable (*la* or *da*) and you should find it closer to melodies you're familiar with. Poland's musical ties, unlike Bulgaria's, are closer to Western European, particularly German folk music. The dance rhythm

is typically Polish. Here the metaphors from the animal world seem to carry

Szta mu-szka po wo - de do zim - ne - go zdro - ju

za - stą - pił jej ko - mar dro - ge nie dat jej spo - ko - ju,

zas - tą - pit jej ko - mar-dro - ge nie dał jej spo - ko - ju

17,7" ♩ = 115

Ko ma - rze, do ma - rze cóż ja to - bie win - na,

za - stą pi - łeś mi dró - żeń - ke gdzie je wo - da zim - na.

17,6" ♩ = 115

Pa - mien-tasz ty mu - szko jak ja był mło - dzień - cem

pa-wie pior - ka za cza - pe - czka z bar - wi-no-wem wien - cem.

Ex. 5–5. *Polish lyric song.* Source: *Czekanowska 1961:160.*

Fig. 5–10. *Polish lyric song.*

A little bug was going to get some cool water.
Along came a mosquito that wouldn't let it rest.
"Mosquito, mosquito, why is it my fault?
Let me get some cool water."
"Do you remember, little bug, when I was young?
Hat with a peacock feather and a colorful wreath."

none of the mythic and fairy-tale weight and of the ritual and narrative songs we have looked at. This is pure fun.

MUSICAL INSTRUMENTS AND
INSTRUMENTALISTS

Mentioning a dance tune brings to mind the sound of fiddle, bagpipe, and drum. However, it would be a mistake to imagine a large group of merry peasants all playing away on their instruments. Instrumental music is different from the song tradition; as Kodály remarks: "Where instrumental music is concerned ... everyone is a listener; performance is the task of a few. Whether the musician is a gypsy or a peasant, he stands alone, or with a few companions, face to face with the listening masses. They are critical and discriminating and can distinguish what is good," (Kodály 1971:126). Nor is the instrumentalists' life an easy one. Kodály's memories are useful here: "In 1912 I was present when a well-to-do Szekely [a region] farmer engaged a gypsy to play at his son's wedding. He was the only musician in Kaszonfetiz, a place of some 10,000 inhabitants. This single fiddler had to play for twenty-four hours in return for food and drink, some kerchiefs, and five forints [about $2.50]" (Kodály 1971:127). No wonder there was a scarcity of performers: "As long ago as the 1880s they 'made do' in quite a number of places ... with a single bagpiper, even for a well-to-do wedding," Kodály writes.

Which instruments are used, what contexts they appear in, and by whom they are played are questions always related to the history and makeup of the local culture (see ills. 5–8, 5–9). History determines what instruments are available and which are preferred. In the Balkans and Greece, many of the instrument types reflect the age-old position of Southeastern Europe as a crossroads between East and West. For instance, Bosnians in Yugoslavia play a long-necked lute they call the *saz*, a close relative of the stringed instrument of the same name found in Turkey, while the Bulgarian shepherd's flute *kaval* is almost identical to the Turkish *kaval*. Newer layers of instruments spread from other directions, most obviously the spread of the hardy accordion from Western to Eastern Europe in the nineteenth century, which drove out or reduced the use of earlier types of instruments.

The organization of instrumental music is based on two principles: gender, and ethnic discrimination of performing ensembles. Kodály's reference to Gypsies above and his use of "he" for musician are not accidental. Women were generally not given access to most musical instruments in peasant cultures, save for occasional exceptions like the tambourine and the Jew's harp (also allowed to village women in the Middle East). Just as the lament is left largely to females, so instrumental music is generally left to males. Certainly the appearance of a female bagpiper or fiddler would have been exceptional, if not shocking in most of traditional Eastern Europe, just as the appearance of female bagpipers is a very recent phenomenon in Scotland.

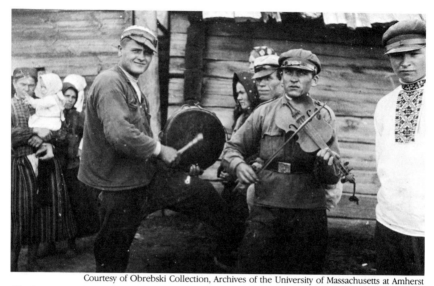

Courtesy of Obrebski Collection, Archives of the University of Massachusetts at Amherst

Ill. 5–8. *Local peasant musicians in the Polesie region of the Ukraine, 1930s.*

Often instrumental assignments are made in terms of ethnic group. Two large marginal non-peasant peoples of Eastern Europe, the Jews and the Gypsies, held a special musical position. In many areas, bands of these two groups once

Ill. 5–9. *Local peasant musicians in the Polesie region of the Ukraine, 1930s.*

Courtesy of Obrebski Collection, Archives of the University of Massachusetts at Amherst

formed standard ensembles for peasant festivities, particularly weddings. Of course, not all instrumental music was left to these groups; the shepherd's flute and horn calls were the province of peasants. It is difficult to get at the root of ethnomusical organization, but it seems to be connected to the usually low status accorded the professional instrumentalist, as opposed to the amateur shepherd or farmer. This bias holds true for some present-day village situations, surviving generational change and the disruptions of two world wars, as Sachs notes for Macedonia:

> Just as Gypsy bands composed of Turkish drum . . . and shawm . . . [oboe] were popular in the heyday of the traditional group, Gypsy bands composed of the same instruments as are contemporary Christian transitional bands are popular with the transitional and acculturative generations today. Gypsies play at village and city festivities and are regarded, like the *griots* of Africa, as professional musicians whose conduct and morals are presumed by Christian Macedonians to be different and worse than their own. (1975:208)

In the past these marginal musicians had a great impact on the peasant repertory. Ethnic interaction in Eastern Europe could be quite complicated, as, for example, in the Bukovina (in present-day USSR), where Rumanians, Hungarians, Jews, Ukrainians, and smaller groups coexisted on the same land. For that region, Kodály (1971:127) notes that Gypsy musicians "play to four or five nationalities," all of whom tend to share the same body of dance tunes. This naturally makes it difficult to determine that a tune is purely "Hungarian," "Rumanian," etc.

Even today, more than two generations after the destruction of six million Eastern European Jews during the Holocaust of World War II, certain "Jewish" or "Sabbath" polkas can be collected from Christian peasants in Poland. One can also hear old-time Rumanian fiddlers who remember songs in Yiddish, a Jewish language. On the other hand, the music of the marginal peoples sometimes represents a radical departure from local peasant music. In the late nineteenth century composers like Brahms and Liszt were so dazzled by the virtuosity and soulful quality of urban Gypsy musicians that they assumed the music represented a "Hungarian" folk quality. Bartók and Kodály had to prove to the Hungarians themselves that the old-style Hungarian peasant music had no connection to the fancy rhapsodies of Gypsy café musicians.

On the Jewish side, there was an impressive body of liturgical, folk, and professional instrumental music and an intricate, many-layered internal social organization of their music-culture (see ill. 5–10). The Jewish music-culture was often completely at odds with the Christian peasant way of thinking about and organizing music, despite centuries of constant Christian influence. Gypsy bands also managed to maintain musical identity while roving over large areas of countryside and being truly international in musical outlook.

Aside from its importance in accompanying songs, instrumental music is significant in its own right as both dance music and music not meant for dance. Non-dance music includes a great variety of pieces, from spring mountain calls

Courtesy of YIVO Institute for Jewish Research, New York

Ill. 5–10. *Eastern European Jewish band of wedding musicians, Vilna, Lithuania, early twentieth century.*

played by shepherds on straight or curled horns of wood or animal horn, or tunes played on ordinary leaves (we will listen to one shortly), fish-scales, or any other small, hand-held object, to the greater rhapsodic Gypsy fantasies just mentioned.

We turn first to dance music. Though also quite varied, dance music is unified by a single function: keeping the beat. The two basic requirements of the good dance band are a large repertoire and a steady beat. Small ensembles of two to several players are typically found in much of Eastern Europe. Dance tunes often fall into clearly marked sections, usually two or three to a piece, that repeat over and over; the same tune can serve for various texts, if songs accompany the dance, and may be stretched over many minutes. The player's individual style is more often reflected in small variations than in the invention of new musical material. This small-scale variability of traditional material is the lifeblood of folk music and eventually leads to musical change.

We will listen to a Jewish wedding dance, featuring clarinet and accordion (recorded selection 29). Recorded in New York, it shows how immigrants hold on to their European roots in America. After a piece is heard straight through, the three principal sections, labeled A, B, and C in figure 5–11, can be heard

Fig. 5–11. *Sequence of sections, Jewish dance tune.*

A A A A B B B B C C A A A A B B B B C C A A

separately for easy identification. Notice the small variations at each repetition, and notice the large differences in the register (high vs. low) and type of scale, as well as accompaniment style, of the three sections.

As figure 5–11 shows, the piece consists of two repetitions of a single scheme—AAAABBBBCC, plus a final two statements of A. This scheme probably indicates that the performers were used to playing a tune just long enough to fit on one side of an old 78 rpm record, which lasted about three minutes. Beginning early in the twentieth century, recordings of folk music were made commercially. In Europe as in America the demands of the technology, as well as of the audience, began to shape the repertoires of folk–professional musicians. At a live dance, the piece given here might last up to forty-five minutes, with the sequence of sections much less predictable than on our recording and with probably even more melodic variety within the framework to keep the players from getting bored. As long as they keep the beat, the dancers will be satisfied.

Though men and women danced at the same time and place, they did not necessarily dance together, either in the Jewish tradition just cited or in some others, such as Rosa, the Macedonian village described by Nahoma Sachs:

> Dancing took place usually in a family's courtyard or in an open area in front of the village church. A man known for his sense of strength, responsibility, and propriety ploughed a large circle ... he ploughed a diameter through the circle as well. The men stood on one side of this furrow, and the women on the other, so that there could be no physical contact between men and women. ... The sexual division in dancing was not limited to traditional Rosans; it was still in practice during the early postwar years. (1975:214)

Not only were the sexes separated, but their movements differed considerably: "Men performed movement sequences with larger, higher steps than did women. ... Womens' style, in contrast, had special steps or movements which emphasized subtlety and smallness" [1975:214].

Sachs's description of the position and role of the Rosan instrumentalist is of particular interest: "The piper stood at the center of the circle ... his centrality made it possible for men or women to call him to their side of the circle. He was the only man who was allowed on the women's side" [1975:214]. This "neuter" role of the musician, who belongs to neither side of the circle, probably symbolizes the marginal, sometimes outcast status of the folk musician, observable in many world music-cultures. There is another, darker side to this ambiguous role. Male musicians could be viewed as a threat to the virtue of respectable girls. This is true of rock musicians in America, and it is true of many musicians in other parts of the world. When they were wanderers, not tied to a farm, musicians were a potentially disruptive element in the conservative life of the village.

The great Yiddish writer Sholom Aleichem, whose stories formed the basis for the musical *Fiddler on the Roof*, once lived with Jewish fiddlers and wrote a fascinating novel about their life-style. He even had to learn the musicians' special secret language to understand them. His book, *Stempenyu*, named for the dangerous fiddler-hero, describes a wedding scene in great detail, including the impact of Stempenyu's playing on the young girls at the wedding feast.

> Stempenyu kept his head thrown to the side with his long mane of hair spread over his broad shoulders; his eyes, those black, burning eyes, looked straight ahead, and the beautiful, shining face used to suddenly grow pale as death. . . . You only see how a hand flies up and down, up and down, and various voices are heard, and all sorts of songs pour forth, all melancholy, sad ones that seize your heart and draw your soul. . . . The heart fills up and tears appear in the eyes. Men sob, sigh, weep . . . as to the girls . . . they stay rooted to the spot like sticks, looking at Stempenyu with his fiddle, not moving a muscle, not batting an eye. Somewhere, on the other side of a corset, hearts are beating: tick-tick-tick—and from there a buried sigh often emerges. . . .

The rest of the novel explores the growing infatuation of Rachel, the heroine, for Stempenyu, which she controls only with great difficulty. Significantly, the book ends with Rachel forcing her small-town husband to move to the big city. Knowing now the excitement of the wandering musician, she insists on leaving the village behind. Stempenyu, ironically, is pinned down to an awful marriage by another girl he has seduced and abandoned.

To round out our picture of instrumental music, let us look at one more example; this time from Hungary (recorded selection 30). The selection is a ballad, first as sung solo and then as played by the same man (a fifty-two-year-old swineherd) first on a birch leaf and then on a small strummed zither. In the first two stanzas (fig. 5–12), we find a very ballad-like confrontation between an upper-class girl and a herdsman, which probably develops into a closer relationship as the ballad progresses. The topic, structure (four-line stanzas are very common for the European ballad), and singing style of the song are in the mainstream of ballad tradition. The melody, however, is purely Hungarian, relating neither to the free Balkan lines, the polyphonic eastern Slavic style, or the Polish–Central European manner we have seen so far. First, the four melodic lines (ex. 5–6), are, on closer inspection, only two lines, A and B, presented in the order ABBA. (The second B has a special ending; it is marked B−).

Second, the scale structure of the song is basically pentatonic. This means that the five notes F, G, B−flat, C, D (and upper F) are the most important ones in the

Fig. 5–12. *Hungarian ballad for instrumental variants.* Source: *Rajeczky 1972. Used by permission.*

1. *The young Lady's herd of cattle is grazing on the beautiful pasture.*
   The young Lady herself is walking out to see the herd.
   From a far distance she calls to the herdsman,
   "My dear Bandi, please spread your overcoat down upon the ground."

2. *"Can I really spread my overcoat down upon the ground?*
   My herd of cattle will be all driven away."
   "Never mind, my dear Bandi, if it's driven away
   For my mother dear will redeem it, I can assure you."

Ex. 5–6. *Hungarian ballad.* Source: *Rajeczky 1972:35. Used by permission.*

song. The other notes, A and E − flat, occur "trapped" between B or F and are less important to the overall sense of tonality. This type of tonality can be found in other parts of the world: the Scottish song "Auld Lang Syne," played for New Year's in America, is pentatonic as is the American hymn, "Amazing Grace," examined in chapter 4. However, the pentatonic structure is especially characteristic of the type of old Hungarian folk tune we are listening to. Third, the song is sung in a very bare, straightforward manner, with only one note for each syllable of text. This is also typical of the songs of this region, as opposed to the ornamented lines of Southeastern Europe, or of the Russian ballad we examined.

Now, how will this very Hungarian song be turned into instrumental music by the singer? The answer is that the two instruments he chooses suggest different types of treatment. On a birch leaf, with its high-pitched continuous, one-line quality, the performer stretches the notes of the tune. Not tied to singing sylla-bles, he twists and bends the melody somewhat, very skillfully making it a bit freer. The strummed zither, however, offers quite different possibilities of in-terpretation. This is a box-shaped instrument with several strings and with char-acteristics like the American folk dulcimer. Here, continuity of sound is not possible; instead, the performer chooses a lively strum, now marking the rhyth-mic aspect of the song more than he did while playing the birch leaf. In addition, he can create a multipart texture, which he does by adding a drone part—that is, a continuously repeated note against which the melody stands out in relief.

So, while there are large, distinctive repertoires of music just for instruments, particularly if designed for dancing, songs can be turned into modest instru-mental works in which the properties of the chosen instrument play an impor-tant role.

NEWER LAYERS OF THE EASTERN
EUROPEAN MUSIC-CULTURE

In the late nineteenth century industrialization and urbanization began to affect Eastern European peasant life. In addition, strong nationalist trends led to the reshaping of musical traditions. As early as the 1880s, V. V. Andreyev rebuilt two vanishing Russian stringed instruments, the *balalaika* and the *domra*, creating new shapes and sizes to form an orchestra of folk instruments. This ensemble is capable of playing arrangements of folk songs in a new, virtuoso manner as well as playing transcriptions of classical music. The accompanying cassette offers a good example of Andreyev's technique in his variations on a Russian folk song, "The Moon Shines" (recorded selection 31). First you hear the theme, then a set of variations displaying different sides of the balalaika orchestra. Note the highly virtuosi playing, the flexibility of dynamics, and the general bravura quality of the performance, all of which go far beyond the capabilities of the average village musician.

This movement toward modernization came at the same time that several generations of Eastern European composers incorporated folk songs into their symphonic compositions. Among them were Dvořák and Smetana in Czechoslovakia, Bartók and Kodály in Hungary, Enesco in Rumania, and Moussorgsky, Borodin, Rimsky-Korsakov, and Stravinsky in Russia. This tendency still echoes in much of the compositional activity in the Soviet Union and elsewhere. It often involves the composers in collecting and studying the folk heritage themselves, as we have seen with Bartók and Kodály. Meanwhile, widespread campaigns for literacy and a growing network of public music schools and conservatories has made this body of publication and composition accessible to generations moving from village to city or, through the media, to those still living down on the farm, a shrinking percentage of Eastern Europeans.

The vast loss of life and dislocation of people caused by two catastrophic world wars (1914–1918 and 1939–1945) made severe inroads on old peasant customs and traditions (see ill. 5–11). In addition, far-reaching political change destroyed the old empires and their social systems, as socialist states were formed, first in Russia (1917), then in the rest of the region (1940–1948). Secularization of much ritual and the politicization of important parts of peasant life combined with modernization (electricity, mechanization of labor) to stimulate the growth of new genres and hasten the death of some old ones.

We can exemplify some of the early stages of the change by looking at the evolution of content in a specific genre of Russian folk song: the *chastushka*. *Chastushki* (pl.) consist of short, snappy verses, often in quatrain (four-line) form, sung and largely composed (usually improvised) by girls. Thousands of these have been collected, though many fewer tunes are used, one melody serving for dozens of local songs. The genre seems to have emerged in the late nineteenth century as a major peasant form taken by villagers to the towns and cities when they migrated to urban centers for jobs. Most are about love, many being bawdy but as they are frequently topical, speaking to the emotions or issues of the mo-

Courtesy of Obrebski Collection, Archives of the University of Massachusetts of Amherst

Ill. 5–11. *Inside a peasant house in the 1930s. Newspapers show the impact of print on oral traditions; note the religious pictures on the wall.*

ment, many other themes are also touched upon. Since they are not directed toward timeless ritual concerns, *chastushki* mirror changing life-styles. For instance, here is one song from the 1930s that simply notes the appearance of a new technological miracle:

> *She went to the telephone*
> *And picked up the receiver.*
> *She called her gray-eyed sweetheart*
> *for a date.*

Others comment on the flight to the cities:

> *Leningrad is beautiful city,*
> *The best of cities.*
> *Why is it a beautiful city?*
> *Because my sweetheart's there.*

Another takes up the transition from field to factory work:

> *I work in the factory*
> *On the night shift.*
> *The motor knocks noisily;*
> *And upsets a girl.*

Still others speak directly to the process of political and cultural change:

> *I'm not going to church today*
> *I'm not the praying kind.*
> *I'm joining the Komsomol (Communist youth organization)*
> *I'll be a Komsomolka.*

Just as the war roused the dormant lament, so it provided material for countless *chastushki* on topics ranging from fear for the sweetheart's life to satirical thrusts against the Nazis:

> *Hitler sits at the table*
> *Gobbling down potatoes.*
> *The little Hitlerites under the table*
> *collect the crumbs.*

Some, composed in German concentration camps, continue the tradition of topical commentary despite the horrors of the situation:

> *I'm not afraid of Germany*
> *But of German rations.*
> *You can't even grease up your tongue*
> *With those two grams of butter they give you.*

The *chastushka* is a favorite genre for state-supported musical activity today, and, though it has declined in the television era, it continues to comment on daily life in Russia.

The post-world War II generations have grown up in a music-culture in which the state, rather than the calendar or the church, provides much of the impetus for music making by sponsoring village dance and instrumental ensembles, regional and national performance competitions and awards, and the message of the state-operated mass media, the only suppliers of music on records, radio, and television. As a result, young people are attuned to the musical values, instruments, and repertoires emanating from the cities. These may reflect international as well as national taste, creating an increasingly eclectic local music culture. Hit songs from *Fiddler on the Roof*, a play that depicts the life of the now-vanished Jewish population of Eastern Europe, can be heard on the radio in villages or at city dances as an import from America rather than as a manifestation of local nostalgia. Recently, dixieland jazz, rock bands, and American country music have become part of the music-culture in relatively isolated Russia, and even more so in the Eastern European countries more open to Western influence, such as Hungary and Poland. The antiestablishment movement of workers and intellectuals in Czechoslovakia in 1977 was sparked by the government's suppression of a rock band. This indicates both that the emotional and political message of a musical style can carry across borders (rock is sometimes antiestablishment in America and Western Europe) and that governments recognize that fact.

For the later stage of modernization we will introduce just one telling example. We mentioned Andreyev, who was inspired in the 1880s to create a new repertoire and ensemble from old Russian folk instruments. His music consisted of arrangements of folk songs on the one hand, and of his own Western European-oriented compositions on the other hand (waltzes, fantasias, etc.) In the present generation we can find the same process at work, even though the innovations seem much more up-to-date. The Leningrad Dixieland Band, interested in a new sound and in imported repertoires, updated Andreyev's approach by playing the "St. Louis Blues" on one track, analogous to Andreyev's imported European compositions, and a set of variations on the same Russian folk song he used, "The Moon Shines" (recorded selection 32).

In 1989, the Eastern European situation as described above changed drastically with the crumbling of Socialist regimes and Communist parties in Poland, East Germany, Czechoslovakia, Hungary, Bulgaria, and Rumania while the forces of nationalism and political change began to undermine the foundations of the Soviet Union itself. It is too early at the time of this writing (early 1990) to assess the impact of this turbulent and dramatic political and social upheaval. However, it is clear that at least partial commercialization of state-run music systems will be inevitable and that the old peasant traditions will be viewed in a new light. Links to the transnational system of commodified music making will doubtless strengthen as hitherto isolated Eastern European lands join the global village. Despite the uncertainties of the new situation, three basic trends will probably continue: deliberate preservation and appreciation of older expressive forms as part of national identity; steady evolution of existing repertoires, concepts, organization, and instruments, perhaps involving the elimination of some genres unsuited to new conditions; and continual creation of new musical styles, contexts, and opportunities.

MARIAM NIRENBERG:
THE LIFE OF A FOLK SINGER

Mariam Nirenberg, now in her eighties, was never a professional folk singer. Like so many others in folk culture, she picked up songs from a wide variety of sources—family, outsiders, records, radio—and sang just for pleasure. In traditional Eastern European societies, a democratic approach to song making and singing meant that people would enjoy hearing a good singer and would encourage music making on an informal basis. For folk singers, this group support was important, as much so as their own feeling that singing helped them get through what was usually a difficult life.

Mariam Nirenberg's life story constantly turns to music, which figures prominently in her memories. She represents just one individual among the millions who left the small towns and cities of Eastern Europe for the United States and Canada at the end of the nineteenth and the early decades of the twentieth century. We will let her speak for herself now, then look at a song from her unusually wide repertoire.

*Mariam Nirenberg's Life History**

When my mother was pregnant with me, when she was in labor, she had a very difficult time. They took her from Tshernovtshits, the town where I grew up, to Warsaw, and in Warsaw she died. She was nineteen years old. They wrapped me in cotton (there were no incubators then) and took me to Brisk [now Brest–Litovsk in the USSR] and found a woman to nurse me. This woman kept me for two years.

Then my father remarried and took me home. They made him a match with a beautiful young woman from Bialystok. She was very good to me. She used to sing all the time. She sang beautifully, mostly old songs. She used to sing songs in Russian too, but I never learned those songs. I only learned the songs she sang in Yiddish [the everyday language of the Eastern European Jews]. She used to sing funny little songs to us when we were small. When I got older I learned her old love songs. I started *kheyder* [Jewish primary school] when I was three years old. We learned to read Hebrew, we learned to pray and write. Mornings I went to the Russian public school.

My stepmother got sick with a lung ailment, with consumption. There were six children counting me. When the smallest child was a year old, she died. My grandfather raised me. He used to be a dairyman. He used to sing a lot and I learned songs from him. Tshernovtshits was a small town. There were about forty houses, mainly Jewish. Brisk was about twelve miles away. The peasants lived in small houses scattered on the outskirts of town. I used to feed the animals and work in the fields. All the peasant girls used to be my girl friends. I used to sing with them. We were like one family, because it was a small town. In the spring we would get up at four in the morning and be in bed by nine at night. I would go with the peasant girls into the forest. We would gather wild raspberries and strawberries. Then we walked the twelve miles to Brisk, singing all the way. In Brisk we sold the berries at the hospital and made a little money. You cannot imagine how different the Old Country was to here [Canada], especially the place I came from. It was a miserable life there, a miserable life.

When the Sabbath came [Friday night and Saturday], there were older girls (seventeen years old) and we used to go to the nicest house in the town to dance. Boys and girls were dancing. We sang and danced. Other times when we got together we had a gramophone with a big horn. There was only one in the whole town. We would dance to that music. Otherwise we sang the tunes ourselves.

We used to dance at weddings. If it's a wedding in a little town, everybody goes. It doesn't matter if it's Jews or if it's Gentiles. They brought the musicians from Brisk. They played fiddle, drum, and trumpet and sometimes there was a *tsimbl* [hammered dulcimer]. And a wedding jester came too. We did all kinds of dances: *kaketke, kozatske, krakovyak, shrayer, sher, broyges tants, mitsve tants,* quadrille, waltz, parade waltz, charleston, tango, polka, fox trot, and other ones. Sometimes they would

* Courtesy of Barbara Kirshenblatt-Gimblett

invite me and my brother to sing. We'd sing songs with a marriage theme during the dinner.

I was singing when I was a kid four years old. My grandfather used to say I would hide behind the door and sing because I was very shy. I used to sing together with my brother Shimen and my sister Itke. We sang songs in Russian, Byelorussian, Ukrainian, Polish, Yiddish, Hebrew. When we sang at home, people would stand at our windows to listen. The town was small after all. If a guest visited, everyone got together. People who came to visit brought songs. When we used to go to another town, we learned new songs and brought them back. We always sang—while we worked, while we walked, when we got together. Sabbath and holidays the family sang *zmires* (songs around the table) at home.

If I like a song, you know, and I hear it, and I really like it, I can't sing it right away. But when I go home and go to sleep, in the morning I know it. But if I don't like it, no. But if I like it, in the morning I know the whole song. I was good at memorizing in school too. Sometimes I add a stanza, or once in a while I may make up new words to a tune I already know.

In 1930 I came to Canada. I was engaged to Lazar at the time. Before I left, my uncle in Warsaw gave me comforters to bring. I also took a few photographs. When I arrived in Canada, I lived in St. Catherine's for the first couple of years. I missed Lazar very much. The whole time I sang my favorite Yiddish love songs. I acted in a Yiddish play and wrote Yiddish poetry for the Jewish newspapers. Lazar came in 1933, and we got married. We moved to Toronto and worked very hard. I had the two boys, Les and Harvey. When they were small, I did ten jobs. I sold dresses in the house, and I mended socks my husband brought me from the shop. Then we got our variety store. We sold newspapers, candy, cigarettes, and other things. We worked seven days a week, even to this day. Here I was too busy to sing very much. In Canada if you work in a shop, you can't sing. I used to go to the Yiddish theater all the time. During the last few years, different Jewish organizations invite me to sing for their luncheons. In the summers I sometimes went to a resort in Muskoka, Ontario, for two weeks. There were about three hundred people at the new Acadia summer resort. Each evening people would sing, including me. On Friday evenings, after the Sabbath meal, everybody would sing *zmires* (table songs), mainly in Hebrew, some in Yiddish.

I learned songs at these resorts. People sang songs from *Fiddler on the Roof.* Very recently I learned a song from a woman in the country. I copied out the words from her. Sometimes I hear songs I like on the radio. At home, I sing to myself all the time when I'm cleaning. My children knew every song that I know. My sons have their own families now. Les, the oldest, is an executive producer and actor, and Harvey is a real estate broker.

Mariam Nirenberg's life story is typical of her generation. Raised in difficult circumstances and physical hardship, she nevertheless formed fast friendships and used music and dance as a central focus of her social life. Emigrating during the Great Depression, her life continued to be extremely demanding for many years, and she continued to sing whenever and wherever possible. Folk singers like Mrs. Nirenberg never stop acquiring new songs—even now she learns them at resorts, from people she happens to meet, from the radio. Although her children know all her songs passively, from years of listening, they do not sing much themselves. Now Mrs. Nirenberg is relatively comfortable, and her children have done well, but she has not forgotten the songs and surroundings of her childhood in Eastern Europe. To close this section, we will look at one of her songs (recorded selection 33; ex. 5–7), "Vinter Iz Geveyn a Groyser Shturem Vind," about World War I (1914–1918). All the peoples of Eastern Europe suffered during that war, as armies crisscrossed the region, spreading destruction in their wake. Her song is not particularly ethnic, and stands for the experience of a whole generation. It is in the narrative tradition discussed earlier, and shows that up through recent decades, people were still making up folk songs about current situations in the style of songs sung hundreds of years earlier. Notice that it opens with a reference to nature ("storm wind"), which reflects the fate of the human beings involved; by now you know that this is typical of older songs, as is the four-line verse structure and the shifting of the narration from one character (the man) to another (the woman) in the last verse (fig. 5–13).

Finally, notice the adaptability that marks Mrs. Nirenberg's entire description of her life. In her small town, she spoke and sang in several languages. Her description of dances is encyclopedic, ranging from Jewish folk dances to the new Jazz Age Charleston. In Canada she learned a new language and added even more variety to her singing. Of course, not all folk singers are as versatile as Mrs. Nirenberg, but the perseverance and resilience she shows is common among the ordinary folk who flooded North America in the great waves of immigration,

Ex. 5–7. *Lyrics, "Vinter Iz Geveyn a Groyser Shturem Vind."*

Vinter iz geveyn a groyser shturem vind.
Oyfn shlakhtfeld hot men mir avekgeshikt.
A farsamte pulye hot mir getrofn
In hospital firt men mir geshvind.

In hospital hot men mir genumen
Oyfn betl hot men mir avekgeleygt.
Tsvey doktoyrim un a sanatarke
Zey hobn mir geratevet fun toyt.

Oy ratevet mir shoyn yo un neyn
Mayn lebn iz mir shoyn alts eynts.
Nor eyn zakh iz mir a shud
Fun aza getraye kale avek tsu geyn.

Mayn kale iz tsu mir gekumen
Un zi hot mi gegebn a kish.
Mayn moyshele ligt on gedanken
Un derkenen derkent er mir shoyn nisht.

In winter there was a great storm wind
They sent me to the battlefield
A poisoned bullet hit me
They quickly took me to the hospital.

They took me to the hospital
And laid me on a bed
Two doctors and a nurse
Saved my life.

O save me, yes or no
My life is all the same to me
Just one thing is a shame
To leave such a faithful bride.

My bride came to me
And kissed me
"My Moyshele is lying unconscious
And he doesn't even recognize me."

Fig. 5–13. ***Lyrics, "Vinter Iz Geven a Groyser Shturem Vind."***

and her flexibility is also typical of many of the musicians we are meeting in our travels through world music.

REFERENCES CITED

Alexandru, T., and A. L. Lloyd
    1963   Notes to *Rumania*. Columbia KL 5799.
Balashov, D. M., and Ilu. Kraskovskaia
    1969   *Russkie svadebnye pesni Terkskogo berega Belogo moria.* Leningrad: Muzyka.

CMPH (Corpus Musicae Popularis Hungaricae)
  1956   Vol. III/B *Lakodalom*, edited by L. Kiss. Hungarian Academy of Sciences

  _____

  1966   Vol. V: *Siratók*, edited by L. Kiss and B. Rajeczky.
Czekanowska, A.
  1961   *Pesni Bilgorajskie*. Wroclaw: PTL.
Kodály, Zoltán
  [1960] 1971.   *Folk Music of Hungary*. Reprint. New York: Praeger.
Kotikova, N. L.
  1966   *Narodnye pesni Pskovskoi oblasti*. Moscow: Muzyka.
Petrovic, Ankica
  1977   "Ganga, a Form of Traditional Rural Singing in Yugoslavia." Ph.D. diss.,
          Queen's University, Belfast, Northern Ireland.

  _____

  1985   *Traditional Music from the Soil of Bosnia-Hercegovina*. DT LP 8149.
Rajeczky, B.
  1972   Notes to *Hungarian Folk Music II*. Budapest: Hungarian Academy of
          Sciences.
Sachs, Nahoma
  1975   "Music and Meaning: Musical Symbolism in a Macedonian Village." Ph.D.
          diss., Princeton University.
Wolf, Eric
  1969   *Peasants*. Englewood Cliffs, N.J.: Prentice-Hall.

ADDITIONAL READING

Works in English on the music cultures of Eastern Europe are still scarce. For a good example of the study of peasant ritual, see two books by Gail Kligman: *Calus: Symbolic Transformation in Rumanian Ritual* (Univ. of Chicago Press, 1981) and *The Wedding of the Dead* (Univ. of California Press, 1988). For general surveys with bibliography see the country entries in the *New Grove's Dictionary of Music* (1979).

ADDITIONAL LISTENING

The suggestions below are for the American market; many more styles are available from smaller European labels. A well-annotated documentary album on Mariam Nirenberg is out: *Folksongs in the East European Jewish Tradition from the Repertoire of Mariam Nirenberg* (Global Village GVM117). The French label OCORA has some titles for Yugoslavia (4558548, 4558572, 4558619) and Rumania (558506, 4559070, 558505), and a very interesting style from Sardinia (4558611). For Hungary, the Hungaroton label has issued several boxed sets and many individual albums of folk music styles. On Folkways, *Lithuanian Folk Music in the US* (FM 4009) is a good example of the preservation of older styles in emigration, and *Music of the Soviet Union* (Smithsonian Folkways SF40002) has examples of Russian, Lithuanian, Estonian, Tuvan, Azerbaijani, and Georgian musics from the USSR. The Columbia Folk and Primitive Music series, edited by Alan Lomax in the 1950s, goes in and out of print and is an excellent source for older styles of a number of European countries.

S I X

♦ ♦ ♦

India/South India

DAVID B. RECK

THE ENVIRONMENT—THE MUSICIAN

The Setting

Imagine in your mind's eye being dropped into the thriving city of Madras in South India. Under the burning tropical sun framed by large white clouds in a brilliant blue sky, beneath rising dust that hangs mistlike over the asphalt streets, palm trees, and whitewashed concrete buildings, you would be faced with a bewildering confusion of elements: the traffic, seemingly chaotic, pits colorful trucks, buses, taxis, and automobiles against a kaleidoscopic array of bicycles, handcarts, motorcycles, and three-wheeled motor rickshaws (see ills. 6–1, 6–2). Streams of people, a human river, pour out from the sidewalks and onto the streets. The pungent odor of curries drifts through the air from restaurants and food stalls. Sidewalk vendors sit by their symmetrical arrangements of wristwatches, cutlery, or plastic toys. Others carry bananas, flowers, or rolls of brilliantly colored cloth in baskets on their heads. A roadside astrologer sits under a tree. A few feet down the street (under the next tree) might be a cobbler or a bicycle repairman.

Modern skyscrapers and high-rise apartments abut mud-and-thatch village style huts. Spacious air-conditioned movie theaters and showrooms for silks, motorcycles, refrigerators, or television sets border crowded bazaars with tiny shops selling jewelry, perfumes, rugs, or spices. Massive mills and factories producing everything from computers to airplanes contrast with the humble establishments of traditional craftsmen working with the tools and methods of generations past.

There are other jarring juxtapositions. A bullock cart with massive wheels creaks under the weight of its load, an electrical transformer. A loinclothed laborer, a turban protecting his head from the sun, stands momentarily next to a businessman holding a briefcase and dressed in fashionable Madison Avenue suit and tie. Hindu religious rites thousands of years old dedicate a nuclear power generator. The old and the new, the indigenous and the transplanted, coexist. It is almost as if the layers of three thousand years of history have been frozen—in people, objects, beliefs, life-styles, buildings—to exist simultaneously in an inexplicable present.

Ill. 6–10.   *Mount Road, one of the busiest commercial streets in Madras.*

The facts about India are staggering. Its population of over 700 million (one-fifth of the world's population) exists in an area less than half the size of the United States. There are fifteen major languages (most with different alphabets)

Ill. 6–2.   *Bunder Street in Georgetown, a section of Madras which grew up around the offices, warehouses, and fort of the British East India Company.*

and dozens of dialects. India's history is a continuous thread going back to the great cities of the Indus Valley civilization (3000–1500 B.C.).

Due perhaps to its geography—a peninsula cut off from neighboring lands by jungles, deserts, and the towering Himalaya mountains—India has developed forms of culture and lifeways that are distinctly its own. Yet because of its size and its variety of terrain there are also great regional differences.

The largest such division is between the Hindi-related language groups of the North and the Dravidian-speaking peoples of the South, a division that is paralleled in the two styles of "classical" music: the northern *hindusthani* style and the southern *karnataka* tradition.

Numerous influences have come into India, the earliest being the immigration of Aryan people from central Asia (beginning in the second millenium B.C. whose Indo-European language was related to the languages of Europe. Perhaps the most important later influences came from the Islamic conquests (beginning the twelfth century A.D.) and the British, who made India "the jewel of their colonies" (seventeenth to twentieth centuries). Cultural ideas, along with technology, came with each group, but a characteristic pattern has emerged each time: the new ideas (and people) were absorbed, assimilated, and digested, emerging finally in a new and undeniably Indian synthesis.

In music this synthesis and transformation can be seen in the relationship between the *ragas* (music/expressive modes)* and forms of India and those of Iran and the Middle East (the Islamic influence), or in the adaptation of the European violin, clarinet, and harmonium—all played in a distinctly Indian manner—from the English.

The arts, along with the sciences and philosophical and religious thought, have flourished in India from the earliest times. Great kings and great dynasties built thousands of magnificent palaces, temples, forts, towers, tombs, and cities. Indian sculpture in stone, wood, or bronze and Indian painting (notably the book-size miniatures) rank among the greatest masterpieces of world art. Traditional literature is dominated by the two major epics—the *Ramayana* and the *Mahabharata* (written down between 400 B.C. and 400 A.D., but believed to exist in oral traditions much earlier). There have been dozens of major authors, poets, and playwrights, however; the most famous was Kalidasa, who lived in the fourth and fifth centuries; and there are numerous collections of stories and fables.

Indian soil has also been the locus of great religious development. The four *Vedas* (believed to have crystalized as early as 1200 B.C.) and the later *Upanishads* contain religious and abstract philosophical thought of such logic and beauty that they have fascinated Western thinkers like Thoreau and scientists like Robert Oppenheimer. *The Puranas* (first century A.D. to the present) are filled with the myths of the Gods and Goddesses of popular Hinduism. Thinkers like Shankara (?788–829) rank among the great philosophers of the world. The ancient physical and mental disciplines of *Yoga* are now practiced by millions of Americans and Eu-

---

* An English equivalent follows the italicized word here and, where appropriate, throughout this chapter.

ropeans and taught in universities and meditation centers, and even on television. In recent times, activist saints like Mahatma Gandhi (1869–1948) have preached nonviolence combined with radical social action to a passive world.

Excellence in the arts continues today in many areas. Musicians like Ali Akbar Khan or Ravi Shankar are as well known in the West as rock and pop stars. Satyajit Ray is one of the acknowledged masters of contemporary cinema; R. K. Narayan's novels, written in English, have won widespread critical acclaim. And there are hundreds of poets, musicians, painters, authors, filmmakers, and thinkers of great depth and skill whose work is not known abroad. Finally, there are the many humble craftsmen, carrying out centuries-old traditions in weaving, fabric painting, embroidery, metalwork, wood carving, jewelry, basketry, and other crafts, who support an export trade of fine handmade goods admired throughout the world.

The problems of modern India are immense. Successive governments have attacked but not completely solved serious problems of overpopulation, terrorism, social order, and an agriculture dependent on monsoon rains which may either bring famine if they fail, or devastating floods and hurricanes if they are too heavy.

The political system (based on British parliamentary rule) is democratic (a rarity in the world today), though it can appear chaotic to an outsider. And change is occurring in the face of the apparent immovable inertia of age-old traditions. There are, therefore, steel mills and locomotive factories and nuclear power plants; there are soft drinks, modern airline and railway systems, computers everywhere, well-equipped armed forces, and a growing and prosperous middle class with world-class competence and brilliance particularly in the sciences, technology, and business. There are subways, skyscrapers, discos, and jazz bars. At the same time there is the juxtaposition of the ancient, the archaic—in customs, lifeways, ways of seeing, and ways of doing. The old, traditional ways survive through all the changes of time and history (see ill. 6–3). This coexistence is part of the amazement and fascination of India—and perhaps also part of its strength.

Many Musics

If we were to stroll through one of the more traditional neighborhoods of Madras, like the section of Mylapore, we might come into contact with many forms of music. The music that we hear would reflect many levels of folk or popular or classical art, many layers of society. It may be built on ancient traditions passed down by generations, or new ones; it may have sprouted and grown on Indian soil, or it may be an exotic transplant, undergoing a process that, unless stopped by outright rejection, will ultimately metamorphose it into an Indian synthesis (see ill. 6–4).

The predominant music here and elsewhere in South India, blasting out of house radios or loudspeakers mounted at the front doors of shops and teastalls, is the sound of "cine music." Listen to the recording of "Engal Kalyanam" ("Our

Ill. 6–30. *The traditional wedding of a young couple is laced with ancient ritual and music. Note the garlanded images of Hindu deities on the wall.*

Wedding") on the accompanying cassette (recorded selection 34; fig. 6–1). Indian pop music is called "cine music" or "film music" because almost all the songs come from hit movies in Hindi, Tamil, or other regional languages. Virtually all movies are musicals. Cine music is a curious and sometimes bizarre blend of East and West: choppy and hyperactive melodies, often in "oriental" scales, are belted out by nasal singers over Latin rhythms and an eclectic accompaniment that may include trap set, electric organs and guitars, violins, xylophones, celeste, bongos, *sitar*, *tabla*, or bamboo flute. More recently some genres of Indian pop music have been crafted to sound exactly like their Western pop counterparts, only their lyrics in Indian languages making them distinguishable from the latest hit tune. The lyrics of cine songs tend to focus on the eternal trivia and complications of love and romance. "Engal Kalyanam" takes a light-hearted look at the commotion and excitement of an Indian wedding, with the ever-present relatives and the joyful feelings of the happy couple.

The same musical characteristics hold for many of the forms of folk music and street entertainments: for snake charmers piping on their *punjis* (a kind of gourd and reed bagpipe), for mendicants playing small gongs or the conchshell *shanku*, for musicians accompanying acrobats and dancers or street theater (see ill. 6–5).

Often forms of music are connected with forms of worship. Each large temple

Ill. 6–4. *A poster advertises Thillana Mohanambal, a popular Tamil movie adapted from a famous novel about the romance and marriage of a dancer and a musician.*

has its musicians: singers of ritual songs, performers of *harikatha bhagavatham* (a kind of storytelling and sermon interspersed with classical and religious song), or the religious ensemble of double-reed *nagaswaram* and drums, which provide music for temple and household ceremonies, processions, and weddings. Part of the ritual to Ayyappan—a god whose temple is located deep in the jungles of the southern mountains—is the sound of the *panchavadyam*, a ten- to twenty-man percussion orchestra. Listen to the recording of this ensemble, turning the volume up to the loudest level possible without distortion (recorded selection 36). This is only a fragment of a performance that you must imagine as lasting all night long. Try to get a feeling for the numbing power of the sound through its complexity, loudness, and continuousness over a long period of time. *Panchavadyam* percussion music is based on long rhythmic cycles marked by ostinato patterns played by the group over which individual soloists alone, or in rapid alteration, improvise. Rhythm and drumming in India are among the most complex in the world.

There may also be unmodified transplants. Student rock bands play hits from England or America; Westernized clubs may have a dance combo or jazz band; Christian churches sing hymns or mount a Christmas production of Handel's *Messiah*. And there is the curious hybrid from the British military bands of the colonial era: the street bands, which—sometimes elaborately uniformed—play Western band instruments (bass and snare drums, cymbals, trumpets, trombones, clarinets, saxophones, and so on). These groups blast mostly unison melodies from the pop music repertoire to claphammer percussion as they march in wedding, temple, and political processions.

Our marriage is a confusion/commotion marriage!
   Sons-in-law spend for the marriage
     and the father-in-law puts up the pandal[1]
     to receive gifts.

Morning is the wedding, and evening is the wedding night.
   Enliven! Love marriage.[2]
Tomorrow won't the marriage altar give the garlands?[3]
   Won't the drums drum with the pipes?

The lovers' story is performed in the eyes.
   How much struggle: to perform in the eyes!
A colorful chariot is running beside me;
   Heaven is coming to us!

Mother-in-law is putting on eye make-up
   And the sons-in-law are staring at the mirror;
Processions wind along the streets with fire crackers,
   And everybody is giving their blessings.

Shall we have ten to sixteen children?
   Shall the trimness of the body be lost?
You hated men,
   (Yet) you gave desire!
    I am the God of Love!
    You are the reason!

Your cheeks are inviting me;
   The thoughts are asking for one.
Eyes are like bright lightning;
   What are the pleasures we haven't experienced?

He (father-in-law) had prayed to the God of Tirupati[4]
   To perform the marriage in Tirupati
    So that they (the bride and groom) might live
    prosperous lives.

Sons-in-law should come home
   and give a send-off to the father-in-law
   so that he can take up sanyasin![5]

                    —translation from the Tamil
                      by S. B. Rajeswari

1. *Pandal*: a temporary wedding canopy of bamboo and palm leaves.
2. A "love marriage" is contrasted with a marriage arranged by parents, often with pragmatic objectives.
3. The bride and groom exchange garlands at an important part of the ceremony. The answer to both questions is "no."
4. Tirupati is the site of the great temple to Lord Venkateswara, the most popular shrine in South India.
5. That is, the new son-in-law should take over the responsibilities of his wife's father who can then retire and take up a religious life (*sanyasin*).

Fig. 6–1. *Lyrics to "Our Wedding."*

Ill. 6–5. *C. P. Saraswathi, a wandering minstrel, accompanies herself on the kudam. A member of a household offers her rice in exchange for her song.*

We might also hear more traditional types of music. Minstrels carrying simple instruments like the one-stringed gourd and bamboo *ektara* or the washtub bass-like *kudam* (literally "clay pot") sing from door to door hoping for a few *paisa* (pennies) or a gift of rice. Listen now to *nagapattu* ("Song to the Snake Deities") sung by C. P. Saraswathi, a minstrel from the Kerala region of South India, as she accompanies herself on the *kudam* (recorded selection 35; fig. 6–2). Musical elements like "oriental" scale, melodic ornamentation, drone, assymetrical phrasing, and a strongly accented rhythmic accompaniment mark this (quite sophisticated) folk song as distinctly "Indian," and connect it to "classical" traditions found in the same culture.

Finally, echoing from concert halls, from temples, from *nagaswaram* piping ensembles, and from radios we would hear *karnataka sangeeta*, the classical music of South India. We call it classical not because it is necessarily more complicated or polished or difficult to perform than many of the folk traditions, but because it has a status as a cultivated high art form in India similar to that of classical, or art, or serious music in the West. This status is today shared by the classical dance traditions such as *bharata natyam, kathak*, or *odissi*.

Listen to the example of *karnataka* music on the cassette (recorded selection 37), or to any of the recordings recommended in the discography. Try to become familiar with the sound and style of *karnataka sangeeta* so that you can form a background for the explorations and analysis that follow later in this chapter. Make a list of some of the characteristics of the music. Try humming or singing along with the slower passages. Best of all, try listening to *karnataka* music intensively over a period of several days (or even a week), even while you

Then, when the dark ages had passed,
It happened thus to Garudan.[1]

A dance and flowers of great beauty were offered,
As salutation to God in those ways (paths).

Garudan's desire to elevate himself to nobility
Had been apparent earlier in the clouds.

The orphans[2] *went to the Mother,*
Bowing down in obeisance to Her.

Whereupon that Mother
Kissed them with great joy.

All the wickedness that had come to pass
Was whispered into Her ear.

"Wickedness has befallen me in this, my child!
The wretch that I am!" Kadru[3] *fearfully declared.*

"Let what is my due
Be fulfilled unto me."

Hearing this, Garudan was alarmed;
"O Mother, what can I do about this?

This web of deceit (iniquity) is spun.
What must I do that it may end?" . . . . . .

> *Partial and free translation—*
> *P. George Mathew*

1. Garudan: the great mythical bird, the mount of the God Vishnu.
2. The orphans: that is, the cobras, snakes.
3. Kadru: mythical mother of the snakes.
The allusions of the songtext are to epic legends concerning the origins of the snakes before time began.

Fig. 6–2. *Song to the Snake Deities.*

read, talk, daydream, or do chores. Try to absorb as much of the music as you can.

A Day in the Life of Ramachandra, a Musician of Madras

Mylapore, one of the older neighborhoods of Madras, like many sections of the great city was originally a town in itself. Built around the great Shiva temple of Kapaleeswara, Mylapore is made up of back-to-back one-, two-, and three-story houses with flat or red-tiled roofs. Its streets are lined with the tiny shops of crafts-men and businesses, and with open-air markets. Here we might notice some of the problems of Madras and other large Indian cities: overcrowding, inadequate sanitation, insufficient water (clusters of women with pots around public faucets), fickle supplies of electricity. We might also notice that everyday life—far from being shut up boxlike in individual houses—spills out into the communal spaces of courtyards, onto the sidewalks and the street. Life is too crowded in individual homes and in the city to be anything but gregarious (see ills. 6–6, 6–7).

In the maze of Mylapore, on a tiny lane approachable only by footpath, is the modest house of Sri Veena Thirugokarnam N. Ramachandra Iyer. As in the case of many South Indians, we can tell much about him by his name: *Sri* means "sir" or "mister"; *Veena* refers to the fact that he is a musician, a master of the seven-stringed plucked *veena*; *Thirugokarnam* is the name of his ancestral village, the place of his birth; *N.* is the initial of his father's given name; *Ramachandra* is his own given name; and *Iyer* is a caste-name signifying that he is a member of the Brahmin caste, that his ancestral ties are to the region of the Tamils (now the state of Tamilnad), and that his religious sect regards Shiva as the supreme deity.

To place oneself by name is very important to South Indians. Everyone is born into a caste that (while things are changing gradually) can predetermine many things: social status, how you speak, whom you can eat with, whom you can marry, and what jobs or profession you may or may not pursue, as well as certain social and religious practices and obligations. Ramachandra's caste, Brahmin, is socially high (though a Brahmin may be poor) and is traditionally associated with the Hindu priesthood, with scholarship and teaching, and (in the South) with music.

Ramachandra is a frail, shy man in his sixties, whose traditional clothes and hairstyle (shoulder length hair tied in a knot) and religious markings signify that he is conservative and traditional. His movements are often birdlike, and neighbors regard him as a little eccentric (an excusable fault for an artist). However, his shyness disappears when he picks up his *veena* and plays or teaches; in fact, he has a ready wit and a good sense of humor. He tries to be "a good man,"

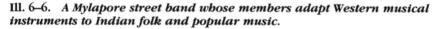

Ill. 6–6. *A Mylapore street band whose members adapt Western musical instruments to Indian folk and popular music.*

Ill. 6–7. *Children play on the small lane in front of Ramachandra's house. Most homes in Madras are similarly built with stucco and brick or concrete. The windows ate laced with metal bars since glass would make the houses too hot in the tropical climate.*

living according to his *dharma*—that is, holding to high ethical standards; but he is confused by the dog-eat-dog mentality, the imperfections, and the instability both of the modern world and of the music scene in Madras.

When Ramachandra was a boy living in a small village in the tiny kingdom of Puddukottai, near Tanjore, his father decided that he was to become a *veena* player, and sent him to study with his uncle, Karaikudi Sambasiva Iyer, one of the greatest virtuosi of modern times. The decision was not a rash one, since his family had included seven generations of *veena* players before him. Many of his ancestors had served as musicians attached to the courts of the *rajas*—the kings and princes—of the area.

After his apprenticeship and marriage, Ramachandra was encouraged by a wealthy patron to move to Madras, then as now the center of the *karnataka* music world. He quickly became established as a teacher, and has supported himself and his family (a wife and three sons) in a manner that has not changed substantially in the past twenty years. Although it was not Ramachandra's fate to become a famous concert musician like his *guru*, he plays occasional weddings and temple concerts and is highly regarded by his colleagues.

A typical day in Ramachandra's household begins around 5:30 in the morning. The women get up first and begin work in the kitchen. The men rise next, washing their faces and brushing their teeth. The children are last.

Ramachandra's household is a "joint" or "extended" family. Besides him and his wife (who make most of the decisions since they are senior members of the family group), there are the eldest and youngest of his three sons, their wives, and four grandchildren (see ill. 6–8). In all, ten people live in the five tiny rooms of the house; and those who have jobs pool their income to help maintain the household.

The house is like thousands of others in Madras. Thick brick and concrete walls, glassless steel-barred windows, and a red tile roof enclose a cavelike space of tiny rooms. Tables, cabinets, chairs, trunks, and a couch encroach upon the limited floor space, since most rooms (except for kitchen and pantry) serve multiple functions throughout the day. The main living room, for example, serves as a bedroom at night, music room during lessons, dining room during meals, and a living space at other times. In the back is a small open-air courtyard adjoined by sheds containing a washroom and a toilet. A single handpump brings water up from the city water pipes, but when water pressure drops (a daily occurrence) water must be carried from a nearby well.

Ramachandra and his family, though they are middle class, have few possessions, especially when compared with habitually acquisitive Americans. A few faded and framed photographs and calendar prints of the Hindu gods hang from nails on the bare concrete. Besides pots and pans, clothes, and other items needed for day-to-day living, only a table radio, a thermos bottle, an electric wall clock, a rotating electric fan, and a television set—some presented to Ramachandra by his students—stand out as "luxury" items. A large cabinet dominating the

Ill. 6–8. *Musical tradition is adsorbed by younger generations through daily contact: Ramachandra and his daughter-in-law Sarawati encourage his grandchild to try his hand at strumming the veena. The family shrine can be seen in the background.*

main living hall contains Ramachandra's most valuable possessions: two magnificent *veenas* of jackwood and brass with ivory inlay. With these instruments in
the cabinet are old music books, pictures of Ramachandra's parents and *guru*,
and the miscellaneous paraphernalia of a musician. At night Ramachandra removes his prized foreign-made wrist watch (an Italian Timex), bought on his
only trip abroad, and locks it with other valuables in the cabinet.

The early morning hours in Madras are among the most pleasant of the day.
Usually a breeze blows in from the Bay of Bengal, rustling the leaves of palm
trees and awakening a noisy population of crows. It is relatively cool—in the 70s.
Ramachandra's family moves through its regular morning ritual of hot coffee or
milk, baths, shaving, getting dressed in fresh clothes, reading the Tamil newspaper (Tamil is the language of Madras), listening to the news or *karnataka*
music on the radio, taking care of the children, marketing, and preparing and
eating breakfast. Considerable logistics are required with so many people moving around in such a small space.

The milkman arrives on his rounds, driving his sleepy herd of buffalo before
him and milking at every doorstep. Ramachandra's daughter-in-law or niece
sprinkles water outside the front door and paints a beautiful symmetrical design
on the ground in front of the house by sifting flour between her fingers. These
designs, done every day by South Indian women, are called *kolams* or *rangoli*
and are considered to bring good luck.

Meanwhile, at around 7:00 A.M., the first of Ramachandra's students arrives. The
two *veenas* are lifted out of the cabinet and placed on straw mats on the floor.
Ramachandra sits facing his student and the lesson begins. Every note, every
ornament, every phrase is taught in the traditional way: Ramachandra plays, the
student watches his hands, listens, and then imitates. Bit by bit the phrases of a
raga or a composition are built up, perfected, and memorized. There is no
musical notation. "This is 'the thousand-times method,' " Ramachandra has said.
"Once you learn something in this way you can never forget it . . . the 'book' is
in your head and in your hands."

Ramachandra's lessons have an air of relaxed formality. It was different in the
old days, the days of Ramachandra's apprenticeship. Then, he remembers, students moved into the household of the *guru*, to live as part of his extended
family. As many as five or ten students might be living with a well-known *guru*
at any given time. In exchange for lessons, students helped out in the household,
and occasional gifts were given by their parents to the teacher. Much of the
learning was simply by "osmosis," by living in an environment filled with music
"twenty-five hours a day."

Discipline was strict and the *guru* demanded the utmost in respect and obe-
dience. Poor students became familiar with the whack of a teacher's hand on the
top of the had or a slap on the hands with a stick. Fear, it was thought, makes you
try harder!

The *guru*, one's principal teacher, is remembered and venerated for a musician's entire lifetime. The reason for this respect is that—unlike the West where
most of our knowledge exists in books and computers—in India, the *guru* is the

ultimate source of all the student's musical knowledge. He holds within him a whole musical tradition stretching into the past, as well as compositions, improvisatory skills, and vocal or instrumental techniques. He is like a living, human library. And what he gives to his students, despite his apparent cruelty or harshness, must ultimately be regarded as a priceless gift.

A music lesson lasts an hour, more or less. And as the morning wears on, other students (mostly children, young girls in their teens, or adult women) appear to wait quietly in a front room until they are called for their lesson. Each pays Ramachandra a monthly stipend, according to his or her family's means. It is not much.

During the lessons, life in the household goes on. The grandchildren are fed and the eldest is sent off to school. The sons and niece and nephew go off to work. Vendors come to the door selling flowers, vegetables, pots and pans, plastic toys, and other items with characteristic and almost musical calls. About mid-morning, maybe around ten o'clock, Ramachandra takes a break from his lessons. It is time for his morning bath, his *puja* (or household worship), and his morning meal.

Ramachandra, cleansed by his bath, goes to a mirror, combs and oils his long, greying hair (tying it into the traditional bun), and applies scented sandalwood paste to his arms, chest, and forehead. He applies a dime-sized circular red spot of *kumkum* to his forehead. Seated on a small wooden pallet and surrounded by ritual objects, he performs his daily *puja*. Before him is a small cabinet, the family shrine, containing framed prints, gold-plated reliefs, and small statues of some of the Gods of the Hindu pantheon. Represented among them are Shiva, the main deity of Ramachandra's sect, Saraswati, the goddess of music and learning, and a photograph of Ramachandra's musical *guru*, whom he venerates along with the Gods. There are also pictures of the famous composers of the *karnataka* tradition.

After the *puja*, Ramachandra eats his morning meal of rice cakes and a spicy sauce with lemon or mango pickles; or simply yogurt and rice. He sits on the floor, eating from a banana leaf "plate" (as is the custom) with his right hand. His wife or daughter-in-law serves, bringing the food out hot from the kitchen.

Dressed in the traditional *veshti* (ankle-length white cloth draped around the waist) and loose-fitting *juba* (or *kurta*, the sometimes embroidered shirts now sold in Indian clothing shops all over the United States), and sandals, Ramachandra walks under the shade of a large black umbrella or boards a cycle-rickshaw or a bus to give lessons in the homes of his wealthier students. On some days he returns home for a mid-afternoon rest. He may then chat with his wife, play with his grandchildren (swinging them in a hammock suspended from the ceiling), help with a little housecleaning, or spread a mat on the floor under the ceiling fan and take a nap. Three days a week he must leave again, after the afternoon *tiffin* (snack) around four o'clock, and travel to a small music school to give group *veena* lessons. On these days he will not get home again until eight or nine o'clock in the evening.

Meanwhile, during the day the women of the household may find moments to rest. They listen to the radio, gossip with their neighbors, or, in late afternoons when the markets are open again, go out to shop. Most women in South India are expected to fill the traditional role of mother and housewife. However, many—if they belong to the middle or upper classes—have had musical training, and they make up much of the audience at concerts. Today many of the most famous performers (voice, *veena,* violin, and flute, but only rarely the drum) in the *karnataka* tradition are women.

Like the early morning, late afternoon is also a nice part of the day in Madras. Shadows lengthen, a sea breeze blows off the heat of the day, and people pour out onto the streets to conduct business, visit friends, shop, worship, or simply take a stroll. The sounds of bells, the double-reed *nagaswaram*, and drums float out of the crowded Hindu temples to compete with a cacophony of radios, loudspeakers, vendors' calls, taxi and bus horns, and bicycle bells. The cooling twilight hangs as if it will never end.

It is at this time of day—around five or six o'clock—that concerts usually begin. Programs are sponsored by *sabhas*, cultural clubs that bring to their members and the general public a series that includes music, dance, Tamil plays, and sometimes even movies. The large and prestigious *sabhas* have their own buildings, often large shed-like structures with open sides to catch the evening breeze. The smaller *sabhas* may meet in the assembly hall of a high school or some other meeting place. The audience sits either in chairs, or, more traditionally, on large striped rugs or mats spread on the floor in close proximity to the musicians, who cluster on a slightly raised platform. The musicians' cronies or fellow musicians tend to sit at the front where they can offer reactions and encouragement through stylized motions like head-shaking or a throwing out of the hands, tongue-clicking, or verbal comments like "Yes, yes!," "Beautiful!," or "Good!"

Concerts are relaxed and (compared to classical concerts in the West) informal. Members of the audience may count time with their hands, periodically converse with friends, or occasionally get up and take a stroll or buy betel nuts or a soft drink at the refreshment stand. There are no printed programs; mature musicians are not likely to preplan their entire program in advance, and a knowledgeable audience is familiar with the repertoire of songs, *ragas*, and *talas* (time cycles). A program may last as long as three-and-a-half or four hours without an intermission. The music (which we shall examine later) is a mixture of precomposed songs and improvisation; the musician is both an interpretive artist and a creator.

Most concerts feature vocal music, and the singer may be accompanied by a second voice, violin, and drums—sometimes with additional percussion. Solo instrumental concerts might feature the violin, the bamboo flute, or the *veena*. When a concert ends there is usually little or no applause; the audience, many of whom might have arrived late and left early, simply files out and heads for home, humming, perhaps, a tune or two, while a few well-wishers congratulate the musicians and chat with each other.

Returning to the daily life of a musician, the working members of Ramachandra's household come back home around 6:00 P.M. Evenings—unless everyone goes out visiting or to a movie—are spent together playing with the children, doing chores, receiving guests, or listening to a favorite radio quiz show or watching a television drama. Often one of Ramachandra's friends drops by, and they may chat for hours about music, religion, or acquaintances in Madras or in the country. Here Ramachandra is most at his ease, laughing, punning, chewing betel nuts and *pan* leaves, confident, through the warmth and admiration of his friends, all of them traditional men like himself and most of them musicians, of the worth of his life as a musician.

On Fridays, a holy day for Hindus, and on festival days, Ramachandra takes his *veena* in the evening and, sitting alone before the family shrine, plays for himself, for practice, and as a meditation, an offering to the gods. Music for him, as for other traditional Indian musicians, is far more than a beautiful art form. Intimately connected with religion, it is a form of *yoga*, a path and a spiritual discipline that can lead to a deep inner experience of Reality, the Truth behind all existence. Musicians, it is believed, through devotion to music and the discipline of their art, can touch the mysteries of *Nada-Brahma*, "God-as-Sound."

Ramachandra and his family eat their major meal—like other South Indians—around 9:00 P.M. Boiled rice surrounded by a variety of vegetarian curries and topped off with chutneys and pickles is the usual fare. After dinner it is time for sleep. The family bedding is brought down from overhead storage and spread on the floor. The lights go out, muffled voices can be heard in the darkness; then, one by one, everyone drops off to sleep.

Perhaps in the stillness before he, too, falls asleep, Ramachandra thinks of his life, of his role as one musician who both connects through his *guru* to a chain of musicians stretching back in Indian history for thousands of years, and also projects himself through his students to the future. Through thousands of musicians like himself *karnataka* music has lived and continues to live. A break in the chain would end it forever. Perhaps in his mind's ear Ramachandra thinks of the hundreds of *ragas* and beautiful compositions stored in his memory. Or perhaps he thinks of the insecurities and mundane worries of day-to-day existence as a musician in Madras. But eventually for him, too, sleep must come. A day in the life of a South Indian musician, Sri Veena Thirugokarnam N. Ramachandra Iyer, has come to an end. Tomorrow will be much the same.

KARNATAKA SANGEETA, THE CLASSICAL MUSIC OF SOUTH INDIA

Ramachandra's tradition—*karnataka sangeeta*—has its roots in the distant past. The earliest extant theoretical work is the *Natya Shastra* by Bharata, a treatise on theater, dance, and music dating from between the second century B.C. to the fifth century A.D. Through the centuries many more important scholarly books on music have been written, perhaps the most noteworthy of which was the medieval *Sangeeta Ratnakara* (c. 1210–1247) by Sarangadeva.

Stone sculpture on the ancient temples and palaces as well as miniature paintings give us a visual record of ensembles, instruments, and the where and how of performance through several thousand years. In addition, there are many references to music in the epics, the *Mahbharata* and *Ramayana*, as well as in stories and religious writings. But the actual sound and practice of Indian classical music, as it grew and developed through generation after generation of musicians working in the courts of kings or in the immense temple complexes, has been lost. One of the characteristics of an oral tradition—such as that of Indian music—is that it lives day-to-day in performance, in human beings, the musicians. It cannot be frozen in time, either by being written down (as words can), or by being preserved as a visual entity (such as a photograph or painting) though today sound recordings and videotape can preserve a particular performance.

From about the thirteenth century, scholars began to notice a difference in India between the classical style of the North (today called *hindusthani* music) and of the South (*karnataka sangeeta*, or Carnatic music). While both styles use *ragas* (melodic modes) and *talas* (metric cycles) and have many similarities, the systems also differ considerably. We might say (simplifying tremendously) that the northern style and its instruments (like the *sitar*, *sarod*, and *tabla*) have been more greatly influenced by Persian and other elements of Islamic culture. In *hindusthani* music seemingly timeless broad improvisations eventually evolve into sections of brilliant virtuosity. By contrast the *karnataka* style of the more orthodox Hindu South is built around an immense repertoire of precomposed songs. The musical texture tends to sound more busy and active, more consistently ornamented.

Try comparing examples of *hindusthani* and *karnataka* music from some of the recordings listed in the discography. Juxtapose vocal selections or instrumental selections in both styles. Try to make a list of similarities and differences.

Karnataka sangeeta began to stabilize into its present shape in the sixteenth century. Purandara Dasa (1484–1564), sometimes called the "Father of *karnataka* music," composed not only many songs but the standard lessons and exercises that are still memorized by every music student today. A "golden age" occurred between about 1750 and 1850 when the forms and performance style that have continued to the present day were set. Thousands of new *kritis* (compositions) were composed, new *ragas* were invented, and the conceptual forms of older *ragas* expanded. Three great saint-composers dominate this period and the *karnataka sangeeta* tradition as a whole: Syama Sastri (1762–1827), Tyagaraja (1767–1847), and Muttuswamy Dikshitar (1776–1836) (ill. 6–9). A clever South Indian proverb compares the music of the *trimurthy*, the "big three." Dikshitar is said to have written music that is like a coconut: the "hard shell" of his brilliantly intellectual musical structures and complex, scholarly, and sometimes esoteric texts "must be broken to taste the sweet nut and milk inside." By contrast, Syama Sastri's music is said to be like a banana: "the fruit is not so difficult to get to, but still one must peel off the bitter skin"—Sastri's complicated rhythms and *talas* (cycles) of five and seven beats—"before enjoying its flavor." But Tyagaraja's songs are said to be like fresh, ripe grapes;

**Ill. 6–9. *Three great saint-composers (left to right): Muttuswamy
Dikshitar, Tyagaraja, and Syama Sastri, as seen in contemporary
prints.***

both poetry and melody are immediately accessible: "to enjoy it one needs
merely to bite into it. Even the skin is soft and sweet." It is no wonder, then, that
Tyagaraja's extraordinarily beautiful songs dominate the repertoire, loved and
held like precious gems in the hearts and memory of musicians and music
lovers alike.

A PERFORMANCE SEGMENT: THE SOUND
WORLD

Now that we have become familiar with the sound and style—and some of the
background—of *karnataka* music, we can begin to explore the music itself, how
it is put together and shaped in performance. What we might call a "performance segment" is a unit in a concert that is built by the musician around the
central core of a precomposed piece, a song. This unit may include various types
of improvisation in the same *raga* and *tala* as the core piece. A concert is made
up of a series of such performance segments (as many as twelve or fourteen),
each in a different *raga* and based upon a different composition.

The individual South Indian musician can exercise great flexibility in his
shaping of each performance segment. That is, he can select from a number of
different options and procedures. We shall look into some of these possibilities
later. But first, listen to the performance segment built upon "Sarasiruha," a song
by the nineteenth-century composer Puliyur Doraisamy Ayyar. The performer is
Ramachandra Iyer playing *veena*, accompanied by his son Ravindran and the
author on second and third *veenas*, and the American *mridangam* player David
Nelson (recorded selection 37). Since this is a house concert and not a studio
recording, you may notice various extraneous noises: the buzzing of the insects
of a Madras night, the humming of ceiling fans, the passing of an automobile, or
at one point the barking of the host's large dogs which give the home its
nickname: "Naymahal," the "Dog Palace." Make a list of the characteristics of

karnataka music style and of the instruments. Then try to chart out the overall structure of the performance. Compare what you have discovered with the analysis that follows.

Instruments

Ramachandra Iyer's instrument is the seven-stringed *veena*, a plucked lute that took its present shape in the sixteenth century (ill. 6–10). Its ornate body, inlaid with deer horn or ivory, is carved out of jackwood. A natural or papier-mâché gourd is attached to the upper neck as a resonator. The brass frets are set chromatically in black wax, and tuning is by means of large pegs. A dragon's head decorates the end of the neck. Of the seven strings, four are playing strings used for playing the melody, and three are unstopped by the fingers, providing an unchanging drone (as in a bagpipe or five-string banjo). The playing style combines fingerings on the frets, various slides and flickerings, and deflection (pulling, "bending") of the string to increase its tension and produce higher notes, subtle intonation, and ornaments. The *veena* is played today held semihorizontally in

Ill. 6–10. *Ramachandra Iyer and his brother Krishnamurthy playing their veenas.*

Photo: © D.B. Rama, 1989.

front of the musician (who sits cross-legged on a rug on the floor or stage) with the gourd-end resting on his left knee. The *veena*, with its soft mellow sound, is a quiet instrument best suited for intimate chamber music. In the large concert halls of today it must be heavily amplified, often through use of a contact mike.

David Nelson's instrument, the barrel-shaped double-headed *mridangam*, is the principal drum of South Indian classical music. Its body is made from a hollowed-out log of jackwood. The leather skins of the two drumheads are held by leather strapping buttressed by movable pegs jammed beneath to aid in tuning. Both heads are made from multiple layers of leather, the outer layers cut with circular holes in the middle. The lower (untuned) left-hand head has a blob of wet wheat paste applied in the center to give it a booming sound. The center of the right-hand head (which is tuned to the tonic note, the *sruti*, of the soloist—in this case, the *veena*) has a hard, metallic black spot made from many finely polished layers of rice paste and other ingredients. The sophistication of these drumheads, combined with the hand and finger techniques of the drummer, makes possible up to fifteen or more distinct sounds (many at different pitches)! The use of the fingers as miniature drumsticks allows the drummer to play passages of incredible speed and complexity. The *mridangam* is propped horizontally in front of the player, resting between knee and ankle, as he sits on a mat on the floor.

Scholars in ancient India classified instruments (*vadyas*) by their acoustical properties. It is interesting that the modern classification of musical instruments devised by Eric M. von Hornbostel and Curt Sachs in the twentieth century is based on the ancient Indian system. The divisions are as follows:

1. *tata vadyas*: the sound is produced by stretched strings that are plucked, bowed, or hit (e.g., lutes, fiddles, and zithers).

2. *sushira vadyas*: the sound is produced by breath or wind (e.g., flutes, oboes, clarinets, and trumpets).

3. *avanaddha vadyas*: the sound is produced by stretched skin (e.g., drums).

4. *ghana vadyas*: the sound is produced by striking solid objects (e.g., cymbals or gongs).

In the *karnataka* music tradition, *tata vadyas* (or chordophones, i.e., strings), are the *veena*; the *gottuvadyam*, like the *veena* but played with a slide, much in the manner of a Hawaiian, or, steel, guitar; the *tambura*, a plucked four-string drone lute; and the violin, adapted from the West but played with a distinctly Indian manner and sound.

Sushira vadyas (or, aerophones, i.e., winds) include the bamboo open-holed flute; the *nagaswaram*, a large double-reed pipe with a sound something like a saxophone; the clarinet, adapted from the West; and the *sruti*-box, a tuned-reed drone harmonium.

Avanaddha vadyas (or membranophones, i.e., drums), include, besides the double-headed *mridangam*, the *kanjira*, a tambourine made of lizard skin; and (occasionally) the North Indian double drum, the *tabla*.

Ghana vadyas (idiophones, i.e., solid—non-drum—percussion) are the *ghatam*, a large clay pot held in the lap of the bare-chested player; and the *morsang*, a metal jew's-harp. Both of these instruments can play all the rhythmic patterns of the *mridangam*. In dance and temple ensembles the *talam*, or finger-cymbals, are also used to keep time.

Many more instruments in all categories may be found in the folk and religious traditions of South India.

The Ensemble

One way of looking at the music of India is to divide the musical texture (and the instruments) into functional layers. On the recording, you may have noticed that the *veena* plays drone notes (to be discussed next) and melody notes. There is no harmony, that is, not in the way that we in the West are used to. When the *mridangam* enters, a new functional layer appears: the rhythmic. Thus we might draw a picture using symbols for each functional layer (fig. 6–3)

In our recording, two musicians on only two instruments—the *veena* and *mridangam*—could take care of all the functions necessary in the texture of *karnataka* music. But one of the marvels of the tradition is that instruments and musicians can be added to each functional layer. For example, two additional *veenas* back up the principal *veena* in recorded selection 37. Or if a vocalist is the principal soloist, he or she may be joined by a backup singer, and by an accompanying violinist (who echoes and shadows what the vocalist does). The melody layer would then have three musicians. The drone layer could include several special instruments: one or two *tamburas* and/or the reed organ *sruti-*box. On the percussion layer, the *mridangam* player could be joined by performers on the clay pot *ghatam*, the *kanjira* tambourine, or the jew's harp *morsang*. One could thus—in a large ensemble—have as many as ten musicians working within the three functional layers (see fig. 6–4). Because each layer is strictly defined by function and because within each layer there are traditionally

Fig. 6–3. *The three layers of the musical texture, filled by veena and mridangam.*

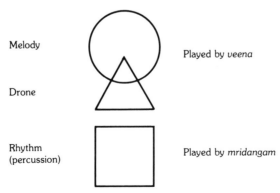

Melody   Played by *veena*

Drone

Rhythm   Played by *mridangam*
(percussion)

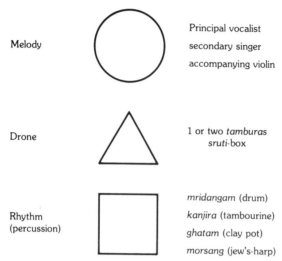

Melody — Principal vocalist / secondary singer / accompanying violin

Drone — 1 or two *tamburas* / *sruti*-box

Rhythm (percussion) — *mridangam* (drum) / *kanjira* (tambourine) / *ghatam* (clay pot) / *morsang* (jew's-harp)

Fig. 6–4. *Layers of the musical texture with added instruments.*

accepted ways of doing things, ways for the musicians to relate to each other, there is never any confusion. There is not even (among professionals) a need for rehearsals. Musicians simply appear for a concert, sit down, and play (see ill. 6–11).

Try listening to some of the suggested recordings in the discography. Map out what the instruments are and how they fit into each of the three functional layers, melody, drone, or rhythm.

Ill. 6–10. *A vocal music ensemble. The singer is B. Rajam Iyer, the violinist is M. S. Gopalakrishan. The string tambura provides a drone, as does a sruti-box which is partially obscured behind the singer. M. A. Easwaran plays the mridangam.*

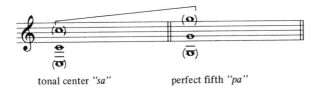

tonal center *"sa"*　　　　　　perfect fifth *"pa"*

sa　　pa　　sa　　　　　pa　　sa　　sa　　sa

drone notes (strings) on the *veena*　　　drone notes (strings) on the South Indian *tambura*

Ex. 6–1. *The tonal center and perfect fifth as drone notes.*

Sruti (the Drone)

Central to the texture of much of India's music, folk and classical, is the idea of the drone, an unchanging tone or group of tones against which the melody moves. (We in the West are familiar with drone notes in bagpiping, five-string banjo playing, fiddling, and the mountain dulcimer.) The drone, or *sruti*, marks the tonal center—the center of gravity—for the melody and its *raga*. Unobtrusive, calm, quiet, static, the drone is like the earth from which the melodies of the musicians fly, from which they start and to which they return. It is like a blank movie screen on which images, actions, and colors are projected; the screen in essence does nothing, but without it the movie would be lost, projecting into nothingness.

In our recording you have probably noticed that Ramachandra Iyer strums a single note or a drone chord from time to time. (In other recordings you will recognize the continuous nasal, buzzing sound of the *tambura* or the reedlike *sruti*-box.) In *karnataka* music the notes used for the drone are the tonal center and the perfect fifth above it. Indian musicians may choose whatever tonal center is convenient for their instrument or their vocal range. For simplicity we have written our notation in concert C, although the *sruti*, the tonic or tonal center, is not fixed, but can be transposed to any pitch (ex. 6–1).

Each note of a *raga* relates to drone notes in varying degrees of consonance and dissonance. The dissonant notes tend to "pull" (almost as if in a gravitational field) toward tones that blend with the drone. Try singing the *raga* scales (ascending and descending) in example 6–2 against a drone (played or sung). Hold each tone for a full breath, giving yourself time to see how it blends with or pulls against the drone. The first *raga* scale in example 6–2, *Mayamalava-gaula*, is the first *raga* learned by students in the *karnataka* music tradition.

Raga (the Expressive Mode)

Listen again to the first two and one-third minutes of the performance segment by Ramachandra Iyer (recorded selection 37). For convenience you may want to

*Pronounced "sah," "ree," "gah," "mah," "pah," "dah," "nee," "sah."

Ex. 6–2. *Singing exercises, raga scales against drones.*

use a stopwatch or a wristwatch (with hour, minute, and second hands starting at twelve o'clock) to help identify sections in our analysis.

The *veena* begins alone (without the drum) in a kind of free-flowing melodic improvisation called *alapana*. The melody evolves gradually, without a sense of beat or time cycles. Pauses between musical phrases are filled in with drone notes. There are slides and pulls and tremolos and vibratos. Many of the tones are sharper or flatter in pitch than those we are used to in Western classical music. The intervals of the scale are also quite different.

An *alapana* is an improvised exposition of a *raga*. The ancient texts define a *raga* as being "that which colors the mind." In fact, in Sanskrit the primary meaning of the word, *raga*, is "coloring, dyeing, tingeing." This connection with generating feelings and emotions in human beings, "coloring the mind," is important because a *raga* is much more than what we in the West might call a "scale." A *raga* is in some ways a kind of mystical expressive force with a musical personality all its own. This "musical personality" is, in part, technical—a collection of notes, scale, intonations, ornaments, characteristic melodic phrases, and so on. Each *raga* has its rules and moves, something like the game of chess. While some of the facts about *ragas* can be verbalized and written down, a musician does not memorize a *raga* or learn it from a book. (*Ragas* are too elusive for that!) Rather, one gets to know a *raga* gradually—by contact with it, hearing it performed by others, performing it oneself—almost as one gets to know a friend by his or her face, clothes style, voice, and personality.

Traditionally *ragas* are said to have "musical-psychological resemblances." A particular *raga* may be associated with certain human emotions, (actual) colors, various Hindu deities, a season of the year, a time of day, or with certain magical properties. Contemporary South Indian musicians are not overly concerned with these associations, but they are aware of the expressive force of *ragas*, their power, and their capability to create deep feelings in the human heart.

Now let us return to Sri Ramachandra's *alapana* exposition of a *raga*. Roughly transcribed, his opening passage is as shown in example 6–3. The phrases, the scale, the intonation, and the ornaments mark the raga as *Natai*, the *raga* set by the song which forms the core of the performance segment.

*durations approximate

Ex. 6–3. *Opening passage, alapana.*

Natai is an ancient and powerful *raga*. Literally *Natai* means "dance" or "drama," and it has associations with the God Shiva in his manifestation as Nataraja (Lord of Dance), whose cosmic dance is seen as the embodiment and manifestation of the eternal energy and cycles of the universe. Medieval paintings of *Natai* often picture a brave warrior, sword in hand, riding a horse or elephant, engaged in a ferocious battle. The emotions personified are the heroic and furious, and the predominant color is red. *Natai* is considered a *ghana raga*, that is, it is solid and rocklike; it is particularly appropriate for the improvised form known as *tanam*.

Scale, Natai Raga

The *Natai* scale is shown in example 6–4. In ascent it usually moves as a five-note scale—*sa ga ma pa ni sa*—although *ri* (D#) is sometimes used. *Da* (A#) occurs, but very rarely. In descent—*sa ni pa ma ri sa*—phrases skip *ga* (E) and move through a *ri* (D#) marked by an oscillation. This *ri* (D#) is in fact the "life note" of the raga: fluctuating with *ga* (E) it gives *Natai raga* a characteristic of the major-minor third that listeners associate with the African-American form

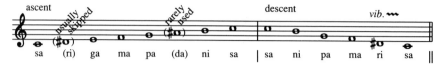

Ex. 6–4.   Scale, Natai raga.

known as the blues (see chapter 4). Besides *ga* (D#) many other notes are decorated with oscillations, slides, bends, flickering, turns, and sliding glissandos: a network of ornaments—*gamakas*—that also give *Natai* its personality. The subtlety of these ornaments cannot be shown in our staff notation, but they may be heard if you listen closely.

Try singing or humming along with the opening passages of the *alpana* (recorded selection 37). You can notice two things from this example (and from the recording). First, a "note" in *karnataka* music is not necessarily just a single tone (as in one piano key); rather, it can be a whole constellation of tones, a miniature universe of sound. Second, movement between tones tends not to be in discrete steps like a staircase (as in a piano keyboard), but rather continuous, with portamentos and glissandos (fig. 6–5).

Returning to the characteristics of *Natai raga*, certain notes are characteristically stable. Melodic phrases tend to come to rest on these tones, to center on them, and to extend them into notes of longer duration. We might call these important centering notes "pillar tones" (example 6–5).

Finally, there are special note groups and musical phrases that characterize

Fig. 6–5.   Notes and melodic movement, veena compared with piano.

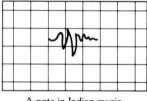

A note in Indian music

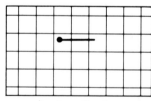

A note on the piano

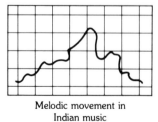

Melodic movement in
Indian music

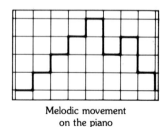

Melodic movement
on the piano

Ex. 6–5. *"Pillar tones" in Natai raga.*

Natai raga. These are like the face and physical features of a person (example 6–6).

In Indian musical notation only the first letters of the note names are used. Thus: s = *sa*, r = *ri*, g = *ga*, m = *ma*, p = *pa*, d =*da*, n = *na*. A dot above the letter indicates the upper octave; a dot below the letter indicates the lower octave. (No added dot indicates the middle octave.) Capital letters are double the durational value of small letters; a line over any letter halves its durational value. Longer durations are shown by the addition of commas and semicolons; a comma increases the previous note value by the equivalent of a small letter, a semi-colon increases the previous note value by the equivalent of a capital letter. There are no signs for rests.

Indian theory books sometimes give model exercises for the phrases of a specific *raga*. A model for *Natai raga* written by the theorist P. Sambamoorthy is given in example 6–7. Spend some time singing or playing the exercise. Your teacher may sing each phrase several times, imitated by the class (as in the traditional Indian manner). Sing the names of the notes or the syllable "ah." The rhythm should be flexible and liquid, not rigid.

While our working with *Natai raga* cannot match a performance by a South Indian musician, still it can bring us closer to Ramachandra Iyer's *alapana.* The model exercise is, in fact, a capsule *alapana*, a brief sketch of the *raga.*

If Ramachandra Iyer's performance were being timed, at about 2:21 on the stopwatch, his improvised *alapana* comes to an end, and he moves into the improvised form known as *tanam.* Now the texture and the melodic movement is more active and rhythmic (though there is no recurring meter), as the musician shapes combinations and permutations of note-groups into somewhat formulaic rhythmic structures.

Tala (the Time Cycle)

At around 5:42 on the stopwatch the *tanam* comes to an end and there is a brief pause. It is at this point that a drummer may check the tuning of his *mridangam.* Then the rendition of the *kriti* ("composition") begins. The *kriti* "Sarasiruha" is of course in the same *raga* as the *alapana*, since (as we have seen) the core piece sets the *raga* for the entire performance segment. But a new element has

Ex. 6–6. *Some characteristic phrases in Natai raga.*

* m r m r m P ;   -   p   m g m R ;   s - p N   m P ;

Ex. 6–7. *Model Natai raga.*

been added (with the drum): a *tala*, or time cycle. Ramachandra Iyer marks the *tala* by striking the drone strings of his *veena* (ex. 6–8). The *tala* in this case is *Adi*, a time cycle of eight beats subdivided 4 + 2 + 2. *Adi tala* may also be counted with the hands, as shown in figure 6–6. The *tala* cycle, once it has entered along with the *mridangam* drum, will continue now until the end of the performance segment. Try counting the *tala* along with the recording.

Karnataka music theorists have listed dozens of possible *talas*. However, only a few are commonly in use today. Practice counting the *talas* listed. See if you can count along as you listen to some of the recordings in the discography (usually the *tala* of a performance segment will be identified).

Ex. 6–8. *Marking the tala with the drone strings.*

Adi tala: 4 + 2 + 2 = 8 beats

```
  1    2    3    4    /5    6    /7    8 //
```

Clap ﹀﹀﹀ Clap   Clap

       Finger Count*   Wave   Wave

*2nd beat = little finger and thumb.
3rd beat = ring finger and thumb.
4th beat = middle finger and thumb.

Fig. 6–6. *Counting in Adi tala.*

Many *tala* cycles also occur in slow tempo. In this case one would add an extra pulse, an "and" between each beat, as in figure 6–7.

You may have noticed that the *tala* cycles of *karnataka* music differ from the meters of Western music (time signatures of 4/4, 3/4, 2/4, 6/8, and so on) in a very significant way. *Talas* are built from uneven groupings of beats (4 + 2 + 2, 1 + 2, and so on). These groupings are marked by the hand claps (fig. 6–8). Even *talas* with the same total number of beats—such as the last two examples in figure 6–9, *Misra Chapu tala* and *Triputa tala*—may sound different because of the different accents created by the beat groupings and by the hand claps. (Try performing these two *talas*, and comparing their sound.)

Musical Structure: Improvisation

The classical music of India—North and South—has two facets: *kalpita sangeeta*, or precomposed music, and *manodharma sangeeta*, improvised music. We have seen that in a typical concert there is a balance between the tasteful and beautiful rendering of the composition of the great masters, and the contemporary musician's exploration of his own creative imagination and skill. These balances work through an intricate framework of procedures and possibilities, and the musician's improvisation itself works within the limits of a kind of "musical tool-kit" handed to him by his tradition.

There are four major types of improvisation found in *karnataka* music:

1. *Alapana* is a free-flowing gradual exposition and exploration of the *raga*, its facets, characteristic *gamaka* (ornaments), and moods—cycles—and its

Fig. 6–7. *Counting in slow tempo with added pulses (compare with fig. 6–6).*

Adi tala (slow tempo)

```
  1  .  2  .  3  .  4  .  /5  .  6  .  /7  .  8  .  //
```

   (&)   (&)   (&)   (&)   (&)   (&)   (&)   (&)

Clap ﹀﹀﹀﹀﹀﹀Clap   Clap

       Finger count   Wave   Wave

phrases evolve in prose-like "breath rhythms." It is improvised before a composition and introduces the *raga* mode of the composition.

The *alapana* follows a general plan set both by the tradition as a whole and by the individual improvisational habits of the musician. Both combine to make the musician's tool kit. *Alapanas* are often shaped by a centering on "pillar tones" that are progressively higher and by a gradual climb to the highest range of the instrument or voice. There is then a quick descent back down to the middle register with an ending on the tonal center. The slower phrases are occasionally broken by quick virtuoso bursts of fast notes called *brikkas.*

2. *Tanam* is a more rhythmic exposition of the *raga*, a lively and strongly articulated working through permutations and combinations of note-groups. Although *tanam* is not restricted by the cycles of any *tala*, it does have a strong "beat sense." Its highly rhythmic phrases tend to fall within constantly changing patterns of twos and threes (♫'s and ♫♫'s), setting up melodic/rhythmic units of asymmetrical length. *Tanam* is shaped like an *alapana*, moving from low phrases to a high peak, followed by a descent. *Tanam* occurs after the *alapana* and before the composition.

3. *Niraval* is an improvised variation on one melody line, or phrase, of the song. It takes the words and their rhythmic setting as a basis, spinning out gradually more and more elaborate and virtuosic melodic variations. (In an instrumental performance, the words are thought of by the performer though they are not, of course, "heard" by the audience.) Since the same words appear over and over again in different melodic contexts, an almost mystical transformation occurs: new meanings take shape and disappear, hidden associations emerge, and subtle nuances come into focus.

Niraval occurs within the composition—following the melody line upon which it is based. It fits within the *tala* cycle of the piece (as well as the *raga* mode).

4. *Svara kalpana* ("imagined notes") occurs after *niraval*—that is, in the middle of a composition—or after a complete run-through of the song. It fits into both the *raga* and the *tala* of the composition. *Svara kalpana* is without a text; instead, it is sung to the names of the notes: "*sa*," "*ri*," "*ga*," "*ma*," and so on. The improvised sections return again and again to the "island" of a theme taken from the composition. *Svara kalpana* improvisations increase in length gradually from being a few notes (before the theme) to being extended passages many cycles in length and full of complicated rhythmic and melodic invention and clever calculation. In some respects *svara kalapana*, especially when sung, is similar in sound to the "scat singing" of jazz.

MUSICAL STRUCTURE: THE KRITI

All compositions in *karnataka* music are songs, melodies with words. The composer is also a poet (though his poetry may be in the "prose" of free verse),

Ata tala: 5 + 5 + 2 + 2 = 14 beats

| 1 | 2 | 3 | 4 | 5 | /6 | 7 | 8 | 9 | 10/11 | 12 | /13 | 14 | // |

Clap ⌣⌣⌣⌣⌣⌣ Clap ⌣⌣⌣⌣⌣⌣ Clap   Clap

    Finger count*   Finger count*   Wave   Wave

2nd beat = little finger and thumb.
3rd beat = ring finger and thumb.
4th beat = middle finger and thumb.
5th beat = index finger and thumb.
(same fingers for beats 7 through 10)

Fig. 6–8. *Counting in Ata tala.*

Fig. 6–9. *Counting in some additional talas.*

Rupaka tala: 1 + 2 = 3 beats

| 1 | /2 | 3 | // |

Clap Clap

    Wave

(Khanda) Chapu Tala: 2 + 3 = 5 beats

| 1 | 2 | /3 | 4 | 5 | // |

Clap * Clap Clap *

*space (i.e., nothing)

Misra Chapu tala: 3 + 2 + 2 = 7 beats

| 1 | 2 | 3 | /4 | 5 | /6 | 7 | // |

Clap Clap * Clap * Clap *

Triputa tala: 3 + 2 + 2 = 7 beats

| 1 | 2 | 3 | /4 | 5 | /6 | 7 | // |

Clap ⌣⌣⌣ Clap   Clap

    Finger count* Wave   Wave

2nd beat = little finger and thumb.
3rd beat = ring finger and thumb.

and his text—even when it deals with love—is usually of a religious nature. The thousands of songs of the tradition have been passed down from generation to generation like jewels on a string. But because they are not precisely notated, rather taught and learned orally, there is no definitive version of a song (in the sense that a symphony or sonata by Beethoven or Mozart exists in an "original," which has been written and can be printed on paper). As it passes through different lines of teachers and disciples, *gurus* and *sishyas*, on its journey from the composer to the present, the same composition may take different shapes. Yet a composition, a song, remains itself—different versions coexist—just as a jazz tune remains itself despite the many interpretations of different singers and musicians over the years.

The *kriti* (composition), is the major form of South Indian concert performance.* It is amazingly flexible, almost liquid in its structure and expressive potential; some *kritis* are tiny, others are massive pieces extending ten or fifteen minutes in length. Most of the major composers—like the "big three" of Tyagaraja, Dikshitar, and Syama Sastri—have concentrated on *kritis* for the expression of their musical and poetic thought. Each treats the form in his own way, with his own touch. The *kriti* may be performed alone on a concert program, for its own intrinsic beauty, or it may serve as the core piece for improvisations that are woven before, in the middle of, or after it.

The *kriti* has three sections:

1. *Pallavi* ("the sprouting," "blossoming"): the opening section. The name of the *kriti* comes from the first several words of the *pallavi* "Sarasiruha" in the *kriti* of Ramachandra Iyer's performance. The *pallavi*—both melody and words—is extremely important because part of it recurs rondo-like after the next two sections. Its size is often expanded through *sangati* (variations) on its melody lines.

2. *Anupallavi* ("after the sprouting, blossoming"): a secondary, contrasting section, often pushing to a kind of climax before a return to the *pallavi* theme. It also may be expanded through composed *sangati* (variations) on its melody lines. In some *kritis* there is a recapitulation of the tune of the *anupallavi* (but not its words) to form the last part of the next section, the *charanam*.

3. *Charanam* ("verse" or "foot"): usually a more relaxed, tranquil section. Occasionally it is a series of energetic "verses" that alternate with the *pallavi* theme. As noted above, the latter half of the *charanam* may incorporate all or part of the melody of the *anupallavi*, giving the impression of a kind of recapitulation. There is a rondo-like return to the *pallavi* theme at the end.

An additional section, lively and highly rhythmic—called a *chitta svaram* (if it has no words) or a *svara sahityam* (if it has a text)—may be interposed after the

---

* Other forms are the *varnam*, a kind of "concert etude"; the slow and stately *padam* and the lively *tillana* and *javali* (all three adapted from the dance tradition); the *bhajana*, a devotional song; and the *pallavi*, a single melodic phrase expanded through manipulation and improvisation. See the recordings in the discography for examples of all these forms.

anupallavi and/or after the *charanam* before the rondo-like reprise of the *pallavi* theme. Often this section will be added by a later composer or musician.

We can map out the form of the *kriti* as shown in figure 6–10. There are, of course, any number of diversions from this scheme. But many of the *kritis* of the *karnataka* music tradition can fit into or otherwise relate to our map. The three major sections are set off in performance by a pause, during which the drummer comes to the forefront with cadential rhythmic patterns.

All in all, the *kriti* as a composition is a magnificent form, balancing repetition, reprises, and melodic recapitulation of larger units with variation and new and unexpected material. Its poetic text gives it an extra dimension, as does the *raga*, the "mystical expressive force" from which its melodies are spun.

The Song Text

"Sarasiruha," the core piece of the performance segment, has a devotional song text in Sanskrit addressed to Saraswati, the Hindu goddess of music and learning (ill. 6–12). A free translation by vocalist and Sanskritist Dr. Indira Peterson is as follows:

Fig. 6–10. *Structure of the kriti.*

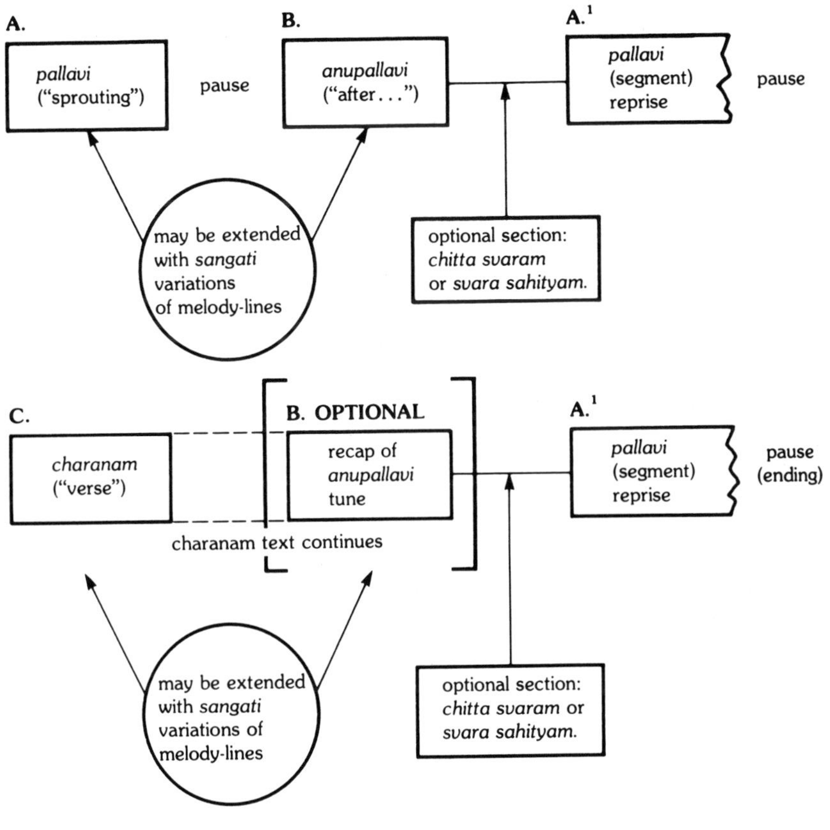

Ill. 6–12. *Saraswati, the goddess of music and learning, seen in a contemporary print.*

PALLAVI: O mother who loves the lotus-seat,
            Ever delighting in the music of *veena*,
            Ever joyful, and ever merciful to me.

ANUPALLAVI: Save me who have taken refuge in you!
            O you with feet as tender as sprouts,
            You charm the hearts of poets,
            You dwell in the lotus,
            You of the jeweled bracelets.

CHARANAM: Lotus-eyed mother who is gracious to the lowly who seek your
            mercy,

Mother with a face as lovely as the autumn moon,
Pure lady! O Saraswati, chaste,
    ever fond of learning,
Lady with breasts like ceremonial vessels,
Complete Being, who holds a book in the hand which bestows all
    dominion.

Of course, in an instrumental performance the words are not audible as they would be in a vocal performance. Yet both the musicians and the more sophisticated members of the audience will know the song text (much as we may reflect upon the lyrics of a Beatles or Tin Pan Alley tune performed in an instrumental arrangement). In fact, some traditional *veena* players may sing at times as they play. The importance of song text can be seen at the stopwatch point 11:12 in the performance when Ramachandra Iyer elaborates around and repeats a single phrase; the text at this point is the name of the Goddess: "Saraswati."

Svara Kalapana in the Performance

After the performance of the complete *kriti* (12:34 on the stopwatch) Ramachandra Iyer begins trading *svara kalpana* improvisations with his accompanists. These improvised *svaras* always return to the opening phrase of the *kriti* (ex. 6–9).

The phrase in a specific *kriti* around which *svara kalpana* are woven is called the *idam*, the "place." This place has two aspects: (1) the raga note on which the phrase starts (in "Sarasiruha": *pa* [G]), and (2) the portion of the *tala* cycle in which it begins (in this case, one-half beat after the first beat). The musician must shape his improvisation so that the *svaras* lead smoothly back to the *idam*.

Svara kalpana may occur in two degrees of speed. In the first speed the predominant movement is two articulated notes per beat (there may also be some notes held longer). In the second speed, the predominant movement shifts to a double-time of four articulated notes per beat (fig. 6–11).

In Ramachandra Iyer's performance, he begins immediately with the second speed. His *svara kalpana* begins (12:34 to 13:14) with three cycles in each of which he improvises briefly within the last four beats of the 8-beat *tala*. (His accompanists alternate with him after each turn.) At 13:15 he stretches his improvised *svaras* to one and one-half cycles. At 13:43 he completes the *svaras* with an extended passage that stretches through about four and three-quarter *tala*

Ex. 6–9. *Opening phrase (idam) of "Sarasiruha."*

[Song text: "sa - ra - si - ru-ha . . ."]

The svara kalpana begins in the first *kala*, or, the first degree of speed. This means that the predominant movement is in eighth notes (two to a beat):

Notice how the improvisations keep returning to the "island" of the theme taken from the charanam ("verse"):

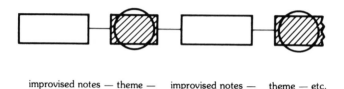

improvised notes — theme —   improvised notes —   theme — etc.

The *svara kalpana* improvisations shift gears and move into double-time. In this "second *kala*," or second degree of speed, the predominant movement as in sixteenth notes (four to a beat):

Fig. 6–11. *The Svara kalpana.*

cycles before returning to the *pallavi* theme. Though the *svara kalpanas* of this performance segment are succinct, they demonstrate the characteristic pattern of increasing length and complexity.

After *svara kalpana* the performer finishes off the *kriti* and brings the performance segment to a close. The drummer marks the ending with a rhythmic closing formula.

An Ear Map

To summarize, Ramachandra Iyer's performance of "Sarasiruha" might be charted as shown in figure 6–12. It is interesting to note that the composed song, the *kriti*, fills about 7:06 minutes of the performance, while Ramachandra Iyer devotes about 8:25 minutes to the three types of improvisation utilized.

On another occasion, at another performance, Sri Ramachandra might decide—using the same *kriti* as a core piece—to choose another set of balances. Drawing from his musical tool kit the procedures and ideas and performance habits stored in his memory, as well as from his conceptual image of the *raga*, much in his successive performances might be the same. But much, sparked by

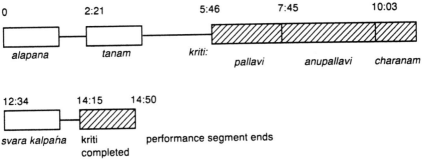

Fig. 6–12. *Complete kriti performance.*

the creative instinct, would be new or different. That is one of the wonders of the *karnataka* music tradition.

The Drummer's Art

Until now we have concentrated on the melodic aspect of *karnataka* music. But drumming in India is important not only in the texture of performance; it is fascinating, complicated, and exciting in itself as well. The *mridangam* drummer or other percussionists (on the *tavil* [drum], *morsang* [jew's-harp], *kanjira* [tambourine], or *ghatam* [clay pot] play in an improvisatory style based on hundreds or thousands of rhythmic patterns which they have memorized, absorbed, and stored in the memory of their brains and hands. In the "heat" of a performance the percussionist may use precomposed patterns, arranging them like a master of collage in predictable or unpredictable groupings. Or he may create entirely new groupings or patterns, spontaneous, yet within the limits and grammar of his rhythmic language (see ill. 6–13).

At the basis of the *mridangam* drummer's art are between fifteen and seventeen drum-strokes—distinctive individual tones produced on different parts of the drumheads by different finger combinations or parts of the hands. These strokes, individually and when put together into rhythmic patterns, can be expressed in *solkattu*, spoken syllables that imitate the sound of the drum-stroke and precisely duplicate each rhythmic pattern. Normally spoken *solkattus* are used only in learning and practice, but there is also a tradition in South India to recite *solkattu* as part of a concert performance.

Simplifying greatly, we might map out the various levels of the South Indian drummer's art, beginning with the microcosm of the individual drumstrokes and ending with the macrocosm of an entire performance-segment accompaniment or a percussion solo (called a *tani avartanam*); see example 6–10.

Now listen one more time to the performance segment (recorded selection 37) of *veena* and *mridangam*. This time focus on David Nelson's drumming. Like the melodic soloist, the South Indian drummer (and his accompanying percussionists, if any) follows a kind of "map" of procedures. At times he may simply keep time, keep *tala*. Or he may "shadow" or reflect the subtle rhythms

Ill. 6–13.   *Drummers in a religious procession in Madras. Even folk musicians such as these play rhythmic patterns of great complexity.*

and phrases of the melodic soloist. A good drummer knows the repertoire of songs in the *karnataka* tradition, he knows their flow and feeling, and he shapes his accompaniment to what we might call "the rhythmic essence" of each song.

The drummer emerges from the background during pauses or long-held notes in the melody; he also emerges at cadential points, marking the endings and "joints" of sections (as we have seen) with his formulaic *mora* (ending) or cadential patterns with their threefold repetitions. And if an improvising melodic soloist pops into a formulaic pattern, an alert drummer is quick to recognize the pattern, duplicate it with an ornamental drum version, and carry it to the end.

It is important to remember that the South Indian percussionist (like the

LEVEL I:

Basic drumstrokes and sound on the *mridangam*—2 or 3 for the left hand, about 14 for the right hand and fingers.

ta - di - tom - nam - etc.

LEVEL 2:

Tiny cell-like rhythmic patterns, such as:

connected with various stroke arrangements:

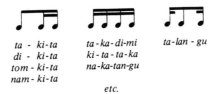

ta - ki-ta	ta-ka-di-mi	ta-lan - gu
di - ki-ta	ki-ta-ta-ka	
tom-ki-ta	na-ka-tan-gu	
nam- ki-ta		
	etc.	

LEVEL 3:

Brief rhythmic patterns of several (or more) beats built from combinations of rhythmic cells, like:

na-ka-tan-gu   ki - ta - ta-ka

or:

din - ta-din - ta - ta-din - ta - ta-din - ta - ki - ta

LEVEL 4:

Longer strings of rhythmic pattern combinations, and *moras* (3-times-repeated ending formula) like:

di - tan - ki - ta   na-ka-tan-gu   ki - ta-ta-ka   tom- -

tan-gu   ki - ta-ta-ka   tom- -

tan-gu   ki - ta-ta-ka   tom-   (x 3)

(The above *mora* pattern repeated three times fits 16 beats, 2 cycles of *adi tala* (4 + 2 + 2 = 8 x 2). If done right, the final *"tom"* should come on the downbeat of the 17th beat.)

Ex. 6–10. *Map of South Indian drummer's art.*

LEVEL 5:

Large sections improvised/composed/arranged on the spot, or pre-planned/pre-composed/memorized. One such larger pre-composed section in *Adi tala (4 + 2 + 2 =)* is given below:

Adi tala

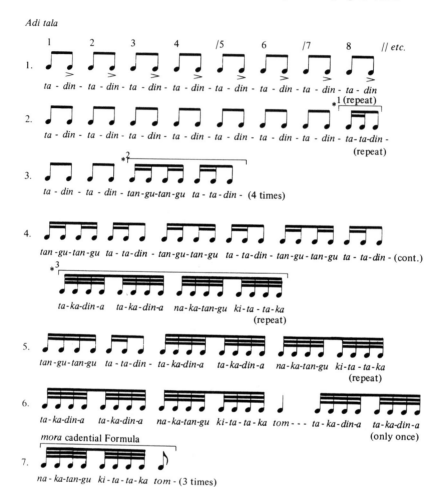

We can learn a number of things about South Indian drumming from the above exercise complicated though it seems, taken from the elementary lessons for drum students. First, changes or variations are added gradually to repetitions of familiar materials. Notice how the new elements (marked *¹, *², and *³) are tacked on to the ends of the repeating rhythmic patterns.

Second, different speeds of patterns are used structurally. Notice in our example how the ♩♪'s are replaced by patterns of ♫♫♫'s and then ♫♫♫'s. Often the same rhythmic pattern will be played at double-time or triple-time (or it will be slowed down to half-time) giving it in essence "a new face."

Ex. 6–10. *(Continued)*

Third, try fitting the exercise into *Adi tala* (4 + 2 + 2 = 8) time cycles (with the beat = ♩). You will find that as the patterns progress they begin to shift and pull against the clockwork regularity of the *tala* cycles. This pull is called "counter-rhythm" or "cross-rhythm" and it is one of the essentials of Indian drumming. There is a constant working away from, a contradicting of, the beat and/or the *tala* cycle.

Finally, you will notice that the exercise—like all larger sections—ends with a *mora*, a cadential formula repeated three times. If you have counted correctly the last "*tom*" of the *mora* (on the third repetition) will come on a downbeat of a *tala* cycle.

LEVEL 6:

Accompaniment of a *kriti* or of an entire performance segment. Improvisation of a *tani avartanam* (percussion solo.)

Ex. 6–10. *(Continued)*

melodic soloist) is not merely "playing off the top of his head." Through years of training and study and listening his brain is, in a sense, preprogrammed with hundreds of building blocks, formulas, and possibilities of larger combinations. He is also calculating constantly, like a master mathematician, how his formulas and patterns of asymmetrical lengths will fit into or against the *tala* cycles, how they will come out right at the end (on the downbeat of the *tala* cycle or the beginning of a song melody line).

But the drummer is much, much more than a manipulator, merely shifting around and arranging pieces of an invisible rhythmic jigsaw puzzle. Rather, *he is creating within a system.* And in the process he may compose variations, superimpose (sometimes) startling juxtapositions, flow from easy time keeping to mind-boggling complicated patterns or sections, stop for meaningful pauses (and start again), support a melodic soloist (or work cleverly against him), or stamp out the identity of cadences—the "joints" and endings of sections of compositions.

Though we have only touched the surface of the drummer's art, we can begin to appreciate what must be a rhythmic system as complicated as any in the world, a system that balances beautifully with the complexities of melody seen in the *ragas.* As an old Sanskrit verse says:

श्रुतिर्मता लयः पिता

Sruti marta layah pita
"Melody is the mother, rhythm is the father."
(after P. Sambamoorthy)

INSTRUMENT BUILDING AND
PERFORMANCE

We are by now familiar with much of the sound-world of *karnataka* music. We have taken a brief glance into its environment and history, we have traced a musician's day in the city of Madras, we have listened to snippets of various types of nonclassical music, and we have explored one performance—in the classical tradition—in all its intricacies. But listening, observing, rationalizing about, untangling concepts expressed in words on a page, looking at them from the outside, can carry us only so far. To begin really to understand a musical culture we must bring the music into ourselves, into our own imaginations, into our voices, and into our hands.

What music really is (we all know) is something of a mystery. It transcends the metaphors of words and analysis. It moves in the beautiful but invisible world of feeling and human expressivity. In India this expression, this magical transference of sound into feeling, into human emotion, is called *bhava*. Without it, music—no matter how proficient technically—is considered to lack life, to lack warmth, to lack "a heart."

The instruments that we shall make or adapt cannot, of course, compare with the exquisitely crafted instruments of an Indian artisan utilizing the skills passed down for generations and a lifetime of experience. We should not expect them to. Rather, our instruments—like the many folk instruments of India—will be functional: they can make the music we want to make on them. And they can teach us.

Similarly, our performances cannot compare with those of *karnataka* musicians who have undergone years of exacting training and apprenticeship and who have grown up in the tradition. Still, our own involvement will help us gain some insight into the way a performance in South Indian classical music works; it will give us first-hand contact with some of the techniques and skills contained in the musician's tool kit, with *ragas*, with improvisational and compositional forms, in short, *with the music itself*, how it flows and how it feels.

Instrument Building

For the accompaniment of singing you will need an instrument to provide a background of *sruti* (drone). For instrumental performance you will need an instrument capable of providing both a single-line melody and a *sruti*.

For either purpose a guitar (or banjo, or other stringed instrument)* may be adapted. Simply retune the guitar so that all the strings are either on the tonal center (*sa*) or on the perfect fifth (*pa*) (ex. 6–11). Most music shops carry an adapter (costing a few dollars), which raises the strings of an ordinary guitar, making it more suitable for slide or "bottle-neck" guitar. You can also buy (or make—see page 151) a slide to use with a guitar or with the instrument you make.

---

* A violin or other fretless bowed or plucked instrument may also be used.

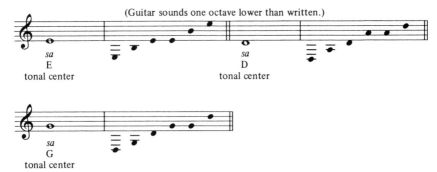

Ex. 6–11. *Retuned guitar for sruti (drone).*

Making a Slide Veena (fig. 6–13)

Materials needed:
  a piece of wood 2½ to 3 feet in length (1 × or 1 × 4)
  a piece of wood (1 × 1 or 1 × 2) the same length
  2 plastic gallon apple cider or milk jugs (or other, similar resonators)
  about 1 foot of corner molding
  4 to 6 guitar or banjo machine-heads
  4 to 6 guitar strings (D, G, B, and several E strings)
  4 to 6 beads or washers
Tools needed:
  hammer and a variety of small nails
  drill (hand or electric) with a variety of bits, one at least as large as the rod of
    the machine-heads
  Elmer's, Weldwood, or Hyde glue
  C-clamps
  (a chisel and a rat-tail file, if necessary, for the fitting of the machine-heads)

Playing Technique

Place your *veena* in front of you on the floor or on a table (fig. 6–14). Pluck or strum with the fingers of the right hand. In the left hand slide a bought slide, a small cylindrical glass bottle, a piece of metal tubing, or the back of a knife blade or handle to achieve different notes. Be sure to damp the nonsounding part of the string with the side of your hand holding the slide to prevent unwanted sounds.

The drone strings will always be played as open strings. You will touch the slide only to one or the other of the two playing strings.

Practice playing notes on your instrument, alternating them with occasional strums of the drone strings. Try playing various *gamakas* (ornaments): sliding from one tone to another, oscillating between two tones, or putting a heavy vibrato on a tone. After you have developed some mastery of the playing tech-

STEP 1

In the center of either end of what will be the underside of the neck/fingerboard (the 1 x 3, or 1 x 4):

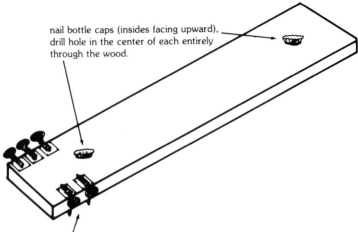

nail bottle caps (insides facing upward), drill hole in the center of each entirely through the wood.

Drill holes for and nail in guitar machine-heads. You may need to enlarge the holes with a rat-tail file, and do some chiseling to make insertion of the playing strings possible.

STEP 2

On the underside of the neck/fingerboard:

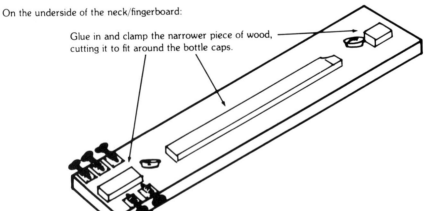

Glue in and clamp the narrower piece of wood, cutting it to fit around the bottle caps.

This is for added strength.

Fig. 6–13. *Steps in making a slide veena.*

STEP 3

Cut 2 bridges from the corner molding.
Make them the width of your neck/fingerboard.
Add a tiny notch to hold each string.

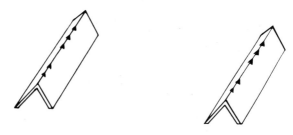

STEP 4

Install the strings.

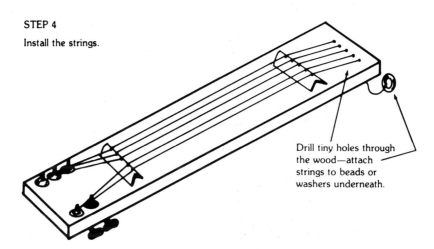

Drill tiny holes through
the wood—attach
strings to beads or
washers underneath.

Two possibilities for string size:

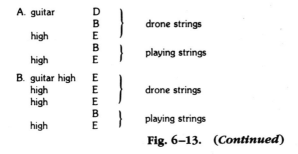

A. guitar   D
           B   }   drone strings
  high   E
           B   }   playing strings
  high   E

B. guitar high   E
  high   E   }   drone strings
  high   E
             B   }   playing strings
  high   E

Fig. 6–13. *(Continued)*

In the case of possibility B, attach 2 screws long (high) enough to hold the tension of the 2nd & 3rd drone strings in the following way:

1/3 length of string from the left (that is, between the bridges
1/2 length of string

STEP 5

Tune the strings, as follows:

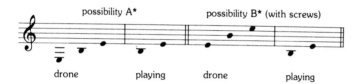

*Or an equivalent transposed tuning.

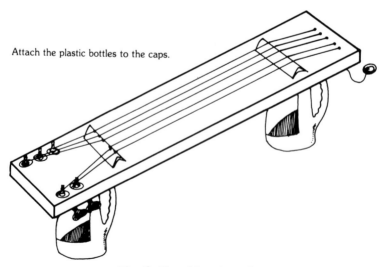

Attach the plastic bottles to the caps.

Fig. 6–13. (*Continued*)

STEP 6

Mark the chromatic scale with a colored felt-tipped pen on the wood underneath the playing strings, left to right.

You will want to make additional markings (in a different color or removable) to show where the notes of your *raga* lie on the fingerboard.

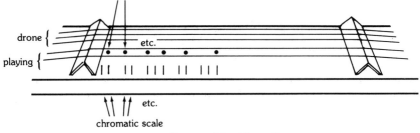

Fig. 6–13.   (*Continued*)

nique of your instrument, you are ready to apply yourself to the lessons that follow.

INVENTING A RAGA

Each *raga* (expressive mode)—"that which colors the mind"—is built from a complex combination of elements that combine to produce a unique musical personality. In this section we shall look at some general characteristics of *ragas* in the South Indian tradition.

Scales

The Melakarta System

The *melakarta* system sets up seventy-two basic "parent" or "generative" scales. Each of these scales (or *melas*) has seven tones. The system is based on a

Fig. 6–14.   *Veena, playing position.*

gradual permutation of the tones of the chromatic scale, each parent scale arranged (and numbered) in a logical order. We can simplify the system as shown in figure 6–15 (as before, all examples are shown with a tonal center of C; the tonal center may be transposed to any pitch).

Try discovering some of the seventy-two possible parent scales of the *melakarta* system. Simply read figure 6–15 from left to right following the grid of possible channels. Once you find several scales that you like, try improvising in them; get familiar with their sound and explore their possibilities.

Janya (Derived) Ragas

The *melakarta* scales are still only scales; they do not have the fully developed musical personality that would make them into *ragas*.

A *melakarta raga* is a seven-note *raga* whose ascending and descending scales (in regular order) are the same as the parent *melakarta*. The addition of ornaments, special intonation, and characteristic melodic turns and phrases gives it a complete musical personality.

By contrast, *janya* (derived) *ragas*, though descended from parent *melakarta* scales, differ from them in one of the following ways:

1. *Varja ragas* omit some notes in ascent or descent (the scales of *ragas* may be the same going up and coming down, or they may differ!). One may have any combination of seven-, six-, or five-note scales; see example 6–12.

Try inventing some *varja raga* scales, omitting notes from the parent *melakarta* in ascent or descent (or both).

2. *Vakra ragas* take a zigzag melodic movement either in ascent or descent, or both (see ex. 6–13).

Try your hand at inventing several *vakra* (zigzag) *raga* scales.

Fig. 6–15. *Melakarta system showing raga scales.*

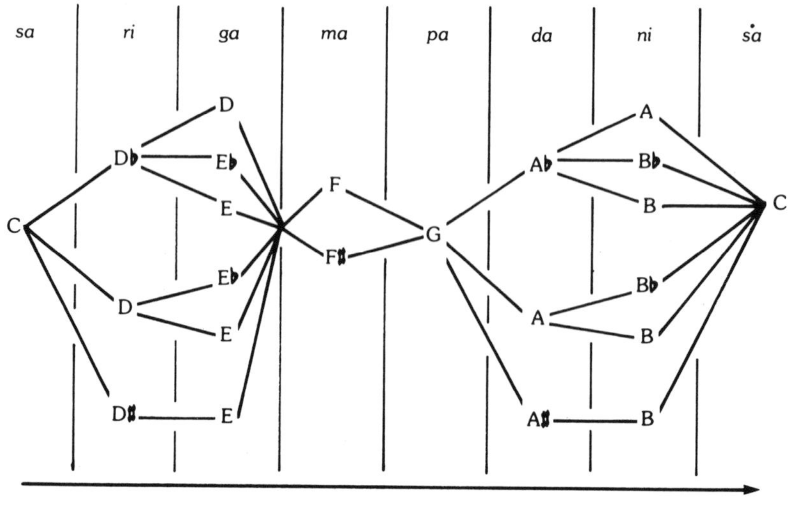

Ex. 6–12.   ***Some varja ragas, with parent scales.***

3. *Bhashanga ragas* can have a "visiting note," an accidental note belonging to the parent scale from which it is derived. The visiting note usually does not occur often, but usually appears in special places or within special musical phrases (see ex. 6–14).

Again, try inventing a *raga* scale with a visiting note.

Finally, a *raga* scale may combine all of the above possibilities: a single *raga* could be *varja* (omitted notes), *vakra* (zigzag), and *bhashanga* (visiting notes) at the same time.

Tones

One of the popular myths about Indian music is that is based on scales of microtones, "intervals in the cracks of a piano keyboard." We have just seen that

Ex. 6–13.   ***Some vakra ragas, with parent scales.***

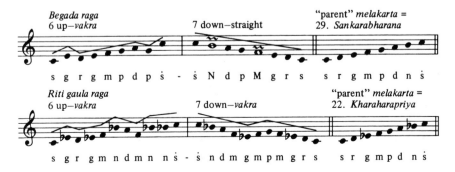

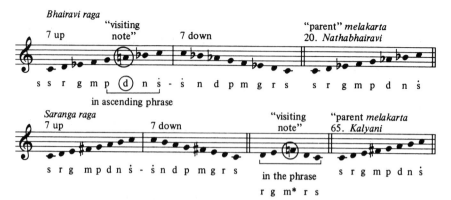

Ex. 6–14. *Some bhashanga ragas, with parent scales.*

raga scales usually have a maximum of seven notes, and often have fewer. The microtones in Indian music, then, have less to do with the scale itself than with the fine tuning of individual tones in the scale.

We have also noted earlier how each tone may be performed with all kinds of little things happening in it: subtle twists and turns, slides, oscillations, and touches of other notes. This *gamaka* (ornamentation) is essential to the "musical personality" of the *raga*. As an ancient sage and theorist, Bharata, has written:

> *Music without gamaka*
> *Is like a moonless night,*
> *A river without water,*
> *A vine without flowers,*
> *And a lady without jewelry.*

> *[After P. Sambamoorthy]*

Within a given *raga* the *gamaka* is not rigid. Each tone may be ornamented in a variety of ways depending upon the musical context or the mood or invention of the performer (staying within, of course, a range of possibilities proper for a specific *raga*).

Contrasting with *gamaka* are tones (often *sa* [the tonal center] or *pa* [the fifth]) that are sung or played plainly, without any vibrato or oscillation whatsoever.

Finally, the tones in a *raga* may exist in a kind of hierarchy. There are important tones that seem to exert a "gravitational pull" on other notes which rotate around them almost like the sun, planets, moons, and asteroids of a solar system. Earlier we called these important tones "pillar tones." Indian theory classifies tones in the following way:

jiva svara: the mystical "life-note" of a *raga*.

amsa svara: the predominant note, resting note.

raga chhaya svara: the "shadow note" that reveals the individuality of a *raga*.

dirgha svara: a note that can be held for a long time, emphasized.

alpatva svara: a very unimportant note that must be only lightly touched, or passed over.

Many of the above categories are interchangeable, and the same tone in a *raga* could fall into several categories.

Try adding more subtle characteristics to certain tones in your *raga* scale: intonation, *gamaka*, and a hierarchy of pillar tones and lesser notes. Search especially for a *jiva svara*, a "life-note," which in its uniqueness captures the essence of your *raga*.

Phrases

A large part of the "musical personality" of a *raga* (its *svarupa*, "own image") is made up of a collection of characteristic phrases, as recognizable as the face or particular way of walking (or talking) of a human being. Just as in people, there are *ragas* that are powerful, deep, and complicated (with many phrase possibilities) and there are *ragas* that are simple and straightforward (with fewer phrase possibilities). And there are also *ragas* that are highly eccentric "oddballs."

Especially characteristic phrases are classified as

ranjaka: "sweet," the musical equivalent of a dish of ice cream.

chaya: "shadowing" the inner essence of the *raga*.

rakti: "charming," "especially pleasing."

visesha: "unusual," used only several times in a performance.

Besides the special phrases, there are the workaday phrases that move up and down through the scale and ornamented notes of the *raga*, that is, through the rules and the labyrinth of possibilities set by our musical game.

In general, the phrases of Indian music tend to work within limited pitch areas and to rotate around the *raga's* pillar tones. They tend not to have the neatly balanced boxlike phrase shapes of Western classical and folk music. Rather, the melodic phrases in Indian classical music can be angular and asymmetrical, or spin out seemingly endlessly like the thread on a weaver's loom. They can rest and balance on a single tone, or explore the infinite possibilities of two or three tones subtly varied. Or they can dart like insects or butterflies, or explode into sudden fireworks. But here we are talking as much about style as about *raga*.

Explore your own *raga*(s). Try to discover what seem to be "sweet" or important musical phrases. Make a catalog of them.

Psycho-Acoustics

On the one hand (I am sure we will all agree by now) *ragas* are a complex technical musical machinery with many "rules" and "moves." But in our original definition, "a *raga* is that which colors the mind." A *raga* then—beyond its technical characteristics, like a human being beyond his or her appearance and anatomy—is a mystical expressive force, a "something beautiful" creating emotional response.

There are many stories about the power of *ragas*. It is said that *Deepak raga* ("lamp"), performed by exceptional musicians, can light the wicks of lamps or cause heat and fire; *raga Megha* ("cloud") can bring rain; *raga Vasanta* ("spring") can bring a cooling breeze; or *Nagavarali raga* ("most excellent snake") can charm cobras (see ills. 6–14, 6–15).

Theoretical works of the Middle Ages consistently assign *ragas* to times of the day when it is most appropriate to perform them. The eight watches of the day were

1. Early morning (before light and dawn)
2. Sunrise
3. Morning
4. Noontide (midday)
5. Afternoon
6. Sunset
7. Early evening
8. Nocturnal (late night)

Example 6–15 shows the scales of two *karnataka ragas* associated with a time of day. Try performing them during their "proper hour."

The old texts also assigned *ragas* to the six seasons of the Indian climate: winter, spring, summer, rainy season, autumn, and early winter. Especially important (musically, and in poetry and painting) is spring, with its festivals of renewal and the blossoming of flowering trees, the return of tropical birds, and the erotic buzzing of bees. Summer, the hot season, comes in April and May. Intolerable heat (up to 120 degrees Fahrenheit) scorches trees and fields, and brings human activity to a standstill. But the coming of the monsoon in June with its billowing clouds and torrential rains changes everything almost overnight. The temperature drops 20 or 30 degrees, the earth turns green again, crops are planted, human activity begins anew. The rainy season is connected with the "storms" of human passion and love, and thus finds echoes in poetry, painting, and in *ragas*.

Try performing within the scales of the two *ragas* given in example 6–16 associating them, in your mind with the appropriate seasons.

Many of the beautiful *ragamalas*—miniature paintings of *ragas*—take advantage of the imagery offered by seasonal connections: the lush, blooming foliage of spring surrounding beautiful women in colorful *saris*, for example, or lovers reclining in a palace chamber while outside the rain pours from billowing black clouds cut by jagged bursts of lightning.

Finally, *ragas* have been attached to specific emotions—the nine *rasas*, or "sentiments." The word *rasa* literally means extract or juice, flavor; in fact, one can go into a South Indian restaurant and order *rasam*, a hot, spicy soup! The most important modes associated with music are

Ill. 6–14. *A raga painting depicting Raga Vasanta (Spring). Here the God Krishna, renowned for his flute-playing, and his female accompanists celebrate the joys of Spring.*

love (in all its aspects)
sadness, loneliness
strength, heroism
peace, tranquillity

Ill. 6–15. *An itinerant snake-charmer, R. Vedan, plays the punji, an instrument traditionally associated with the charming of snakes, in this case a python.*

(The other *rasas* are wonder, horror, the comic, disgust, and anger.)

Two other moods often believed to be expressed in music are

bhakti (pure, religious devotion)

gana rasa (abstract aesthetic enjoyment)

Now, see if the *ragas* you have been building seem to express a time of day, a season, or an emotion or mood. Choose a name for your *raga*(s).

Ex. 6–15. *Scales, Bauli and Nilambari ragas.*

By now you will have nearly concluded inventing a *raga*. Here again are the factors you must take into consideration:

1. *melakarta*: "parent" scales
2. *janya*: "derived" scale
    a. *varja*: five, six, or seven notes up
        five, six, or seven notes down
    b. *vakra*: zigzag scale up and/or down
    c. *bhashanga*: "visiting note(s)" not belonging to the parent *melakarta*
3. tones: intonation, *gamakas* (slides, vibratos, oscillations, turns, mordents, grace-notes, and so forth), pillar tones, the *jiva svara* ("life note")
4. phrases: characteristic, sweet, or rare phrases
5. psychoacoustical properties: mood, time of day, season, magical qualities, and so on
6. name of *raga*.

Spend some time with your *raga*, singing or playing it, exploring its characteristics, working within its rules and moves until they become almost second nature. Get to know its "mystical expressive personality," its idiosyncrasies. Then you will be ready to try to shape a brief *alapana*.

Ex. 6–16. *Scales, Vasanta and Megha ragas.*

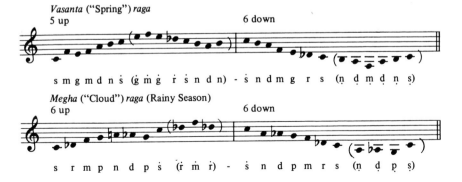

REFERENCES CITED

Isaac, L.
   1967   *Theory of Indian Music.* Madras: L. Isaac.
Peterson, Indira
   1979   Personal communication, song translation.
Mathew, P. George
   1989   Personal communication, song translation.
Raghavan, Ramnad V.
   1971   Personal communication, drumming lessons.
Rajeswari, S. B.
   1989   Personal communication, song translation.
Ramanujachari, C.
   1966   *The Spiritual Heritage of Tyagaraja* (Translations of songtexts by Tyagaraja.)
Reck, David B.
   1983   "A Musician's Toolkit: A Study of Five Performances by Thirugokarnam Ramachandra Iyer." Ph. D. diss., Wesleyan University.
Sambamoorthy, P.
   1963   *South Indian Music*, Book IV. Madras: Indian Music Publishing House.

———

   1964   *South Indian Music*, book III. Madras: Indian Music Publishing House.
Viswanathan, T.
   1975   "Raga Alapana in South Indian Music." Ph.D. diss., Wesleyan University.

CLASSROOM RESOURCES

Kumar, Kanthimathi, and Jean Stackhouse
   1988   *Classical Music of South India: Karnatic Tradition in Western Notation.* Stuyvesant, N.Y.: Pendragon Press. (Beginning lessons and simple songs with free translations of song texts.)
Nelson, David
   1989   *Madras Music Videos.* (Videotapes of concert performances of South Indian music.) Available from D. Nelson, 340 Westhampton Road, Northampton, Mass. 01060.
Viswanathan, T. (with David Reck)
   1990   *The Music of South India: A Classroom Work-Kit.* (Text with cassette tape) Available from Ganesh Publishers, P.O. Box 475, Amherst, Mass. 01004.

ADDITIONAL READING

Basham, A. L.
   1959   *The Wonder That Was India.* New York: Grove Press.
Brown, Robert E.
   1971   "India's Music" in *Readings in Ethnomusicology*, edited by David P. McAllester, 192–329. New York: Johnson Reprint.

Edwardes, Michael
   1970   *A History of India.* New York: Universal Library.
Lanmoy, Richard
   1971   *The Speaking Tree: A Study of Indian Culture and Society.* New York: Oxford.
Shankar, Ravi
   1968   *My Music, My Life.* New York: Simon and Schuster.
Wade, Bonnie
   1988   *Music of India: The Classical Traditions.* Riverdale, Md.: Riverdale Co.

ADDITIONAL LISTENING

Write to the sources listed below for catalogues.

The World Music Institute, Inc., 109 West 27th Street, Room 9C, New York, N.Y. 10001, has an extensive catalogue of Indian (and world) music, including most of the recordings listed below.

Another resource is Earth Music, P.O. Box 2103, Norwalk, Conn. 06852.

Nonesuch (Explorer Series) CD and phonograph recordings: performances by T. Visvanathan (flute), K. V. Narayanaswamy (vocal), Ramnad Krishnan (vocal), Ram Narayan (*sarangi*) and others with excellent notes.

Folkways (ethnic series) field recordings of folk music.

The French labels CBS and Ocora (available from the above sources) offer excellent recordings of Indian folk and classical music.

Oriental Records, Inc., P.O. Box 1902, Grand Central Station, New York, N.Y. 10017. Compact discs, phonograph recordings, and cassettes. Recommended performances include those by Alathur Srinivasa Iyer (vocal), T. N. Krishnan (violin), Namagiripettai Krishnan (*nadhaswaram*) and *karnataka* music performed on saxophone, mandolin, *jalatharangam* (porcelain bowls), and guitar. North Indian music by Ravi Shankar (*sitar*), Ali Akbar Khan (*sarod*), Hariprasad Chaurasia (flute), Nikhil Bannerjee (*sitar*), Shivkumar Sharma (*santoor*), Parween Sultana (vocal), and others.

Ravi Shankar Music Circle, 7911, Willoughby Avenue, Los Angeles, Calif. 90046. CDs, L.P.s, and cassettes by many of the top performers of Indian classical music. Besides those noted above are Lakshmi Shankar (vocal), Imrat Khan (*surbahar* [bass *sitar*]), L. Subramanian (violin), U. Srinivas (mandolin), T. Viswanathan (flute), S. Balachander (*veena*), and an anthology of South Indian music. Many are reprints of out-of-print recordings from the 1960s. Also available are some innovative experiments using synthesizers, jazz, and unusual instrumental combinations.

Indian grocery stores often carry cassettes of Hindi or regional pop music; many also offer video rental of Indian movies, some with subtitles. Ask the clerk for recommendations.

S E V E N

◆ ◆ ◆

Asia/Indonesia

R. ANDERSON SUTTON

Indonesia is a country justly proud of its great cultural diversity. Nowhere is this diversity more evident than in the stunning variety of musical and related performing arts found throughout its several thousand populated islands. Known formerly as the Dutch East Indies, Indonesia is one of many modern nations whose boundaries were formed during the centuries of European colonial domination, placing peoples with contrasting languages, arts, systems of belief, and conceptions of the world under a single rule. The adoption of a national language in the early twentieth century was a crucial step in building the unity necessary to win a revolution against the Dutch (1945–49). More recently, a pan-Indonesian popular culture is contributing to an increased sense of national unity, particularly among the younger generation. Nevertheless, though we can identify some general cultural traits, including musical ones, shared by many peoples of Indonesia, it is problematic to speak of an "Indonesian" culture, or an "Indonesian" style of music. Regional diversity is still very much in evidence.

Most Indonesians' first language is not the national language (Indonesian), but instead one of the more than two hundred separate languages found throughout this vast archipelago. And though many Indonesians are familiar with the sounds of Indonesian pop music and such Western stars as Michael Jackson, Sting, and Bruce Springsteen, they also know, to a greater or lesser extent, their own regional musical traditional. Many kinds of music exist side by side in Indonesia, in a complex pluralism that reflects both the diversity of the native population and the receptiveness of that population to centuries of outside influence. Indonesia is, then, a country that can truly be said to be home to worlds of music.

What sort of impressions might you first have of this country? You would probably arrive in the nation's capital, Jakarta, a teeming metropolis of about eight million people—some very wealthy, most rather poor. Jakarta is near the western end of the north coast of Java, Indonesia's most heavily populated (but not largest) island (see fig. 7–1). The mix of Indonesia's many cultures is nowhere more fully realized than in this special city. Many kinds of music are heard here. Western-style night clubs and discos do a lively business until the early hours of the morning. Javanese *gamelan* (percussion ensemble) music accompanies nightly performances of *wayang orang* theatre (an elaborate type of dance-drama from central Java). You might also run across Jakarta's own

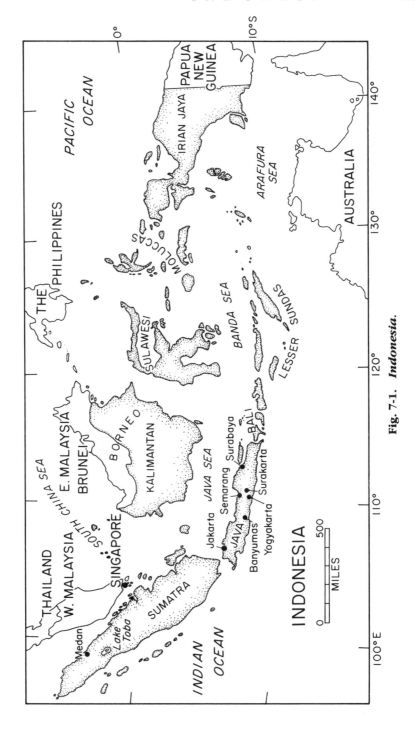

Fig. 7-1. *Indonesia.*

gambang-kromong (small percussion ensemble), and perhaps a troupe from Bali, Sumatra, or any of the many other islands performing traditional music and dance at the national arts center Taman Ismael Marzuki. Once you get your bearings, learn to bargain for taxis or motorized pedicabs, and develop a taste for highly seasoned food, you can get a sense of Indonesia's many cultures by roaming this complex city. But much of what you encounter here has stronger roots in the various regions from which it has been derived.

CENTRAL JAVA

Java is an island of just less than 50,000 square miles—very nearly the size of Czechoslovakia or New York state and slightly smaller than Nepal. With close to 100 million people, it is one of the most densely populated regions in the world. (Indonesia's total population is about 170 million.) Most of the central and eastern two thirds of the island is inhabited by Indonesia's largest ethnic group, the Javanese, 60 to 70 million people who share a common language and other cultural traits, including music, though some local differences persist. In the western third of the island live the Sundanese, whose language and arts are distinct from those of the Javanese. Despite its dense population, Java remains mostly a farming society, with wet-rice agriculture as the predominant source of livelihood. While most Javanese profess to be Muslim, only a small percentage follow orthodox practice. More adhere to a syncretic blend of Islam with Hinduism and Buddhism (introduced in Java over one thousand years ago), and with what most scholars believe to be a still earlier layer of belief in benevolent and mischievous spirits and in ancestor veneration. The world view that embraces these many layers of believe is often referred to as *kejawèn*—literally, *Javanese*, or *Javaneseness*, a term that indicates its importance in Javanese self-conception.

From Jakarta a twelve-hour ride on bus or train through shimmering wet-rice fields, set in the plains between gracefully sloping volcanic mountains, leads to Yogyakarta (often abbreviated to "Yogya" and pronounced "Jogja"), one of two court cities in the cultural heartland of Central Java. The other, less than fifty miles to the northeast, is Surakarta (usually known as "Solo"). Most Javanese point to these two cities as the cultural centers where traditional *gamelan* music and related performing arts have flourished in their most elaborate and refined forms. These courtly developments are contrasted with the rougher styles associated with the villages and outlying districts.

Yogya is a sprawling city with a population of about 350,000. It has few buildings taller than two stories. Away from the several major streets lined with stores flashing neon signs and blaring loudly amplified popular music, Yogya is in many ways like a dense collection of villages. Yet at its center is one of Java's two major royal courts (*kraton*), official home of the tenth sultan (His Highness Hamengku Buwana X). Unlike any Western palace or court, the *kraton* is a complex of small buildings and open pavilions, appropriate for the warm, tropical climate. Its design is not merely for comfort, however. The *kraton* is endowed with mystical significance as an earthly symbol of the macrocosmos, the ordered universe, with orientation to the cardinal directions. And the ruler, whose residence is located at the very center of the *kraton*, is, like the Hindu-Javanese kings of many centuries ago, imbued with divine powers.

In many of these pavilions are kept the court *gamelan* ensembles. Some date back many centuries and are used only for rare ritual occasions; others were built or augmented more recently and are used more frequently. Most of these, like other treasured heirlooms belonging to the court, are believed to contain special powers and are shown respect and given offerings. Also kept in the palace are numerous sets of finely carved and painted *wayang kulit* (shadow puppets made of water buffalo hide) used in all-night performances of highly sophisticated and entertaining shadow plays. Classical Javanese dance, with *gamelan* accompaniment, is rehearsed regularly and performed for special palace functions.

Though the *kraton* is still regarded as a cultural center, it is far less active now than it was prior to World War II (during which the Japanese occupied Indonesia). Much activity in the traditional Javanese arts is to be found outside the court, sponsored by private individuals and also by such modern institutions as the national radio station and public schools and colleges. In the rural villages, which long served as a source and inspiration for the more refined courtly arts, a variety of musical and related performing arts continue to play a vital role in Javanese life.

Gamelan

The word *gamelan* refers to a set of instruments unified by their tuning and often by their decorative carving and painting (see ill. 7–1). Most *gamelan*s consist of several kinds of metal slab instruments (similar in some ways to the Western vibraphone) and tuned knobbed gongs. The word *gong* itself is one of the very few English words derived from Indonesian languages. (Two others are ketchup and amok.) In English, gong may refer to any variety of percussion instrument whose sound-producing vibrations are concentrated in the center of the instrument, rather than the edge, like a bell. In Javanese it refers specifically to the larger hanging knobbed gongs in *gamelan* ensembles and is part of a family of words relating to largeness, greatness, and grandeur—*agung* (great, kingly), *ageng* (large), and *gunung* (mountain). In addition to gongs and other metal instruments, a *gamelan* ensemble normally has at least one drum and may have other kinds of instruments: winds, strings, and wooden percussion instruments (xylophones).

Some ancient ceremonial *gamelan*s have only a few knobbed gongs and one or two drums. The kind of *gamelan* most often used in central Java today is a large set, comprising instruments ranging from deep booming gongs three feet

Ill. 7–1. *The gamelan Kyai Kanyut Mèsem ("Tempted to Smile") in the Mangkunegaran palace, Surakarta, Central Java. In foreground: gong ageng and gong siyem. (Photo courtesy of Arthur Durkee, Earth Visions Photographics.)*

in diameter to sets of high-pitched tuned gongs (gong-chimes) and slab instruments, with three drums, several bamboo flutes, zithers, xylophones, and a two-stringed fiddle.

Instruments in the present-day *gamelan* are tuned to one of two scale systems: *sléndro*, a five-tone system made up of nearly equidistant intervals, normally notated with the numerals 1, 2, 3, 5, and 6 (no 4); and *pélog*, a seven-tone system made up of large and small intervals, normally notated 1, 2, 3, 4, 5, 6, and 7. Some *gamelan* are entirely *sléndro*, others entire *pélog*, but many are actually double ensembles, combining a full set of instruments for each system. The two

Ex. 7–1. *Western scale and representative pélog and sléndro scales. Based on measurements of gamelan Mardiswara, Wasisto Surjodiningrat et. al., 1972:51–53.*

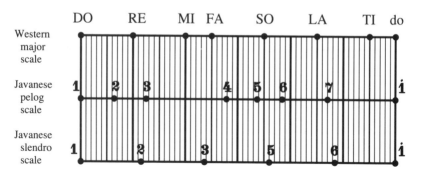

scale systems are incompatible and only in a few rare cases are they played simultaneously. The tones of neither of these scale systems can be replicated on a Western piano. Example 7–1 shows the chromatic intervals of Western music (the black and white keys of the piano) in comparison with sample intervals for one instance of *sléndro* and one of *pélog* (these are not entirely standardized, as I shall explain below).

The instrumentation of a full *sléndro-pélog gamelan* varies slightly but usually includes all or most of the instruments given in the list below. Most of these are illustrated in figure 7–2.

Knobbed Gong Instruments

GONG AGENG:	largest of the hanging gongs, suspended vertically from a wooden frame; one or two in each *gamelan*; often simply called *gong*; played with a round, padded beater.
SIYEM:	middle-sized hanging gong; usually from one to four in each *gamelan*; also called *gong suwukan*; played with a round, padded beater.
KEMPUL:	smallest hanging gong; from two to ten per *gamelan*; played with a round, padded beater.
KENONG:	largest of the kettle gongs, resting horizontally in a wooden frame; from two to twelve per *gamelan*; played with a padded stick beater.

Fig. 7–2.   *Central Javanese gamelan instruments. (Illustration by Peggy Choy.)*

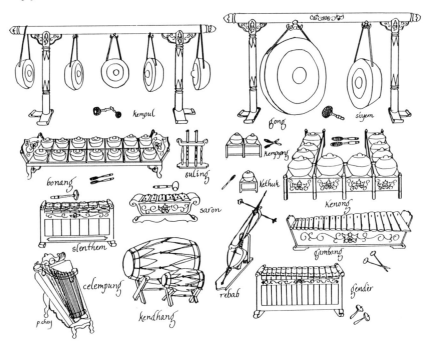

KETHUK: small kettle gong; one for each scale system; played with a padded stick beater.

KEMPYANG: set of two kettle gongs, smaller than *kethuk*; used only for *pélog*; played with two padded stick beaters.

BONANG BARUNG: set of ten, twelve, or fourteen kettle gongs resting horizontally in two parallel rows in a wooden frame; one set for each scale system; often simply called *bonang*; played with two padded stick beaters.

BONANG PANERUS: smaller member of the *bonang* family; same as *bonang barung* but tuned an octave higher; one for each scale system.

Metal Keyed Instruments

SARON DEMUNG: largest member of the *saron* (single-octave metallophone) family; six or seven thick metal keys resting over a trough resonator; usually one or two for each scale system; often simply called *demung*; played with a wooden mallet.

SARON BARUNG: like *saron demung*, but an octave higher; usually from two to four for each scale system; often simply called *saron*.

SARON PEKING: like *saron barung*, but an octave higher; often simply called *peking*.

GENDÈR SLENTHEM: six or seven thin metal keys suspended by strings over cylindrical resonators made of bamboo or metal; one for each scale system; often simply called *slenthem*; played with a padded disc beater.

GENDÈR BARUNG: thirteen or fourteen thin metal keys, suspended over cylindrical resonators; one for *sléndro*, two for *pélog*: *bem* (with tones 1, 2, 3, 5, and 6 in each octave) and *barang* (with tones 2, 3, 5, 6, and 7 in each octave); often simply called *gendèr*; played with two padded disc beaters.

GENDÈR PANERUS: like *gendèr barung*, but an octave higher.

Other Melodic Instruments

GAMBANG: seventeen to twenty-three wooden keys resting over a trough resonator; one for *sléndro*; one or two for *pélog* (if two, like *gendèr barung* and *gendèr panerus*; if only one, exchange keys enable player to arrange instrument for *bem*—with 1s— or for *barang*—with 7s); played with two padded disc beaters.

CELEMPUNG: zither, usually supported at about a thirty-degree angle by four legs, with twenty to twenty-six strings arranged in ten to thirteen "double courses" (as on a twelve-string guitar); one for *sléndro*, one or two for *pélog* (cf. *gambang*); plucked with thumb nails.

SITER:	smaller zither, resting on floor or in horizontal frame, with from ten to twenty-six strings in single or double courses; one for *sléndro*, one or two for *pélog* (cf. *gambang* and *celempung*); plucked with thumb nails.
SULING:	end-blown bamboo flute; one for *sléndro*, one or two for *pélog*.
REBAB:	two-stringed fiddle; one or two per *gamelan*.

Drums

KENDHANG GENDHING:	largest of the hand drums; two leather heads, laced onto a barrel-shaped shell; one per *gamelan*.
KENDHANG CIBLON:	middle-sized hand drum, like *kendhang gendhing*; often simply called *ciblon*.
KENDHANG KETIPUNG:	smallest hand drum, often simply called *ketipung*.
BEDHUG:	large stick-beaten drum; two leather heads, tacked onto a cylindrical shell; one per *gamelan*.

There is no standard arrangement of these instruments in the performance space, though almost without exception they are placed at right angles to one another, reflecting the Javanese concern with the cardinal directions (see ill. 7–2). Generally the larger gong instruments are in the back, with the *saron* family immediately in front of them, *bonang* family and *bedhug* drum to the sides, other melodic instruments in front, and the *kendhang* drums in the

Ill. 7–2. *Gamelan musicians in the Kraton Kasunanan (royal palace) in Surakarta, Central Java. In foreground: bonang (left) gendèr (right). (Photo courtesy of Arthur Durkee, Earth Visions Photographics.)*

center. The placement of the instruments reflects their relative loudness and their function in the performance of pieces, which I will discuss shortly.

The *gamelan* instruments are normally complemented by singers: a small male chorus (*gérong*) and female soloists (*pesindhèn*). Java also supports a highly developed tradition of unaccompanied vocal music (*tembang*), which serves as a major vehicle for Javanese poetry. In fact, the word *tembang* is best translated into English as "sung poetry." Although Javanese have recorded their *tembang* in several writing systems for over one thousand years, these are normally neither read silently nor read aloud in a speaking voice, but sung. Even important letters between members of the nobility were, until this century, composed as *tembang* and delivered as song. Though the postal system has eliminated this practice, vocal music, whether with *gamelan* or unaccompanied, enjoys great popularity in Java today.

The relation between vocal and instrumental orientations in *gamelan* music is reflected in the two major groupings of instruments in the present-day Javanese *gamelan*: "loud-playing" and "soft-playing." Historical evidence suggests that these two groupings were once separate ensembles and were combined as recently as the sixteenth or early seventeenth centuries. Loud-playing ensembles were associated with festivals, processions, and other noisy outdoor events, and were strictly instrumental. Soft-playing ensembles were intended for more intimate gatherings, often indoors, and involved singing. Even today, performance style distinguishes these two groupings. In loud-playing style, only the drums and louder metal instruments are used, as listed below in the column on the left. In soft-playing style, these instruments, or most of them, are played softly, and the voices and instruments listed below in the column on the right are featured.

Loud-Playing Instruments	*Soft-Playing Instruments*
gong agng	gendèr barung
siyem	gendèr panerus
kempul	gambang
kenong	celempung
kethuk	siter
kempyang	suling
bonang family	rebab
saron family	
slenthem	
kendhang family	
bedhug	

Gamelan Construction

Bronze is the preferred metal for *gamelan* manufacture, due both to its durability and to its rich, sweet sound quality. Brass and iron are also used, especially in rural areas. They are considerably cheaper than bronze, easier to tune, but less sonorous. Bronze *gamelan* instruments are forged (some cast in their basic shapes and then forged) in a long and difficult process. Though the metal worker in many societies occupies a low status, in Java he has traditionally been held in very high regard. The act of forging bronze instruments not only requires great skill but is also imbued with mystical significance. Working with metals, transforming molten copper and tin (the metals that make bronze alloy) into sound-producing instruments, is believed to make one especially vulnerable to dangerous forces in the spirit world. It is for this reason that the smiths make ritual preparation and may actually assume mythical identities during the forging process. The chief smith is ritually transformed into Panji, a powerful Javanese mythical hero, and the smith's assistants become Panji's family and servants (Kunst 1973:138).

The largest gongs may require a full month of labor and a truckload of coal for the forge that heats the metal. Only after appropriate meditation, prayer, fasting, and preparation of offerings does a smith undertake to make a large gong. The molten bronze is pounded, reheated, pounded, reheated, and gradually shaped into a large knobbed gong that may measure three feet or more in diameter. A false hit at any stage can crack the gong and the process must begin all over.

Gamelan Identity

A *gamelan*, particularly a bronze set with one or two fine large gongs, is often held in great respect, given a proper name, and given offerings on Thursday evenings (the beginning of the Muslim holy day). Though *gamelan* makers have recently begun to duplicate precise tuning and decorative designs, generally each *gamelan* is unique set, whose instruments would both look and sound out of place in another ensemble. Formerly, attempting even to copy the tuning and design of palace *gamelan* instruments was forbidden as these were reserved for the ruler and were directly associated with his power.

The variability in tuning from one *gamelan* to another is certainly not the result of a casual sense of pitch among Javanese musicians and *gamelan* makers. On the contrary, great care is taken in the making and in the occasional retuning of *gamelan* sets to arrive at a pleasing tuning—one that is seen to fit the particular physical condition of the instruments and the tastes of the individual owner. I spent one month with a tuner, his two assistants, and an expert musician as they gradually reached consensus on an agreeable tuning, and then altered the tuning of the many bronze gong and metal slab instruments through a long process of hammering and filing—all by hand. Bronze has the curious property of changing tuning—rather markedly during the first few years after forging, and more subtly over a period of twenty to thirty years, until it is finally "settled." It might seem that the lack of a standard tuning would be cause for musical chaos, but the actual latitude is rather small.

Gamelan Performance Contexts

Despite the changes wrought by modern institutions (formal musical instruction in schools and dissemination through the mass media) in the contexts of music making and the ways music is understood, Javanese music is more closely interrelated with other performing arts and more intimately bound to other aspects of life than are the arts in the West. "Concerts" of *gamelan* music simply do not occur, at least not in anything like the circumstances of a concert of Western classical music. The closest thing to a *gamelan "concert"* in Java is *uyon-uyon* (or *klenèngan*), but these are better understood as social events that involve *gamelan* music. They are usually held to commemorate a day of ritual importance, such as a birth, circumcision, or wedding. Normally a family sponsors such an event and invites neighbors and relatives, while others are welcome to look on and listen. The invited guests are served food and are expected to socialize freely through the duration of the event. No one expects the guests to be quiet during the performance of pieces or to pay rapt attention to them the way an audience does at a Western concert. Rather, the music, carefully played though it may be, is seen to contribute to the festiveness of the larger social event, helping to make it *ramé* (lively, busy in a positive way). Connoisseurs among the guests will ask for a favorite piece and may pay close attention to the way the ensemble or a particular singer or instrumentalist performs, but not to the exclusion of friendly interaction with the hosts and other guests. While the music is intended to entertain those present (without dance or drama), it also serves a ritual function, helping to maintain balance at important transitional points in the life of a person or community.

More often, *gamelan* music is performed as accompaniment for dance or theater—a refined female ensemble dance (*srimpi* or *bedhaya*), a flirtatious female solo dance (*gambyong*), a vigorous, martial lance dance (*lawung*), or an evening of drama based on Javanese legendary history (*kethoprak*), for example (see ills. 7–4, 7–5). A list of traditional genres currently performed in Central Java with *gamelan* accompaniment would be long. Some are presented primarily in commercial settings, with an audience buying tickets. Others are more often part of a ritual ceremony.

The genre held in the highest esteem by most Javanese, and nearly always reserved for ritual ceremony, is the shadow puppet theatre (*wayang kulit*), which dates back no less than one thousand years (see ill. 7–6). Beginning with an overture played on the *gamelan* during the early evening, shadow puppet performances normally last until dawn. With a screen stretched before him, lamp overhead, and puppets to both sides, one master puppeteer (*dhalang*) operates all the puppets, performs all the narration and dialogue, sings mood songs, and directs the musicians for a period of about eight hours, with no intermission.

The musicians do not play constantly throughout the evening, but must be ever-ready to respond to a signal from the puppeteer. He leads the musicians

Ill. 7–3. *Musicians playing the gamelan Kyai Kanyut Mèsem. Mangkunegaran palace, Surakarta, Central Java. In foreground: Sarons, kempul, and gongs on left; saron peking and bonangs on right. (Photo courtesy of Arthur Durkee, Earth Visions Photographics.)*

and accents the action of the drama through a variety of percussion patterns that he plays by hitting against the wooden puppet chest (*kothak*) to his left and by clanging metal plates (*kecrèk, kepyak*) suspended from the rim of the chest. If he is holding puppets in both hands, he uses his foot to sound these signals. He must be highly skilled as a manipulator, director, singer, and storyteller.

What the puppeteer delivers is not a fixed play written by a known playwright, but rather his own rendition of a basic story—usually closely related to versions performed by other puppeteers, but never exactly the same. It might be a well-known episode from the *Ramayana* or *Mahabharata*, epics of Indian origin that have been adapted and transformed in many parts of Southeast Asia and have been known in Java for one thousand years. The music is drawn from a large repertory of pieces, none specific to a single play and many of which are played in other contexts as well.

A good musician knows many hundreds of pieces, but the pieces, like the shadow plays, are generally not totally fixed. Many regional and individual variants exist for some pieces. More important, the very conception of what constitutes a *"gamelan* piece" or *"gamelan* composition" (in Javanese: *gendhing*) is different from the Western notion of musical pieces, particularly as that notion has developed in the Western art music or "classical" tradition.

Ill. 7–4.   *Dancers at Pujokusumuan in Yogyarkarta perform a srimpi, female court dance. (Photo by Peggy Choy.)*

Ill. 7–5.   *Dancers at the Pakualaman palace in Yogyakarta perform a bedhaya, female court dance (here with innovative costumes). (Photo courtesy of Arthur Durkee, Earth Vision Photographics.)*

Ill. 7–6.   *Puppeteer Ki Gondo Darman performing wayang kulit at the ASKI performing arts academy in Surakarta. (Photo courtesy of Arthur Durkee, Earth Vision Photographics.)*

Gamelan Music—A Javanese Gendhing in Performance

We can best begin to understand what a Javanese *gendhing* is by considering one in some detail—how it is conceived and how it is realized in performance. Listen to "Bubaran Kembang Pacar" on the accompanying cassette (selection 38). This is from a tape I made in a recording session in Yogya with some of the most highly regarded senior musicians associated with the court. It was played on a bronze *gamelan* at the house of one of Yogya's best known dancers and choreographers, Dr. Soedarsono, who founded the National Dance Academy (ASTI) in Yogya. You will note that it is an example of loud-playing style throughout. And you might have guessed that it is in the *pélog* scale system, with small and large intervals. It uses the *pélog bem* scale— tones 1, 2, 3, 5, and 6, with an occasional 4, but no 7. But what about its structure: How are the sounds organized in this piece—or, more precisely, this performance of this piece?

Unless they are connected directly to a previous piece in a medley sequence, Javanese *gendhing*s begin with a solo introduction, played on one instrument or sung by a solo singer. Here a short introduction (*buka*) is played on the *bonang barung* by the well-known teacher and musician Pak Sastrapustaka. During the latter portion, the *bonang* is joined by the two drums *kendhang gendhing* and *ketipung*, played (as is customary) by one drummer—in this case, the *kraton* (palace) musician Pak Kawindro. The drummer in the Javanese *gamelan* acts as a conductor, controlling the tempo and the dynamics (the relative levels of loudness and softness). He need not be visible to other musicians, since his "conducting" is accomplished purely through aural signals. He does not stand in front of the ensemble, but sits unobtrusively in the midst of it.

Although we discussed the choice of "Bubaran Kembang Pacar" at this recording session, experienced musicians recognize the identity of the *gendhing* from the introduction and do not need to be told what piece is about to be performed. The *bonang* player (or other musician providing an introduction) may simply play the introduction to an appropriate piece and expect the other musicians to follow. At the end of the introduction, most of the rest of the ensemble joins in, the large gong sounds, and the main body of the *gendhing* begins.

The structure of this main body is based on principles of balanced, binary (duple) subdivision and of cyclic repetition. The basic time and melodic unit in *gendhing* is the *gongan*, a phrase marked off by the sound of either the largest gong (*gong ageng*) or the slightly smaller gong *siyem*. For most *gendhing*s, these phrases are of regular length as measured in beats of the *balungan*, the melodic part usually played on the *slenthem* and the *saron* family—almost always some factor of two: 8 beats, 16 beats, 32 beats, 64 beats, 128 beats, 256 beats. (In the genre of pieces that serve as the staple for accompanying dramatic action, as we shall see below, *gongan*s are of irregular length and the regular unit is marked instead by the smaller gong *kempul*.) A *gongan* is subdivided into two or four shorter phrases by the *kenong*, and these further subdivided by *kempul*, *kethuk*, and in some lengthier pieces by *kempyang*.

The result is a pattern of interlocking percussion which repeats until an aural signal from the drummer or one of the lead melodic instruments (*bonang* in loud-playing style, *rebab* in soft-playing) directs the performers to end or to proceed to a different piece. Whereas in Western music composers must provide explicit directions for performers to repeat a section (usually by means of notated repeat signs), in Javanese *gamelan* performance repetition is assumed.

As we speak of "phrases" in describing music, borrowing the term from the realm of language, Javanese also liken the *gongan* to a sentence and conceive of the subdividing parts as "punctuation." For "Bubaran Kembang Pacar," after the gong stroke at the end of the introduction, the pattern of gong punctuation shown in ex. 7–2 is repeated throughout. The time distribution of these punctuating beats is even, but the degree of stress or weight is not (even though no beat is played louder than any other on any single instrument). Javanese listeners feel the progression of stress levels indicated in ex. 7–3, based on the levels of subdivision.

The strongest beat is the one coinciding with the largest and deepest sounding phrase marker, the *gong* (G), and with the *kenong* (N)—at the end of the phrase. Javanese would count this as one, two, three, **four**, etc., with the strongest beat being the sixteenth. This is the only beat where two punctuating gong instruments coincide. It is this "coincidence" which gives a sense of repose, a release of the rhythmic tension that builds through the course of the *gongan*.

Although in the West one may dismiss events as "mere coincidence," in Java the simultaneous occurrence of several events, the alignment of days of the week and dates (like our Friday the 13th), can be profoundly meaningful. It is not uncommon to determine a suitable day for a wedding, or for moving house, based on the coincidence of a certain day in the seven-day week with a certain day in the Javanese five-day market week, and this in turn within a certain Javanese month (in the lunar calendar rather than the solar calendar used in the West.) And the simultaneous occurrence of what to Westerners would seem to be unrelated (and therefore meaningless) events—such as the sounding of a certain bird while in the course of carrying out a particular activity—can be interpreted in Java as an important omen.

This deep-seated view of the workings of the natural world is reflected in the structure of *gamelan* music, where coincidence is central to the coherence of the music. The sounding of the *gong* with the *kenong* marks the musical instant

```
t = kethuk
N = kenong          ṫ  ẇ  ṫ  Ṅ  ṫ  Ṗ  ṫ  Ṅ  ṫ  Ṗ  ṫ  Ṅ  ṫ  Ṗ  ṫ  Ṅ
P = kempul                                                          G
G = gong or siyem
w = rest
  = one beat in balungan melody
```

Ex. 7–2. *Interlocking punctuation pattern in "Bubaran Kembang Pacar."*

SUBDIVISIONS

full gongan:															G
1st level:			N			N			N				N		
2nd level:	w			P			P				P				
3rd level: t		t		t		t		t		t		t		t	

----

wk	md	wk	str	wk	md	wk	str	wk	md	wk	str	wk	md	wk	xstr

beat
no.   1   2   3   4   5   6   7   8   9   10   11   12   13   14   15   16

(wk = weak; md = medium; str = strong; xstr = very strong)

Ex. 7–3.   *Stress levels in punctuation pattern of "Bubaran Kembang Pacar."*

of greatest weight and is the only point at which a *gendhing* may end. Yet other lesser points of coincidence also carry weight. If we consider the piece from the perspective of the *balungan* melody, it is at the coincidence of the *balungan* with the *kenong* strokes that the next strongest stress is felt. And in pieces with longer *gongans* (e.g., 32, 64, or 128 beats), where there are many more *saron* beats and therefore many of them do not coincide with any punctuating gong, each *kenong* stroke and even each *kethuk* stroke may be an instance of emphasis and temporary repose.

The ethnomusicologist Judith Becker and her student Stanley Hoffman have found it useful to represent the cyclic structure of *gendhings* by mapping patterns onto a circle, relating the flow of musical time to the recurring course traced by the hands on a clock. The pattern used in "Bubaran Kembang Pacar," then, can be notated as shown in example 7–4. Becker has argued convincingly that the cyclic structure of Javanese *gendhings* reflects the persistence of Hindu-

Ex. 7–4.   *Punctuation pattern of "Bubaran Kembang Pacar" represented as a circle.*

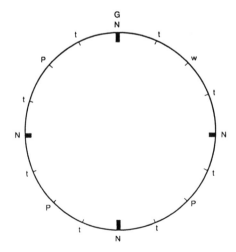

Buddhist conceptions of time introduced to Java during the first millennium A.D. and not wholly eliminated by the subsequent adoption of Islam. (For an elaboration of this theory, see Hoffman 1978, Becker 1979, and especially Becker 1981.)

Today, the players of most of the punctuating instruments have a choice of pitch in performance of many pieces. Their choice is normally determined by the *balungan* melody tone played simultaneously, or the one about to be emphasized in the following phrase. However, when performing pieces in loud-playing style it is not unusual to use a single pitch throughout, reflecting earlier practice, when only one *kempul* and one or two *kenong* were made for each *gamelan*. Here the musicians opt for this older practice; they use *kempul* tone 6 throughout, and a special *kenong* (called *kenong japan*) tuned to tone 5 in the octave below the other *kenong*. The *kethuk*, as is customary in Yogya, is tuned to tone 2. The gong player chooses to sound the *gong ageng* only for the first and last gong strokes; otherwise he plays the smaller gong *siyem*, tuned to tone 2.

The punctuation pattern and its relation to the *balungan* melody is indicated in the first word of the full nomenclature of a *gendhing*. In fact, the way Javanese refer to *gendhing*s normally includes their formal structure (in this case "bubaran"—sixteen beats per *gongan*, four *kenong* beats per *gongan*), the name of a particular melody (in this case "Kembang Pacar"—a kind of red flower), the scale system (*pélog*), and the modal category (*pathet nem*).

Let us now consider the *balungan* melody of this piece, notated as performed on the *saron demung, saron barung*, and *slenthem* (ex. 7–5). The system used here and elsewhere in this chapter is the cipher notation system now widely used throughout central and eastern Java. Dots in place of numerals indicate a rest—or, more correctly, the sustaining of the previous tone. Dots below numerals indicate the lower octave and dots above indicate the higher octave. An extra space or two is often given after groups of four beats as a means of demarcating the unit known as *gatra* (roughly equivalent to the Western notion of "measure" or "bar"—though in Java almost always four beats long and with the stress on the *last* beat, not the first). Nowadays many Javanese musicians refer to notation to learn or to recall particular pieces, but they do not generally read from notation in performance. And what is notated is usually only the *balungan* melody and introduction; the parts played on other instruments are

				G N
Introduction (on bonang):	5 3 5 .	2 3 5 6	2 4 5 4	2 15555

				G
Main Body				
punctuation (same each gongan):	t w t N	t P t N	t P t N	t P t N
1st gongan:	3 6 3 5	3 6 3 5	3 6 3 5	6 5 3 2
2nd gongan:	6 5 3 2	6 5 3 2	6 5 3 2	5 3 5 6
3rd gongan:	2 1 2 6	2 1 2 6	2 1 2 6	3 5 3 2
4th gongan:	5 3 5 .	2 3 5 6	2 4 5 4	2 1 6 5

Ex. 7–5. *Introduction and balungan melody for "Bubaran Kembang Pacar."*

recreated in relation to the *balungan* melody and are open to some degree of personal interpretation.

The piece consists of four *gongan*s (each, of course, with the same *bubaran* structure), played one after the other. Each of the first three begins with a *gatra* that is played three times in succession and ends on the same tone as the previous gong tone. This kind of regularity enhances the balanced symmetry provided by the punctuation structure. The fourth *gongan*, which stands out with its one rest (fourth beat) and different *gatra*s, is melodically very similar to the introduction and leads right back into the first.

The whole main body can be repeated as many times as the drummer desires, or as is appropriate to the context in which it is performed. Pieces in *bubaran* form usually are played at the end of performances—*bubar* means to disperse. The guests or audience are expected to leave during the playing of the piece; thus the number of repetitions may depend on the length of time it takes those in attendance to get up to leave.

Already we have a fairly good understanding of the structure of this piece as performed. Let us focus our attention now on the part played by the drummer, using the smallest and largest drums in combination. Throughout the piece he plays a pattern specific not to this particular piece, but, like the punctuating pattern, generic to the *bubaran* form. That is, the drumming for any of the forty or so other pieces in this form would be the same: a particular introductory pattern, several variant patterns for the main body, and a special contrasting pattern reserved only for the playing of the final *gongan* and which, together with the slowing of tempo, acts to signal the ending. The patterns are made up of a vocabulary of drum strokes, each with a name that imitates onomatopoetically the actual drum sound. (ex. 7–6). It is the drummer who first begins to play faster, thereby signaling the ensemble to speed up at the end of the second time through the large cycle of four *gongan*s. As warning that he intends to end, he alters the last few strokes in the penultimate *gongan* (from dDdD dD. to dDdD TdD). This way the other musicians all know they are to slacken the tempo, though the precise rate is determined by the drummer. The playing of the ending pattern through the last *gongan* confirms his intentions.

We have seen how the punctuating gong parts and the drumming fit with the *balungan* in "Bubaran Kembang Pacar." We can now turn to the elaborating melodic instruments—here the *bonang barung* and *bonang panerus*—which normally play at a faster rate, subdividing the *balungan* part and providing variations based on the *balungan* melody. In pieces with *balungan* played at slower tempos, the *saron peking* also provides a limited degree of melodic elaboration, but in Yogyanese court style the instrument is sometimes omitted (as it is here).

It was mentioned earlier that the only part normally notated is the *balungan*. Other melodic parts are derived through processes generally understood by practicing musicians. Ideally all musicians can play all the parts. In reality, this is true only in the best professional groups; but most musicians have at least a

Introduction: N /G
  5   3   5 .   2   3   5   6   2   4   5   4   2   1 5 5 5 5
                                       T   T   d   D   T   d d .

Main Body:

	t	w	t	N	t	P	t	N	t	P	t	N	t	P	t	N/G
(e.g.)	3	6	3	5	3	6	3	5	3	6	3	5	6	5	3	2
A:	d	d	d D	.	d	d	d D	.	d	d	d D	.	d D d D	d D	.	

(played in 1st, 2nd, & 4th *gongan*)

	2	1	2	6	2	1	2	6	2	1	2	6	3	5	3	2
B:	T d D	. T d D	.	T d D . T	d D	.	T d D	. T d D	.	d D d D . d D	.					

(played in 3rd *gongan*)

	5	3	5	.	2	3	5	6	2	4	5	4	2	1	6	5
Ending:	T d d	d	D	T d dD	Td	D	d DT	d Td	T	D d	D	d d	.			

(played in 4th *gongan*, last time)

d =   dung (a high, resonant sound produced by one or two fingers striking the larger head of the *ketipung*)

T =   Tak (a short, crisp sound produced by slapping the smaller head of the *ketipung* with the palm)

D =   Dang (a deep sound, produced by hitting the larger head of the *kendhang gendhing*, often in combination with Tak on the *ketipung*)

Ex. 7–6. *Drum patterns for "Bubaran Kembang Pacar."*

passive knowledge of the workings of all the instruments and know how to respond to various signals and subtler nuances.

The two *bonang*s here perform in a style called *mlaku* (literally "to walk"), usually alternating left and right hands in sounding combinations of tones derived from the *balungan*. The *bonang barung* part played the first time through the four *gongan*s is notated in ex. 7–7. The arrangement of kettle gongs on the instrument is given in the upper portion of the figure, and the notation below (with the same cipher system used to notate the *balungan*).

In subsequent repetitions the *bonang barung* part remains similar, but not identical. The variations reflect the sensibilities of the player, who both adjusts to tempo changes and alters his patterns purely for the aesthetic enjoyment of variation. He has not learned a particular *bonang* part or set of variations, note for note, for this one piece. Rather, he has thoroughly internalized a vocabulary of patterns (called *céngkoks*) which he knows by tradition to fit with certain phrases of *balungan*. What he usually will have learned about the particular piece, other than its *balungan*, is the octave register in which to play his variations (e.g., 3 6 3 6 rather than 3̇ 6̇ 3̇ 6̇).

The *bonang panerus* plays similar sorts of variations of the *balungan* melody,

Kettles on bonang:

4̇	6̇		5̇	3̇	2̇		1̇	7̇
1	7		2	3	5		6	4

Bonang Playing in *Bubaran Kembang Pacar*:

```
balungan:   3   6   3   5   3   6   3   5   3   6   3   5   6   5   3   2
bonang:   3 6 3 6 3 5 3 5 3 6 3 6 3 5 3 5 3 6 3 6 3 5 3 5 3 5 6 5 3 5 6 . 6 .
                                                                      2   2

balungan:   6   5   3   2   6   5   3   2   6   5   3   2   5   3   5   6
bonang:   6 5 3 5 6 . 6 . 6 5 3 5 6 . 6 . 6 5 3 5 6 . 6 . 5 3 5 3 6 6 6 .
                2   2           2   2           2   2                 6

balungan:   2   1   2   6   2   1   2   6   2   1   2   6   3   5   3   2
bonang:   2̇ 1̇ 2̇ 1̇ 5 6 1̇ 6 2̇ 1̇ 2̇ 1̇ 5 6 1̇ 6 2̇ 1̇ 2̇ 1̇ 6 6 6 . 3 3 3 . 2 2 2̇ .
                                                            6         3           2

balungan:   5   3   5   .   2   3   5   6   2   4   5   4   2   1   6   5
bonang:   5̇ 3̇ 5̇ 3̇ 5 5 5̇ . 2̇ 3̇ 2̇ 3̇ 5 6 5̇ 6̇ 2 4 2 4 5̇ 4̇ 5̇ 4̇ 2̇ 1̇ 2̇ 1̇ 6 5 3 5
              5
```

Ex. 7–7. *Bonang barung part played in "Bubaran Kembang Pacar."*

but at twice the rate of the *bonang barung*. Example 7–8 gives *balungan*, *bonang barung*, and *bonang panerus* for the first *gongan*. The arrangement of kettles is identical to that of *bonang barung*, though each is tuned an octave higher than the corresponding *bonang barung* kettle. You can see in this figure how the two *bonangs* vary by repetition: 3 6 in the *balungan* becomes 3 6 3 6 in the *bonang barung* part and 363.3636 in the *bonang panerus* part—all heard simultaneously. Yet it is not simply a matter of mechanical replication throughout, for alternate tones can be substituted (e.g., 6 5 3 5 instead of 6 5 6 5) and other choices can be made. Still, we can understand why the Javanese refer to the *saron* and *slenthem* melody as *balungan*: the term literally means "outline" or "skeleton." And it provides just that for the elaborating instruments and, in soft-playing style, for the voices as well. The degree to which the *saron* and *slenthem* part actually sounds like an outline depends on its tempo and the resulting levels at which it is subdivided by the elaborating instruments.

Irama Level

In this performance of "Bubaran Kembang Pacar," the *bonang barung* plays at twice the density of the *balungan*, subdividing it by two. This ratio defines one

```
balungan:     3   6   3   5   3   6   3   5   3   6   3   5   6   5   3   2
bon. bar.:   3 6 3 6 3 5 3 5 3 6 3 6 3 5 3 5 3 6 3 6 3 5 3 5 6 5 3 5 6 . 6 .
                                                                      2   2

bon. pnr.:   363. 3636353. 3535363. 3636353. 3535363. 3636353. 3535656. 6535626. 626.
```

Ex. 7–8. *Bonang barung and panerus parts for "Bubaran Kembang Pacar," first gongan.*

of five possible levels of *balungan* subdivision known as the *irama* level. If the tempo had slowed sufficiently (as we shall see in the next piece), the *bonang barung* would double its ratio with the *balungan*, subdividing each beat by four. Ward Keeler aptly likens the process to a car shifting gears, in this case down-shifting as it goes up a steep grade (Keeler 1987:225). And the *bonang panerus*, in order to maintain its relationship with the *bonang barung* would double as well, resulting in an eight-to-one ratio with the *balungan*. At the slowest *balungan* tempo, the *bonang barung* would have a ratio of sixteen beats to one *balungan* beat; and the *bonang panerus*, along with several of the soft instruments, would play a full thirty-two beats for each *balungan* beat!

Performing Your Own Gamelan Music

All you need is a group of seven or eight people in order to get the feeling of *gamelan* ensemble performance. They can use any percussion instruments available, such as Orff instruments, or simply use their voices. Start by assigning each punctuating instrument to one person. The gong player can simply say "gong" (in a low, booming voice), the *kempul* player "pul" (middle voice) the *kenong* player "nong" (long and high) and the *kethuk* player "tuk" (short and low). Another can be assigned to play the drum pattern (saying the syllables given in the patterns in example 7–6 above). Then the remaining performers can divide among themselves the *balungan* melody and, if they are inclined, some *bonang* elaboration. With a larger group, people can double up on all instruments, except the drum.

First try the piece we have listened to, since the tune is familiar. The "drummer" should control the tempo and play the ending pattern, slowing down to end. Try different versions with different numbers of repetitions. You can end at any gong tone; it does not have to be at the end of the fourth *gongan*. Then try the piece given in example 7–9, called "Bubaran Udan Mas" (literally, Golden Rain). You can hear it on the recording *Javanese Court Gamelan from the Pura Paku Alaman* (Nonesuch H–72044). The gong punctuation is the same as in

```
Introduction:                                                     N/G
                  7   7   7   5   6   7   2̇   2̇   7   6   5   6   7   6   5
                                        T   T   d   D   T   d   d

Main Body:
                  t   w   t   N   t   P   t   N   t   P   t   N   t   P   t   N/G
  (balungan:)     6   5   3   2   6   5   3   2   3   3   2   3   6   5   3   2

    (bonang:)   6 5 6 5 2 . 2 . 6 5 6 5 2 . 2 . 3 3 3 . 3 3 . . 6 5 6 5 2 . 2 .

  (balungan:)     7   5   6   7   5   6   7   2   2   7   6   5   6   7   6   5

    (bonang:)   7 5 7 5 6 7 6 7 5 6 5 6 7 2̇ 7 2̇ 2̇ 7 2̇ 7 6 5 6 5 6 7 6 7 5 5 5 .
```

Approximate equivalents in Western pitches for *pélog* scale:
(1 = D), 2 = E, 3 = F, (4 = A^b), 5 = A, 6 = B^b, 7 = C (1 and 4 not used here)
Ex. 7–9. *"Bubaran udan mas," pélog pathet barong—for performance.*

"Bubaran Kembang Pacar," but the melody is different. The sequence is as follows: introduction, first *gongan* twice, second *gongan* twice, first *gongan* twice, etc.—until your drummer signals an ending. Try to learn it well enough so that you are not reading notation, but, like a Javanese musician, using your ears, rather than your eyes.

A Javanese Gendhing in Soft-Playing Style

Listen to the next piece on the cassette, "Ladrang Wilujeng," *pélog pathet barang* (selection 39). The title word, "wilujeng," translates literally as "safe," "secure." This piece is often performed at the beginning of ceremonies or rituals to ensure the safety not only of the community involved but also of the ceremony or the performance itself. The recording was made at the house of my teacher Suhardi, who lives just outside of Yogya and directs the professional *gamelan* musicians at the Yogya branch of the national radio station (Radio Republik Indonesia, or R.R.I.). Some of the performers are professional musicians (at R.R.I. and elsewhere); others are Suhardi's neighbors who gather at his house for regular weekly rehearsals on his *gamelan*.

The instruments, which fill much of his modest house when they are spread out for playing, are mostly iron and brass. Perhaps you noticed the contrast in sound quality as the metal percussion instruments first enter. But for soft-playing style, the quality of singing and of the various soft-sounding instruments is what matters most, rendering the contrast between bronze and other metals far less significant than in loud-playing. It is for this reason that some Javanese say the soft-playing music is more a music of the common people (who cannot afford large bronze ensembles) and the loud-playing music more a music of the court and nobility.

This example contrasts with the previous one on the cassette in many ways. It is in soft-playing style, with voices and the various soft-sounding instruments featured. The introduction is played on the *rebab* (fiddle), with the subtle slides and nuances one could not produce on a fixed-pitch instrument such as the *bonang*. The pattern of punctuation (*ladrang*) is nearly the same as in the previous piece, but expanded to fit with *gongan* phrases thirty-two beats in duration, rather than sixteen. The players of the *kempul* and *kenong* do not limit themselves to one tone but instead use a variety of tones, matching or antici- pating important tones in the melody (see notation in example 7–10).

Pathet

This piece uses the *pélog* scale system, as did "Bubaran Kembang Pacar," but is classified as *pathet barang*. Javanese generally identify three *pathet* in each of the two scale systems, ordered in relation to the progression in which they are featured in the all-night shadow puppet performances:

Introduction: 7̣ 3 2 6̣ 7̄2̣. 3 7 7 3 2 7 6̄7̄2̄7̄6̄

N/G (above the overline near end)

A: (*umpak* section)

t	w	t	N3	t	P6	t	N5	t	P3	t	N6	t	P3*	t	N6/G
2 7 2 3		2 7 5 6		3 3 . .		6 5 3 2		5 6 5 3		2 7 5 6		2 7 2 3		2 7 5 6

*(if going to *ngelik*, P6)

B: (*ngelik* section)

t	w	t	N6	t	P7	t	N6	t	P6	t	N7	t	P6	t	N6/G
. . 6 .		7 5 7 6		3 5 6 7		6 5 3 2		6 6 . .		7 5 7 6		. 7 3 2		. 7 5 6

Ex. 7–10. *"Ladrang Wilujeng," pélog pathet barang.*

	sléndro pathet	*pélog pathet*
ca. 9:00 P.M. - midnight	nem	lima
ca. midnight - 3:00 A.M.	sanga	nem
ca. 3:00 A.M. - 6:00 A.M.	manyura	barang

In actual shadow puppetry today the first phase may start before 9:00 and last until well after midnight. The second begins as late as 2:00 A.M. and the third as late as 4:30. Several schemes are given for music performed outside the shadow puppet context, but current practice indicates little relation between time of day and *pathet*. Instead, pieces in *sléndro pathet nem* or *pélog pathet lima*, which are usually calm and subdued in mood, tend to be played relatively early in a performance, regardless of the time of day.

Much effort has been spent in defining *pathet* with reference to the melodies of *gamelan* pieces, particularly the *balungan*. The famous Dutch ethnomusicologist Jaap Kunst noted that certain phrase finals were more common in one *pathet* than another, especially for pieces played primarily in *sléndro* (Kunst 1973). Mantle Hood, one of Kunst's students and a major force in establishing ethnomusicology in the United States, devoted an entire book to the subject, concluding that *pathet* can be distinguished by different cadential patterns in the *balungan* part and the avoidance of certain tones (Hood 1954).

With a larger body of data than was available to Hood, Judith Becker found *pathet* to be "based upon three interlocking factors; (1) melodic pattern, formula, or contour, (2) the pitch level of that pattern and (3) the position of the pattern within the formal structure of a piece" (Becker 1980:81). In *sléndro*, for instance, a *gatra* with the contour of three conjunct steps downward can occur in any *pathet*. *Gatras* beginning on tone 5 and descending to 1 (5 3 2 1) are relatively common in both *sléndro pathet manyura* and *sléndro pathet sanga*, but in *manyura* they normally do not end in a strong position (e.g., with a gong stroke), whereas in *sanga* they often do. *Gatras* with the same descending contour, but beginning on tone 6 and descending to 2 (6 5 3 2) are common in both *pathet manyura* and *pathet nem*, but those ending in gong position are more likely to be *pathet nem*.

Javanese often speak of register or pitch level in relation to *pathet*, likening it in some ways to Western concepts of key. Indeed many *gendhing* are played in several *pathet*, just as Western popular tunes are often transposed from one key to another. The relationship to "key" is most apparent not in the single-octave *balungan* melody but in the parts played on instruments with wider ranges, and in the singing. Instrumentalists and singers learn a vocabulary of melodic patterns (*céngkok*), which they can readily transpose up or down—and even between scale systems. For example, the *céngkok* one uses to arrive at tone 6 in *sléndro pathet manyura* can be realized one tone lower, with the same physical processes (i.e., the same hand movements of the player) to end on 5 in *sléndro pathet sanga*. In fact, most Javanese say that pathet sanga is simply *pathet manyura* down one tone. But *sléndro pathet nem*, said to be the lowest of the three *sléndro pathet*, is often described by musicians as consisting of an ambiguous mix of phrases from the other two *sléndro pathet*, as is the case in our third example (discussed later).

Pélog pathets are understood slightly differently. *Pathet barang* is easily distinguished by the presence of tone 7 and the avoidance of tone 1. Differentiating *pathet lima* from *pathet nem* presents greater problems, since both avoid tone 7, employ the other six *pélog* tones, and do not seem to be simply one or more tones above or below the other. Javanese musicians often disagree over which of these two is the correct *pathet* category for a given piece. Perception of a piece's mood, which is determined by other factors beside melodic contour and register, may also contribute. The calmer pieces would be classified as *pathet lima* and livelier ones as *nem*.

These few preceding paragraphs have not been sufficient even to present a thorough survey of the many ideas about the concept of *pathet*. But at least you realize that, though it is usually translated as "mode" in English, *pathet* is somewhat more complicated than its Western counterpart. The word *pathet* literally means "limit" and is related to other Javanese words for stopping or delimiting. In many ways it indicates something about the limitations of the piece in question—the tones that will be played or emphasized in the *balungan* melody, the pitch level of the other parts, the mood, and (especially for shadow puppetry accompaniment) the time of day or night at which it is appropriately played. Though the association with mood and time of day suggest comparison with Indian *raga* (see chapter 6), *pathet* is actually a very different concept. *Ragas* are differentiated from one another by details of interval structure and ornament, as well as contour, and not by register. Hundreds of *ragas* are known, thousands theoretically possible. Indian musicians do not, to my knowledge, transpose pieces from one *raga* to another, since the *raga* is so essential to the aesthetic impact of the piece. *Pathet* is a far more general concept. Only a few *pathet* are identified for each of the two scale systems, and transposition from one *pathet* to another occurs with some frequency.

Instrumental Playing
in "Ladrang Wilujeng"

Now we can return to the example "Ladrang Wilujeng" (selection 39)—a piece that is often performed in *sléndro pathet manyura* as well as *pélog pathet barang* simply by transferring the melodic patterns from one system to the other. Notation is given in example 7–10, above for the introduction, the *bal-ungan*, and the gong punctuation (with pitch choices for *kempul* and *kenong*).

This piece is considerably more challenging to follow than the previous one. It slows and changes *irama* level in the third *gatra* (3 3 . .), settling by the end of the first *gongan* to a tempo of about thirty-six *balungan* beats per minute. The *umpak* is played twice, then the *ngelik* once, then *umpak* twice again, *ngelik* again, and so on, ending in the *umpak*: A A B A A B A A B A. For the final two *gongans*, the tempo first speeds up (but with no change in *irama* level) to about 42 beats per minute, and then slows gradually to the final *gong*. A solo *pesindhèn* sings for most of the first two *gongans*. At the beginning of the first *ngelik* and from then on, all the singers join to sing in unison, a style known as *bedhayan*. And the *balungan* part is no longer played explicitly! Instead the *balungan* instruments play simple variations based on the *balungan*.

It will be helpful in following the flow of the piece to use a stop watch, starting with the introduction. Elapsed time is given for the end of each *gongan* and for other significant events:

	(minutes:seconds)
Beginning of introduction, on *rebab*	0:00
Gong at end of introduction, ensemble enters	0:07
Change of *irama* level	0:19
Gong at end of first *umpak*	0:51
Singers enter in unison	1:44
Gong at end of second *umpak*	1:45
Gong at end of first *ngelik*	2:39
Gong at end of third *umpak*	3:34
Gong at end of fourth *umpak*	4:30
Gong at end of second *ngelik*	5:24
Gong at end of fifth *umpak*	6:19
Drummer signals acceleration in tempo	6:54
Gong at end of sixth *umpak*	7:10
Gong at end of third *ngelik*	7:56
Drummer signals gradual slackening in tempo	8:24
Final gong at end of seventh *umpak*	8:53

The drummer, with the same two drums used in the previous example (*ken-dhang gendhing* and *ketipung*), plays standardized patterns specific to *ladrang* formal structure: a *ladrang* introduction, a *ladrang* slowing down pattern (in the first *gongan*), standard *irama dadi* (literally "settled" *irama* level—i.e., four *bonang barung* beats per *balungan* beat) patterns for most of the rest of the performance (with a standard *ngelik* variation each time the *ngelik* is played), and finally an ending pattern during the final *gongan*. In accord with the soft-playing style, the drumming is softer and sparser than in loud-playing. Example 7–11 gives the standard pattern used, with minimal variation, throughout all the *umpak gongans* but the final one.

Other instrumentalists play variations of the *balungan* melody, producing such a complex heterophony that some scholars prefer to identify *gamelan* music as "polyphonic," noting the stratification of layers: parts moving at a wide variety of tempi—some at a much faster rate or higher density than others. Generally it is the smaller, higher-pitched instruments that play at the faster rates and the larger, deeper ones at the slower rates. You can get a sense of this stratification by considering the frequency with which the gong is struck, comparing it to *kenong* (here four times per gong), then *balungan* (here eight beats per *kenong*), and then the subdividing parts (*bonang barung* and *saron peking* four times per *balungan* beat, *bonang panerus* and many of the soft-playing instruments eight times per *balungan* beat). Thus, the instruments playing at the fastest rate, mostly those of higher pitch, actually play 256 beats for every one beat of the gong!

Above I indicated that in this example the *balungan* is varied even on the instruments that usually sound it explicitly. After the first two *gongan*, where the balungan is played normally, the *saron barung* usually plays the second *balungan* tone on the first and second beats, and the fourth *balungan* tone on the third and fourth. The *saron demung* sounds these tones of the *saron barung*, but inserts "neighbor" tones (the next highest or next lowest tone) between the beats. And the *slenthem* plays the *saron demung* part, but delayed by a quarter of a *balungan* beat to interlock with the *demung* (ex. 7–12). Variations occur, particularly when the *balungan* is "hanging"—that is sustaining one tone (e.g., 3 3 . . ; or . . 6 .).

The combination resulting from the interlocking of *slenthem* and *saron demung* here is identical to what the much higher-pitched *saron peking* plays, duplicating and anticipating the *balungan* tones in a manner that also resembles closely the walking style of *bonang* playing. This means of varying the *balungan* characterizes *peking* playing generally and is not limited to the few cases where the *balungan* is only implied (ex. 7–13).

Throughout "Ladrang Wilujeng" the *bonangs* play in walking style, mixed with occasional reiteration of single tones or octave combinations, as we found

```
   2  7    2  3    2  7  5  6    3    3    .        .  6  5    3  2
   .  . . . .    . . d    d . d D . .    . .    .  d  .    d    . d Dd . Dd . . . d D    . d D

   5  6    5  3    2  7  5  6    2    7    2    3  2  7    5  6G
   d D . d . dD . T    d d d D d . dD d    . dD    dD . dD .    dD . dD . . . d . dD d D
```

Ex. 7–11. *Drum pattern for "Ladrang Wilujeng," irama dadi.*

```
(balungan:      3    5    6   7P   6    5    3    2N — not played)

saron barung:   5    5    7    7    5    5    2    2
saron demung:   3 5 3 5 6 7 6 7  6 5 6 5 3 2 3 2
slenthem:       3 5 3 5 6 7 6 7  6 5 6 5 3 2 3 2
```

Ex. 7–12. *Variation by "balungan" instruments in "Ladrang Wilujeng."*

```
(balungan:      3    5    6   7P    6    5    3    2N)

saron peking:   3355335566776677   6655665533223322
```

Ex. 7–13. *Saron peking part for passage in "Ladrang Wilujeng."*

in the first example. The lengthier time interval between *balungan* beats here, however, provides opportunity for greater melodic and rhythmic independence from the *balungan* melody. The phrase shown in example 7–14 is played (with occasional variation) on the *bonang barung* with the *balungan* 2 7 5 6.

The various soft-playing instruments provide more elaborate variations, more independent of the *balungan* part and often inspired by phrases in the vocal parts. It is difficult to hear clearly all the soft instruments, since they blend together in the thick texture of soft-playing style. As an example, let us consider the *gambang* (xylophone), which plays mostly "in octaves"—the right hand usually sounding the same tone as the left, but one octave higher. The excerpt is from the middle of the *umpak* section, fourth statement (4:05 to 4:20 on the stop watch) (ex. 7–15). In other statements of this passage, the *gambang* part is similar, but not identical. Good players draw from a rather large vocabulary of patterns and vary the repeated passages in performance with a degree of individual flexibility, though not with the range of spontaneity we associate with improvisation in jazz or Indian music. The *gambang* player, like the other *gamelan* musicians whose part is not completely fixed, operates with a system of constraints (not quite "rules" or "laws"). At the end of a *gatra*, the *gambang* and *balungan* tones almost always coincide; at the midpoint (second beat), they usually do; on other beats they often do not, even though the *gambang* sounds eight (or in some cases as many as thirty-two) times as many tones as the *balungan*.

Singing in "Ladrang Wilujeng"

Solo singing with *gamelan* is also based on notions of flexibility and constraint. During the first two *gongan* one of the female vocalists sings florid vocal phrases that weave in and out of the balungan part. Although her part employs a much freer rhythm than the steady pulsation of most of the instruments (e.g., the

```
balungan:       2    7    5   6N

bonang barung:  2 7 755 5 7 . . 5 7 75. 6 7 . 6
```

Ex. 7–14. *Bonang barung part for passage in "Ladrang Wilujeng."*

balungan:	5	6	5	3P
r.h.	2323553553535353562765335276662273			
l.h.	2323523523532353562765335276762673			

balungan:	2	7	5	6
r.h.	3567627656327327727276533535656656			
l.h.	3567627656327327327276533535656356			

Ex. 7–15. *Gambang playing in "Ladrang Wilujeng."*

gambang discussed above), her melody is also constructed from phrases that usually end on the same tone as the *balungan* phrase, even though in current practice she often reaches that tone a beat or two later than most of the other instruments. Her phrases resemble those of other singers, but in at least some small way they are her individual *céngkok*. The vocal text used by the solo singer (difficult to determine in this recording) is not specific to the piece, but one of many in a well-known verse form fitted to the structure of this *ladrang* and to many pieces in this and other forms.

In contrast to the soloist, the chorus sings a precomposed melody. The text, although agreed upon before performance, is again a generic one, used in many *gamelan* pieces and having no connection with the meaning of the title of this piece. To a great degree, Javanese melody and Javanese texts lead independent lives. A single melody, for example, may be sung with a variety of texts; and a single text may be heard in a variety of *gamelan* pieces—depending on the wishes of the performers or sometimes (but rarely) the requirements of a particular dramatic scene.

The choral text is one of many *wangsalan*, in which the meaning of seemingly unrelated phrases in the first part suggests the meaning or sound of words or phrases in the second part. This kind of literary indirection is greatly loved in Java and can be seen as an aesthetic expression of the high value placed on subtlety and indirection in daily life. To "get" the connections, one must know traditional Javanese culture rather well: history, legends, nature, foods, place names (in both the real and the mythological worlds), and the Javanese shadow puppet tradition with its many hundred characters. Javanese poetry is difficult to render in English. The Javanese is given first, with word-by-word translation second (with some double meanings), followed by a freer translation underneath (fig. 7–3). Some of the *wangsalan* riddles here are obscure even to most Javanese. An explanation of two of them should suffice to give you an idea of how they work. In the first line of verse I, the words "satriya ing Lésanpura" (a knight in the kingdom of Lésanpura) suggest the sound of the first word of the second line "setyanana," as the shadow puppet character named Setyaki is a well-known knight who came from Lésanpura. "Kala reta," in the first line of verse III, suggests not the sound, but one meaning of the root particle in the compound "Mbang-embang" in the second line. Though the two-word expression "kala reta" can mean "centipede," the two words translate individually as "time" (kala) and "red" (reta). "Bang," the root of "mbang-embang," is another

I. *Manis rengga,*   *satriya ing Lésanpura*
   sweet decoration (colorful sweet snack), knight of/in Lésanpura
   Beautifully adorned, the knight from Lésanpura [a kingdom in the *Mahabharata*]

   Setyanana yèn laliya marang sira
   Be loyal   if   forget   to   you.
   You should be loyal, even if you forget yourself.

II. *Tirta maya, supaya anyar   kinarya*
    Water pure, so that quickly be made
    Beautiful clear water, let it be done quickly

    Ning   *ing   driya, tan na   ngalih amung sira*
    purity/emptiness of/in heart, not exist move   only you
    With the purifying of my heart, there is nothing that moves, only you.

III. *Kala reta,*   *satriya ngungkuli jaya*
     Time red (centipede), knight   surpass   glory/victory
     At dawn, the knight proves exceptional in his glory

     Sun mbang-embang hamisésa   jroning pura
     I   hope/yearn for   have power within domain/palace
     I yearn to exercise power here in this domain.

Fig. 7–3. *Choral text in Javanese and English.*

word for red and "bang-bang wétan" (literally "red-red east") is a Javanese expression for dawn.

In this example, as is common in pieces where male and female singers join to sing in unison (*bedhayan* style), the text is interspersed with extra words and syllables whose meaning may be obscure (underlined in example 7–16) and portions of the text may be repeated. These characteristics strongly suggest the relatively greater importance of what we would call the "musical" elements (pitch and rhythm) over the words, with the word meaning often obscured and the words serving primarily as vehicles for beautiful melody. The notation in example 7–16 shows the scheme for the first verse (with *bal-ungan* and gong punctuation given above the vocal line). The second verse operates the same way, with repetition of the last four syllables at the end of one *umpak* and repetition of the first four syllables of the second line in the next *umpak*. Only the final verse (here the third, but this could have gone on for many more verses) ends after one *ngelik* and one *umpak* and thus does not reach the "Adèn, adèn" interjections and the repetition of the first four syllables we would expect in the next *umpak* if the performance did not end where it does.

Chorus enters at end of second <u>umpak</u> (1:45 on stopwatch):   6 6N/G
                                                                                    Andhé

ngelik:

```
    .    .   6   .     7   5   7   6N   3   5   6   7P   6   5   3   2N
   - - - - - - - - - - - - - - -7- - - -2- - -    2- 376- - - - - - -    2- 327- - - - - -675- - - -6532
                     é                  ba- bo                    Ma- ni s           r eng-  ga


   6   6   .   . P   7   5   7   6N   .   7   3   2P   .   7   5   6N/G
  - - - - - - - - -  6- 535- - - -6- 722- - - -3276- - - - -  567-  5- 632- - - -  723- - 223276
                     sa- t r i-     ya     i ng               Lé- s an          pu- ra,
```

umpak:

```
    2   7   2   3   2   7   5   6N   3   3   .   . P   6   5   3   2N
   - - - - - - - - -           2- - 3232- - 76- - - 53- - - -  3- 566- - - - -5675- - - -6532
                              Ba- bo ba- bo                Se- t ya-     na-    na


    5   6   5   3P   2   7   5   6N   2   7   2   3P   2   7   5   6N/G
   - - - - - - - -   6- 753- - 2- 2- 2- - - 232- 376- - - - - -  2- - 33- - - - - -722- - - -3276
                     yèn  l al i ya marang si- r a           ma- r ang      s i -      r a
```

umpak:

```
    2   7   2   3   2   7   5   6N   3   3   .   . P   6   5   3   2N
   - - - - - - - - -           2- - 3232- - 76- - - 53- - - -  3- 566- - - - -5675- - - -6532
                              A- dèn a- dèn               Se- t ya-     na-    na


    5   6   5   3P   2   7   5   6N   2   7   2   3P   2   7   5   6N/G
```
(no vocal, until end of line, where next verse begins):   6 6
                                                                                   An- dhé

Ex. 7–16. *Vocal part (Bedhayan style) for "Ladrang Wilujeng," first verse.*

Biography of Ki Nartosabdho—A Gamelan Musician, Composer, and Puppeteer

To this point we have focused mostly on musical sound and its structure. But what of the people who are most drawn to this music—the musicians themselves? Javanese and foreign scholars alike have often mentioned the close interrelationship among the arts in Java. In fact, the status of "musician" does not preclude one from dancing or performing puppetry. Many of the better performers in one art are quite competent in several others. In the following several pages I am going to let a consummate artist, one famous as a *gamelan* musician, composer of new pieces, and shadow puppeteer, speak for himself. The biography I provide is based on an interview my wife and I conducted with the late Ki Nartosabdho in 1979. (His music is discussed at length in Becker 1980.)

We began by asking him how he became a shadow puppeteer and he proceeded to tell us the story of his life from early childhood memories with very little interruption from us. I have chosen to omit my wife's and my occasional questions, some of which merely sought clarification of vocabulary. Only toward the end did our questions seek to fill in some details concerning his musical experiences. I have also chosen to omit Ki Nartosabdho's occasional questions about our background and about the English words for various Indonesian and Javanese words and concepts.

> Ki Nartosabdho: Since I sat at my school desk in second grade, I had a knack for the arts. Which ones? Painting. A child's paintings, but even so, with cubist style, realism, expressionism, and my own creations: for instance, a lamb being chased by a tiger, things like that. Now, they really did not give lessons in those kinds of painting for children my age, but I made every effort to see duplications of pictures made by other painters at that time. After beginning to learn to paint, I began to learn classical style dance. I'd dance the role of a monkey, an ogre, and so forth. We actually learned a lot about classical dance—not everything, but a good deal. At that time I lived in my small village, in the Klatèn area [between Yogya and Solo]—called Wedhi. I was born in Wedhi on August 25, 1925. There, when I was twelve years old and in third grade, we had a teacher who gave dance lessons. He was from Solo. We studied so hard that we were able to put on quite an impressive show. It was really rare for village children to have the opportunity to study with a "classical" dance teacher from Solo.
>
> After dance, I began to learn Western music—violin, guitar, cello, and *keroncong*. [Author's note: The *keroncong* is a small chordophone, like an ukulele, played in the Western-influenced Indonesian genre of the same name. The violin, guitar, and cello he studied were for this same genre, and not for "classical" Western music]. By village standards I did just fine, but not by city standards. After that, I studied *gamelan* music. All these interests took their toll—requiring one to spend time, emotions, and especially money. Especially for musical instruments, what was I to use to purchase one? A guitar in 1937 cost six gulden—Dutch money—or we would say six rupiah [Indonesian currency]. I was the eighth of my brothers and sisters, I was the youngest. And I was born into a family that was poor, lacking in possessions, in work, and especially in education. So it is clear that, no matter how much I wanted something, I could not continue my education without any income. My father died just after I began second grade, and my mother, a widow, was already old. So I earned money by making masks—yes, masks—in order to be able to continue school. And I managed to finish fifth grade. And I used to have Dutch language classes after school, but they cost 1.25 gulden each month, so I only took Dutch for two months. They threw me out—because I couldn't pay!
>
> Now, rather than hang aimlessly about the house, when I was a teenager, I took off, without even asking my mother's permission. Where in the world would I go, I didn't know. Like a bird in flight, not knowing where I might perch. It was as if I needed some time to suffer—Excuse me, I don't usually come out with all this about myself, but today I am—Anyway, like a bird in flight, no idea where I should perch. I might

even be called a *gelandangan* (homeless street person). If not a *gelandangan*, then an outcast, or a forgotten soul.

I felt that the perch I should take was only to join and follow performing groups: both *kethoprak* [musical drama, with stories from Javanese legendary history] and *wayang orang* [musical dance-drama, based on the same Indian epics as shadow puppetry]. First I joined a *kethoprak* group, working as an actor and as a *gamelan* musician. But what I got for it was very minimal—both artistically and financially. And what was more, the coming of the Japanese reinforced my feeling that I had to keep drifting. A life of wandering about, and in tattered clothing. There were lots of clothes then that no human being should have to wear [burlap bags, etc., as the Japanese took much of the cloth during their occupation], but like it or not, circumstances required it. In Javanese there is a saying: *nuting jaman kalakoné* ["following the times is the way to act"— cf. "go with the flow"]. There are lots of sayings and stories that still have mystical content in Indonesia, still plenty. And you should know, even though in your country there is so much great technology, in Indonesia traditional and mystical matters still persist and are even gaining in strength.

So, I played with about ten *kethoprak* groups, only one month, then move, three months and move, at the longest, only four or five months, then move. It is called *lècèkan*—not taking care of oneself. Then one day I was playing *kendhang* for a *kethoprak* group named Sri Wandowo, playing in Klatèn. This was in 1945, just before the Proclamation of Independence [August 17]. There was a manager, the manager of the Ngesthi Pandhawa *wayang orang* troupe, who happened to be eating at a little eating stall (*warung*) behind the *kethoprak* stage where I was playing. As he ate, he heard my drumming and it made an impression. After going home—from eating frogs' legs—he called three of his troupe members and asked them to find out who it was playing *kendhang* for the *kethoprak*. After that, in brief, I left Sri Wandowo and joined Ngesthi Pandhawa. And what startled the other members was that I was the only member who was nervy enough to play *kendhang* at his first appearance. I had lots of experience drumming, but what I knew needed "upgrading."

Now, this guy named Narto [i.e., Nartosabdho] was a man without upgrading. Three-quarters of the Ngesthi Pandhawa members scorned me, ridiculed me, and seemed disgusted by my behavior. A new member already nervy enough to direct and play *kendhang*? Now, in the old days, Ngesthi Pandhawa was just an ordinary *wayang orang* troupe, with lots of free time in its schedule. Well, I took steps for "evolution"—not "revolution," but "evolution." Where was our "evolution"? On the stage of Ngesthi Pandhawa, both in the *gamelan* music and in the dance, and in the new pieces I composed—I should say "'we" composed. These were very popular with the public, with the audience. From village tunes to new tunes unknown in Java, such as waltz-time. [Several other composers have also experimented with *gamelan* music in triple meter, including the Yogyanese Hardjosoebroto. It is not clear who can rightfully claim to have done it first.] The piece was "Sang Lelana" (The Wanderer). Also there was "Aku Ngimpi" (I Dream) and "Sampur Ijo" (The Green Scarf), even for dance!

And [the vocal parts] for these waltz pieces could be duet or trio: one, two, or three voices [singing different melodies]. When we tried these out at Ngesthi Pandhawa, there were people who predicted that I would go crazy. My response was that we are all human. God gives us cattle, not beefsteak. Once we are given cattle by God, we have the right to transform it into something that is appropriate and useful, in accordance with our taste. All the better if we can bring in rhythms (meters) from outside Indonesia, as long as we don't change or destroy the original and authentic Indonesian rhythms. For example [he taps—on the "x"s—and hums (ex. 7–17), yes, three-four. Now in the old days this didn't exist. And even now, when it does, it causes hassles for all the instruments played with two hands—*kendhang, gendèr, gambang*—hassles, but it turns out it is possible. At first [they played] only the simplest of patterns; now it is enjoyed by many listeners: experts [players] and those who only wish to listen. Now obviously I faced some defiance, lots of criticism that I was destroying [tradition]. I was called "destroyer." But I didn't take it just as criticism, but rather as a whip—to push me to find a way. Indeed the criticism was justified. So maybe not only in my country, but in yours too, if there is something startling and seemingly irrational suddenly applied [e.g., in the arts], it gives rise to much protest and criticism, right? So maybe the life of mankind everywhere is the same. What differs is just their appearance, their language, their traditions, but life is the same, right?

As it turned out I did okay. My manager gave me something: not money, but a name. Before, I had been Sunarto, now Nartosabdho [from *sabda*—see below]. I gratefully accepted this honor, though not without careful consideration of its justification. In Indonesia often a name is taken from one's profession. For example, Pak Harja Swara (*swara* = voice, sound) was a vocalist, *gérong*. Then Harjana Pawaka. *Harjana* means "safe" (cf. *wilujeng*), and *pawaka* means "fire"; he was on the fire brigade [he uses the Dutch *brandweer*], someone who puts out fires. Wignya Pangrawit: *wignya* means "skilled," and *pangrawit* "a *gamelan* player"; so he was someone skilled at playing *gamelan*. Then Nyata Carita: *nyata* is "clear," "evident," and *carita* is "story"; he was a puppeteer who was accomplished, skilled in story-telling. And I was given the addition *sabda*. *Sabda* is "the speech of a holy man." But here I was a composer and drummer at Ngesthi Pandhawa, specializing in *gamelan* music. It did not seem possible that I would utter such speech. I taught singing and *gamelan*. So I wondered how my profession might fit with this name *sabda*.

[*Author's note*: In *wayang orang*, one person sits with the musicians and acts as a "*dhalang*"—not operating puppets, but providing narration

```
       x   x   x   x   x   x   x   x   x
Gong . . 3 5 7 6 6 . 5 3 6 5 5 . 3 2 7 2 . . 5 6 5 3N
       . . 7 2 6 7 7 . 3 2 7 2P
```

Ex. 7–17. *Excerpt of Nartosabdho piece in triple meter.*

and singing the mood songs known as *sulukan*. We learned from interviewing other members of the Ngesthi Pandhawa troupe that one night when the usual *dhalang* was unable to preform, Nartosabdho took over and, to the amazement of the audience, showed himself to have a fine voice, facility with the somewhat archaic *dhalang's* language, and a thorough knowledge of the story. This preceded his debut as a *wayang kulit dhalang*.]

Well, on April 28, 1958, I earned the title *"dhalang'* [here, puppeteer for *wayang kulit* (ill. 7–7) not *wayang orang*] in Jakarta, at R.R.I. People heard that I was learning to do shadow puppetry, and in January 1958 I was called by the broadcast director, Pak Atmaka—he's still alive. Would I do a broadcast? [Javanese shadow puppetry, though it uses beautifully carved and painted puppets, is often broadcast over the radio. The audience follows the story by recognizing the particular vocal quality given to each character by the puppeteer, and can also enjoy the music.] I replied that I would not be willing right away. The broadcast would be heard all over Indonesia, maybe even outside the country. This was before all the private radio stations, so broadcasts from the central studio could be heard clearly [at great distances]. I agreed to perform in a few months, in April. What shape should my puppetry performance take, how classical, how innovative? Could I match the quality of my accomplishments in *gamelan* music? How to proceed, it is always a puzzle. There was a woman, a singer (*pesindhèn*) who made a promise: if I could perform shadow puppetry all night, she would give me a kiss. A kiss of respect, right, not an erotic kiss, not a "porno" kiss!

Ill. 7–7. *Ki Nartosabdho as puppeteer (dhalang), performing wayang kulit. (Photo courtesy of Judith Becker.)*

Sometime after coming home to Semarang from performing in Jakarta, I had a guest. His name was Sri Handaya Kusuma, and he came on behalf of the Medical Faculty in Yogya. He wanted a performance around Christmas time. [*Author's note*: Though few Javanese are Christian, Christmas is a holiday, and schools are normally on a short break beginning shortly before Christmas and lasting until after the New Year.] I was asked to perform a "classic" story. Now requests began to come in one after the other: Jakarta, Yogya, Surabaya, Solo. Yes, I was earning money, but more important, I was also earning my name. Nowadays I perform once or twice a week, but have more requests than that. I have even played at the presidential palace in Jakarta for Pak Harto [President Suharto] four times.

How did I learn? I am what you would call an "autodidact" ("*otodidak*"). I read and so forth, but it also took looking at a lot of shadow puppetry performances. I would watch all the puppeteers I could, not only the older ones, but also the younger. And each performance, by whatever puppeteer, offered something new that I could and should incorporate in my own performance.

What about musicians? When I first played in Jakarta, it was the R.R.I. musicians who accompanied me. Elsewhere, I would take a few of those closest to me, my *gendèr* player, Pak Slamet, who came from Yogya and still plays at R.R.I. Semarang. And my drummer was the late Pak Wirya. Since 1969 I have had my own group, Condhong Raos, mostly younger musicians, under thirty-five years of age.

In the early 1970s I began to make cassettes, first of my new *gamelan* pieces, then of full-length shadow puppet performances. There were some discs produced by Lokananta [the National Recording Company] in the 1960s, too. My first set of *wayang* cassettes was the story "Gatutkaca Sungging," recorded in 1974, if I remember correctly. Not so long ago. I don't really have a favorite story—how can you say one is better than another? If someone wants to hire a puppeteer and asks for "Parta Krama" [Parta, i.e., Arjuna, gets married], for example, no puppeteer should say he doesn't like that story. That wouldn't be very good!

What changes do I foresee in the next five or ten years? It may be possible to predict changes in technology, but not in culture, not in the arts. Some people think *wayang kulit* should be given in the Indonesian language. To me, if a change adds to the beauty of the art, then it can be accepted. If not, then it cannot be. In Javanese there are many ways to say "eat," or "sleep" [He goes on to give examples. Different honorific levels of vocabulary permeate Javanese but are almost entirely absent from Indonesian. Nartosabdho implies, without stating explicitly, that he finds *wayang* more beautiful in Javanese and would like to keep it that way.] I have taken *gamelan* music from various areas of Java, even Sunda and Bali, and used them in the *gara-gara* [a comic interlude occurring at the beginning of the *pathet sanga* section, ca. 1:00 A.M.]. Not only have I studied these different songs, but I have even taken liberties with them. But other aspects of my puppetry have not been influenced by other regional styles. My style is basically Solonese. Who can predict if it will change, or how it will change?

The preceding few pages have presented my English translation of much of what Ki Nartosabdho told my wife and me when we visited him in his modest home (certainly modest for a performer of his status and popularity) in Semarang. Though he was still giving one or two strenuous all-night *wayang* performances per week, he was already suffering from a kidney disease. In late 1985, Ki Nartosabdho died and left a legacy of hundreds of new *gamelan* vocal pieces, hundreds of musical recordings, and close to one hundred recordings of all-night *wayang* performances. His group Condhong Raos still performs music, but at present no one stands out as such a clear "superstar" within the world of traditional Javanese performing arts—a world which, until the era of mass media, really knew no "'star system" at all.

Gamelan Music and Shadow Puppetry

Now that we have had a glimpse of a man deeply involved in both *gamelan* music and shadow puppetry, it is fitting to consider some of the music most closely associated with shadow puppet performance. Both the pieces we have studied so far are most often played for *uyon-uyon*, and less often for dance or dramatic accompaniment. The musical staples of the shadow puppet repertory are pieces with dense *kenong* and *kempul* playing, and *gongan* of varying length—pieces that generate a level of excitement, partly because of the dense gong punctuation. For each *pathet* there are at least three of these staple pieces: relatively calm (*ayak-ayakan*), somewhat excited (*srepegan, playon*) and very excited (*sampak*). The gong punctuation is densest in the very excited pieces and less so in the calm pieces. Which piece is to be played is determined by the puppeteer, who must be just as thoroughly at home with the *gamelan* music as he is with the many hundreds of characters and stories that make up this tradition.

We are going to listen to two versions of one of these pieces, the Yogyanese "Playon Lasem" *sléndro pathet nem* (selections 40 and 41). Depending on the mood the puppeteer wishes to establish, the piece can be played in loud-playing style or in soft-playing, or switched at any point. (*Ayak-ayakan*, the calmest of the three, is usually in soft-playing style; and *sampak*, the most excited, is always performed in loud-playing style.) Also, the length of the piece can be radically tailored to suit the needs of the dramatic moment. Sometimes it may go on, through repetition of a central section, for five or ten minutes. The first instance we will hear takes a little over a minute, only beginning to repeat when the puppeteer signals the playing of a special ending phrase. All the musicians must know one or two of these ending phrases for each gong tone and be ready to tag the appropriate one onto any *gongan* if the signal comes.

Example 7–18 gives *balungan* notation for the entire piece. The *gong ageng* or *siyem* sound at the end of each line, as written. The *kenong* plays on every *balungan* beat, the *kempul* every second beat (except where the gong sounds), and the *kethuk* between the beats. Notice that here the frequency of "coinci-

Introductory portion: (signal . . . .) 5	Length of Gongan
6 5 6 5 6 5 2 3 5 6	10 beats
1 6 5 6 2 3 5 3 2 1 2 1	12 beats
2 1 2 1 3 5 6 5 2 3 5 6	12 beats
1 6 5 6 5 3 2 3 1 2 3 2**	12 beats
Repeated portion:	
[: 5 6 5 3 5 6 5 3 6 5 2 6 5 2 3 5*	16 beats
3 2 3 2 6 5 2 3	8 beats
5 3 5 3 5 2 3 5 1 6 5 3 2 1 3 2	16 beats
6 6 1 2 3 5 6 5	8 beats
2 1 2 1 2 1 3 2 5 6 1 6	12 beats
3 2 5 3 6 5 3 2 :]	8 beats

Endings:
*   from gong tone 5 (first rendition); 2 1 3 2 1 6
** from gong tone 2 (second rendition): 5 3 2 1 2 6

Punctuation Pattern for <u>playon/srepegan</u> form:

kempul & gong:	P (repeat × ?) G	e.g.:	P P P P G
kenong & kethuk:	tNtN (repeat × ?) tNtN		tNtNtNtNtNtNtNtNtN
balungan:	. . (etc.)	. .	6 5 6 5 6 5 2 3 5 6

Ex. 7–18. *"Playon Lasem," sléndro pathet nem.*

dence" between gong punctuators is very high: every second beat! To Javanese, this makes for exciting music, appropriate for scenes charged with emotion, even for fights. Quick rapping on the puppet chest signals the musicians to play. The drummer, playing the middle-sized drum (*ciblon*), and sometimes the *kenong* player as well, enter just before the rest of the ensemble.

During the course of the all-night performance at which I recorded these examples, the puppeteer (Ki Suparman) signaled this piece to be played eighteen times—all, of course, within the *pathet nem* section of the night, which lasted from about 9:00 A.M. until about 1:30 A.M. the first rendition you hear (selection 40) begins in soft-style, but speeds and gets loud by the end of the first *gongan*, then proceeds through the entire melody, begins to repeat the main section and ends, on signal, after the first *gongan*. In the second rendition (selection 41), entirely in loud-playing style, the musicians never even reach the "main" section. To add variety to this rendition, played quite late during the *pathet nem* section (ca. 12:30 A.M.), the *saron* players play variant phrases for some of the *gatra* notated above, though the *slenthem* player holds to the previous version.

Even without such change, we can see that this one piece has the potential for a great variety of renditions, through changes in tempo, instrumentation, and ending points. This is the essence of shadow puppet music—a very well-known piece, played over and over, but uniquely tailored each time to fit precisely with the dramatic intentions of the puppeteer, and kept fresh by the inventiveness of the instrumentalists and singers who constantly add subtle variations.

BALI

Lying just east of Java, separated by a narrow strait, is the island of Bali, whose unique culture and spectacular natural beauty have fascinated scholars, artists, and tourists from around the world. It is also a place where almost everyone takes part in some activity we would call artistic: music, dance, carving, painting. And while the Balinese demonstrate abilities that often strike the Westerner as spectacular, they maintain that such activities are a normal part of life. The exquisite masked dancer by night may well be a rice farmer by day, and the player of lightning-fast interlocking musical passages accompanying him may manage a small eating stall.

Most of the several million people inhabiting this small island adhere not to Islam, Indonesia's majority religion, but to a blend of Hinduism and Buddhism resembling that which flourished in Java prior to the spread of Islam (ca. 15th–16th centuries A.D.). Though it would be a mistake to believe that what exists in Bali today represents a living museum of Javanese Hindu-Buddhist culture, the Balinese and Javanese share elements of a common cultural heritage. As in Java, we find percussion ensembles known as *gamelan* (or *gambelan*), with metal slab instruments and knobbed gong instruments that look and sound very similar to those of the Javanese *gamelan*. Some of the names are the same (*gendèr, gong, gambang, saron, suling, rebab*) or similar (*kempur, kemong*). Most ensembles employ some version of the *pélog* scale system (some with all seven tones, others with five or six). The accompaniment for Balinese shadow puppetry (as in Java, called *wayang kulit*) employs the *sléndro* scale system, although the instruments used consist only of a quartet of *gendèrs* (augmented by a few other instruments for Ramayana stories). Many Balinese pieces employ gong punctuating patterns similar in principle to those of Java. The Balinese play *gamelan* for ritual observances, as in Java, though usually at temple festivals, or in procession to or from them, rather than at someone's residence.

Nevertheless, certain characteristics clearly distinguish the music of these two neighboring cultures. One fundamental difference is that the Balinese maintain a variety of ensembles, each with its distinct instrumentation and associated with certain occasions and functions. There is no single large ensemble that one can simply call "the Balinese *gamelan*." Still, the style of music one hears performed on most ensembles in Bali is (1) strictly instrumental, (2) characterized by changes in tempo and loudness (often abrupt), and (3) requires a dazzling technical mastery by many of the musicians, who play fast interlocking rhythms, often consisting of asymmetrical groupings of two or three very fast beats. People often comment that Balinese music is exciting and dynamic in comparison to other Indonesian musics, exploiting contrasts in the manner of Western art music.

They may also comment on the shimmery quality of the many varieties of bronze ensembles. This quality is obtained by tuning instruments in pairs, with one instrument intentionally tuned slightly higher in pitch than its partner. When sounded together, they produce very fast vibrations. In the West, piano tuners rely on these same vibrations, called "beats," to "temper" the tuning, though on a piano it is intervals that are made intentionally "out of tune," rather than identical strings sounding the same tone. Of course, the intentionally "out-of-tune" pairs of metallophones are perceived to be "in tune" (i.e., "culturally correct") in Bali, just as the piano is in our culture.

The most popular ensemble in Bali today is the *gamelan gong kebyar*, which only developed during the early twentieth century, along with the virtuosic dance it often accompanies (also called *kebyar*—literally "flash," "dazzle"). *Kebyar* music is indeed "flashy," requiring not only great virtuosity of the players, but also a consummate sense of "'ensemble"—the ability of many to play as one. This music can be heard on any of a number of commercially available recordings (see Discography).

Rarer today, though making something of a comeback in modified form after its near extinction sixty years ago with the decline of the Balinese courts, is the *gamelan semar pegulingan* (ill. 7–8). The name has been rendered in English as *"gamelan of the love god."* It was formerly played for the king's pleasure within the court during the late afternoon and evening, and with slight modification became the favored ensemble to accompany the famous *lègong* (an intricate dance performed by three young girls). It is a rather delicate sounding ensemble, and yet unmistakably Balinese. It is this ensemble which the late composer and scholar of Balinese music, Colin McPhee, heard by chance on early recordings and which enticed him to travel in 1931 to Bali, where he stayed to study Balinese music for nearly ten years.

Ill. 7–8. *The gamelan semar pegulingan of Teges, Kanyinan, Pliatan, Bali. (Photo courtesy of Richard Wallis.)*

Listen to "Tabuh Gari" (selection 42), which serves in Bali as a closing piece, a counterpart to the *bubaran* pieces in Java. "Tabuh Gari" begins with an introduction (*pengawit*) in two sections. The first starts in free rhythm (without steady pulse) on the *trompong*, a set of fourteen kettle gongs, like the Javanese *bonang*, but in a single row. The second section (*penyumu*) begins as other instruments join and establish a pulse: at the first sound of the *kempur*, the largest gong in the ensemble, similar to the Javanese *siyem*.

At the next sound of the *kempur* (32 beats after the first), the full ensemble plays the main section (*pengawak*). The main body, which resembles the Javanese *balungan* in its regular, even rhythm, is played on single-octave *gendèr*-type instruments known as *jublag*s (or *calung*s). Every fourth tone is stressed by the *jegogan*s, which are like the *jublag*s, but an octave lower. Delicate and skillful interlocking is preformed on higher-pitched instruments of the *gendèr*-family (*kantilan*s and *gangsa*s). Four bamboo flutes (*suling*s) double the faster instrumental parts. Other percussion instruments provide secondary punctuation and emphasis. The *pengawak* stops momentarily at the next *kempur* stroke, only to start up again and repeat. A second pause leads on to the final, livelier section, the *pengecèt*, which is played over and over. The tempo is controlled throughout all sections but the first by the interlocking patterns of two drummers, each playing a double-headed cylindrical drum (*kendhang*).

The Balinese have long used a system of notation for recording the melodies of their most sacred pieces, though they do not use notation in performance. The system is based on contrasting vowel sounds, naming tones *dong*, *dèng*, *dung*, and *ding* (with variants for six- and seven-tone melodies). Since you have already had to learn one new notation system in this chapter, and since it is readily applicable to Balinese as well as Javanese *pélog*, I have decided on notation in Javanese cipher for the main melody (*jublag* part) in the *penyumu*, *pengawak*, and *pengecèt* sections (ex. 7–19). This may not sound like the "main" melody at first hearing, since the faster moving and more rhythmically varied elaborations of this melody are more audible throughout. The tempo is roughly forty-eight beats per minute in the *penyumu*, thirty-six beats per minute in the *pengawak*, and sixty-six beats per minute for most of the *pengecèt* (speeding toward the end).

```
Introduction (on trompong):                        . . . 5P        P = kempur
        Penyemu:   1 3 6 3    1 3 1 5    2 5 2 6    5 6 3 6
                   5 6 2 3    5 2 3 5    6 5 3 2    5 3 2 6P


        Pengawak:  5 6 1 2    *3 2 5 6   5 6 1 2    3 5 3 5      — = jegogan
                   6 5 3 5    2 3 5 6    5 6 3 5    3 6 5 3
                   1 2 3 2    5 6 5 3    5 3 1 2    1 6 5 3
                   5 3 5 6    5 6 3 5    6 5 3 6    5 3 1 2
                   6 1 5 3    2 6 1 2P   (1st time: . . . 2, return to *3, above)
                                        (2nd time: . 5 . 2P, move on to pengecèt)


        Pengecèt:  3 5 3 2P   3 5 3 2P   1 6 3 2P   1 6 3 2P (repeat many times)
```

Ex. 7–19. *"Tabuh Gari," played on gamelan Semar Pegulingan.*

Even in this piece, representing a style of considerable age and what might be called the quieter side of Balinese music, you can hear the shimmering metallic filigree, the asymmetrical rhythms, and the changes in tempo so important to Balinese music. I hope this one brief example has whetted your appetite to explore the incredible variety of Balinese music, which, more than any other Indonesian tradition, is well represented on records commercially available in Europe and North America (see Additional Listening).

NORTH SUMATRA

From Bali or Java to North Sumatra is a considerable distance, both culturally and geographically. Though influenced to some degree by Indian culture during the first millennium A.D., the Batak people, the main inhabitants of the province of North Sumatra, now have largely converted to Protestant Christianity or to Islam. The Christian Bataks sing hymns at their Sunday church services with an exuberance and an accuracy of pitch that would put most Western congregations—and even many choirs—to shame. Be that as it may, a variety of indigenous musical genres still thrive among the Batak, and many of these are central to rituals that are only marginally related to Christianity or Islam, if at all. Just as the majority of Javanese Muslims partake in rituals involving *gamelan* music and Hindu-based shadow puppetry, so the Batak Christians adhere in varying degrees to beliefs and ritual practices that were prevalent prior to the coming of Christianity.

Most celebrated of the Batak ensembles are the varieties of percussion and wind ensembles known as *gondang* or *gordang*, which usually include a set of tuned drums that, from a Southeast Asian perspective, can be seen as counterparts to the kettle-gong chimes (*bonang* or *trompong*). These can be heard on several fine recordings available commercially (see Additional Listening). Our brief encounter with music in North Sumatra is from a ritual observance I attended among the Karo Batak, living in the highlands west of Medan and north of the large and beautiful Lake Toba.

A woman in the town of Kabanjahe was planning to open a beauty parlor in part of her house and wished to have the space purified and to secure blessing for her new business by seeking harmony with the spirit world. This she hoped to accomplish by sponsoring and participating in a ceremony involving music and dance and during which she contacted her immediate ancestors through the help of a spirit medium (*datu*). Members of her family gathered, along with sympathetic neighbors (some more orthodox Christians were not so sympathetic), and even a few foreign visitors, including myself. To my surprise I was urged to take photographs and record the event, and with what little equipment I had brought with me, I did so.

The ceremony lasted for nearly five hours, with several long sections of continuous music. Family members and some neighbors joined the woman in a traditional line dance. The *datu* sang incantations, sometimes while dancing. He spoke gently to the woman and sometimes loudly to the spirits. With some difficulty the woman was eventually able to go into trance and the evening was deemed a success.

The musical group engaged for the evening was a small ensemble performing *gendang keteng-keteng*, a form of traditional Batak music employing a small two-stringed, boat-shaped lute (*kulcapi*), two bamboo tube zithers (*keteng-keteng*) and a porcelain bowl (*mangkuk*). On each of the tube zithers, thin strips had been cut and stretched, forming taut filaments. To one filament on each was attached a small bamboo disc. These remarkable instruments sound a kind of interlocking percussive filigree. But in addition, when the filaments with the discs are struck, they vibrate over a hole cut in the bamboo and produce a deep, vibrato sound remarkably like a small gong. The ensemble played continually for many hours, with the *datu* singing part of the time. Melody, filling in, gong punctuation—here were the essential elements, it seemed, for music making not only throughout much of Indonesia but also much of Southeast Asia.

The few excerpts I provide on the tape (selection 43) cannot give a real sense of the long ritual, but at least they offer an introduction to musical sounds that contrast with the *gamelan* ensembles we have heard and yet bear a certain distant likeness to them. The first excerpt is from the early part of the ceremony. The *kulcapi* player, Tukang Ginting, provides what is basically a repeating, cyclic melody that he varies (see ill. 7–9). The "clickety" sounds are the two percussionists playing the bamboo *keteng-keteng* instruments, filling in the texture to give a constant "busy" sound, which seems to characterize much music throughout Indonesia (see ill. 7–10). What is especially remarkable, in light of the other music we have heard, is the way in which the porcelain bowl and the gong sound relate. The gong sound occurs at regular time intervals, as one so often finds in Java and in Bali. It is subdivided by the porcelain bowl sound, which we hear coinciding with the gong sound and at the midpoint between them—like a *kenong* subdividing and coinciding with a gong in Java.

The second excerpt is taken from a climactic moment in the evening when the woman first thought she was going into trance. (She did not succeed at this point, but did an hour or so later.) The musical intensity has increased by compressing the time interval between gong beats; the tempo speeds and then doubles during this excerpt. The porcelain bowl consistently subdivides the time between gong beats, even in the very fast portion, resembling structurally the *wayang kulit* music of Java (like the "Playon" we studied earlier).

With its gong punctuation, coincidence, cyclic melody, binary rhythms, and fast-moving and dense percussion playing, this music seems clearly a relative of the *gamelan* music we heard earlier. I have intentionally stressed the similarities, but it is important to realize that these are *structural* similarities, easy to identify from a theoretical perspective. However, the differences are profound enough that the Batak and Javanese care little for each other's music. To the Javanese, clacking bamboo is no substitute for the varied drum strokes of the *kendhang*, the interlocking melodies of the *bonang*, or the heterophonic wanderings of the various soft-ensemble instruments in the Javanese *gamelan*. To the Batak, the thick-textured and often mighty sound of the full Javanese *game-*

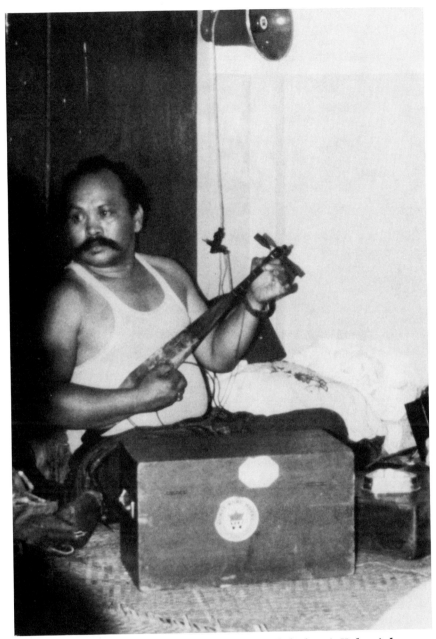

Ill. 7–9.   *Tukang Ginting plays the Karo Batak kulcapi, Kabanjahe, North Sumatra. (Photo by R. Anderson Sutton.)*

Ill. 7–10. *Members of Tukang Ginting's gendang keteng-keteng group, playing the bamboo tube zither (keteng-keteng), Kabanjabe, North Sumatra. (Photo by R. Anderson Sutton.)*

lan cannot afford the personal intimacy of the small *kulcapi* ensemble, nor the spontaneity of the *kulcapi* player that we hear in these excerpts.

Perhaps with these few examples of traditional music from several regions of Indonesia you begin to gain an understanding of the national motto *Bhinneka Tunggal Ika*—a phase in Old Javanese meaning "Unity in Diversity." In the arts we indeed find great variety, but underlying elements shared by these arts attest to the appropriateness of the motto. As we turn to examples of recent popular music, we find another layer of Indonesia's musical diversity—one to which many Indonesians are exposed and one which is especially meaningful to younger Indonesians from many regions.

INDONESIAN POPULAR MUSIC

Most of the music Indonesians would identify as "popular" is, like most popular music anywhere in the world, characterized by the use of at least some Western instruments and Western harmony (see Hatch 1989). It is disseminated through the mass media, performed by recognized stars, and is essentially a "commercial" genre. Without going into the interesting history of Western-influenced music in Indonesia, which has primarily been in the popular vein, I would like to introduce two varieties of contemporary popular music that represent contrasting orientations within the "pop" music world in Indonesia. We will consider one key representative super-star from each.

The first is called *dangdut*, in imitation of the sound formerly made on hand drums and more recently on trap set and electric guitar. The musician known during the 1970s and 1980s as the "king of *dangdut*" is Rhoma Irama. Born in 1947 in West Java, he learned to play electric guitar and showed greater interest in music than in the formal schooling his mother was struggling to pay for. In his late teens he dropped out of school and joined the underground music movement, heavily influenced by Western rock (and banned by then-president Sukarno).

Rhoma soon became disenchanted with rock. By his own account, he then consciously set out to create a sound that would satisfy the craving of Indonesian youth for a "modern" musical style, but that would at the same time sound clearly Indonesian (or at least "Eastern") in contrast to Western rock (Frederick 1982:109). He turned to a Western-influenced genre, "Orkès Melayu" music, whose origins are traced to the urban areas of North and West Sumatra and which incorporated influences from the soundtracks of the many Indian films that have long enjoyed wide popularity in Indonesia (compare "Engal Kaly-anam" from chapter 6). Even with its quasi-Western harmonic basis, this music was clearly "Eastern," characterized by highly ornamented singing and flute playing.

Rhoma Irama set out to make a commercial mark, and he succeeded spectacularly. Like most pop stars, he has sung about love, but he has also presented forthrightly his own ideas about his country and, perhaps most persistently, about his religion. He was one of the first Indonesian popular artists to make the pilgrimage to Mecca, and has used both his music and his films to spread his Islamic message. One of his first hits (1977) was a piece about greed, entitled "Rupiah" (the national currency). It was banned by government officials who thought it "debased the national currency" (Frederick 1982:117). Another early song, also banned, was "Hak Azasi" (Basic Rights), which described human rights—including freedom of religion and freedom of speech.

Listen to "Begadang II" (selection 44; fig. 7–4) which was the most popular song of 1978 and established Rhoma as a star. The song bears the same title as the hit film for which it served as the theme song. *Begadang* is a Jakarta term for staying up all or most of the night, usually to socialize with friends. Not only does this serve as a typical example of the *dangdut* musical sound as Rhoma Irama developed it, but the text shows his clear orientation toward lower-class youth. Like most of his music, it appeals to the youthful urge to dance and is often used to accompany popular social dancing akin to rock or disco dancing in the West.

Twelve years after this big hit, Rhoma Irama is still producing top-selling cassettes and has starred in a number of films in which—to the chagrin of more conservative Indonesian Muslims—he proselytizes for Islam through his loud, electric *dangdut* music. Unlikely as it may seem, then, Rhoma Irama is an Islamic rock star, and an enormous commercial success. His passion for communicating his vision of a more perfect society, holding closely to the teaching of Islam, has led him into the realm of politics. In 1982 he endorsed the Islamic opposition party and played at a rally in Jakarta that erupted in violence shortly before the

Apa artinya malam minggu	What good is Saturday night
Bagi orang yang tidak mampu?	For those who are not well-to-do?
Mau ke pesta tak beruang;	Want to go to a party, but have no money;
Akhirnya nongkrong di pinggir jalan.	Wind up squatting by the side of the road.
Begadang, marilah kita begadang,	Stay up, let's stay up,
Begadang sambil berdendang;	Stay up and sing;
Walaupun kita tidak punya uang	Even though we don't have money
Kita juga bisa senang.	We can still have fun.
Bagi mereka yang punya uang	Those who have money
Berdansa-dansi di nite club;	Dance at night clubs;
Bagi kita yang tak punya uang	Those of us who have no money
Cukup berjoget disini.	Just dance here [by the road].
Bagi mereka yang punya uang	Those who have money
Makan-makan di restoran;	Always eat in nice restaurants;
Bagi kita yang tak punya uang	Those of us who have no money
Makannya di warung kopi.	Just eat at makeshift roadside stalls.

Fig. 7–4. *Lyrics to "Begadang II."*

elections took place. Yet recently he has, most likely with some reluctance, joined the incumbent party and even played at functions of the very body that has represented the clearest threat to Islamic political power in Indonesia: the army.

From Rhoma's *dangdut*, we now turn to a genre sometimes known as *pop berat* (literally "heavy pop," see Hatch 1989), represented by Guruh Sukarno-putra. Contrasting in many ways with Rhoma Irama and the many other *dangdut* singers, Guruh is of the elite. He is the youngest living son of the founding father of the Republic of Indonesia, president Sukarno. Born in 1953, Guruh was raised in the presidential palace in Jakarta, college educated, and formally trained not only in piano, but in traditional Javanese and Balinese *gamelan*. Like his father, Guruh feels an intense patriotism that at times seems to blind him to the glaring inequities in contemporary Indonesian society. And, like his father, Guruh is far from orthodox Islam and sees Indonesia's culture as pluralistic and inescapably mixed with influences from the West. But where president Sukarno wielded power like a latter-day god-king with a matchless gift of oratory, Guruh does so through his music.

It was after his father's death in 1970 that Guruh began his musical career, playing first with a pop music group in Jakarta. After several years of architectural study in Holland, he formed his innovative and highly acclaimed Guruh Gipsy group. In early 1977 he released the *Guruh Gipsy* cassette, which one critic later called the most important Indonesian cassette of the 1970s. Here Guruh demonstrates musically his penchant for unusual juxtapositions and superimpositions of Western and Indonesian elements. And he also demonstrates a worldly musical sophistication, with arrangements drawing on a full spectrum of American popular styles from circus music to Motown, 1930s crooning to 1970s heavy metal. Where Rhoma Irama's music is consistently *dangdut*, with little variety in instrumentation or conception, the music of Guruh Gipsy sounds radically different from one cut to the next and often even within one single piece. It is a music for listening, not for casual social dancing.

Listen to the several excerpts from a lengthy (16 minute) piece entitled "Indonesia Mahardhhika;" which translates as "Indonesia [is] Free," using an intentionally archaic word for Free: the Sanskrit-sounding Mahardhika, rather than the modern Indonesian "merdeka" (selection 45; fig. 7–5). The first excerpt combines acid rock, a gapped scale closely resembling *pélog*, and Old Javanese poetry. The second presents a combination of interlocking Balinese metallophones (*gangsas*) with electric guitar and synthesizer, and the third an optimistic, patriotic text with episodic breaks. Traditional Javanese court poets often incorporated their names within their poems by means of a device known as *sandhi asma* (literally hidden name), whereby the first syllable of each line was part of the author's name. Guruh uses the device, constructing the lines of poetry so that the first syllables or first letters conceal the first names of members of Guruh Gipsy: Oding, Roni, Chris, and Guruh.

Since the release of this important cassette, Guruh's music has become increasingly less experimental, but remains both sophisticated and eclectic. More recent cassettes show influences from driving disco music, sassy Broadway musicals, soft Brazilian sambas, stirring Sousa marches, late Romantic opera, and even the dissonant orchestral sonorities of twentieth-century Western concert music. He has mounted a number of spectacular performances, which combine such blatant signs of patriotism as red and white costumes (the national colors) and incessant flag-waving on stage, with music performed by a variety of popular stars. These shows have been fantastically expensive by Indonesian standards, some costing over $100,000, with tickets priced far beyond the reach of any but the most wealthy. Guruh's musical expressions of patriotism have drawn considerable criticism from the press, who have labeled it both "elitist" and "naive."

A: (In Old Javanese language)
Om awighnam astu
DINGaryan ring sasi karo
ROhinikanta padem
NIcitha redite prathama ...

B: Instrumental (Balinese *gamelan* with electric guitars and synthesizer)

C: (In Indonesian language)

Cerah gilang gemilang	Clear and bright
Harapan masa datang	The hope for the coming era
Rukun damai mulia	Harmonious, peaceful, glorious
Indonesia tercinta	Beloved Indonesia
Selamat sejahtera	Safe and prosperous
GUnung langit samudra	Mountain, sky, ocean
RUH semesta memuja.	The whole spirit worships.

Fig. 7–5. *Excerpts from "Indonesia Mahardhhika."*

Guruh and Rhoma Irama are but two of several hundred pop stars in Indonesia today. The contrasts between them and between their musical sounds can begin to give you an idea of the complexity of Indonesia's popular music—still mostly unexplored by research scholars. Despite his recent political shift, Rhoma is a strong Muslim. His roots are humble and he speaks to the disenfranchised masses. Guruh's public persona is enigmatic, even meek, his religious beliefs more syncretic. His tastes in songwriting and stage production, combined with his direct descent from a leader of mythical stature (the father of the country) make him a very different sort of pop figure altogether. Rhoma's songs are more straightforward than Guruh's. The texts are clearly audible, like the throbbing beat of his *dangdut* music, and their meaning obvious. Guruh's are more complex; he often chooses obscure words and unusual musical elements. Where Rhoma's music has consistently and consciously been molded by mass taste and has been popular throughout the entire nation, Guruh's has had to build its own following, mostly among urban elite youth on Java.

Yet both of these stars have drawn on Indonesia's regional traditions and they have aspired to use their music to do more than entertain. Both offer spiritual guidance to their listeners and followers. Rhoma sees himself as a powerful spokesman for Islam, Guruh for the past glory and future hopes of the nation. Both have expressed some dissatisfaction with things as they are. Ultimately they both acknowledge their social identities in the styles of music they make. Each "knows his social place"—and maintains a separate artistic style as a result. Yet Indonesia prides itself on the ability to tolerate diversity and to achieve coexistence. Through even these two pop music stars we glimpse that diversity and find that it applies not only to traditional regional culture but also to popular music disseminated nationally.

REFERENCES CITED

Becker, Judith
    1979   "Time and Tune in Java." In *The Imagination of Reality: Essays in Southeast Asian Coherence Systems*, edited by A. L. Becker and Aram A. Yengoyan, 197–210. Norwood, N.J.: Ablex Publishing Corporation.

    1980   *Traditional Music in Modern Java: Gamelan in a Changing Society.* Honolulu: Univ. Press of Hawaii.

    1981   "Hindu-Buddhist Time in Javanese Gamelan Music." In *The Study of Time, 4*, edited by J. F. Fraser. New York: Springer-Verlag.

Frederick, William
    1982   "Rhoma Irama and the Dangdut Style: Aspects of Contemporary Indonesian Popular Culture." *Indonesia* 34:103–130.

Hatch, Martin
  1989 "Popular Music in Indonesia (1983)." In *World Music, Politics and Social Change*, edited by Simon Frith, 47–67. Manchester: Univ. Press.

Hoffman, Stanley B.
  1978 "Epistemology and Music: A Javanese Example." *Ethnomusicology* 22(1):69–88.

Hood, Mantle
  1954 *The Nuclear Theme as a Determinant of Paṭet in Javanese Music.* Groningen: J. B. Wolters.

Kunst, Jaap
  1973 *Music in Java: Its History, It Theory, and its Technique.* 2 vols. 3rd rev. ed. by Ernst Heins. The Hague: Martinus Nijhoff.

Surjodiningrat, Wasisto, P. J. Sudarjana, and Adhi Susanto
  1972 *Tone Measurements of Outstanding Javanese Gamelans in Jogjakarta and Surakarta.* Yogyakarta: Gadjah Mada Univ. Press.

ADDITIONAL READING

On Music:

Becker, Judith, and Alan Feinstein, eds.
  1984, 1987, & 1988 *Karawitan: Source Readings In Javanese Gamelan and Vocal Music.* 3 vols. Ann Arbor: Univ. of Michigan Center for South & Southeast Asian Studies.

Hood, Mantle, and Hardja Susilo
  1967 *Music of the Venerable Dark Cloud: Introduction, Commentary, and Analysis.* Los Angeles: Univ. of California Press.

Kartomi, Margaret
  1980 "Musical Strata in Java, Bali, and Sumatra." In *Musics of Many Cultures*, edited by Elizabeth May, 111–133. Berkeley: Univ. of California Press.

Lindsay, Jennifer
  1979 *Javanese Gamelan.* New York: Oxford Univ. Press.

Manuel, Peter
  1988 *Popular Musics of the Non-Western World: An Introductory Survey.* New York: Oxford Univ. Press (esp. pp. 205–220).

McPhee, Colin
  1966 *Music in Bali.* New Haven, Conn.: Yale Univ. Press.

Simon, Artur
  1984 "Functional Changes in Batak Traditional Music and its Role in Modern Indonesian Society." *Asian Music* 15(2):58–66.

Sutton, R. Anderson
  1984 "Who is the *Pesindhèn*? Notes on the Female Singing Tradition in Java." *Indonesia* 37:118–133.

1991 *Traditions of Gamelan Music in Java: Musical Pluralism and Regional Identity.* Cambridge: Cambridge University Press.

Vetter, Roger
1981 "Flexibility in the Performance Practice of Central Javanese Music." *Ethnomusicology* 25(2):199–214.

On Indonesia:

Anderson, Benedict R. O'G.
1965 *Mythology and the Tolerance of the Javanese.* Ithaca, N.Y.: Cornell Modern Indonesia Project.

Becker, A. L.
1979 "Text Building, Epistemology, and Aesthetics in Javanese Shadow Theater." In *The Imagination of Reality: Essays in Southeast Asian Coherence Systems*, edited by A. L. Becker and Aram A. Yengoyan, 211–243. Norwood, N.J.: Ablex Publishing Corporation.

Geertz, Clifford
1960 *The Religion of Java.* New York: Free Press.

Holt, Claire
1967 *Art in Indonesia: Continuities and Change.* Ithaca, N.Y.: Cornell Univ. Press.

Keeler, Ward
1987 *Javanese Shadow Plays, Javanese Selves.* Princeton, N.J.: Princeton Univ. Press.

Ricklefs, M. C.
1981 *A History of Modern Indonesia, c. 1300 to the Present.* Bloomington: Indiana Univ. Press.

ADDITIONAL LISTENING

Java (Central and West):

Gamelan Garland: Music from the Mangkunegaran at Surakarta, Performed on Gamelan Kjai Kanjut Mesem. Fontana 858 614 FPY.

Gamelan Music from Java, recorded in the Kraton, Surakarta. Philips 831 209 PY.

Java: Gamelans from the Sultan's Palace in Jogjakarta. Musical Traditions in Asia. Archiv 2723 017.

Java: Historic Gamelans, Unesco Collection, Musical Sources, Art Music from Southeast Asia Series, IX-2. Philips 6586 004.

Java: "Langen Mandra Wanara," Opéra de Danuredjo VII. Musiques traditionelles vivants III. Ocora 558 507/9.

Javanese Court Gamelan from the Pura Paku Alaman, Jogyakarta. Nonesuch Explorer Series H–72044.

Javanese Court Gamelan Vol. II, recorded at the Istana Mangkunegaran, Surakarta. Nonesuch Explorer Series H–72074.

Javanese Court Gamelan, Vol. III, recorded at the Kraton, Yogyakarta. Nonesuch Explorer Series H–72083.

Music of the Venerable Dark Cloud: The Javanese Gamelan Khjai Mendung, Institute of Ethnomusicology, UCLA. IER–7501. (Performed by UCLA study group, mostly Americans; recorded in Los Angeles.)

Musiques populaires d'Indonésie: Folk Music from West-Java. Anthologie de la musique populaire. Ocora OCR 46. (Various Sundanese genres.)

Sangkala. Icon 5501 (Distributed by Elektra/Asylum).

Street Music of Central Java, recorded in Yogyakarta. Lyrichord LLST-7310.

Bali:

Bali: Court and Banjar Music. UNESCO Collection, Musical Sources, Art Music from South-East Asia, IX–1. Philips 6586 008.

Balinese Theatre and Dance Music. UNESCO Collection, Musical Sources, Art Music from South-East Asia, X–1. Philips 6586 013.

Gamelan Music of Bali. Lyrichord LLST–7179.

Gamelan Semar Pegulingan: Gamelan of the Love God, recorded in Teges Kanyinan, Pliatan, Bali. Nonesuch Explorer Series H–72046.

Music for the Balinese Shadow Play: Gendèr Wayang from Teges Kanyinan, Pliatan, Bali. Nonesuch Explorer Series H–72037.

Golden Rain. Nonesuch Explorer Series H–72028.

Music from the Morning of the World. Nonesuch Explorer Series H–72015.

Other Indonesian Islands:

Les Musiques de Célèbes Indonésie: Musique Toraja et Bugis. Anthologie de la musique des peuples. Société Française de Productions Phonographiques, Paris. AMP 7 2906.

Gondang Toba, Nord Sumatra/Indonesia. Museum Collection Berlin (West) MC 12; 66.28287 01/2.

Gendang Karo, Nord Sumartra/Indonesia. Museum Collection Berlin (West) MC 13; 66.28321 01/2.

The Angkola People of Sumatra. An Anthology of South-East Asian Music. Institute for Musicology, University of Basle. Bärenreiter–Musicaphon BM 30 L 22568 LC 0522.

Cassette recordings of most popular and traditional musical genres from Indonesia are widely available in Indonesia, where they are sold commercially. The Modern Indonesian Cultures Collection at the University of Wisconsin-Madison includes a collection of over 800 such cassettes, representing a broad cross-section of what is available, particularly in Java and Sumatra.

E I G H T

◆ ◆ ◆

East Asia/Japan

LINDA FUJIE

Present-day Japan impresses the first-time visitor as an intense, fascinating, and sometimes confusing combination of old and new, of Eastern and Western and things beyond categorization (see fig. 8–1). Strolling through the Ginza area of Tokyo, for example, you find many colorful remnants of an earlier age sprinkled among the gigantic department stores and elegant boutiques; and always there is the ubiquitous McDonald's (pronounced *Makudonarudosu*). Tiny noodle shops and old stores selling kimono material or fine china carry the atmosphere of a past era. Looming over a central boulevard, in the midst of modern office buildings, is the Kabuki-za, a large, impressive theater built in the traditional style.

As the visitor begins to sense from the streets of Japan's capital, many aspects of Japanese life today—from architecture to social attitudes to music—are an intriguing mix of the traditional and the foreign. Japan has absorbed cultural influences from outside her borders for centuries, many of which originate in other parts of Asia. The writing system comes from China and one of the major religions, Buddhism, is from India, through Korea and China. Connections with Chinese and Korean music and musical instruments are a fundamental part of the history of traditional music in Japan.* In the late nineteenth and twentieth centuries, European and American ideas and objects have also had a major impact on Japanese culture.

Although cultural borrowing has clearly been important in Japanese history, the worn-out stereotype of the Japanese as "mere imitators" must also be laid aside. The Japanese have developed a unique culture, both through their own creativity and by imaginatively adapting foreign elements into their own culture. During much of her history, geographical and political circumstances have isolated Japan to the extent that such independent creativity and adaptation were necessary. A group of islands separated from the Asian continent by an often treacherous sea, Japan set herself apart for several centuries. This isolation reached its height in the Tokugawa, or Edo period (1600–1867), when Japan's borders were mostly closed to the outside world. Many customs and ideas that we consider "traditionally Japanese" were developed during this period. Most

---

* In this chapter, "traditional music" in relation to Japan will refer to those musical genres developed mainly in pre-Meiji Japan—that is, before 1868 and the beginning of a period of strong Western influence on Japanese music.

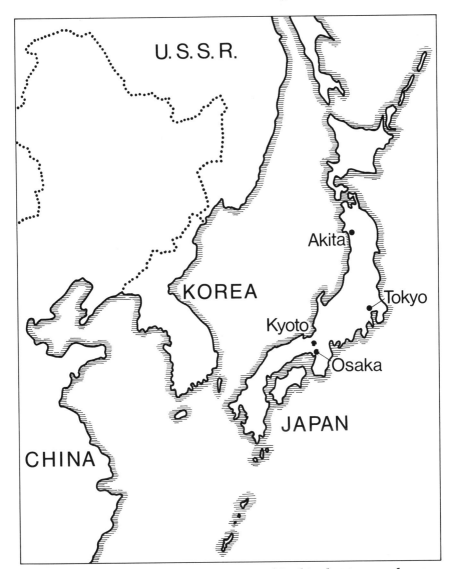

Fig. 8–1. *Map of Japan. Cities mentioned in this chapter are shown.*

traditional music presented in this chapter, for instance, dates from the Tokugawa period, though its roots may go back farther.

On the whole, Japan's culture combines a deep respect for tradition with creativity and flexibility. Many layers of culture, musical and otherwise, exist side by side, different yet harmonious. One sign of this diversity lies in the music the Japanese listen to today.

LISTENING HABITS OF CONTEMPORARY
JAPANESE

In concert halls, theaters, clubs, and bars, Japanese looking for entertainment find all kinds of live musical performances: Japanese traditional music, Western classical music, rock, jazz, punk, country and western, and music from around the world. In addition, television, radio, tapes, and compact discs provide recorded music of every imaginable type.

The kinds of music Japanese most enjoy listening to and performing usually vary by the age of the listener.* Japanese children learn to play the recorder and sing European, American, and Japanese folk songs in their schools; many also take private lessons on a Western musical instrument. Children learn and sing theme songs from television shows and commercials, and these sometimes become hit records. As teenagers, many Japanese listen to the latest hits from the West as well as to Japanese popular music. Teenagers know a great deal about the latest developments in sound technology and spend more on music— recordings and equipment—than any other segment of the population. Among young adults, tastes tend toward the more mellow popular music genres, such as contemporary folk and so-called golden oldies, or Western classical music or traditional folk songs. At this stage in life, singing with the *karaoke* machine (described below) can become an important form of musical entertainment. Middle-aged adults like to listen to older Japanese and Western popular songs, Western classical music, and Japanese folk songs. Along with older people, the middle-aged are most likely to enjoy traditional Japanese music, which they hear on television and at live performances.

Given the high quality of audio and video equipment available in contemporary Japan, it is not surprising that people use the mass media for most of their music listening. About one in four Japanese listens to music solely through television sets (NHK 1982:38). Each week, Japanese public and private television stations broadcast a dozen or more music-variety shows. Many of these feature popular music, but some offer performances of *kabuki* theater, Western opera, or symphonies. Young people in particular listen to music on cassette tape players, compact discs, and the radio (NHK 1982:47). Japanese also listen to many live performances featuring both Japanese and foreign performers. On the whole, however, Japanese listening is similar to that in many other countries: the people listen more to recorded music than to live performances and they are not always fully attentive to it. Music is heard in the background of everyday life, whether it is Muzak in a coffee shop or music coming from a radio or television set kept on while people go about their normal activities.

In the last hundred years, the Japanese have become more involved with new music, devoting less time to traditional music. Since the Meiji period (1868– 1911), Western music has been influential and its spread has been officially

* The following statements are based on the results of a comprehensive survey of Japanese musical tastes made in 1981 (NHK 1982:68–77).

encouraged through the education system. Despite the overwhelming influence of music from outside Japan, however, traditional music remains very viable. The *kabuki* and *bunraku* theaters in the larger cities are still well attended, as are concerts of traditional instrumental and vocal music. Teachers of instruments such as the *shakuhachi* and the *shamisen* still find many interested pupils of all ages, and televised instruction for such instruments in recent years has helped bolster their popularity. Perhaps the large amount of Western influence has made young people more appreciative of the different beauty of Japanese music and its special relationship to Japanese history and culture.

GENERAL CHARACTERISTICS OF JAPANESE TRADITIONAL MUSIC

To begin to understand traditional Japanese music it is helpful to examine its general characteristics. There are exceptions to these generalizations, but they should be used as a point of reference for the musical examples that follow.

Pitch/Scales

Like Western music, Japanese music divides the octave into twelve tones. The Japanese tonal system is based on the Chinese system, which in turn developed in a similar way to the Pythagorian system of the West. These notes, when put in pitch sequence, represent an untempered chromatic scale of 12 semitones. While equal temperament has strongly influenced contemporary performers, the exact intervals between notes still differ in traditional music according to genre, school, the piece performed, and the individual performer (Koizumi 1974:73). No single set of pitches is used by all musicians. For example, the mode system used in *gagaku* (orchestra music derived from T'ang China) differs from that used in music for the *koto* (a thirteen-stringed zither). The *gagaku* modal system is linked to Chinese systems, while the *koto* system developed several centuries later in Japan.

Considering this diversity in scale systems, it is not surprising that music historians have developed a wide range of theories to describe them. According to one of the traditional theories, much Japanese music (excluding older genres like *gagaku* and Buddhist chanting) is based on two pentatonic scales, either with or without semitones. The scale used frequently in music for the *koto* and the *shamisen* (a three-stringed lute) is called the *in* scale and contains semitones (e.g., D, E^b, G, A, B^b). The *yo* scale, without semitones (D, E, G, A, B), is often heard in folk songs and early popular songs like "Nonki-bushi" in recorded selection 50. These scales are shown in ex. 8–1 with their auxiliary notes in parentheses.

A more recent theory holds that the traditional concept of the pentatonic scale (such as the *in* and *yo* scales) does not adequately explain what is found in the music itself. Instead, it is more useful to interpret Japanese music on the basis of

In

b.

Yo

Ex. 8–1. *In and yo scales*

"nuclear tones," located a fourth apart, and the main notes that appear between them (Koizumi 1974:76). Actually, the pitches thus produced are the same in the genres of music mentioned above: the *miyako-bushi* scale applies to *koto* and *shamisen* music and the *minyō* scale is found in folk song (ex. 8–2). What is new in this theory is the emphasis on fourths, as indicated here. In fact, much melodic movement tends to emphasize this interval (e.g., the use of *miyako-bushi* nuclear tones in "Hakusen no," recorded selection 47).

Timbre

The Japanese aesthetic sense favors the use of a broad range of sounds and tone qualities in their music. In particular, "unpitched" sounds are commonly heard in the middle of instrumental melodies. When we hear a sound wave with a stable frequency, it is easy for us to distinguish pitch. But if the frequency varies too quickly, we do not hear a pitch. A cymbal, for example, is unpitched compared to an oboe. In Japanese music, examples of unpitched sound include the very breathy sound made on the *shakuhachi* bamboo flute, or the hard twang produced when the plectrum strikes the *shamisen* lute. Just as Japanese poetry is full of appreciation for unpitched sounds of nature such as water flowing or trees whispering in the wind, Japanese music recreates such sounds for the enjoyment of their listeners. (An example of this characteristic can be heard in recorded selection 46, "Tsuru no sugomori.")

Ex. 8–2. *Miyako-bushi and minyō scales*

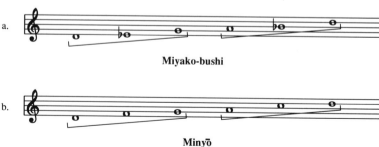

Miyako-bushi

b.

Minyō

Melody/Harmony

The diversity of Japanese melodies makes generalization difficult—the melodies of folk songs differ greatly in rhythm, pitch, and structure from those of *shakuhachi* music, for example. Japanese melodies often contain short motifs that are repeated, in part or in their entirety, throughout a piece. (See, for example, recorded selection 47, "Hakusen no," in which segments of phrases are repeated and varied.) In the theater, quoting melodic patterns from other contexts is a favorite device to inform the audience of the thoughts of a character or to foreshadow an upcoming event. Complete repetition of phrases sometimes occurs at the beginning and end of a piece, such as in the *shamisen* accompaniment to "Hakusen no," thereby lending an air of finality to the conclusion.

In the *shakuhachi* piece (recorded selection 46) the pitch movement in the melody strikes the non-Japanese listener as extremely slow; in fact, the dynamic and timbre changes give the melody its life, rather than rapid changes in pitch. In contrast to this, much vocal music contains elaborate vocal ornamentation, as heard in recorded selections 47 and 48.

The interval of the fourth often appears in the melodic material of Buddhist chanting and in instrumental music such as *koto* and *shamisen* music—even larger leaps occur often in the latter case. In vocal music, both syllabic and melismatic treatment of text can be found, but narrative styles like the music of the puppet theater described later tend toward syllabic text setting, which emphasizes the words.

Only Western-influenced Japanese music uses Western harmony; traditional music is dominated by a monophonic or heterophonic sound. Most common when two or more instruments (or voice and instrument) play together is a heterophonic texture—in which both or all parts play basically the same melody but in slightly different versions.

Rhythm

One distinctive characteristic of Japanese music lies in the flexibility of pulse in many pieces. We sense a pulse in music when we hear notes that are dynamically accented. In Western music, pulses almost always occur at regular time intervals (forming "beats"), and are arranged most commonly in groups of two, three, four, or six (creating a "meter"). Music can also have irregular intervals between the pulses, however, and this is sometimes called "beatless" or "flexible" or "free" rhythm. Those accustomed to Western music may have difficulty at first listening to music that lacks a steady beat because it seems "hard to follow" without the firm rhythmic structure they expect. But this music conveys a powerful expression of feeling because of its freedom and flexibility. Such beatless rhythm is found in many kinds of Japanese music, from folk song to music of the *shakuhachi* (recorded selections 46, 47, and 48). Even when a steady beat is present, there can be a sense of flexibility to it, as in the festival music example presented later.

When there is a sense of beat in Japanese music, those beats usually occur in groups of two, four, or eight. Triple meter is rare, though it can be found in some folk and children's songs.

Japanese music uses a wide variety of tempos, from very slow to very fast. Often, in music associated with the theater, the tempo accelerates as excitement and drama build in the play. A typical musical form called *jo-ha-kyū*, described below, is outlined through changes in tempo.

Tempos are not determined by metronome but are learned through imitation and trial and error. As in a Western classical music ensemble, when a Japanese ensemble sits down together to rehearse, it is not uncommon for one member to say, "That was a bit too fast last time, don't you think?" or "Why did we slow down at that point?" Through negotiation and trial and error, they settle into a tempo and changes in that tempo that are acceptable to most members. Experienced solo performers tend to play the same piece at almost the same tempo each time, though performances of the same work by different performers sometimes show a surprising tempo variance. This variation can be linked to difference in stylistic school or to personal interpretation.

Musical Form

The most common musical form in Japanese music is called *jo-ha-kyū,* and is based mainly on rhythmic rather than melodic changes. Found in music for the *gagaku* orchestra, this form profoundly affected *nō* theater as well as other instrumental and vocal genres.

Jo means "introduction" and is the slow beginning section: *ha* is literally "breaking apart," and here the tempo builds; finally, *kyū,* or "rushing," finds the tempo reaching its peak, only to slow before the piece ends. As a loose form, this tripartite structure applies in some cases to entire pieces as well as to sections of those pieces and individual phrases, as in the "Rokudan" piece described later.

To summarize, the three characteristics of traditional Japanese music that most exemplify its uniqueness and beauty are (1) variety of timbres, including unpitched sounds; (2) heterophonic treatment of voices in an ensemble; and (3) flexibility of pulse found in both solo and ensemble music. These elements occur in most of the traditional music described in this chapter.

In the following sections, several different kinds of Japanese music will be explained, illustrating some of the colorful diversity of musical life in that country today. The first four of these types developed largely during the Tokugawa period. The history of each instrument or musical genre provides a fascinating look into the rich, vibrant life of traditional Japanese cities and villages during the times of the *samurai,* wandering Buddhist priests, and *geisha.*

The *shakuhachi* flute is linked to the social turbulence of early Tokugawa times as well as to Zen philosophy and aesthetics. A *shakuhachi* piece provides an example of free rhythm, one of the most important characteristics of Japanese music. Also during the Tokugawa period, merchants took up the *koto* zither and made it one of the most commonly played instruments. The example of *koto* music displays the *dan* form musical structure as well as the *jo-ha-kyū* principle. The *geisha* and a female composer of the late Tokugawa period were important in the development of the short *kouta* songs. These songs, sung to the accompaniment of the *shamisen,* exemplify heterophonic texture in Japanese music. A description of the *bunraku* puppet theater and its music, *gidayu-bushi,* illustrates the strong connection of music with the theater and describes teaching methods, old and new.

These kinds of music are generally labeled "art" or "classical" music. In comparison to "folk" music, art music has stricter guild systems, more regulation over skill level, and more professionalism. These terms are imported from the West, however, and the dividing line between the two categories has become blurred today as folk musicians become more professionalized.

Next, two kinds of music termed "folk" are described: folk song from northern Japan and instrumental festival music from Tokyo. While both of these date from the Tokugawa period or earlier, they will be described in their contemporary contexts to show the reader how traditional music is faring in modern-day Japan. Musically, the folk song example shows the intricate ornamentation and the use of "microtones" that are characteristic of folk music from this region; the festival music example illustrates ensemble practice. Finally, we will explore present-day Japanese popular music, which shows musical features of both East and West, and the world of *karaoke* singing, in which live singing and technology are mixed in a unique way.

SHAKUHACHI

Considering its range of tones from soft and ethereal to rough and violent, the *shakuhachi* appears surprisingly simple in construction. This flute is made of a length of bamboo from the bottom part of a bamboo stalk, including part of the root. The name *shakuhachi* derives from the length of the standard instrument. *Shaku* signifies a traditional unit of measure (equivalent to about 30 cm.) and *hachi* stands for 8, together meaning 1.8 *shaku,* or about 54 cm. (Players also use different lengths, sometimes to match the range of the other ensemble instruments.) The standard *shakuhachi* has four holes in the front of the instrument and one in the back for the thumb of the left hand.

The *shakuhachi*'s versatility in pitch and tone production is, in fact, due to its construction. Held vertically, the flute has a mouthpiece at the top which is cut obliquely on the side away from the player. By partially covering the fingerholes and changing the angle of the lips to the mouthpiece, a player can produce a wide variety of pitches and tone qualities. Not only does the *shakuhachi* easily produce microtones but it also generates tones ranging from "pure" with few overtones to very breathy, sounding almost like white noise. Many Western-influenced contemporary compositions have been written for the *shakuhachi* because of its varied pitch and tone quality.

Solo *shakuhachi* performance flourished during the Tokugawa period (1600–1867). This was a golden age in Japanese cultural life. It was a time of peace, during which the *shōgun* living in Tokyo ruled over a united country, while the Kyoto emperor held only nominal power. After centuries of violent struggles between different factions of aristocrats and military leaders, Japan welcomed peace and prospered under it.

But long-lasting peace meant trouble for members of the *samurai* class. *Samurai* warriors enjoyed high status during the years of fighting, but afterward many *samurai* of lower rank were released from their duties, becoming *rōnin,* or "masterless *samurai.*"* The Tokugawa regime found it expedient to uphold the social class system established in earlier times: at the top were *samurai,* followed by farmers, craftsmen, and finally merchants. By issuing edicts designed to set up boundaries between these classes, the government tried to prevent movement between them. For this reason, even though they were without a means of support, *rōnin* were not allowed to change their class status as *samurai,* though some managed to do so. A number became teachers or writers, others became farmers, and still others became hired bodyguards for rich merchants. The image of the proud, swaggering, brave *samurai,* as projected in *samurai* movies, is largely based on the *rōnin* of the Tokugawa period, who were actually unemployed *samurai.*

Another option for the *rōnin* was to take religious orders and beg on the streets and highways of Japan. In fact, in Tokugawa society, it was considered more honorable to beg than to "lower" oneself by becoming a merchant or farmer. One group of *rōnin* who took religious orders were called *komusō.* *Komusō* (literally, "emptiness monks") were Buddhist priests who wandered the countryside, playing the *shakuhachi* and begging. The standard *komusō* costume included a large, basket-shaped hat made of cane, through which the wearer could see but not be seen. It was rumored that the *komusō* were government spies, taking advantage of their right to travel throughout the country wearing a costume that shielded their identity (Blasdel 1988:103–107).

These *samurai*-turned-priests made their mark on the *shakuhachi* repertoire. The *honkyoku,* or main solo repertoire for the instrument, derives from the pieces played by the *komusō.* All of these pieces, the most spiritual and meditative of the present-day *shakuhachi* repertoire, have a free rhythm; that is, they lack a regular beat.

Komusō were organized into the Fuke sect of Buddhism, which propagated a Zen basis for *shakuhachi* playing. Zen Buddhism is a philosophy that has spread throughout much of Asia and the world in various forms, but it is based on the idea that intellect is not needed in the pursuit of truth. We can search to know *about* things, but we do not really *know* them. To know them, we must throw

---

* The term *rōnin* has been given a new meaning by the Japanese. High school graduates who fail college entrance examinations and must wait until the following year (or years) to pass the exams are also called *"rōnin."*

away our notions of scientific investigation and logical reasoning and instead rely upon a heightened awareness and intuition about life.

Various means for reaching that state of heightened awareness of enlightenment (*satori* in Japanese) have been proposed. These include pondering *kōan,* or paradoxical riddles (the most famous is "What is the sound of one hand clapping?") and the practice of *zazen,* sitting in silent meditation. In the Fuke sect, playing the *shakuhachi* also was regarded as a means for reaching enlightenment. For this reason, the *shakuhachi* was not called a "musical instrument" by its performers, but a *hōki,* or "spiritual tool." The spiritual approach to the "playing" or use of the instrument is called *suizen,* or "blowing Zen."

According to *suizen,* the goal of *shakuhachi* coincides with the goal of Zen: to reach enlightenment, proceeding into unlimited "knowing." How this is done is not formulated precisely (as it cannot be from the Zen perspective), but one common notion is called *ichōon jōbutsu,* or "enlightenment in a single note." According to this theory, one could reach enlightenment suddenly when blowing a single tone.

Breathing is crucial in *shakuhachi* playing and its connection with Zen. The exhaling of breath is heard in the dynamic level and tone quality of a pitch; at the same time, it carries with it the possibility of instant spiritual enlightenment. Thus, each moment of "performance," whether the intake of breath or its slow release, whether the subtle, delicate shading of a tone or the explosion of air through the instrument, can be interpreted in the context of a larger spiritual life.

The breathing pattern is important in learning to play the *shakuhachi.* Each phrase takes one full breath, with dramatic shifts in dynamic level according to how quickly the air is expelled. The typical phrase in *shakuhachi honkyoku* music follows the natural breathing pattern, the sound growing fainter toward the end of the phrase as the air in the lungs runs out. When this dynamic pattern is broken by a gradual or sudden increase in volume, it makes a pronounced impression on the listener.

The performer of the *shakuhachi* piece in recorded selection 46, Kawase Junsuke, is one of the best-known *shakuhachi* musicians in Japan and the head of a stylistic school of playing (see ill. 8–1). Here he is playing with his sister, Kawase Hakuse, on the *shamisen*—she is also an active performer, particularly in the *kabuki* theater.

This piece, a part of the *honkyoku* (solo) repertory of the Kinko style of performance, is called "Tsuru no Sugomori," or "Nesting Cranes." (The version recorded here is performed in the *kabuki* theater and therefore is accompanied by *shamisen;* this part is not notated in the following transcription.) The music describes a winter scene during which cranes make their nests. The fast trills in the *shakuhachi* imitate the bird's fluttering wings. When played in the *kabuki* theater, "Tsuru no Sugomori" is performed in one of the most famous *kabuki* plays, *Kanadehon Chushingura,* or Treasury of Local Retainers, during a scene when parting lovers suddenly notice the scene outdoors.

Ill. 8–1. *Kawase Junsuke playing the shakuhachi.*

The first time one listens to this piece, it is best just to sit back and relax, appreciating the overall mood. For later listening, the transcription in example 8–3 shows in Western notation the general outline of the piece. Western notation is limited in conveying uneven rhythms, and so the transcription here is only approximate in time values. Phrases—defined by points at which a breath is taken by the musician—are numbered for reference.

After listening to this piece a few times, one may sense that certain phrases are repeated; in fact, this short piece has many repetitions of melodic material. For example, phrase 1 is heard again (with some modifications) in phrases 6, 9, 17, and 24. The group of phrases numbered 1 to 5 are repeated in phrases 9 to 13, and most of the other phrases are variations on previous melodic material.

Ex. 8–3. Transcription, "Tsuru no sugomori."

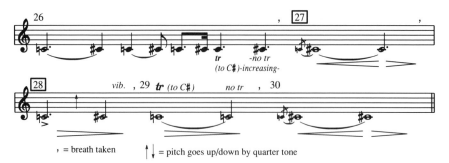

, = breath taken   ↑↓ = pitch goes up/down by quarter tone

Ex. 8–3. (*Continued*)

There is also a clear climax to the piece, created by changes in pitch and dynamics.

One of the most obvious characteristics of this piece is the constant change in dynamics within one phrase. Almost every phrase increases or decreases in volume; in many cases the musician increases the volume on one long note and decreases it on the next one. This careful breath control must be learned and practiced over years to prevent running out of breath too soon and to maintain constant control over tone quality.

A knowledge of some of the techniques used to play *shakuhachi* will help explain how some of the tones in this performance are produced. Sometimes the player flattens or sharpens a pitch by changing the angle of the lips to the mouthpiece. This is called *meri* when the pitch is lowered, producing a soft tone, and *kari* when the pitch is raised. (Occasionally the pitch is lowered and again raised, as at the end of phrase 22.)

The musician changes pitch also through finger techniques, depending on the effect desired. A finger can slowly open or close a hole, it can quickly tap a hole (creating an accent), or cover only a portion of a hole. These techniques are necessary because tonguing is not used to separate notes in *shakuhachi* playing.

Different techniques of breath release into the flute also create interesting effects such as *muraiki,* an explosion of breath into the instrument. In addition, *shakuhachi* players used flutter tonguing, finger tremolos and vibrato—all of which can be heard in the first few phrases of "Tsuru no sugomori". One common technique of producing vibrato is to shake the head while blowing into the instrument, either from side to side or up and down.

This piece shows at least two of the three basic characteristics of Japanese music listed above: a variety of timbres within one piece and a flexibility of pulse. Some notes have a thin sound, while other have a rich, full tone. Some notes sound "purer" to our ears, and others are breathier. The *shakuhachi* player expresses the music through such changes in timbre. With the exception perhaps of contemporary music, this variety of tone quality is rarely found within a single piece written for a Western wind instrument. In terms of Japanese musical aesthetics, however, this contrast of timbres is important to the texture and expression of the piece.

The lack of a regular pulse means that learning a piece requires a good ear and an excellent sense of timing on the part of the student. Most forms of musical notation convey the time durations of notes easily if the music has a steady pulse. But without such a pulse, the original time values are difficult to communicate in a written score. Perhaps this is one reason that musical notation never developed into an important teaching tool in most forms of traditional Japanese music. Because Japanese musicians could not rely on scores to teach them the rhythm of a piece, they used them more as a device to help them remember how the piece should sound. First, of course, performers must acquire this memory by listening to their teacher (and perhaps other students) many times.

The idea of *ma* (literally "space" or "interval") is linked to both rhythm and to the Zen background of *shakuhachi* playing. *Ma* refers to the overall timing of a piece—not just the pauses and rests, but also the relationship between sound and silence upon which all music is fundamentally based. It embraces the idea that sound enhances silence and silence enhances sound. This emphasis on silence conforms with Zen ideas concerning the importance of emptiness and space. The player who is aware of *ma* begins his notes with an instinctive care for the length and quality of the silences before and after. This concept applies particularly to music with a beatless rhythm, since the sounds and silences fall at irregular points and the player is more active in creating those moments.

Performers often link the concept of *ma* to the quality of a musical performance. Musicians speak of "good *ma*" or "bad *ma*," referring to the quality of the sounds and silences and their proportion to one another. When this proportion is deemed appropriate—a subjective judgment that is learned only from years of experience—then the performance has been successful.

Though the Fuke sect priests have long disappeared from the roads of Japan, many players keep the *shakuhachi* tradition alive today, both in Japan and abroad. Because of the instrument's versatility of pitch and timbre, composers and performers like to use it in various contemporary genres, such as jazz, fusion, and "new age" music. At the same time, the meditative, spiritual nature of the *honkyoku* is continually reaffirmed through performances given by several active *shakuhachi* masters, such as Yamaguchi Gorō,* Aoki Reibo, and others.

KOTO

The graceful music of the koto is familiar to many foreigners, since it has become well known outside Japan through concerts, records, and tapes. Whether played as a solo instrument or in an ensemble, with a vocal part or without one, the koto has for several centuries been one of the most popular traditional instruments of Japan.

---

*Japanese names are given in the Japanese order: family name followed by given name.

The contemporary koto is a long (about 1.8 meters), wooden instrument with 13 strings, traditionally silk but now also nylon. Bridges (called *ji*) hold the strings above the surface of the instrument, one for each string. These bridges are movable, so that the player can set them at different places along the string, depending on the desired tuning.

Like the prototype of the *shakuhachi,* the ancestor of the *koto* came to Japan from China during the early centuries of cultural exchange, after which the instrument was gradually adapted to its present form. After several centuries of use by an elite few, during the Tokugawa period the *koto* gradually spread in popularity to different segments of Japanese society. At this time changes in teaching and in the *koto* repertoire stimulated many men and women to learn it (Malm 1959:169). Growing numbers were merchants, the class that officially held the lowest status but which was gaining rapidly in wealth and influence. By the beginning of the Meiji period in 1868, the *koto* could be found in many private homes as well as in teahouses and theaters, and skilled *koto* performance had become a sign of good breeding for young women. Most of the *sōkyoku* (or *koto* music) pieces performed today were written during the Tokugawa period, when new schools and styles of playing arose. At this time the *koto* was used in ensembles with the *shamisen* and later the *kokyū* or *shakuhachi,* combinations that brought an important form of chamber music into Japanese life.

One of the most famous *koto* pieces is entitled "Rokudan," or "Six Sections." It is typical of the *danmono* type of instrumental pieces consisting of several "steps," or sections, known as *dan.* Each *dan* contains 104 beats and is repeated several times, with great variation. A short introduction of four to eight beats (four beats in the case of "Rokudan") begins the piece, and each *dan* follows the last without a break. The first four beats are followed by six *dan,* each 104 beats long.* Hearing the piece one time, however, can indicate that the *danmono* is anything but a simple theme-and-variation form, since the sections are difficult to tell apart. Even after listening to the piece several times, one might not be able to tell where a new *dan* begins because the melody of each *dan* is made up of short figures that are generally difficult to distinguish. The second and third *dan* are perhaps recognizable as related to the first, for they are closer to the melodic content of the first *dan;* after that the similarity in thematic material becomes less clear. Some basic melodic figures are heard again, but in a different part of the *dan,* or in a different range or rhythmic pattern.

Therefore, rather than trying to distinguish each section, it makes more sense to listen for the repetition of the short melodic figures as well as larger overall patterns. Some of the brief melodic-rhythmic patterns that recur include a descending dotted figure and octave leaps. As for larger patterns, the *jo-ha-kyū* structure mentioned in the beginning of this chapter may be applied to the piece as a whole. The first two *dan* make up the *jo,* or introductory section; the second

* Several recordings of this piece are available on LPs and tapes; one is on the record *The Music of Japan.* Record III: Music of the Edo Period. Kassel: Barenreiter-Musicaphon, a part of the series "UNESCO Collection–A Musical Anthology of the Orient." Also, a transcription of this piece appears in Adriaansz 1973:66–93.

Ex. 8–4. *"Rokudan," introductory figure.*

two *dan* find the tempo increasing, as in a *ha* section; and the tempo reaches its height in the final two *dan,* or the *kyū* section. The tempo slows down only toward the end, in the last twenty-two beats or so, ending in a long glissando. This form is also followed in individual *dan,* in which one can also sense a gradual building of tension.

In listening to this stately piece, we hear in the beginning four beats of "introduction" a long note of two beats followed by a descending note a fourth away, and then an interval of a fifth (ex. 8–4). This figure is easy to hear throughout the piece. The following beat of silence represents the first beat of the material repeated in each *dan.*

A careful listener can hear a variety of timbres and interesting tonal effects. Sometimes the pick of one finger sliding down the string creates a pitchless sound; sometimes glissandos brush the strings. There may be changes in pitch that sound like a sliding from one note to the next and back again. This is a result of changing the pressure exerted in the left hand on the string as the right hand plucks it. Such delicate shifting of pitch and tone color give *koto* music a special beauty.

KOUTA

Another of the well-loved Japanese traditional instruments is the *shamisen,* a three-stringed long-necked lute (see ill. 8–2). In contrast to the *shakuhachi,* which has associations with austere spirituality and meditation, the *shamisen* is often used to convey an outpouring of emotion and drama. For this reason it is considered an excellent instrument for the theater, expressing highly dramatic situations in the *bunraku* puppet theater to great effect. It is also used in another major theatrical form, *kabuki,* and sometimes to accompany folk song, as in recorded selection 48. In a more intimate setting, the *shamisen* also accompanies short, evocative songs called *kouta* (literally, "short song").

The present-day *shamisen* is a descendent of a long line of related instruments stretching back to the *sanshin* of Okinawa, the *san-hsien* of China, and perhaps further back to the Middle East or Central Asia.* While the Okinawan *sanshin* is covered with snakeskin, on the Japanese mainland the instrument is traditionally covered with cat skin, or sometimes dog skin. (As these are now expensive, however, plastic is commonly found on *shamisen* used for practice.) There are different kinds of *shamisen,* varying in shape, weight, material, and overall size;

* Theories that the Chinese *san-hsien* derived from Egyptian or Persian sources are summarized in Kikkawa 1981:157–158.

Ill. 8–2. *Geisha performing at a party. The woman on the right holds a shamisen.*

the type used depends on the musical genre played. The instrument used to accompany *kouta* songs, for example, is smaller and lighter than the one used in *bunraku* puppet theater.

The body of the *shamisen* is made of a wooden box roughly square in shape, covered on both sides with skin or plastic. A long piece of wood, forming the unfretted neck, is inserted into his box. Pegs at the top of the neck hold the three strings, each string of a different thickness. In some kinds of music, a large plectrum is used for striking and plucking the instrument. Sometimes in *kouta*, however, the bare fingers, or sometimes the fingernails, pluck the strings, producing a lighter, less percussive, sound.

A rather unusual sound in the *shamisen* confirms the importance of unpitched sounds in Japanese music. This is a special buzz or hum called *sawari* (literally, "touch") which is purposefully added to the instrument when it is made. The lowest string does not rest on the upper bridge but resonates against a special cavity made near the top of the instrument's neck. This string sets a noise in motion, to which the other strings can contribute in sympathetic vibration. The result is a pitchless buzzing sound that is essential to the tonal flavor of the *shamisen*. Whereas such buzzing noises are avoided in instruments used in Western classical music, Japanese instrument makers intentionally build such timbres into their instruments. Buzzing is also deliberately built into many African instruments (see chapter 3).

The *kouta* is a song form that evokes many images and allusions in a short (generally, one- to three-minute) time. *Kouta* as we know it today dates from the mid-nineteenth century, though the same name was used to describe another kind of song in earlier centuries (Kurada 1982:894–895).

The development of the present-day *kouta* is closely linked to the participation of women in Japanese traditional music. One of the earliest composers of *kouta* was O-Yo (1840–1901). The daughter of the head master of *kiyomoto* (a style of *shamisen* music used in *kabuki*), O-Yo was an excellent musician. As a woman, she was not allowed to take over her father's position after his death; instead she married a man who then inherited his title. But O-Yo took up most of his duties.

O-Yo was not allowed to play the *shamisen* on the *kabuki* stage since only males appeared there. She was, nevertheless, an active performer at private parties in teahouses and restaurants. For such private gatherings she probably composed *kouta* such as "Saru wa uki," thought to be the first *kouta* ever composed (Kikkawa 1981:350). Although women were banned from participating in many of the elite forms of music performance in Japan, they played a key role in teaching that music to generations of male performers. O-Yo herself was an important transmitter of the *kiyomoto* tradition of her father, teaching it to many people from all parts of Japan.

O-Yo's musical world and her involvement with both an older form of music (*kiyomoto*) and a new form (*kouta*) can best be understood in the context of the *iemoto* guild system. This system, active also in O-Yo's time, is a powerful influence on the traditional arts—music, dance, flower arranging, the tea ceremony, and many other artistic areas. The guild is the transmitter of knowledge and the legitimizer of teachers and performers in each art form.

In music, several different guilds may be involved with one type of music (for example, music for the *shakuhachi* or for the *nō* theater) but each guild will have its own slightly different performance style and repertoire. By illustration, one who wishes to become a *shakuhachi* performer must decide which style he or she wants to learn, then become affiliated with the guild that follows that style. Often this affiliation lasts as long as the individual performs on the *shakuhachi*.

Guilds not only transmit knowledge; they also control quality. Each guild sets the standards for teachers and pupils. If an individual works diligently, he or she may be given a license to teach and an artistic name from the guild. The *iemoto* system thus provides a structure through which the arts have been taught, performed, and preserved for hundreds of years in Japan.

The hierarchy of this *iemoto* system is rigid, bearing some similarity to the familial-paternalistic social structures found throughout Japanese society. Traditionally, the leader of each school inherits that position and strictly regulates rights to perform or teach. In theory, this system controls the "correct" transmission of musical information, but it also allows some leaders to exploit their helpless students. A greedy leader, for instance, might demand large amounts of money for the licenses required to be recognized as a qualified performer and teacher of his school, and the student would have no choice but to pay.

On the other hand, the number of scrupulous *iemoto* leaders and teachers far outweighs the number of exploitative ones; most teachers provide a great deal of support and encouragement to their students. Overall, the *iemoto* system has contributed positively to maintaining the artistic level in traditional Japanese music. Its strict regulation of performance standards has preserved musical traditions that could otherwise have changed drastically or even died out through the years.

According to the rules of this system, new composition in many genres of music was discouraged or even forbidden. This conservatism is linked to a reverence for tradition in the arts that is still prevalent among Japanese musicians today. Many believe that the "classic" body of music has been handed down with painstaking precision for decades, or centuries, through the toil of countless musicians. The composition of a new piece of music by an individual was for years considered "arrogant self-expression." If a new piece were composed and proved to have merit, it had to be ascribed to the leader of the guild, who in turn might attribute it to an earlier *iemoto* leader. This reluctance to accept new compositions meant that if they were written, they often had no official recognition. For this reason, when someone like O-Yo composed new music, it was in a new genre like *kouta*. Because there was no *iemoto* associated yet with that kind of music, the restrictions that would otherwise apply toward composition did not exist.

Today, among the forms of traditional music we can still see this restriction on new composition to some degree. New pieces are now written for traditional instruments in Japan, but they are often created outside of the traditional genres, such as in a mixture of *kabuki* music and rock known as *"kabuki* rock." Otherwise, as a rule, only high-ranking members of an *iemoto* create new compositions in a traditional mode.

By the end of the Tokugawa period, the *kouta* was linked to the *geisha* of the city of Edo (which became known as Tokyo in 1868) and the life of the teahouses. For many people today, the lively, intense world of Edo during the Tokugawa period epitomizes the Japanese spirit. Though the official Japanese capital was Kyoto, where the emperor resided, Edo was the actual seat of government where the *shōgun* held state in his castle. It was also the most populous city in Japan as well as one of the largest in the world. The influx of people from all over the country, crowded into tenements and wildly pursuing wealth, pleasure, or both, spurred the coining of the phrase "Edo wa tenka no hakidamari" (Edo is the nation's rubbish heap).

The streets teemed with *chōnin,* townspeople who were members of either the merchant or the artisan classes. With the expansion of the economy during the peaceful Tokugawa period, some *chōnin* became wealthy and powerful. They patronized the theaters, teahouses, and brothels, making their increasingly sophisticated mark on the aesthetics of the drama, music, and dance of the period: a sense of style that combines wit, sensuousness, and restraint. The Edo pursuit of momentary pleasure represents the epitome of the *ukiyo,* or "floating world."

The *kouta,* as sung by the *geisha* of such licensed quarters as the Yoshiwara area of Edo, reflects their world of beauty and style. The songs' lyrics often convey romantic or erotic themes, but such references are subtle. Puns, double-entendres and poetic devices appear frequently in *kouta* lyrics and sometimes even a Japanese will miss their suggestive undertones.

In the *kouta* example found in recorded selection 47, entitled "Hakusen no" (A White Fan), both the image of a white fan and the beauty of nature are used as metaphors for romantic commitment. This particular song shows little of the whimsical side of *kouta;* it is considered suitable for performance at wedding banquets or private parties. At the wedding banquet, this song would be sung to the honored couple.

Though declining in numbers, *geisha* are still trained in Japan to entertain at such occasions. The traditional musical instrument of the *geisha* is the *shamisen,* which is used often to accompany vocal music such as the *kouta.* This recording was made by a *geisha* in the 1960s who lived near the former Yoshiwara quarter of Tokyo.

Figure 8–2 shows the lyrics of the *kouta* and an English translation. (The letters on the left-hand side refer to melodic material and will be explained below.)

Traditional Japanese poetry arranges lines according to their syllabic content, favoring lines with five and seven syllables. The lyrics of "Hakusen no" contains alternating lines of five and seven syllables. (Extended vowels and the letter "n" at the end of a syllable count as separate syllables.) A poetic device known as *kakekotoba,* or "pivot word," is found on the sixth line: the word *kagayaku* ("shimmering") can be interpreted as both referring to the silver node of the fan (the pin holding the fan together at the bottom) and to the pine tree boughs, "shimmering" in the shadows. Such pivot words are often found in Japanese poetry and are made possible by the flexibility of Japanese grammar.

Several auspicious symbols appear in the text. The pine tree has a special sym-

Fig. 8–2. *"Hakusen no."*

A	Hakusen no	A white fan
B	sue hirogari no	spreading out
C	sue kakete	lasting forever
B	kataki chigiri no	the firm pledges
(A)	gin kaname	like the silver node of the fan
(B)	kagayaku kage ni	shimmering in shadows
D	matsu ga e no	the boughs of pine trees
E	ha-iro mo masaru	the splendid leafy color of
(B)	fukamidori	a deep green
E	tachiyoru niwa no	the clearness of the pond
(E)	ike sumite	in the garden approached
(B)	nami kaze tatanu	undisturbed by waves of wind,
C	mizu no omo	the surface of the water
B	urayamashii de	What an enviable life,
(B)	wa nai ka na.	don't you think?

bolism for the Japanese as a tree of special beauty and longevity. A clear pond, "undisturbed by waves or wind," also presents a peaceful, auspicious image of the future life of a couple. The words *sue hirogari* literally refer to the unfolding of a fan, but can also mean to enjoy increasing prosperity as time goes on.

Ex. 8–5 is a transcription of "Hakusen no" and, as in the *shakuhachi* example, the difficulties of conveying uneven time values in Western notation are apparent. The vocal part has been inserted rhythmically in relation to the steady beat of the *shamisen,* which is the easiest part to follow:

Ex. 8–5. *Transcription of "Hakusen no."*

Ex. 8–5. *(Continued)*

This transcription shows only the vocal and *shamisen* parts; in the recording, we also hear an accompanying ensemble made up of the *ko-tsuzumi* and *o-tsuzumi* drums and the *nōkan* flute. These instruments, typical of the *nō* theater, were added to the commercial recording of this song; *geisha* also sing "Hakusen no" with the *shamisen* alone. Another sound not transcribed above are the calls known as *kakegoe,* which help to cue the ensemble as well as add to the atmosphere of the song.

Earlier in this chapter a heterophonic relationship between two or more parts was defined as typical of Japanese ensemble music. In recorded selection 47,

Ex. 8–6. *Motif in shamisen part, "Hakusen no."*

such a heterophony characterizes the voice and *shamisen*. Rather than sounding simultaneously on the same beat, the two parts tend to weave in and out; sometimes the voice precedes the *shamisen* in presenting the melody and sometimes the *shamisen* plays the notes first. The result of this constant staggering and shifting is a duet in which the melody is shared and enhanced by both voice and instrument. An example of this heterophony can be found in the third line, as the *shamisen* anticipates several of the sung notes. Listening carefully to the entire song, try to find other such examples. Are there also times when the voice anticipates what the *shamisen* will play?

One of the most interesting aspects of the vocal part is the flexibility of beat, which contrasts to the even beat of the *shamisen*. See, for example, how the rhythm of the vocal and *shamisen* parts fit together in the line beginning "ta-chiyoru ..."; just as the listener thinks a predictable pattern has been established, the rhythm shifts. The sophistication of this kind of rhythmic contrast has appealed for centuries to the Japanese ear. Together, melodic and rhythmic variety in Japanese ensemble music create a complex, often exciting musical texture.

The vocal melody contains several thematic phrases that repeat in slightly varied forms. The letters next to the text in fig. 8–2 show one way of interpreting these phrases. Repeating letters indicate phrases that are repeated exactly or nearly exactly, while letters in parentheses signify more modified repetitions. For example, the seven different phrases marked "B" have in common long, repeated notes followed by a descending interval, highly ornamented, of a third to a sixth, or some part of this combination.

The *shamisen* part opens and closes the song with the same rhythmically emphasized theme and it occasionally plays a short solo phrase between lines of text. Occasionally, small motifs are repeated; one that occurs several times is shown in example 8–6:

This and other similar motifs in the *shamisen* part stress the notes D and G. The scale used in"Hakusen no" is the *in* scale (shown in Ex. 8–1), based on D. However, there are constant shifts to the same scale based on G, which is closely related to the D scale. A prominent difference between the two scales lies in the A-flat found in the G scale, whereas the D scale contains an A-natural. Another scale shift takes place in the line "kagayaku ...", which stresses the notes G - D^b - C, denoting a temporary change to the C-based *in* scale. Such rapid changes from one scale to another is common in Japanese music even in short songs like *kouta*.

Hearing this song, the listener is drawn into the refined yet playful atmosphere of the Tokugawa teahouses. Now we shall turn to a more dramatic atmosphere, the highly charged puppet theater.

GIDAYU-BUSHI: MUSIC OF THE PUPPET
THEATER

During the Tokugawa period, theater was one of the most popular forms of entertainment among the townspeople. While *nō* was a favored pastime of the elite, attendance at *kabuki* and *bunraku* (puppet theater) was restricted to members of the artisan and merchant classes (Ernst 1956:10). This restriction did not prevent members of the higher *samurai* class from sneaking into the theaters, sometimes wearing large hats or scarves over their heads to hide their identity.

Music is important in *kabuki* and *bunraku* theater, both as a background to the actions on stage and as an essential element of the play itself. In *bunraku*, for example, two musicians—a narrator-singer and a *shamisen* player—tell the story, speak and sing for the puppets, and provide scenes with background music (see ill. 8–3).

Japanese puppet theater utilizes elaborately costumed, large-sized dolls that are brought almost to life by skilled puppeteers and musicians. The *bunraku* plays include some of the most beautifully written works of Japanese drama, expressing intense emotions that appealed to the tastes of the Tokugawa towns-people. The skillfully manipulated dolls, realistic scenery and emotion-packed music, all part of a passionately dramatic scene, often reduced audiences to tears (ill. 8–4).

Ill. 8–3. *Bunraku stage. From this high view, we can see the sunken stage, not normally seen by the audience. The doll on the left plays the shamisen.*

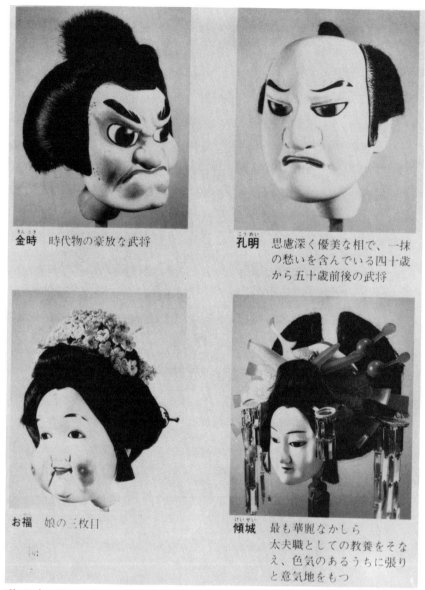

金時　時代物の豪放な武将

孔明　思慮深く優美な相で、一抹
　　　の愁いを含んでいる四十歳
　　　から五十歳前後の武将

お福　娘の三枚目

傾城　最も華麗なかしら
　　　太夫職としての教養をそな
　　　え、色気のあるうちに張り
　　　と意気地をもつ

**Ill. 8–4.   *Bunraku doll heads. On the upper left is a tough samurai, on
the upper right is a more refined samurai, on the lower left is a plain
young girl of the merchant class and on the lower right, the elegant
head of a young beauty.***

Important puppets require three manipulators: one for the head and right
hand, one for the left hand, and one for the feet. Apprentice manipulators
normally require several years of training on the feet, and then several more

三味線

文楽の三味線は太棹三味線と呼ばれ、胴も棹も糸も撥も、一番大きく出来ている。そのため、音も重くボリューム感があり、豊かな表現力をもつ。

三味線は単なる伴奏ではなく、「模様を弾く」つまり「情」が観客のこころに響くように弾くことが大切とされる。情景、季節、心理あらゆるものを、撥先に込めて表現する。

緊迫感

大夫と三味線は、どちらか片方が指揮者の立場に立つわけではなく、むしろ競演という形で演奏を進めていく。この緊迫感の積み重ねが、人形を息づかせる。

大夫・三味線・人形のいわゆる三業が、ひとつに燃え上がるとき感動の舞台となる。

大夫

文楽は、大夫・三味線・人形の三つの要素から成り立っている。

その中でも、魂のない人形に命を吹き込むとき、大夫の占める役割は大きい。

大夫は「情を語る」つまり登場人物のこころを観客に伝えることが大切とされる。

三百年の伝統を基礎に、鍛練を重ねた結果が、今日の大夫の技巧につながる。

「判官切腹の段」を弾く鶴澤清治
三味線はすべて暗譜である。

「判官切腹の段」を語る竹本越路大夫
見台と呼ばれる台の上に床本（台本）をのせる
目遣いからも、浄瑠璃のこころぐみがうかがえる

Ill. 8–5. *Music of bunraku. On the left, the shamisen player, and the right, the tayu narrator.*

years on the left hand before they become chief manipulators who are allowed to manipulate the head and right hand. These manipulators wear black, with hoods over their heads, so as to "disappear" in the background.*

To the right of the main stage is a smaller stage on which the narrator-singer (*tayū*) and *shamisen* player sit. At the beginning of the performance, or in the middle of a play when a change in musical personnel is needed, the wall of the smaller stage rotates to reveal the musicians on the other side. (For some scenes, more than one *tayū* or *shamisen* player may be needed, and these make their entrance from the wings of the stage is a less dramatic way.) Before beginning the play, the *tayū,* who is sitting on the floor, lifts the text from the lacquered lectern on which it rests and bows with it—a sign of respect and a prayer for a good performance (see ill. 8–5).

Together, the narrator and the *shamisen* player try to fill the puppets with life, expressing emotion that is sometimes blatant and exaggerated, or sometimes

---

* Well-known manipulators can appear with their faces exposed, and even in festive costumes, but the emotional content of the scene ultimately dictates the costumes of manipulators. In solemn scenes, for example, all manipulators will normally appear hooded and in black.

subtle and subdued. As one *tayū* states: "The whole point of *bunraku* is to portray human emotions and situations in life so that people's hearts are moved, so that they feel something special about the particular aspect of life the play deals with, whether loyalty, sacrifice, one of the many forms of love, or a dilemma one encounters in life" (Adachi 1985:65).

Working toward this goal, neither *tayū* nor *shamisen* player is regarded as more important than the other; instead, they form a closely cooperating team. Sensing each other's feelings (as well as those of the audience), the two make subtle adjustments in their singing and playing in order to convey emotion through the dolls as effectively as possible. One narrator working in Osaka (the traditional capital of *bunraku*) told me: "When I play with a *shamisen* player that I've known and performed with for many years, we are so accustomed to sensing each other's moods and feelings from performing on stage that I can tell as soon as we sit down together whether or not he's had a fight with his wife that morning!"

To a listener unfamiliar with *bunraku*, the energetic narration of the *tayū* can sound startlingly exaggerated. Indeed, it seems amazing that one man can have the stamina to shout, growl and sing out for such a long time, filling the hall with his large voice.* Developing this kind of stamina takes years of training, and sore throats are not uncommon among those in this profession. One narrator describes his training this way:

> No matter how big the theater, we never use a microphone; all is produced from our bodies alone. You must practice producing the voice from your lower abdomen. When we become narrators, we're told "Make your voice come from your *hara* (lower abdomen)!" And we wonder how that is possible. We learn abdominal breathing, a breathing movement in your stomach. You take in big breaths and let out just enough. You must feel in every part of your body that the voice accompanying the breath is there. But before you understand how the voice can come out of the abdomen, you really have to suffer a lot.†

Some *tayū* even use a small bag of sand, inserted inside the kimono near the stomach, which they use as a kind of "leverage" for their hands and stomach muscles to obtain the air they need.

Traditional training of the *tayū* and *shamisen* player were more strict than at present. Until the early part of this century, the apprentice narrator or *shamisen* player normally moved into his teacher's home at the age of six or seven. After years of helping with household chores, he was permitted to help his master prepare for performances and then, finally, to receive lessons himself. In the meantime, before beginning his own lessons, the apprentice had already listened to thousands of hours of lessons and performances of those around him, absorbing much about the music. In actual lessons, it was important for him to

---

* The *tayū* is referred to as a male here, but there have been female narrators as well, particularly from the mid-nineteenth to the early twentieth century. Today, female amateur *tayū* perform in some small theaters throughout the country (Motegi 1988:206–20).
† Personal communication with Toyotake Sakitayu, April 26, 1986.

learn to imitate what he heard quickly since new material might be presented only once or twice before he was expected to have memorized it. The *shamisen* player Tsuruzawa Juzō, born in 1899, describes his training in the following way:

> Nowadays people ask about the hardships of my early training. At the time I didn't think a thing about it. Life was that way then and young people were used to discipline, punishment, and grueling training. . . . My teacher would play a passage, maybe fifteen minutes long, just once. I was expected to play along with him. Next I was made to play the passage solo. My teacher would sit there scowling at me, scolding, sometimes hitting me in the face. Knowing the punishment that lay in store, I learned quickly to listen very, very carefully, straining every fiber in my body to absorb everything I possibly could with eyes, ears and mind.
>
> In those days, our whole life was Bunraku. We had no movies, no coffee shops, no radios, no popular music to distract us. . . . Our heads were full of Bunraku and only Bunraku. (Adachi 1985:79)

After World War II, however, this teaching process changed dramatically. The *bunraku* theater itself went through difficult times after 1945, partly because of a decline in the wealth of its former sponsors, and partly from an overall decrease of interest in the traditional arts. As professional *bunraku* performers found it more difficult to make a living, new trainees declined in number. Furthermore, even those who were willing to study for a career with such an uncertain future were often discouraged by the rigorous training involved. To counter these trends, new teaching methods were developed to ensure that *gidayū-bushi* would be passed on to future generations. These methods rely on relatively short training hours; one can finish the *tayū* training course of the National Theater in two years, for example.* New features of this training course include the use of standardized instructional methods, scores, and tape recorders to record lessons and performances. While these methods do produce an adequate narrator or *shamisen* player in a short amount of time, the resulting uniformity of performance and interpretation is deplored by older musicians:

> They [the performers trained by the new methods] make no distinction in their playing between scenes with different settings. Even the same melody should have different emotional tones, depending on the context. It all comes from practicing with tapes, without giving any thought to the meaning of the text. They master the form but cannot express the content. With tapes you can practice in your sleep. (Motegi 1984:105)

The modern methods used to transmit *bunraku* music allow students to learn faster and with less pain. But the new training produces a different quality of performer.

All of the musical genres described in this chapter so far are closely tied to the social life of the Tokugawa period from which several common threads emerge.

---

* The National Theater of Japan is a government-sponsored institution that contains facilities for the presentation of traditional theater, dance, and music, as well as for the training of future artists.

For one, we see how the four-tiered class system shaped and defined various aspects of musical life. Many musical and art forms were limited, even by official decree, to a specific class: the *shakuhachi* to the *rōnin* priests, or the *kabuki* and *bunraku* to the merchant class. Social change during the Tokugawa period also reflected changes in music and class, as formerly elite instruments like the *koto* were spread to the lower merchant class.

The next two kinds of music that we will examine, folk song and festival music, traditionally have belonged to the farming class or the poorer merchants in the cities. But people from many levels of society, in Tokugawa times as now, know these musics. Folk and festival music are still found in many everyday locations: in the streets, in the fields, and at social occasions of both the city and countryside.

FOLK SONG

In traditional Japan, people sang folk songs, or *minyō,* while they planted the rice in spring, threw their fishnets into the sea, wove cloth, and pounded grain. Folk songs accompanied many daily activities—to relieve boredom, to provide a steady beat for some activity, as encouragement for a group working at some task, as individual expression, or as a combination of these.

While the everyday uses of folk song have not entirely disappeared from Japan, fewer contemporary Japanese are finding them relevant to their lives. Seventy-six percent of the Japanese population lives in cities, where everyday activities involve riding crowded trains and sitting at desks all day rather than planting rice and weaving cloth (Sōri-fu 1982:22). Still, based on a 1982 survey of musical preferences, folk song, or *minyō,* is one of the most popular forms of music in Japan today (NHK Hōsō 1982:68).

The continuing popularity of folk songs is tied to their identification with the countryside and a sometimes romanticized vision of rural life on the part of city dwellers. Folk songs evoke a past thought to be simpler and more natural, and this appeals to many Japanese today.

In addition to an association with rural life, many Japanese folks songs connect to a specific region of the country. This is the case in "Nikata-bushi," in recorded selection 48, from the region of Akita in northwestern Japan. With the growth of industry in the years after World War II, many Japanese left the rural areas to find work in the cities, and today people from a particular region—or their descendants—gather in many of these urban areas and sing folk songs as reminders of the villages from which they came.

> Despite increasing geographic mobility and cultural homogenization, the Japanese identification of people and songs with their original home areas is still very strong: a Tokyo laborer whose family roots are in the northern prefecture of Akita will be expected to enliven a festive gathering with an Akita folk song. (Hughes 1981:30)

Furusato, or the concept of a home community, maintains a strong emotional grip on today's urban dwellers—even if they left home several decades earlier. The folk song, with its associations and allusions to a particular region, expresses their nostalgia for a faraway place. Thus, nostalgia not only for a different time, but for a different place as well underlies their popularity.

Finally, perhaps because *minyō* were traditionally sung by ordinary people, not trained professionals, the Japanese still find them easy to learn and appreciate—for the Japanese not only listen to folk songs, they usually learn to sing a few as well, either from family and friends or in elementary school. Often they sing them at parties, when they are called on to sing a favorite song. Real enthusiasts take lessons with a good singer and attend folk song clubs or other gatherings where they can perform in front of other enthusiasts. Amateur folk song contests have become a regular feature on Japanese television, presenting folk singers from around the country. In these contests, singers give their renditions of folk songs which are then evaluated by a board of "experts," who might tell the singer his or her vibrato is too broad or hand gestures too dramatic for that particular song.

Folk song preservation societies have sprung up around the country. These societies are formed by amateurs who aim to "preserve" a particular local song and a style of performing that song. The activities of these clubs help foster pride and a sense of identity among the dwellers of a village or a neighborhood within a city (Hughes 1981).

Folk song performance has become more professional and standardized in recent years due to televised *minyō* and the changing tastes of the public. For example, *kobushi,* the sometimes complex vocal ornamentation of a melodic line, is frequently used to separate the good performers from the bad. One critic of this trend claims: "There is a tendency to think that the most excellent kind of folk song is that sung by a person with a good voice who can produce interesting kinds of vocal ornamentation. But if folk song is valued only for interesting ornamentation, it becomes nothing more than a 'popular song'" (Asano 1966:211). The critic noted, however, that national tastes and way of thinking have changed so much since 1945 that perhaps there is no way of avoiding change in folk singing.

Training to sing folk song at a professional level demands years of study. In recent years, folk song has developed its own *iemoto*-like system, modeled after that found in traditional art music. Asano Sanae, the singer on recorded selection 48, for example, has been a pupil of the *shamisen* player, Asano Umewaka, for several years (see ill. 8–6). In the manner of the *iemoto* system, she received her artistic name from him, including her teacher's last name. As a teenager, she moved from Osaka to Akita to become his apprentice and she now participates regularly in concerts and competitions. Her teacher, in his seventies at the time of this recording, grew up in the Akita area and spent most of his life as a farmer, while slowly gaining a local and then a national reputation as a fine player of the *Tsugaru shamisen,* a type of *shamisen* used for virtuoso accompaniment of folk

Ill. 8–6. *Folk singer of Akita. The woman on the right is Asano Sanae, who sings recorded selection 48. A fellow apprentice, Asano Yoshie, stands in the middle. This picture was taken in 1986 at the Folklife Festival of the Smithsonian Institution, Washington, D.C.*

song. His former students live throughout Japan and teach his style of *shamisen* playing and singing.

According to Sanae, Asano himself can be hard taskmaster, but he teaches his pupils with great care. She underwent a kind of apprenticeship, helping with household chores and her teacher's performances while receiving lessons. Therefore, she experienced the everyday exposure and learning from repetition that the *gidayu-bushi* apprentices of earlier times had (see ill. 8–7).

Listening to recorded selection 48, a song called "Nikata-bushi," we hear first the sound of the *shamisen,* but with a stronger tone than we heard in the *kouta* example. This *shamisen* is indeed different in construction, with a larger body, longer neck, and thicker skin. The first notes sound on the open strings, allowing the player to tune his instrument before beginning the piece. (You can hear the pitch change slightly as the player adjusts the strings.) The same "tuning" occurs later, in the instrumental interlude between verses.

The song text is composed of two verses, each set in the syllabic pattern typical of folk song: 7–7–7–5 (fig. 8–3).

The text of each verse is set to almost identical music, even down to the ornamentation used. Similarly, the patterns heard in the *shamisen* part between the two verses almost repeat the patterns played in the introduction.

As in the *kouta* example, the instrument plays a more or less steady pulse while the voice has a flexible rhythm. Look, for example, at the long notes and

Ill. 8–7. *Asano Umewaka before singing Akita folk songs at the Folklife Festival of the Smithsonian Institution, Washington, D.C.*

ornamentation in the vocal part, as seen in this transcription of the beginning of the second verse (ex. 8–7). In the transcription a time line underneath follows the regular beats of the *shamisen* part, so that the vocal part can be seen in relation to a steady unit of time.

This transcription was made at half speed, in order to catch the different

Nikata tera-machi	The temple town Nikata
no hana baasama	a woman selling flowers
hana mo urazu ni	she doesn't sell them
abura uru.	but enjoys herself instead.

Takai o-yama no	On a high mountain
goten no sakura	a cherry blossom tree at a mansion
eda wa nana eda	has seven branches
yae ni saku.	and blossoms abundantly.

Fig. 8–3. *"Nikata-bushi" (folk song).*

pitches that normally hit our ears at a rapid pace. Pitches that are discernible at that speed are notated; vibrato within a range of less than a semitone is simply marked "vib." Looking at the different methods of ornamenting notes, we find many instances of rapid fluctuations between the note just voiced and a new note, before the new note is sounded and held. We also find several instances (for example, during the word *o-yama*) when a trill is performed between two notes that are as far apart as a perfect fourth. This technique of ornamenting the line requires great vocal control.

The perfect fourth and perfect fifth are important intervals in many Japanese folk songs. In the transcribed section, for example, the longest notes are D", G' and D', and these tones are the pivotal notes throughout the song. Both the *yo* scale and *minyo* tetrachords can be discerned here. Just before the voice enters with each verse, the *shamisen* player makes an exclamation that sounds like "huh!" This is another example of *kakegoe,* as first heard in the *kouta* selection.

Sanae's elderly teacher might be considered a "true," old-fashioned folk singer and *shamisen* player in this Tsugaru style, having learned it from childhood in his own native area. On the other hand, Sanae has studied purposefully to become a professional folk singer. This training is reflected in many ways in her performance, such as her ornamentation, precision, clarity of voice, and general presentation. Her singing of *minyō* interests us, however, because Japanese increasingly value these qualities today in a *minyō* singer.

FESTIVAL MUSIC: MATSURI-BAYASHI

Strolling down the street, visitors to Japan may be lucky enough to run into a boisterous crowd celebrating a *matsuri,* or Shinto festival. As people spill over from the sidewalks into the streets, a parade marches by with people dressed up in *kimonos,* some riding in floats or carrying huge portable shrines. In the heart of all the activity is a Shinto shrine, with the distinctive red *torii* gate, where scores of vendors are selling steaming noodles and old-fashioned toys, or offering chances to win a goldfish. In the background, the music of the festival,

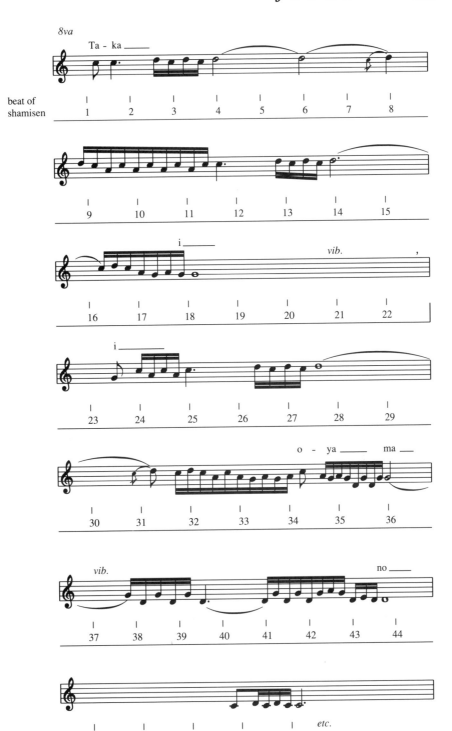

Ex. 8–7. *"Nikata-bushi."*

matsuri-bayashi, adds life and gaiety to the scene as the sounds of a graceful bamboo flute and booming drums fill the air (ill. 8–8).

Even in Tokyo, the capital and largest city of Japan, Shinto festivals are still held within the business districts and small neighborhoods scattered across the city. In every corner of the city—even in the most expensive commercial districts—a Shinto shrine can be found that serves as the tutelary or guardian shrine for that area. By offering prayers and festivities to the god-spirit, or *kami,* housed in the shrine, the residents receive the spirit's blessings for the year.

Although there is no legal or official relationship between a Shinto shrine and its neighborhood, many residents still feel it is important to help sponsor and participate in the traditional festival each year. They form committees and raise money to buy costumes, repair the parade floats, and so on. The festival is usually maintained in older neighborhoods with a stable population because of tradition—the residents have enjoyed their neighborhood *matsuri* for several generations. In Japanese cities, the neighborhood has been traditionally an important social unit—neighbors all knew one another and helped each other when needed, through both formal neighborhood associations and informal ties.

Since the end of World War II, however, there has been a dramatic rise in the mobility of the population as well as an increase in the white-collar sector of the population. As a result, urban neighborhood social ties have become more fragile because of shallower acquaintances with neighbors and fewer professional ties between them. Thus, some neighborhoods with a high turnover of

Ill. 8–8.   *A Tokyo festival. The grounds of the Shinto shrine are covered with the booths of food and game vendors.*

population are also finding the traditional *matsuri* a good way to encourage a feeling of neighborhood friendliness.

With the high cost of living in Tokyo, families with roots in that city are moving in greater numbers to the suburbs. But there still remain some people like the Ueno family, who have lived in Tokyo for several generations. Teachers and performers of festival music, they live in the heart of *shitamachi,* or the "downtown" area. This is the older commercial area, long since passed up in large-scale development projects, where narrow streets are still lined with small, two-story wooden houses. Tokyo has some of the highest land prices in the world, and most houses seem to take up an unbelievably small amount of land. They are built so that their sliding front door comes right up to the sidewalk, leaving no land left unused. To provide some greenery in their surroundings, many residents put out pots of flowers and small trees on the sidewalk. Because the walls of the house are so thin, one can often hear, just walking by, all that goes on within—the television blaring, arguments between children, dishes being washed, and so on. Some of the buildings have small shops on the first floor, above which the shopkeepers and their families live. The women go shopping for groceries at the neighborhood stores, though they also sometimes shop at the big department stores outside their neighborhood. If there are no bath facilities in the house, the whole family bathes in the neighborhood public bathhouse. Bringing soap and plastic bucket with them, they spend time there each day chatting with friends. This close proximity and everyday contact with neighbors brings about a spirit of cooperation and solidarity within the community rarely seen in the suburbs of Tokyo.

When it is time to hold a festival at the small neighborhood shrine, much of the neighborhood becomes involved. The festival is usually held over two or three days. On a stage on the shrine grounds, a musical group—the *matsuri-bayashi* mentioned earlier—plays throughout the day as a musical offering to the *kami* spirit. At some shrines, mimed skits and dances are performed as well to musical accompaniment.

The main event of the festival is a parade that winds through the neighborhood streets. Its principal element is the *mikoshi,* a portable shrine in which the *kami* of the shrine has been temporarily installed. The *kami*'s ride through the neighborhood blesses it for the coming year. The shrine is elaborately decorated in gold and black lacquer and sometimes weighs as much as two tons (making it less "portable" than the translation of the term suggests). From fifty to more than one hundred men (and, lately, women too) hoist it on their shoulders and, tossing it up and down, carry it through the streets for several hours. Shouting repeatedly *"was-shoi,"* or some such exclamation to coordinate their movements, the *mikoshi*-bearers make a colorful sight, dressed in traditional cotton jackets and pants. Along the parade route, spectators cheer them on. During this often rowdy parade, several festival music groups play at different locations: some remain at the permanent shrine, some perform on platforms along the parade route, and others play in floats in the parade (ill. 8–9).

Five musicians play the music of the *matsuri-bayashi* of Tokyo: two play the

Ill. 8–9. *Matsuri-bayashi ensemble in the festival parade.*

shallow double-headed drums called *shimedaiko* (or, more commonly in Tokyo, *shirabe*); one plays the *ōdaiko,* a deep-barreled drum; one the *shinobue,* a
transverse bamboo flute; and one the *yosuke,* a hand-held gong. In other parts
of Japan, different instruments are used for festival music, but these almost
always include flutes and drums (see ill. 8–10).

A close musical relationship is crucial to the performance of *matsuri-bayashi.*

Ill. 8–10. *Matsuri-bayashi of Tokyo. The two shimedaiko drums are on the right, the ôdaiko on the left. This was a performance at Columbia University, New York.*

Each of the musicians, while specializing on one instrument, must learn them all to become proficient. Only then can each one listen to the others' parts and know exactly where every player is in the piece. This degree of familiarity is important because the different instruments often "bend" the rhythm slightly by either holding back or speeding up their tempos. The gong player must keep an absolutely steady beat, though not sounding all the possible beats. After treating the constant beat so flexibly throughout most of the piece, all the instruments should meet exactly together at the end of each phrase. When well done, this simultaneous finish is regarded as the sign of a truly skillful ensemble. But if a member of the ensemble gets "lost" while playing with the beat in this way, the result can be disastrous. Only the best ensembles, with years of experience performing together, can carry off this rhythmic game properly.

The example of *matsuri-bayashi* heard in recorded selection 49 is called "Yatai" and is the opening and closing section of a longer piece called "Kiribayashi" by the Ueno group. (The *yatai* is the wagon used to carry the *matsuri-bayashi* musicians in the festival parade.) The highly ornamented flute melody leads in and out of each section, while the vigorous drum patterns resound at increasing tempi. The main part of this section, after a short introduction, consists of seven repeated phrases (sometimes with variations thrown in) which accelerate with each repetition. At the end of one of these cycles the flute signals for the group to enter a final "coda" section.

In "Yatai," the first drum that enters is a *shirabe;* it sets the tempo for the entire piece. The flute enters with its introductory phrase, joined soon after by the two *shirabe* drums; finishing this section is a two-beat stroke by the large *ōdaiko* drum.

Even in this piece, with a heavy regular beat provided by the *shirabe* drums, the flute part and the deeper *ōdaiko* can vary the tempo just a little in order to make the rhythm more interesting. The flute's heavy ornamentation masks some of this rushing and holding back, but still the player is expected to meet the others at the end of each phrase.

This is the first piece taught to a new pupil in *matsuri-bayashi* by the Ueno family of downtown Tokyo: rapid repetition occurs, student copies teacher. Comparing their typical *matsuri-bayashi* lessons to the lessons in *gigayu-bushi,* we see some similarities to the past but without the pressure of the old days. A lesson with Ueno Mitsuyuki and his son Mitsumasa might proceed as follows.* The student slides open the front door and calls out, "Good evening." Upon being invited to enter, the student immediately removes his shoes and takes a big step up to the level of the first floor of the house. There, on the *tatami* mats, the student bows to Ueno-*sensei* (*sensei* means teacher) and his family, who are all seated in an inner room. The lesson takes place in the room entered by the front door, and since musical instruments and household items are stacked along the walls, the sitting space is only about two meters by two meters. The family is still eating dinner and talking loudly to each other over the sound from the television set.

The teacher likes to chat with students before beginning a lesson. He might talk about his experiences in Tokyo during the war, or the latest *kabuki* performance he attended, or a recent argument with a neighbor. Then, after more students have arrived, either he or his son begins the lesson. In place of a real drum they use an old tire because of the neighbor's complaints about late-night practice sessions. This tire is placed in the middle of the tiny front room. Students and teacher sit on their knees around it, sticks in hand. The teacher begins to teach a new phrase of a piece by hitting the tire in mirror image to the way the performer normally plays, so that the students looking at him can easily learn the correct hand movements.

While striking the "drum" (the *shirabe,* or small drum, part is normally taught first), the teacher also calls out syllables to help the students remember the rhythm of the phrase they are playing. When there is no drum part, he hums or sings the flute melody and inserts some of the *ōdaiko* beats as well by hitting the side of the tire with one of his sticks. All parts are taught through a type of solmization (the syllables that stand for pitch or rhythm). Most genres of traditional Japanese music have their own solmization systems.

In matsuri-bayashi, the solmization of the *shirabe* part in the main section of the recorded selection is shown in fig. 8–4.

It is not difficult to reproduce this rhythmic pattern by tapping a flat surface with the fingers. Begin each phrase with the right hand and do not use the same hand for two consecutive beats, except at the beginning of a new phrase (which

---

* The elder Ueno passed away in 1983, but the present tense is used here to refer to his life and work.

Fig. 8–4. *"Yatai" (matsuri-bayashi).*

should start with the right hand again). Comparing this solmization (which is sometimes called *shōka* in Japanese) to the Western notation shown, we can see that "ten" equals two half-beats, "tsu" equals a half-beat rest, and "ke" equals a half-beat following a half-beat rest. (No syllables are spoken on the last beat of the phrase, though a rest of one beat occurs there.)

Students write down these syllables to help them remember the rhythmic patterns of the drums, and a similar system helps them to memorize the flute melody. However, merely hearing the syllables, without hearing them performed, gives only a vague notion of how they are to be played. The "score" that results is at best a memory device to help the student recall what was taught. As a consequence, Japanese music characteristically lacks a detailed notation system. The teacher is critical to a student's mastering any musical form. Without teachers who are willing to convey a great deal of their musical knowledge, students would be helpless, for scores do not give them access to real musical knowledge.

A good relationship with a knowledgeable teacher is also essential if a student wants to learn any *hikyoku,* or secret pieces. Found in many genres of traditional music, including *matsuri-bayashi,* the secret repertoire consists of rarely performed pieces handed down only to the most trusted of pupils. In the style of festival music taught by the Ueno family, the secret pieces were described by the son as not technically difficult but valued mainly because of their exclusivity. In the past, this knowledge was so guarded that some *hikyoku* have disappeared because teachers have died before finding pupils worthy of learning their secrets.

The lives of Ueno Mitsuyuki and his son vividly exemplify the traditional and contemporary backgrounds of those who love Tokyo festivals and festival music. *Matsuri-bayashi* is traditionally performed by amateurs such as the Uenos, while *kagura,* the mimed plays based on Shinto themes, is carried out by professional actors and musicians (ill. 8–11). According to the father, performing *matsuri-bayashi* strictly as an amateur is important because it is really a pious act of offering entertainment to the gods, not a "performance" or "show." Therefore, he performs only at the festivals themselves. The son, however, while preferring to play at festivals, also plays occasionally with some of the professional *kagura* musicians who have learned how to play *matsuri-bayashi.* These musicians are frequently hired to provide a musically festive atmosphere at secular occasions such as wedding receptions and department store openings.

For both father and son, however, *matsuri-bayashi* remains secondary to their

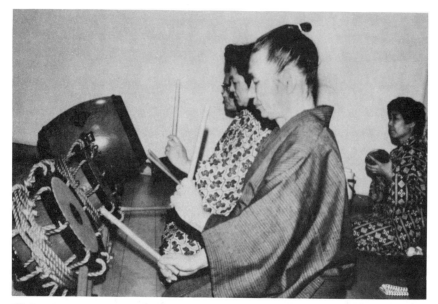

Ill. 8–11. *Ueno Mitsuyuki playing matsuri-bayashi.*

main profession, which is *chōkin,* or metal carving. This intricate art uses silver and gold to create jewelry (such as pins and ornaments for the *kimono*), sword guards, Japanese pipe holders, and small elegant statues of Buddha. The technique, a combination of engraving and inlay, requires years of training and great patience.

The life of Ueno Mitsuyuki epitomizes the spirit of the Edo *matsuri-bayashi.* Born in 1900 in the old downtown area of Tokyo, Ueno proudly tells of his family's long history in Edo. They came to Edo at the beginning of the Tokugawa era (in the early seventeenth century) from Aichi Prefecture. His grandfather was of the *samurai* class, which was dissolved with the class system during the Meiji period. In the 1880s, Ueno's father learned metal carving and *matsuri-bayashi.* Ueno's mother, as the daughter of the priest of an important shrine in the area, was active throughout her life in their own neighborhood festival.

At the age of fourteen, Ueno began to study metal carving seriously, dropping for a time all other hobbies and interests. After he had finished his metal carving training with his father, Ueno studied *matsuri-bayashi* with his uncle, a talented musician. Ueno says: "In the old days, the teacher told the students they were stupid and played poorly and maybe even hit them, but without explaining exactly what was wrong. In this way, I learned both *matsuri-bayashi* and metal carving—the technique became a part of my bones. But these days, people want to be told exactly what is wrong so that they can learn the art quickly and start making money from it." He learned *matsuri-bayashi* easily and soon became well known for his flute-playing style.

Ueno was too old to be accepted in the military during World War II, and he became active in the neighborhood association, which organized drills and fought fires in his area. He recalls the many times American planes dropped bombs on Tokyo, which quickly set afire the closely packed wooden houses, leaving thousands homeless within minutes. But he also blames the military leaders of Japan for dragging their country into such a bloody war, and laments the loss of life on all sides.

When he was thirty-six, relatively late in life, Ueno married a woman from his own neighborhood in Tokyo. His son Mitsumasa was born in 1953, when Ueno was already in his fifties, and he was therefore determined to teach the boy the skills he knew as early as possible. Knowing how long it would take to learn the intricate arts of metal carving and *matsuri-bayashi,* Ueno was afraid there would not be enough time for him to teach everything he knew to his son. He began teaching Mitsumasa the drum part of *matsuri-bayashi* when the boy was three, and metal carving when he was seven. Lessons were conducted every day for one hour after school. By the time he was fifteen, Mitsumasa had become proficient enough in both arts to satisfy his father that his skills had been faithfully transmitted to the next generation.

Ueno told me that he was never bored. Every day he rises after only four or five hours of sleep and, no matter what the weather, strolls to the various shrines in his neighborhood at 4 A.M. to offer prayers. He then begins his work day upstairs in his workshop, together with his son. Sitting side by side, they work almost every day of the week. Father and son stop for a meal at midday; in the early evening, with the disappearance of daylight, they finish their day's work. (Because the work is so intricate, working by daylight is much easier than by artificial light.) Around 7 at night three days a week, the first pupils arrive and the music lessons begin. As there is a great deal of chatting and serving of tea, the lessons sometimes go on until 10 or 11 P.M.

The father exhibits a characteristic typical of the *Edokko,* or "child of Edo"—a nonchalant attitude toward money. For instance, he refuses to sell pieces of his metal carving of which he is especially fond. Also, he readily turns down commissions for work, even when in need of it, if making the requested object does not appeal to him. As Ueno put it: "If you had the choice between gold and silver or paper (money), which would you prefer? And we're not talking about just plain gold and silver, but something you've created out of them which is unique in the world." Then he gave a self-deprecatory laugh and said, "Do you believe there are such innocent people left in the world as myself?" By the same token, the Uenos accept only a small amount of money for the music lessons they give. The father once confided that they would rather give the lessons free, but found that people did not take them seriously if they did not pay something for them.

In spite of their relative poverty and busy lives, the Uenos still find the materials and the time to create with their own hands many of the items needed for the annual neighborhood festival. These include masks and costumes for the mimed plays in which they participate, as well as the drawing of designs to be dyed into the material of the musicians' *kimonos.*

Ueno feels that his profession of metal carving and his hobby of *matsuri-bayashi* have one important quality in common. This is the feeling, as a practitioner, that one is never "finished," or has reached a point of perfection. "This is what makes life interesting: that which you want to do is never in a state of perfection, so you always have to strive to do better. That's why I enjoy metal carving and why I enjoy *matsuri-bayashi.*"

As for the son, Mitsumasa, from the earliest moment he can remember, his father reiterated the importance of his learning both metal carving and *matsuri-bayashi* as soon as possible. In the beginning, Mitsumasa says, he was actually not very interested in carving; but his father said, "Just give it a try." And so, he says, "I've been giving it a try for over 25 years now!

Now the son is proud of carrying on the work of his father, both the metal carving and the festival music. Mitsumasa is one of the few young practitioners of metal carving, and already has won many prizes for his work. As for *matsuri-bayashi,* he says, "I've got that music in my blood now, so as long as I'm around, I want to be playing it." As was the case with his father, the son's flute playing has become well admired and professional musical troupes seek his services.

Today, both folk song and festival music are becoming professionalized and standardized. Folk song in particular seems to be adopting the standards of the "art" genres like *shakuhachi* and *koto* music, with their *iemoto* systems, rankings, and artistic names. As for *matsuri-bayashi,* not only the younger Ueno, but many other Tokyo *matsuri-bayashi* players feel the lure of professional troupes, aware of the income and prestige they could attain as a member of such a company. As musicians join *iemoto* and professional organizations, the pressure to conform to certain performance standards increases.

POPULAR MUSIC

The traditional music genres described up to now had been conveyed from performer to audience without electronic media for many centuries. At a single performance the audience of these traditional genres was relatively small, and establishing rapport with that audience was crucial to success. Today, music performances are regularly presented on radio, television, and other media. A single recorded performance may be heard by millions of people who are unseen to the musicians.

In addition to changing the ways traditional music is played and perceived, mass media and technology have also stimulated the growth of a new kind of music in Japan, which we shall call here "popular music."* Since 1907, when the first commercial music recording was released in Japan, the composition, performance, and appreciation of music has changed dramatically. Music recorded specifically for commercial release in Japan, with the aim of appealing to the mass audience, exhibits several characteristics:

---

* Popular music is defined here as music primarily created for and transmitted by the various mass media. While some genres of so-called popular song that flourished among the masses in pre-Meiji Japan also have exerted an impact on the popular music of today, only those genres particularly linked to contemporary popular genres are discussed here.

1. Performance within a set time limit (generally three to five minutes).

2. A focus on themes that appeal to a broad public (though regional or specialty audiences are also sometimes targeted).

3. Stanza form and a steady beat, making the music more accessible to the Japanese who have become more accustomed to Western music.

4. In live performance, performers aim to reproduce the recorded version of the music so as to fulfill audience expectations.

5. Music rises and falls dramatically in popularity over time.

This "Top 40" mentality was novel to the Japanese; in their previous experience it was common for many kinds of music dating from different eras in Japanese history to survive side by side as vital elements of the country's musical life. Now, through the association of songs with a specific point in time, generations have begun to identify with "their" songs, with the result that music can be used as an age marker.

Through the mass media, music performed by "others" (particularly professionals) became more available to more people than ever before. Today, there is scarcely a home in Japan without a radio, television set, or stereo, and many have all three. As people listen to the same recordings and to the same performance of a song, they are united by a common musical experience; they also develop certain expectations as to what music should sound like.

Of course, a similar process has occurred worldwide as popular music has penetrated all corners of the globe. In Japan, the spread of music through records, tapes, and compact discs has advanced very rapidly. In fact, since the mid-1970s, their combined sales have exceeded "those of all other capitalist nations, except the USA" (Mitsui 1984:107). Furthermore, the Japanese have far more opportunities to hear American and European popular music than Western listeners generally have to hear non-Western popular music. One industry survey shows that since 1970, about two-fifths of all popular music recordings produced in Japan were recorded by foreign musicians, most of whom were American or European (Mitsui 1984:107).

Historical Background

The types of popular music found in today's Japan developed as the modern Japanese state emerged. It is interesting that the present-day music scene has evolved into an exceedingly diverse one in a country known in the past for its high degree of cultural homogeneity. The rise of this contemporary heterogeneous music-culture and specifically "Japanese" popular music can be traced to the latter half of the nineteenth century. At this time, wide-ranging reforms were introduced to Japanese society to enable the country to deal with Western powers. The traditional class system was abolished and the authority of the Tokugawa regime was replaced by a government headed by the Emperor Meiji. He left Kyoto and set up a new capital in what was now called "Tokyo," or

Eastern Capital. This government introduced a constitutional monarchy and made many structural changes in the society to allow a mercantile and industrial economy to flourish.

After their long era of isolation, the Japanese felt it necessary to "modernize" life around them, which for a while meant adopting Western models. Leaders rapidly installed a system of compulsory education and decided, from reading about the Dutch and French school systems, that Japan also needed compulsory singing in its schools. In the late 1870s, Izawa Shuji, a Japanese school principal who had studied in Massachusetts, and Luther Whiting Mason, an American who was director of music for the Boston primary schools, developed a plan for music instruction in Japanese public schools.

In the following years *shōka* songs were introduced to meet a goal of teaching songs that blended Japanese and Western elements. The newly composed songs utilized melodies based on a traditional Japanese scale within the structure of a stanza form and a regular meter. Other songs introduced in the schools contained Western melodies such as "Auld Lang Syne" and "Swanee River" set with Japanese texts. Through songs like these, both *shōka* and Western songs, the Japanese masses were introduced to Western musical structure, scale, and rhythm.

In the last decades of the nineteenth century, different opinions emerged over Japan's future direction. According to one faction, Japan should aim toward a democracy similar to that of the United States. Others, however, supported a strong monarchy and political power for the small group of advisers around the emperor. These people believed that the emperor should stand as the symbol of the nation and its long history and spirit; he would lead the Japanese to a new era of world leadership.

In the end, those who supported the monarchy gained political supremacy, and their spiritual descendants eventually led Japan to political and military expansion and World War II. But during the Meiji period, these arguments were still far from settled, and the public became highly involved in them. In the 1880s, when the People's Rights Movement urged further democratization through the establishment of a parliament, a new kind of song called *enka* evolved to express the goals of the movement. The words of one such song, "Oppekepe," written in 1887, show how political the early *enka* were:*

> I'd like to make those who dislike "rights and happiness" (for the people) drink the water of freedom. Those in their fancy Western hairdos and hats, who dress in stylish garb, their outward appearance may be fine but their political thinking is inadequate; they don't understand the truth of the land. We should sow the seeds of freedom in their hearts.†

The very title of another song, popular from 1886 to 1888, indicates its incendiary purpose: "Dynamite Song." Its first verse reads:

---

* Actually, the words to this song are not so much "sung" to a melody, but recited like a rhythmic chant.
† Author's translation.

Yamato [meaning "Japanese"] spirit is polished with rain
From the tears of the advocates of People's Rights.
Promote the national interest and the people's happiness
Foster the National Resources
Because if this is not done—
Dynamite! Bang! (Malm 1971:278)

These deeply political *enka* songs were transformed through the decades to become sentimental songs full of nostalgia and longing; but their early influence on the development of Japanese popular song as a whole is unmistakable.

The *enka* song called "Nonki-bushi" (Song of the Lazy Man) was composed in 1918, and was an early "hit." (Recorded selection 50.) Its composer was Soeda Azembo, one of the most famous of the early Japanese popular music composers. Soeda began his career as an *enka* singer, but by the early twentieth century the *enka* had already changed in character dramatically, as you will realize from listening to this selection. The lyrics exemplify a typical "silly" song that was popular in the vaudeville halls of the day and reappeared many times over the years in Japan (fig. 8–5).

The singer of this original recording, Ishida Ichimatsu, also wrote the lyrics to this song. Ishida, born in 1902, was studying law in Tokyo when he met Soeda through a musical club. He then began his career in song writing and singing, producing many 78 rpm hit records. In the post-World War II years, Ishida entered politics and was re-elected several times to the National Diet before his death in 1956.

Comparing this song to the earlier examples of Japanese vocal music found in this chapter, we find some astonishing differences: a steady beat in the melody, the repetition of stanzas, the quality of the voice and the narration of small stories in each verse. The effects of Western popular music here are obvious. On the Japanese vaudeville stage, the repetitive structure was convenient because it allowed the performer to add new verses—perhaps pertaining to timely political issues, or making fun of someone in the audience—as he desired.

One aspect of Japanese vocal music that remains, however, is a vestige of the rich tradition of ornamentation. Listen for the quick ornaments placed over some notes in this verse and in following verses. Recreating these ornaments is to this day still considered essential in the performance of *enka*, even among amateurs.

In the transcription of the first verse (ex. 8–8), a short introduction is played by a violin based on the melody of the last phrase, "He he, nonki da ne" (Ha ha, how lazy). This same phrase appears briefly between each verse and at the conclusion of the song. Otherwise, the violin follows the vocal line with only slight embellishments. When "Nonki-bushi" was written, the practice of harmonizing *enka* with chords had not yet replaced the single string instrument—first *shamisen,* then the violin, in later years the guitar—in supporting and occasionally embellishing the melodic line.

In the 1990s, the *enka* still has many fans, but it has undergone several

Nonki no tōsan
o-uma no keiko
o-uma ga hashirihajimete
tomaranai.
Kodomo wa omoshirosō ni
Tōsan, doko e yuku.
Doko e yukun da ka
o-uma ni kiito kure
He he nonki da ne.

The lazy man
rides a horse
and it begins to run
and won't stop.
A child enjoys this, asking
"Hey, where are you going?"
"If you want to know where I'm
going, better ask the horse!"
Ha, ha, how lazy!

Nonki na tōsan no
bōya ga hadaka de
kaachan ga kimono o
kiyo to shikattemo
bōya wa iya da to itte
kimono o kinai
... Choito Tōsan, bōya ga
hada de komarimasu wa yo.
Nanda nanda bōya kaze o hiitara
doo surun da
dete kita tōsan ga maruhade

He he nonki da ne.

The lazy man—
his son was naked
and the mother scolded him
to put on his kimono.
The boy said he wouldn't
put on his kimono.
"Hey, Father, our son is naked—
     do something!"
"What's this! Son, what will
you do if you catch a cold?"
said the father, coming out
     stark naked.
Ha ha, how lazy!

Nonki na tōsan
O-mawari-san ni natta kedo
Saaberu ga jama ni natte
arukenai
ichido koronde mata mata
korobi
Sakki okinakereba yokatta
     mono ni to sa
he he nonki da ne.

The lazy man
became a policeman but
his saber got in the way
and he couldn't walk.
He fell once, then again
and again.
"It would've been better if
I hadn't gotten up again!"
Ha ha, how lazy!

Nonki na tōsan
teppo katsuide
haruka kanata o naganureba

tsugai no hato poppo ga
narande tomatteru.
Aida o neratte uttara
dotchika ataru daro.
he he nonki da ne.

The lazy man
carries his rifle
looking at a far-off tree
     branch
a pair of pigeons are
sitting together.
"If I aim for the middle, I
should hit one, I guess.!
Ha, ha, how lazy!

Fig. 8–5. *"Nonki-bushi."*

Nonki na tōsan
koe hariagete
mina kite miro taihen da
hayaku kite miro
mattaku taihen da
are miro suita densha ga
tōtteiru
he he nonki da ne.

The lazy man
shouted to the others,
"Everyone, come and see—
come quickly and see
it's incredible!
Look there—an empty train
is going by!"
Ha, ha, how lazy!

Fig. 8–5. (Continued)

transformations since the days of "Nonki-bushi." In the years after World War II, *enka* became a highly sentimental song genre which most commonly evoked images of *sake* bars, with the ubiquitous red lantern hanging outside, port towns (the site of many sad farewells), and foggy or rainy, lonely evenings.

Ex. 8–8. *"Nonki-bushi," first verse.*

One might imagine that the older generation would be most likely to appreciate such nostalgic expressions of sadness. Indeed, for many younger people who grew up with rock music, *enka* sounds too old-fashioned and sentimental for their taste. By the mid-1970s, the audiences for *enka* were growing older, and the genre did not seem to hold much appeal for younger listeners. But then a new phenomenon called *karaoke* appeared on the scene, reinvigorating the *enka* and bringing it to a new, younger audience.

Karaoke means "empty orchestra" and designates the technological development that allowed anyone with the proper equipment to sing their favorite songs to a full orchestra accompaniment. A typical set-up includes a cassette tape playback machine on which is played a prerecorded tape of the musical accompaniment to a favorite song, and one or two microphones for amplifying the voice as the amateur sings the melodic line.

Enka were, and continue to be, the songs of choice for most *karaoke* users. Other kinds of music found on *karaoke* tapes include Japanese folk and contemporary "pop" songs, as well as Western popular songs, but the majority are some kind of *enka*. A *karaoke* singer may either sing the lyrics of these songs from memory or consult a book containing the lyrics to hundreds of songs.

A large variety of *karaoke* machines are produced in Japan, ranging in price (in 1986) from about $100 to $3,000, but averaging about $1,000. The difference in price is determined by the machine's features. The more expensive models are used in restaurants, bars, wedding halls, and banquet rooms. At these places, customers or guests sing songs of their choice from a wide selection available on tape, singing either alone or in couples. Models priced in the middle range are often installed in smaller bars as well as touring buses and trains so that Japanese traveling in groups can sing to each other on long trips. The inexpensive models are designed for home use, so that users can practice for these "public" performances. There are even battery powered models for outdoor use.

Sales of *karaoke* machines indicate how widespread its popularity has become. In 1978, 100,000 sets were sold, but within five years, this figure had jumped to 1,100,000 sets, resulting in $625 million in sales. A report in *Time* magazine noted that this is more than was spent that year in the United States on gas ranges (Closet Carusos, 1983:47).

The *karaoke* technology made available to the consumer was developed to support and enhance his or her voice as much as possible. One can adjust the volume of the vocal part in relation to the instrumental background, and even switch on an echo device when desired (to add a kind of "singing-in-the-shower" effect). Some equipment is digitized, permitting singers to change the key of the original accompaniment tape to one in their own register. Even the musical accompaniment is designed to be helpful to the singer; the orchestra stays in the background to avoid stealing the show from the singer, but one instrument reinforces the melodic line, in case the singer becomes lost.

This equipment has reinforced the traditional Japanese custom of group singing. Japanese feel that singing helps to establish a relaxed atmosphere and feeling of closeness with others. Social groups—based on professional, school, familial, or community relationships—are important in Japanese life, and the Japanese put much effort into harmonious relationships within these groups. For example, to improve relations among company employees, management organizes special activities such as group tours to spas and drinking parties. On these occasions, *karaoke* is used to break down the social barriers created by the company hierarchy. For this purpose, mere conversation, even when mixed with drinking, does not suffice because it is based on knowledge and wit. But *karaoke* is a different kind of socializing, and the most sentimental, nostalgic idea can be expressed—and are even encouraged—when sung through the *karaoke* machine.

Karaoke singing also reinforces group harmony through the expectation that each member of a group will participate by singing in front of the group. Even if someone feels embarrassed and wants to refuse, he or she usually gives in and sings at least one song in order to maintain the spirit of group harmony. To be sure, some Japanese dislike the idea of singing in public under any circumstances, but most of them have fewer inhibitions about singing before others than people of the United States, for example.*

Karaoke technology works also as an outlet for stress. For instance, the echo feature gives singers a sense of removal from their everyday identity. One Japanese, living in America, stated: "Americans don't know the enjoyment of singing *karaoke* with a mike; it's great to hear your own voice, resounding throughout the room. You feel all your tension disappear." Some businessmen in Japan enjoy going to *karaoke* bars after work just for that purpose; to relieve the accumulated stress from a day of work by belting down a few drinks and belting out a few songs. One survey shows that *karaoke* is most popular among male, white-collar workers between the ages of twenty and forty-nine; the same survey also found that, within any age group, those who enjoyed *karaoke* the most were "those who like to sing" and "those who like to drink" (NHK Hōsō 1982:24–25).

Even Japanese businessmen living abroad find *karaoke* bars in which they can spend their afterhours. In New York City, for example, where a large population of Japanese businessmen work, some twenty or more *karaoke* bars had sprung up by the mid-1980s, and a fierce competition had broken out among them to install the latest technological developments in *karaoke*. One such development is the laser disc video machine, which shows a series of video-taped scenes to accompany each song. Besides the added visual stimulation, it is said that this apparatus also has the advantage that the singers need not have their heads buried in the lyric book but can look up at the screen and at their listeners.

While the content of the music is quite different, there is an interesting similarity in the way *enka* songs (as sung over *karaoke* machines) and traditional music are learned. Both involve aural skills—listening very carefully to an "original" version (of the recording in the case of *enka,* and of the teacher in

---

* Japanese manufacturers have tried for years to market the *karaoke* machine in the United States on the same scale as in Japan, but their failure is perhaps linked to this individual sense of inhibition where public singing is concerned.

traditional music) and imitating it as skillfully as possible. These days, some notation can also be involved. Real *karaoke* enthusiasts can even study with a teacher for pointers or technique but, for the most part, singers become familiar with the melody and interpretation of a song after listening to a recorded professional version many times.

At the top level of performance, though, *karaoke* performances are expected to produce more than exact imitations of another's performance. For example, more expensive models of *karaoke* machines can automatically score a performer on a scale of 1 to 100. One enthusiast told me that in his experience "exact" reproduction of a song in its original interpretation might bring you a score of 98 or 99, but not 100. For the highest score, an element of "personal expressiveness" is necessary, while at the same time one must show complete mastery of the original version. In the traditional music genres described earlier, we have seen this same standardization of music performance among the lower ranking performers, with expectations for more personal creativity at the master level.

By the same token, master performers of *gidayū-bushi* music, festival music, and other kinds of music discussed here also should go beyond imitating their teachers. For most, however, simply meeting the criteria of imitation—as promoted at most levels of the *iemoto* system—is a lifelong task. Few performers reach the stage where personal interpretation is acceptable, and even then it can be controversial.

Karaoke's impact on the musical life of the typical Japanese should not be underestimated. The use of these machines by people of all ages has widened the average person's song repertoire. The musical generation gap, prompted by the growth of popular music, has narrowed somewhat as a result of *karaoke* activity. Within one social group, members of different generations hear and learn songs from one another's repertoires. Singing together encourages this intergenerational learning process.

The music industry has had good reason to be pleased with *karaoke's* popularity. This technology not only provides a new avenue for merchandizing recorded music (the *karaoke* tapes) but in some cases stimulates sales of the original version of a popular song—when people like a song sung by someone at a bar, they sometimes purchase the record themselves in order to learn it.

Enka's popularity has spread to younger age groups because of social *karaoke* singing. At the same time *enka* composers have adapted their songs to the tastes of the younger generation. Background accompaniment ranges from the earlier simple guitar accompaniment to sophisticated orchestral arrangements to heavier, rock-type beats. More "up-beat" *enka* have been issued, with faster tempos and more optimistic lyrics, though these are still in the minority. Finally, vocal ornamentation, so emphasized in earlier *enka,* is toned down in the newer versions because the youth are more accustomed to hearing Western-style vocalization.

The *enka* song found in recorded selection 51 ("Naite Nagasaki," or Crying Nagasaki) is typical of the more old-fashioned variety of *enka* meant for a middle-aged audience. Recorded in 1988 by a *geisha,* the mournfully romantic theme of the song, its orchestra background and vocal style appeals to people who visit a bar with a *karaoke* machine after a long day at work and want to indulge in a little emotionalism. The text (fig. 8–6) describes a woman alone in her room as she contemplates the departure of her lover.

Several images brought out in the song are common to many *enka* songs. The setting of the port town of Nagasaki conjures up romantic associations and particularly the sadness of lovers parting. The scenes of drowning oneself in *sake,* crying in the windy night, and—on top of all that—rain are also found in hundreds of other *enka* songs. For such themes, the Japanese prefer to use a

Fig. 8–6. *"Naite Nagasaki" (Crying Nagasaki).*

Saka no mukō ni	On the other side of the hill
yogisha ga mieru	I can see the night train.
Anata noseteku	Taking you away,
nobori no ressha	the northbound train.
Okuritai kedo	I want to send you off
okureba tsurai	but if I do it will be painful.
Heya no mado kara	From the window of my room
te o furu watashi	I wave goodbye to you.
Naite naite naite	Crying, crying, crying
Nagasaki	Nagasaki,
Ame ni narisō, ne.	It looks like rain, doesn't it?
Wakarenakereba	That you were someone
naranaihito to	with whom I'd have to part—
shitte inagara	although I knew this,
moyashita inochi	a burning fate,
sugaritsukitai	wanting to cling to you,
Maruyamadōri	along the Maruyamadōri
jitto koraete	with steady endurance,
aruita watashi	I walked:
Naite naite naite	Crying, crying, crying
Nagasaki	Nagasaki.
Ame ni narisō, ne.	It looks like rain, doesn't it?
Minato yokaze	The night wind from the port
fukikomu kabe ni	blows against the wall
furete setsunai	making flutter
anata no heyagi	your robe hanging there.
nigai o-sake o	I drown myself
abiteru watashi	in bitter sake.
Naite naite naite	Crying, crying, crying
Nagasaki.	Nagasaki.
Ame ni narisō, ne.	It looks like rain, doesn't it?

natural minor scale, sometimes with the sharped seventh added. At times, the melody too emphasizes the sad mood, for example in the setting of the words "Naite, naite...," as though the singer were sobbing (ex. 8–9).

The form of the song is also typical of *enka,* as we have already seen in "Nonki-bushi"—a simple strophe with a refrain. It opens and closes with instrumental sections, which also recur between strophes. As soon as the voice enters, the background accompaniment becomes minimal, consisting mainly of a bass guitar playing a bass line and other orchestral and electronic instruments filling in the harmony. This accompaniment begins to expand towards the end of the stanza as the vocal part reaches the climax at "Naite, naite ..."

Harmonically, *enka* tend to use a conservative progression of chords, like most Western popular music. There is a brief modulation to the relative major (on the last "Nagasaki"), but otherwise the main movement is between the tonic, sub-dominant and dominant of A minor.

Compared to "Nonki-bushi," "Naite Nagasaki" contains far more complicated orchestration, the use of background singers, and other elements indicative of Western popular music influence. However, the occasional use of vocal ornamentation reflects Japanese taste in vocal quality. Examples can be found in the slight tremolo heard in the voice in the line "nobori no densha," the occasional use of vibrato before the end of a stanza and the final ornamented fall from the B to the A at the end of the transcribed stanza.

The large Japanese music industry produces many other kinds of popular music in addition to *enka.* Some are strongly influenced by Western genres, and some show connections to Japanese musical traditions. The term *kayōkyoku* describes Japanese popular song as a whole, and particularly the songs, including *enka,* that mix Western and Japanese musical elements. This combination is usually a blend of Japanese melodies made from pentatonic scales with Western harmonic progressions and metrical organization. Since the mid-1970s, however, many of the contemporary songs have been written in Western scales, especially major modes, conforming to the imported music listened to by Japanese youth.

The labels identifying different kinds of Japanese popular music are very confusing (as they can be in Western popular music as well) because they are so often inconsistently applied; but these are the most common:

Gunka

Literally "military songs," *gunka* were first composed and gained popularity during the Russo-Japanese War of 1904–1905. More songs were composed in succeeding military engagements. People in their sixties and seventies now strongly associate such songs with their youth during World War II and therefore are still extremely fond of them. Influenced by military music of the West, these songs are written in stanza form, often with trumpet and other brass instruments in the instrumental accompaniment. Not all are enthusiastic about fighting and war. Some songs were written from the point of view of a lonely mother waiting

Ex. 8–9. *Transcription of "Naite Nagasaki" (first verse).*

for her soldier-son to come home, or of a soldier on the front who has just lost his best friend in battle.

Folk Song

Fōku songu can apply to either Western "new" folk songs, as sung by musicians like Joan Baez and Bob Dylan, or to the Japanese songs written mainly in the 1960s and 1970s that were influenced by such music. Japanese folk singers of this period typically wrote the words and music of the songs they sang. This practice was different from the separation of songwriter, lyricist, and singer that had formerly predominated in Japanese popular music. Musically, these songs can scarcely be differentiated from their Western counterparts; the lyrics, however, sung in Japanese, often refer to social or political issues that are specifically Japanese.

New Music

Also written phonetically to imitate the English words (*nyuu myuushiku*), this term developed in the late 1970s to designate a music that had grown out of the "folk song" style. Represented at first by singer-songwriters such as Yoshida Tokurō and Minami Kōsetsu, "new music" songs generally convey an introverted, personal point of view that appeals to today's young people. In these types of songs, the melody, usually written in the natural minor scale and in short phrases, is given more importance than the presence of a strong beat.

Pops

Appearing from the late 1970s and aimed at a teenage audience, music of this kind is ordinarily sung by teenagers themselves, some as young as fourteen. These singers, mostly female, are discovered by production companies that send talent scouts all over the country. Upon locating a promising candidate, the company decides on the appropriate image for the singer, trains her to sing in a certain way, and choreographs her performances. Television is an important medium for these teenaged performers, as a new singer can gain instant fame with an appearance on one of the numerous musical variety shows. Performing in costumes that accentuate an image of youth and innocence, dozens of these singers rise and fall in the Japanese music business each year, while a few lucky ones manage to maintain long-term careers.

These songs are usually Western sounding in arrangement and melody and, to add a touch of sophistication and exoticism, often include a few words of English in the lyrics. Typically, English words or phrases are alternated with Japanese lines, but the English may not be strictly idiomatic. Figure 8–7 shows an example from one song, with the Japanese phrases translated in parentheses.

In addition to *gunka, fōku songu,* new music, and pops, there are easy

> *I had understood your heart*
> *Ima made wa kotoba ga nakuta tie*
> *(Up to now, without any words)*
> *Oh, please tell me your heart*
> *Ima sugu ni ... ru, ru, ru, ru*
> *(Right away, ru, ru, ru, ru)**

Fig. 8–7. "Himitsu no kata."

listening, rock, punk, and many other kinds of popular music, mostly based on Western models but sometimes deviating from those models in interesting ways.

We have reviewed a small sample of the wide variety of music heard in Japan today. This sample contains many examples of the mixture of native with foreign elements in the evolution of new musical forms. The *shakuhachi* was developed from an instrument of Chinese origin that entered Japan around the eighth century. The Zen philosophy that underlay the instrument's use in meditation also originated in China. The prototype of the *shamisen*, used to play *kouta*, music of the puppet theater and to accompany traditional folk song, can be traced to Okinawa, China, and beyond. Most of the instruments of the festival music ensemble also originated in China, and underwent adaptation in Japan. Finally, popular music as a whole is based in form, rhythmic and harmonic structure and instrumental accompaniment on Western music; only the melodic component and the lyric content in some cases reflect Japanese traditions.

Of course, one can question the concept itself of "tradition" or the "traditional culture" of a nation or people, especially in terms of "purity" of origin. What culture group in the world has not borrowed cultural elements from another, with the roots of that borrowing going so far back that few think of the idea or custom as "borrowed"?

We find, in examining Japanese musical culture, the expression of some aspects of the varied Japanese character. For instance, popular nonsense songs like "Nonki-bushi" (recorded selection 50) find their roots in a certain outlandish sense of humor that the Japanese sometimes indulge in. (Anyone who has watched Japanese television for any length of time, particularly game shows, can attest to this.) On a more sober note, the idea of emptying one's soul and reaching a state of selflessness as preparation for the performance of both *shakuhachi* and the music of the *bunraku* theater reflects the strong underlying influence of Zen thought in Japanese culture. This influence touches many other areas of Japanese daily life, not only in mental preparation for a future task, but also with stress on self-control and self-discipline. Finally, the indulgence in pathos and extreme emotional anguish, as expressed in *enka* songs as well as in the music of the puppet theater, reveals another side of the Japanese character. Listening to Japanese music and learning about its connections to past and present society, we become aware of the richness of Japanese life.

* From the song "Himitsu no kata," sung by Iijima Mari. Victor Records VDR–6, 1984.

REFERENCES CITED

Adachi, Barbara
  1985   *Backstage at Bunraku: A Behind-the-scenes Look at Japan's Traditional Puppet Theater.* New York: Weatherhill.
Adriaansz, Willem
  1973   *The Kumiuta and Danmono Traditions of Japanese Koto Music.* Berkeley: Univ. of California Press.
"Closet Carusos: Japan Reinvents the Singalong."
  1983   *Time,* 28 February 1983, 47.
Asano Kenji
  1966   "Nihon no Minyō" (Folk Song of Japan). Tokyo: Iwanami Shinsho.
Blasdel, Christopher Yohmei
  1988   *The Shakuhachi: A Manual for Learning.* Tokyo: Ongaku no Tomo Sha.
Crihfield, Liza
  1979   *Kouta: "Little Songs" of the Geisha World.* Rutland, Vt.: Charles E. Tuttle Co.
Dalby, Liza Crihfield
  1983   *Geisha.* Berkeley: Univ. of California Press.
Ernst, Earle
  1956   *The Kabuki Theatre.* Honolulu: Univ. Press of Hawaii.
Herd, Judith Ann
  1984   "Play it again, Isamu!" *Mainichi Daily News,* 9 July 1984, 9.
Hughes, David
  1981   "Japanese Folk Song Preservation Societies: Their History and Nature." In *International Symposium on the Conservation and Restoration of Cultural Property,* edited by Organizing Committee of I.S.C.R.C.P. Tokyo: Tokyo National Research Institute of Cultural Properties.
Kikkawa Eishi
  1981   *Nihon Ongaku no Rekishi* (The History of Japanese Music). Osaka: Sōgensha.
Koizumi Fumio
  1974   *Nihon No Ongaku* (Japanese Music). Tokyo: National Theater of Japan.
Kurada Yoshihiro
  1982   "Kouta." In *Ongaku Daijiten* (Encyclopedia Musica), edited by Shitanaka Kunihiko. Tokyo: Heibonsha.
Malm, William
  1959   *Japanese Music and Musical Instruments.* Rutland, Vt.: Charles E. Tuttle.
  1971   *Modern Music of Meiji Japan.* In *Tradition and Modernization in Japanese Culture,* edited by Donald H. Shirley. Princeton, N.J.: Princeton Univ. Press.
Mitsui Toru
  1984   "Japan in Japan: Notes on an Aspect of the Popular Music Record Industry in Japan." *Popular Music* 3:107–120.
Motegi Kiyoko
  1984   "Aural Learning in *Gidayu-Bushi:* Music of the Japanese Puppet Theatre." *Yearbook for Traditional Music* 16:97–107.

———— 1988 *Bunraku: Koe to Oto to Hibiki* (Bunraku: Voice and Sound and Reverberation). Tokyo: Ongaku no Tomo Sha.

NHK Hōsō Seron Chōsajo, eds.
1982 *Gendaijin to Ongaku* (Contemporary People and Music). Tokyo: Nippon Hōsō Shuppan Kyōkai.

Sōri-fu (Prime Minister's Office)
1982 *Population of Japan: 1980 Population Census of Japan*. Tokyo: Statistics Bureau.

ADDITIONAL READING

Brandon, J., W. Malm, and D. Shively
1978 *Studies in Kabuki: Its Acting, Music and Historical Context*. Honolulu, Hi.: Univ. Press of Hawaii.

Fujie, Linda
1986 "The Process of Oral Transmission in Japanese Performing Arts: The Teaching of *Matsuri-Bayashi* in Tokyo." In *The Oral and the Literate in Music*, edited by Yoshihiko Tokumaru and Osamu Yamaguti. Tokyo: Academia Music.

Kishibe Shigeo
1984 *The Traditional Music of Japan*. Tokyo: Ongaku no Tomo Sha.

ADDITIONAL LISTENING

A Bell Ringing in the Empty Sky: Japanese Shakuhachi Music—Goro Yamaguchi. Nonesuch H72025.

Gagaku: Ancient Japanese Court Music. Everest 3322.

Japan—Traditional Vocal and Instrumental Music, Ensemble Nipponica. Nonesuch H72072.

Japan 5: Musique du Nō. Ocora 558 629.

Koto Music of Japan—Katsunuma Takasago. Nonesuch H72005.

Koto Music of Shakuhachi—Ralph Samuelson. Music of the World. (no number)

Music from the Kabuki. Nonesuch H72012.

UNESCO Collection: The Music of Japan, IV—Buddhist Music. Musicaphon BM30–L2015

Yoshitsune: Songs of a Medieval Hero Accompanied by the Biwa. BMG Victor CR10080–81.

NINE

◆ ◆ ◆

Latin America/Ecuador

JOHN M. SCHECHTER

Latin America is a region of many regions. It is a continent and a half with more than twenty different countries in which Spanish, Portuguese, French, and dozens of native American languages in hundreds of dialects are spoken. It is, at once, the majestic, beautiful Andes mountains, the endless emptiness of the Peruvian-Chilean desert, and the lush rain forests of the huge Amazon basin. Latin American cultures are also enormously diverse, yet most share a common heritage of Spanish or Portuguese colonialism and American and European cultural influences. Several ports in Colombia and Brazil were major colonial centers for the importation of black slaves; Latin America remains a rich repository of African and African-American music-cultural traditions, including rituals, musical forms and practices, and types of musical instruments. Native American cultures that were not eradicated by European diseases have in many cases retained certain distinctive languages, dress, musical forms, and music rituals.

In Latin American culture, mixture is the norm, not the exception. When you walk through the countryside of Ecuador, for example, you hear a Spanish dialect sharing many words from Quichua, the regional Native American language. The local Quichua dialect, conversely, uses many Spanish words. South of Ecuador, in the high mountain regions of Peru, the harp is considered an indigenous instrument, although European missionaries and others in fact brought it to Peru. In rural areas of Atlantic coastal Colombia, musicians sing songs in Spanish, using Spanish literary forms, but these are accompanied by African-style drums and rhythms and by Amerindian flutes and rattles. In northern Ecuador, African-Ecuadorians perform the *bomba,* a type of song that features African-American rhythms, Quichua Indian melodic and harmonic features, and Spanish language—with one Quichua word. It is hard to maintain strict cultural divisions because the intermingling of Spanish (or Iberian, to encompass also the Portuguese), African, and Native American strains is so profound in the Latin American experience.

When you first think of Latin American music, you might hear in your mind's ear the vibrancy of the rhythms in salsa. There is an enormous variety of beaten and shaken rhythm instruments, such as claves, bongos, congas, and maracas,

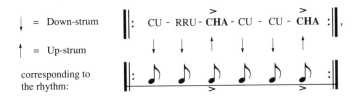

Fig. 9–1. *Cuatro strumming pattern.*

both in salsa and throughout Latin America. In distinctive sizes and shapes, the guitar is prominent in Latin American folk music. In Peru and Bolivia, for example, a type of guitar called the *charango* may have as its body the shell of an armadillo. There are other kinds of Latin American music with which you might also be familiar, including bossa nova, the calypso, and the tango.

VENEZUELAN JOROPO

Listen to recorded selection 52, "Pajarillo." What is most impressive about it? Is it the very fast tempo—with the basic quarter-note beat going beyond the top marking (208) on the metronome? Or is it the way the guitarist (here playing a *cuatro,* in Venezuela a small four-string guitar) strums his chords not only with remarkable speed and agility but also in an apparently fixed rhythmic pattern? The variety of percussion of the salsa band is now concentrated in a single instrument, the maracas, resounding with machine-like precision. The singer skillfully delivers his text ("Ah, fly, fly, little bird, Take wing, if you want to fly away . . .") in a free, declamatory style, yet uses mostly pitches that fall within the two principal chords in the piece, D minor (tonic) and A major (dominant).

This is an example of the *joropo,* the national dance of Venezuela, heard here in a 1968 recording made by Luis Felipe Ramón y Rivera, Isabel Aretz, and Álvaro Fernaud. One standard *joropo* ensemble is the one we hear: *cuatro,* maracas, and harp. To understand the apparently fixed rhythm we can use an onomatopoeic device (like the *sang si sang sang si sang si* pattern taught students of *Kete;* see chapter 3) taught to *cuatro* players in Venezuela to try to capture the character and rhythmic feel of *joropo*. The *cuatro* strumming pattern is vocalized as shown in figure 9–1. Rolling your r's on *RRU* as best you can, speak CU-RRU-*CHA*-CU-CU-*CHA* about as fast as you can, along with the recorded selection, and you will find yourself in sync with the *cuatro*'s rhythmic strumming. You will find yourself chasing after—and hopefully beginning to catch—Venezuelan *joropo*.

The harp's function is related but somewhat different. Here outlining a three-quarter meter (shown in ex. 9–1), sometimes with closely related rhythmic

Ex. 9–1. *Rhythmic pattern played by harp.*

Ex. 9–2. *Harp patterns in the Venezuelan joropo, "Pajarillo."*

forms, the harp provides not only rhythmic but melodic and ultimately harmonic underpinning, with patterns such as those shown in example 9–2. After establishing these basic patterns, however, the harpist improvises their melodic contours and syncopates their rhythms, to contribute to the unique motoric sound of *joropo.* The harp is vital in Venezuelan *joropo;* it has been essential in Latin American music making for hundreds of years.

NUEVA CANCIÓN: "EL LAZO," BY VÍCTOR JARA

Although the guitar is played in ensembles, by itself it accompanies solo folk song throughout Latin America. As in the Venezuelan *joropo,* the instrument usually provides a characteristic regional rhythm. Moving from north to south on the South American continent—from Venezuela to Chile—we listen to "El Lazo," a powerful folk song composed (ca. 1964) and performed on guitar by a great figure in Chilean modern music, Víctor Jara (recorded selection 53).

The regional rhythm in example 9–3 is not the driving CU-RRU-*CHA*-CU-CU-*CHA* of the Venezuelan *joropo,* but a variant of the *cueca,* a Chilean folk dance. This pattern can be felt in either three-four or six-eight time. The text and music of "El Lazo" are presented in example 9–4.

As a frame for the piece, there is a speech-like section, identical at the beginning and end of the song. The thought is somber: "When the sun bent low"; "on a dark ranch"; "on a humble ranch"; and the picture stark: an old man (so we soon find out) at sunset, on a poor ranch, in Lonquén, Víctor Jara's home village. The melody is similarly stark and hesitant, in the minor key, chant-like; sing the first three lines to get the feeling of the mood Jara is setting. Like the song itself, the "spoken" section is framed, beginning and ending with the same text-couplet, set to the same musical line.

With the stage set, Jara spins the details, through strophes 1 through 6, and through the mid-song "speech" section, which is halting in character like the

Ex. 9–3. *Cueca rhythmic pattern.*

Ex. 9–4. *Transcription of "El Lazo," words and music by Victor Jara. Copyright © 1976 Mighty Oak Music Ltd., London, England. TRO–Essex Music International, Inc. controls all rights for the U.S.A. and Canada. Used by permission.*

(2) El lazo como serpiente
se enroscaba en el nogal
y en cada lazo la huella
de su vida y de su pan.

(3) Cuanto tiempo hay en sus manos
y en su apagado mirar
y nadie ha dicho—está bueno
ya no debes trabajar.

Las sombras etc. . .

(4) Sus lazos han recorrido
sur y norte, cerro y mar,
pero el viejo la distancia
nunca la supo explicar.

(5) Su vida deja en los lazos
aferrados al nogal.
Después llegará la muerte
y también lo laceará.

(6) Qué importa si el lazo es firme
y dura la eternidad,
laceando por algún campo
el viejo descansará.

Cuando el so etc. . .

The Noose

When the sun was setting
I found him.
In a gloomy hut
in Lonquen.
In a poverty stricken hut
I found him.
When the sun was setting
in Lonquen.

His hands, although so old,
were strong in their plaiting.
They were rough and they were tender
with the animal skin.

The shadows fell interlacing
the last light of the day
The old man weaves some verses
to capture some gaiety.

How much time is contained in his hands
and in his patient gaze
and nobody has said: "That's enough,
you should not work anymore."

The plaited noose, like a snake,
curled around the walnut tree
and in every mesh was woven
his life and his bread.

His nooses have travelled
south and north, coast and mountain,
but the old man never learnt
what distance really means.

He leaves his life in plaited leather
knotted to the walnut tree
Soon death will come
and that too will be plaited in.

What does it matter if the noose is firm
and lasts for eternity.
Intertwined with some country place
the old man at last will rest.

When the sun was settting
I found him. . . .

Ex. 9–4. (Continued)

opening "spoken section," if different musically. The tale concerns an aged man, portrayed with hands old yet strong, rough yet tender, plaiting whips and lassos. In the Latin American countryside one often comes upon older men and women plaiting animal hide for whips, or cactus or wool fiber for use as rope, sandal tops, bags, or blanket ends. This type of work requires great skill and enormous patience. Jara's admiration for the craftsperson's talent and patience is undisguised. The man of Lonquén is known far and wide for his whips, and their creation is his very life.

Listening to "El Lazo" we become aware of the constant *musical* "plaiting" as well: Jara weaves a variety of arpeggiations into a cohesive musical fabric. We feel the musical shuttle moving nearly continuously, through both the strophes and the middle "spoken" section, or recitative. The music acts as a metaphor for the rope-plaiting activity—the musical gesture evoking the plaiting gesture.

Jara further interweaves the music with the metaphors and similes in the text. The plaited lasso, like a snake, is curled around the walnut tree, the shadows tie together the final daylight, and the old man himself braids verses to bind up joy. We also admire the man of Lonquén because his work is *firme:* it will endure. Jara exalts the skill and dedication of the plaiter of Lonquén and, by association, of Chilean rural craftspersons, in general. The musician-poet is given to humble admiration for rural artists in other songs, too, such as his "Angelita Huenumán," (1964) in which he sings the praises of a Mapuche Indian woman (Jara's mother, Amanda, was of Mapuche ancestry) who dedicates her life to making beautiful blankets. Once again, focus on the hands.

Why does Jara glorify the creative genius of rural Chileans? The answer lies partly with Jara himself—a man of Lonquén, rural Chile; it lies partly with his place in the modern song movement of Chile, and—sometimes with different names—of all Latin America: *Nueva Canción,* or "New Song."

Nueva Canción is a song movement that stands up for one's own culture, for one's own people, in the face of oppression by a totalitarian government or in the face of "cultural imperialism" from abroad, notably the United States and Europe. It developed first in the "southern cone" of South America—Argentina, Chile, and Uruguay—during the 1950s and 1960s, and it has spread throughout Latin America. The 1960s in particular witnessed violent upheavals. Assassinations and urban violence in the United States were echoed in Latin America: nearly every country in South America, as well as Cuba and the Dominican Republic in the Caribbean, saw revolution, massacre, underground warfare, or other forms of violent social and political confrontation.

Nueva Canción artists seek to reinvoke and revalidate traditional lifeways of forgotten persons and peoples. These musicians also express their social consciousness. They speak out in a clear voice against conditions of oppression, advocating social change. Víctor Jara's "Preguntas por Puerto Montt" (1969), notably <u>devoid</u> of metaphor and speaking in a direct and accusatory tone, is a stream-of-consciousness monologue decrying a March 6, 1969, government-sanctioned attack on unarmed peasant families in this Chilean port city. In the 1970 Chilean Presidential campaign, Quilapayún, an important *Nueva Canción* ensemble formed in the mid-1960s, accompanied speakers for Salvador Allende's broad-based Popular Unity party, which had brought together workers, peasants, and students into a mass movement. In 1973, the elected Marxist government of President Allende was overthrown; Allende and some 2,800 others lost their lives, hundreds disappeared, and thousands were jailed. On September 18, 1973, a young man ushered Joan Jara into the Santiago city morgue, where she found the body of her husband, Víctor Jara, "his chest riddled with holes and a gaping wound in his abdomen. His hands seemed to be hanging from his arms at a strange angle as though his wrists were broken. . . ." (Jara 1984:243). The singer who had cried out in word and song on behalf of "him who died without knowing why his chest was riddled, fighting for the right to have a place to live" (lyrics to "Preguntas por Puerto Montt"), the singer whose songs had so often lauded eloquently the hands of his people (in "El Lazo" and "Angelita Huenumán") had met his fate—in a stroke of terrifying irony—his own chest riddled with holes, his own hands made lifeless.

Numerous *Nueva Canción* musicians were imprisoned or remained in exile, but to gain support for human rights in Chile they continued to spread the message of *Nueva Canción* in performances abroad. Within Chile, the movement went underground and was transformed into *Canto Nuevo.*

After the overthrow of Allende, the music of *Nueva Canción* was prohibited on the airwaves and removed from stores and destroyed. Certain prominent folkloric instruments associated with *Nueva Canción,* such as the *charango,* were also prohibited. In the repressive political and cultural atmosphere, the metaphoric character we have seen in the songs of Víctor Jara now became exaggerated and intensified, expressing thoughts that would have been censored if stated directly. In "El Joven Titiritero" (The Young Puppeteer), by Eduardo Peralta, for example, a puppeteer's departure and hoped-for return served as a metaphor for exile and renewed hope.

The status of *Canto Nuevo* was precarious. The government issued permission to perform a concert, but the permission was abruptly revoked; radio programs featuring its music were established, then eliminated; Jara cassettes were at one moment confiscated and soon after sold openly in stores. With changing political conditions, exiled musicians such as Inti Illimani have been permitted to return to Chile.

New Song is still a living international movement. It is traditional and regional in its roots, yet modern and socially conscious in its musical style and message. It reacts to penetration by foreign cultures, seeking instead to draw attention to the people—often the forgotten people—and to their struggles for human dignity.

BOLIVIAN K'ANTU

Certain *Nueva Canción* performers chose the *zampoña,* or panpipes, among other traditional instruments, to symbolize their esteem for the native traditions of the Andes. Although panpipes are widely known outside of South

America, the depth of the panpipe tradition in South America is remarkable. Today, we can find a huge number of named varieties of panpipes among native peoples from Panama down to Peru, Bolivia, and Chile. In Peru and Bolivia, cultures dating back some 1500 years knew and played panpipes of bamboo or clay.

Listen to recorded selection 54, "Kutirimunapaq," performed by Ruphay, a Bolivian ensemble. They are playing a type of ceremonial panpipe music from the altiplano, called *k'antu*. Using Western notation, we could notate what seems to be one melody line, at least, as shown in example 9–5. The entire piece is played three times. Sing the melody to get a feel for the rhythm and flow of this *zampoña* music. Listening again, you'll note that the sound seems richer than on first hearing; you hear a panpipe ensemble playing what seems to be the same melody at various pitch levels, one at an octave below the original pitch level, another a perfect fourth above that lower octave, or a perfect fifth below the original octave (ex. 9–6).

"Kutirimunapaq," which means, roughly, in the Quechua language, "So that we can return," is music of the Kallawaya people, who live on the eastern slope of the Bolivian Andes, north of Lake Titicaca, close to the Peruvian border. (In Peru and Bolivia the language is called "Quechua"; in Ecuador the dialects are called "Quichua.") The Kallawaya *campesinos* (farmers or peasants) live at different altitudes in the Charazani Valley—from 9,000 to 16,000 feet above sea level. Those at the lower elevations speak Quechua and cultivate potatoes, barley, and beans; at the upper elevations they speak Aymara and keep llamas, alpacas, and sheep. Perhaps some 3,500 years ago, Quechua and Aymara were a single language. The Incas adopted Quechua as their official language and spread it with them throughout their empire (ca. 1200–1533). Today, from 5½ to 8 million Andeans in Bolivia, Peru, Argentina, and Ecuador speak Quechua (or Quichua), while a minority speak Aymara. "Kutirimunapaq" is a *k'antu* from the community of Niñokorin, at 11,000 feet.

The Kallawaya musicians term these bamboo panpipes (*zampoña* in Spanish) *phukuna,* from the Quechua verb *phukuy,* to blow. The *k'antu* ensembles, for which the Charazani region is famous, each comprise twenty to thirty *phukuna*-playing dancers, who move in a circular pattern. Some of them simultaneously

Ex. 9–5. *One melody line of the K'antu "Kutirimunapaq."*

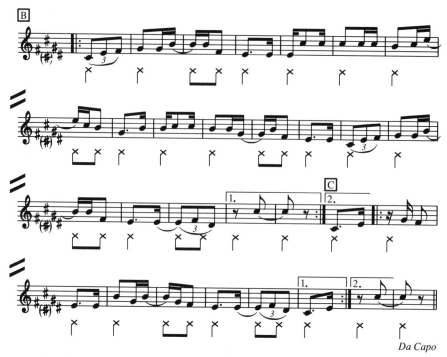

Ex. 9–5. (*Continued*)

beat a large, double-headed drum, called a *wankara.* The triangle (in Quechua, *ch'inisku*) player heard in recorded selection 54 is often present, as well.

The Kallawaya play the *phukunas* in their dry season, which lasts roughly from June to September; they play transverse flutes (played horizontally, like the Western silver flute) or duct flutes (played vertically, and constructed like a

Ex. 9–6. *Ensemble playing in "Kutirimunapaq."*

Ex. 9–6. (*Continued*)

recorder) during the rainy season, which lasts from November to at least late February. The preference on the altiplano for duct flutes, in particular, during the rainy season may be related to the belief that their clear sound attracts rain and prevents frost, necessary conditions for the growth of crops.

Our ensemble consists of *phukunas* of different sizes, yet all with the same basic construction, in terms of numbers of tubes. Each musical register is represented by one named pair of panpipes, consisting of an *ira* set of pipes (considered in the Bolivian altiplano to embody the male principle, and serving as the leader) and an *arca* set of pipes (considered to embody the female principle and serving as the follower). In our context, the *ira* set has six pipes, the *arca* set has seven; we may refer to this type as 6/7-tubed. The different-sized instruments play the same melody, which results in the rich musical fabric of parallel octaves, fifths, and fourths.

There are at least two especially interesting aspects of this music. One is the doubling of the melodic line; the other is the way a melody is produced. Doubling the melody at a fixed interval (parallel fifth, parallel fourth, parallel octave) was used in medieval plainsong. By the ninth century plainsong (one-line Christian liturgical chant) was being accompanied either by one lower part at the octave below or by a lower part at the fourth or fifth below. Another alternative augmented the two-voice complex to three or four voices by doubling one or both lines at the octave. Thus, early medieval Europe had musical textures with parallel octaves, fourths, and fifths very similar in the intervallic structure (if not in rhythm) to what we hear in twentieth-century Bolivian *k'antu*. In twentieth-century Africa, songs in parallel fourths and fifths are found among groups that have the tradition of pentatonic, or five-pitch, songs, such as the Gogo people of Tanzania.

Many peoples have used, and continue to use, the performance practice of hocketing. Performing music in hocket is a uniquely communal way of making music. Hocket music is social music, for you cannot play the entire melody yourself—you need one or more partners to do it with you. You may have already studied the hocketing of Kasena musicians (chapter 3) in their *jongo* flute music, where the highest flute played the beginning of the melody and was answered by the lower-pitched flutes for the rest of the melody. Also in chapter 3, the *akadinda* xylophone music of the Baganda people of Uganda was in strict hocket, the seventeen-key *akadinda* being played by three musicians who created a "resultant" melody by dovetailing the two basic parts of the music, the *okunaga* and the *okwawula*. In Africa the hocket technique also appears among horns and panpipes and with voices among the Bushmen and Pygmy peoples. Hocketing with panpipes also appears closer to our modern Bolivian music. In Panama, the Kuna Indians play a six-tube *guli* panpipe. Each person holds one tube with melody distributed among all six players. The Kuna also play *gammu burui* panpipes. Each fourteen-tube set is bound into two groups, or rafts, of seven tubes, the melody distributed between the two seven-tube players in hocket technique (Smith 1984: 156–59; 167–72).

As among the Kuna, in Bolivian *k'antu* the hocket procedure is integral to the overall musical fabric. In fact, hocketing is actually required by the way the *phukunas* are constructed. Although there are types of altiplano panpipes with from three to seventeen tubes, a very widely used type is 6/7-tubed—that is, the "total" instrument has thirteen tubes, consisting of one line, or rank, of six tubes (the *ira*) and one rank of seven tubes (the *arca*). This *phukuna*, or *siku* (the name used by the Aymara Indians, who inhabit the upper elevations of this same altiplano zone), is tuned in E minor (or in another perspective, G major), as shown in figure 9–2. The type of *phukuna* shown in this figure has made an accommodation to European-derived scales. All *zamponas* of the altiplano are not tuned in this diatonic manner; many have different scales. This basic tuning

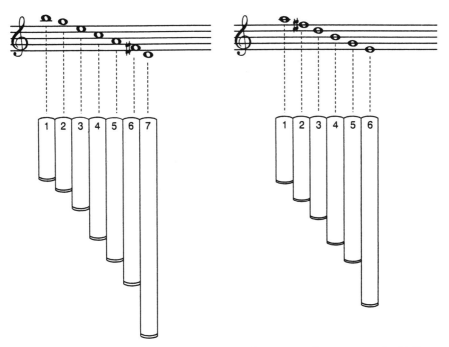

Fig. 9–2. *Example of phukuna tuning. Left: seven-tube arca rank. Right: six-tube ira rank.*

is nonetheless widely found among both Quechua-speaking and Aymara-speaking peoples.

When the full instrument is combined (six- and seven-tube ranks joined together or played by two people) we have a thirteen-tube E-minor scale, over the space of an octave and a half with subtonic below (D), or a thirteen-tube G-major scale, going up to the tenth above and down to the perfect fourth below (D) (fig. 9–3).

The formal structure of this *k'antu* is A B C, each section repeated, then the entire piece repeated twice, for a total of three times. This is a characteristic structure for the Bolivian *k'antu*, accommodating the continuous dancing that goes with the music-making. Counting the number of different notes that sound in the *k'antu* we find that, within the octave, five notes predominate: C♯, E, F♯, G♯, and B. Then, the C♯ and E come back in the upper octave. There is one more note used: D♯; notice, though, that it comes in only at the end of Sections A, B, and C—once each time. This *k'antu* is primarily five-pitch, or pentatonic. We will find later in the chapter that many traditional dance musics in the Andes region are similarly pentatonic, though certainly not all of them. "Kutirimuna-paq" is strongly rhythmic, with the steady beat of the *wankara* supporting the beat. Andean dance music, from Bolivia up to Ecuador, has this powerful rhythmic cast, underscoring its dance function.

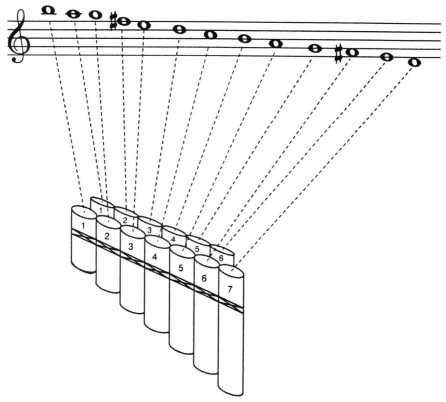

Fig. 9–3. *Tuning of full thirteen-tube phukuna.*

Hocketing panpipes, with rhythmic melodies played in parallel fifths and octaves and with strong, steady rhythm on a large drum, begin to distinguish this Bolivian altiplano stream of Latin American music. The evocation of Native American cultures such as this high-Andean one, through use of Andean instruments, begins to demarcate *Nueva Canción*. New Song is not only nostalgic, though. It is also politically committed and international. Above all, it speaks of and on behalf of the people—characteristically, the forgotten people.

North of Chile, Bolivia, and Peru is a nation of many other unsung (or, less-sung) persons and peoples, a country itself frequently overlooked in discussions of Latin America: Ecuador.

THE QUICHUA OF THE NORTHERN ANDES
OF ECUADOR

We can best appreciate the traditional nature of northern Ecuadorian Quichua music by knowing something of the traditional setting in which Quichuas live. The musicians we will be listening to live in *comunas*, or small clusters of houses, on the slopes of Mt. Cotacachi, one of several volcanoes in the Ecuadorian Andes. These *comunas* lie outside the town of Cotacachi, in Imbabura Province (see fig. 9–4). The Quichua spoken in Cotacachi-area *comunas* was spoken there four hundred years ago. Today in Ecuador more than one million people speak the language.

In addition to the language, the agriculture and material culture (a society's physical objects and artifacts) of the Andes around Cotacachi are traditional. In this rich green countryside dotted with tall eucalyptus, at 8,300 to 9,700 feet above sea level, maize has been the principal cultivated crop for hundreds of years. You have already seen how Latin Americans braid natural fibers into useful objects; Cotacachi Quichua use the thick trunks of the local cactus, *cabuya*, to make stools for the home. The harpist who plays all night in the home of a recently deceased Quichua infant (see below) sits on a *cabuya* stool.

Quichua homes typically have one room, often with a covered patio, both with dirt floor. Regional Quichua homes have been constructed this way for four hundred years. The home of twelve-year-old harpist, César, and his parents, Mama Ramona and Miguel Armando, in the *comuna* of Tikulla outside Cotacachi, is shown in illustration 9–1.

Styles of dress have also remained basically the same since the sixteenth century. Everyone covers his or her head to protect it from the intense heat and light of the near-vertical sun at midday (Cotacachi is almost precisely on the Equator). Women wear cloths, and men wear hats. Quichua women wear embroidered blouses, over which they drape shawls (in Quichua, *fachalina*). Their two skirts, one blue and one white, are secured by two woven belts: a wider, inner belt, called the *mama chumbi* (mother belt) and a narrower, outer belt, called the *wawa chumbi* (child belt). These belts are designed in this region usually with names of Imbabura towns, and they are woven on home back-strap looms by Quichua families in various *comunas*. Men and boys wear a white or blue shirt, white pants, and dark poncho. Any large gathering of Quichua, such as for Saturday market or a Palm Sunday procession, is a sea of blue and white.

In illustration 9–2 we see three generations of father-son relationships within the same family. Of the grandfather's traditional dress, his adult son retains the white sandals, white shirt, pants, and hat, while his grandson wears Western-influenced clothes.

Quichua homes on Cotacachi's slopes are not located on roads but are interspersed along a network of footpaths called *chaki ñanes*. Without telephones families communicate only by foot, along *chaki ñanes*, which bear the weight of Quichua women carrying infants, brush, and food to and from market, and of Quichua men carrying potatoes, milled grain, or perhaps a harp (see ill. 9–3). For all Quichua, the way around the slopes on *chaki ñanes* is second nature; the harpist contracted to play at a *wawa velorio*, or child's wake, is able to reach the home of the deceased child, one and a half hours up Mt. Cotacachi, from his own home, at night, with no illumination other than the moon. Walking (in Quichua, *purina*) is so vital in daily life that it finds its way into speech and song.

Fig. 9–4. *Ecuador.*

Ill. 9–1. *Home of Mama Ramona and Miguel Armando in the comuna of Tikulla outside Cotacachi.*

Ill. 9–2. *Three generations of Quichua men.*

Ill. 9–3. *Chaki ñan (Ecuadorian footpath).*

THE MUSICAL TRADITION: SANJUÁN

The common language, dress, material culture, daily labor, and importance of *purina* all find a musical echo in *sanjuán*. The term, *sanjuán*, may be found at least as early as 1860. At that time, it referred either to a type of song played at the festival of St. John (San Juan) the Baptist held in June or to a type of dance performed at that festival.

Today, the instrument Cotacachi Quichua often use to perform *sanjuán* is the harp without pedals, often referred to as diatonic in English. This is a harp tuned usually to one particular scale and not capable of being quickly changed to another. Quichua have been playing the harp in the Ecuadorian highlands for hundreds of years; in the eighteenth century it was the most common instrument in the region. The harp's popularity in the Andes is not limited to Ecuador; in the Peruvian highlands it is so widespread among Quechua that it is considered a "native" instrument.

Brought from Europe initially by several different groups of missionaries, especially the Jesuits, and even by the first Conquistadors, the harp has been in Latin America for more than four hundred years. In Chile, the tradition of women harpists is strong; this is a heritage of sixteenth-century Spain, when women were virtuosos on the instrument. Elsewhere in rural South America, including Ecuador, harp performance by folk musicians follows the gender principle of organization in instrumental music so that women have rarely been included. Most Latin American diatonic harpists have always been male. However, in other musical endeavors, such as *Nueva Canción*, women have been in the forefront.

Ill. 9–4. *Imbabura harp.*

The Imbabura harp is common only in Imbabura Province (ill. 9–4). It appears as an oddity among harpists in central highland Ecuador, where musicians play a larger instrument. The type of harp shown here is made of cedar, and it uses wooden nails. The sound emanates through three circular holes on top of the "soundbox"; they are always found in the pattern shown in figure 9–5, on either side of the column, or pole, that connects the neck to the soundbox.

Fig. 9–5. *Schematic diagram showing position of sound holes in an Imbabura harp.*

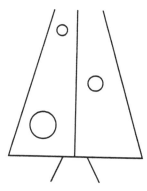

The instrument seems to have an unusual shape, compared to Western harps you may be familiar with. The Imbabura harp's column is straight but short, creating a low "head," or top, of the instrument. Its soundbox is distinctively arched, wide, and deep. On older harps in this region, bull's-hoof glue was used. The tuning pegs are made of iron or wood. There is a single line of strings that typically is a combination of gut, possibly nylon, and steel. The gut strings—used for the bass and middle registers—used to be made by the Quichua themselves from the cut, washed, dried, and twisted intestinal fibers of sheep, dog, cat, or goat. Sometimes musicians use nylon strings for the middle register, or range, of notes. The steel strings, closest to the performer, play the treble register, or melody line. Once again relying on their environment for necessary materials, Quichua musicians may use the leg bone of a sheep (in Quichua, *tullu*: bone) to tune the pegs on the harp neck.

This Imbabura harp is a descendant of sixteenth- and seventeenth-century Spanish harps, as shown by shared features of tuning, construction, configuration, and stringing. Based on what we know now, the Imbabura harp has remained essentially unchanged in appearance for one hundred to two hundred years, and possibly longer.

Recorded selection 55 is a *sanjuán* entitled "Cascarón," played in April 1980 by Quichua master harpist Efraín in the patio of his home in the *comuna* of Saltamora, outside Cotacachi. Harpists play the higher, or treble, strings (treble clef part, below) with their stronger hand, the lower, or bass, strings (bass clef part, below) with their weaker hand. Efraín, left-handed, plays treble with the left hand, bass with the right hand (ill. 9–5). The musical transcription of "Cascarón" appears in example 9–7. Each transcription of Cotacachi Quichua music will begin with a small stemless pitch; this corresponds either to the pitch to which that harp is tuned by that harpist on that day, or to that singer's tonic on that occasion. For comparison, all transcriptions of Cotacachi Quichua music are given in the key of D minor.

In general, the form of "Cascarón" is typical of Cotacachi Quichua *sanjuanes*. It is fundamentally a repetitive form, in which one or two different phrases are perhaps irregularly inserted into an otherwise similar phrase pattern. In *sanjuán*, the primary motive (the A phrases in "Cascarón") predominates. These are the melodies you identify with a particular *sanjuán*. The *sanjuán* phrase often lasts eight beats and frequently the rhythm of the first half of the phrase is identical, or nearly identical, to the rhythm of the second half. Figure 9–6 diagrams "Cascarón" in eight-beat phrases; we use A for primary motive, B for contrasting motive, and T for triadic arpeggiation that usually comprises either introductory or transitional materials. The A motive predominates in this song. The consecutive A statements are varied by a rather fixed sequence of one, one and one-half, or two T statements followed by two B statements. Although not in quite as regular a fashion as Efraín's "Cascarón," most performances of *sanjuán* follow this general pattern, with A statements predominating, and sometimes without any B statements at all.

Look at *A1* (the first statement of the eight-beat A phrase) and sing the eight

Ill. 9–5. *Harpist Efrain.*

quarter-note beats. Then sing *A2* and *A3*. You will begin to sense the feeling of
sanjuán: eight-beat phrases, usually without rests, with the consecutive statements of the primary motive slightly varied. Note that in this case *A1* differs from
A2 only in the first sixteenth note of each statement. Nevertheless, the first two
notes, A and D, respectively, fall within the tonic key of D minor. The *A3* version

Ex. 9–7 *Transcription of the sanjuán, "Cascarón," played by harpist Efraín.*

Ex. 9–7. **(*Continued*)**

Ex. 9–7. (Continued)

Ex. 9–7. (*Continued*)

T 1/2T B B
AAAAAAAATBB
AAAAAT1/2TBB
AAAAAT1/2TBB
AAAAATBB
AAAATT chord

Fig. 9–6. ***Phrase structure, Efrain's sanjuan, "Cascarón."***

partakes of the T phrase, with the first beat now identical to the first beat of *T*. Typically in *sanjuán* varied numbers of consecutive *A* phrases will alternate with two *B* phrases, and often these stress the note a perfect fourth higher than the tonic (here, G, related to D). In October 1990 discussions, Efraín told me that these *B* phrases are called "esquina" (in Spanish, corner) phrases: reflecting the pattern of the *sanjuán* dance, at these "B" moments, dancers turn and begin to move in the opposite direction.

Sanjuán also provides interesting details of interval structure and rhythm. In the *A* statements, the three notes D–C–A and their intervallic relationships (major second and minor third) are prominent. Compare this with the *B* statements, G–F–D, the same intervallic series, now a perfect fourth higher. Listen also to the rhythm of all the statements—*T*, *A*, and *B*—and note that in all cases the rhythm of the eight-beat phrase is the same (ex. 9–8). The rhythm of the first four beats (the first half) of the phrase is echoed by the rhythm of the second half. Example 9–9 illustrates how regular these rhythmic features are. This collection, recorded in Cotacachi comunas in 1979–1980, also gives you a dozen *sanjuanes* to learn and practice singing. Note the eight-beat patterning and the equal rhythm halves; "Cascarón" is number three. Certain *sanjuanes*, such as "Ilumán Tiyu," are often sung, while others such as "Cascarón" and "Carabuela" are typically played instrumentally. After singing or listening to all twelve of these *sanjuanes*, you will begin to sense that some combination of two (or all three) of the motives shown in example 9–10 is strongly characteristic of *sanjuanes*. Just as the major second minor third pattern is distinctive for melody in *sanjuán*, so also are these patterns distinctive for *sanjuán* rhythm.

As to harmonic relationships, "Cascarón's" melody and Efraín's accompanying bass line illustrate the prominence of the minor tonic key and its relative major key: the arpeggios (Ts) stress the minor key (D minor), the *A* sections emphasize the relative major (F Major). The high B-flat of the B statements, together with the D and F in the bass, suggest a feeling of the key of B-flat major—the subdominant key, or IV, of the relative major, F. The musics of many Andean peoples reflect this close relationship of the minor to its relative major. We will call this relationship bimodality.

Ex. 9–8. ***Sanjuán rhythmic pattern.***

Beat number: 1   2   3   4   5   6   7   8

Ex. 9–9. *Twelve Cotacachi Quichua sanjuánes.*

In Cotacachi Quichua *sanjuán* the music is basically repetitive with one, identifiable motive predominating, often eight-beat phrases, first-half rhythm and second-half rhythm very close or identical, characteristic pitch and rhythm motifs, and harmonic support demonstrating the bimodal relationship of minor

Ex. 9–10. *Characteristic rhythmic figures.*

to relative major. These features give many of these twelve *sanjuanes* a similar sound, and provide the grammar of the musical language of Cotacachi Quichua *sanjuán*.

SANJUÁN AND COTACACHI QUICHUA LIFEWAYS

Do Quichua speakers throughout the Ecuadorian Andes know "Cascarón"? How is *sanjuán* performed on the Imbabura harp? On which occasions is it performed? What are the characteristic verse structures when *sanjuanes* are sung? How do these structures or the specific texts reflect aspects of daily Cotacachi Quichua lifeways?

For students of music-cultures, Imbabura Province and the region around Cotacachi in particular are special, even unique, sites. A lyre on the flag of Cotacachi county suggests the central role music occupies in the region, and an author of a recent book on Imbabura traditions even suggests that, to speak of Ecuadorian music is to speak of the music of Cotacachi (Obando 1988: 155). This feeling came also from the Imbabureños themselves, both Quichua- and Spanish-speaking. They insisted on the uniqueness of their own music in relation to that of every other region. In response to questions about the spread of a particular *sanjuán*, for example, Cotacachi Quichua answered "*cada llajta*." "*Cada*" is Spanish for "every," and "*llajta*" is Quichua for "community." *Cada llajta* is the idea that every community has its own music, or its own mortuary customs, or its own dress, or its own dialect of Quichua. *Cada llajta* extends even to the way Quichua is to be written, in Ecuador. In 1980 meetings, representatives of various Quichua communities decided to permit the "speakers of each dialect to determine their own form of writing the language." (Harrison 1989: 19). *Cada llajta* seems to operate elsewhere in Ecuador. In April 1980, my wife and I moved from the northern to the central highlands; I sang and played on the Imbabura harp *sanjuanes* well known in Cotacachi to Quichua speakers in this new region. Although they had never heard these songs before, they came to learn and enjoy the pieces. When *sanjuanes* are imported into other regions, the *indígenas* often name them with reference to their origin: "*Sanjuán* from Cotacachi," or "*Sanjuán* from Otavalo" (a town near Cotacachi).

Cada llajta also dictates the performance media and the performance practices. *Sanjuanes* are sung and/or played by Cotacachi Quichua of all ages, by women and men, girls and boys. They are performed by unaccompanied voice(s), by vocal duos, by voice and harp—with *golpeador* (one who beats rhythm on the harp), by solo harp and *golpeador*, by voice and guitar, by solo *kena* (vertical notched flute), by solo *bandolín* (a fretted mandolin), or by ensembles of various instruments. When you hear *sanjuán* played on the Imbabura harp, you will also see a person kneeling in front of or alongside the harp. This is the *golpeador* (in Spanish, *golpear*: to hit), who beats the lower part of the harp soundbox in rhythm to the *sanjuán*. Illustration 9–6 shows

Ill. 9–6. *Miguel Armando in golpeador posture, César playing harp.*

Miguel Armando, regular *golpeador* for his two harpist sons, César and Sergio, assuming a *golpeador* posture for César. Ramona, the harpists' mother, is alongside.

All Cotacachi Quichua harpists remark that the *golpeador* and his dependable metronomic rhythm are essential to proper *sanjuán* performance. The *golpe* is the bedrock on which the harpist's concentration rests. Without it, he cannot work. The hitting of the harp soundbox, in rhythm, is not unique to Cotacachi, Ecuador; it appears in diverse harp traditions in central highland Ecuador, Peru, Argentina, Chile, and Mexico.

The treble register (the strings closest to the harpist) of the Imbabura harp is tuned to a six-pitch, or hexatonic, scale in the natural minor key, omitting the second scale degree. For example, in our D-minor scale, the harpist will tune his treble register to the following pitches: D, F, G, A, B-flat, C, and D (upper octave). This tuning permits him to play the full range of mostly pentatonic *sanjuanes* in his repertoire, as well as the occasional hexatonic one—for example,"Ilumán Tiyu," normally played with G minor, not D minor, as tonic. The hexatonic pitches present on the harp permit the use of A—the second degree in the key of G minor. "Ilumán Tiyu" requires that second scale degree. The middle register typically is likewise hexatonic. The bass register is tuned so that the harpist may play the minor tonic triad—with upper and lower octaves—in alternation with (i.e., one or sometimes two hand-positions away from the minor) the relative major triad (ex. 9–11). He uses four fingers of the hand (ex-

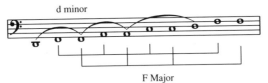

Ex. 9–11. *Tuning of bass register of Imbabura barp.*

cluding the little finger), skipping one string between each finger, often two strings between index finger and thumb.

In the *comunas* outside Cotacachi, the *arpero* (harpist) and *golpeador* perform *sanjuanes* in at least three festive contexts: *matrimonio* (wedding), *misai* (private Mass), and *wawa velorio* (child's wake). Quichua in this region celebrate a five-day wedding. Within the Saturday to Wednesday cycle, Sunday or Monday sees the *ñavi maillai*, a ritual washing of feet and face, at which harp music is present. A *misai* is a private Mass held to a saint: after the Mass in the cantonal church, the statue of the saint—the *santo*—is returned to its altar in its owner's home; a meal is prepared for the Mass-offerer and a musical fiesta is celebrated through the night. In *wawa velorio*, held all night at the deceased child's home, *sanjuán* music predominates.

Sanjuán at *wawa velorio*—as elsewhere—is dance music. You can do the *sanjuán* dance-step as you practice from your list of twelve *sanjuanes*. Men and women hold their hands behind their backs and stomp to each quarter-note beat. Step forward with your left foot, joining with the right foot on the next beat. Then move your right foot back first, followed by your left foot. When dancing *sanjuán*, keep your upper torso stiff, your knees bent and your lower body relaxed, with a good bounce and stomp. The signal to turn around while dancing is (shouted) "Tigrashpa!" or "Tigrapai!"

We can view the *sanjuán* dance-step as an emphatic back-and-forth walking, a stomp, to the music. At the child's wake this stomping is performed all night as the *arpero* plays *sanjuanes*, sometimes several strung together without interruption. As a forceful walk-ing to music, *sanjuán* emphatically asserts the action of walking. It serves as a kinetic endorsement for both the walking and the Quichua way of life that depends upon it. Let us delve further into Cotacachi Quichua walking, which, as we have already observed, is vital to communication, to daily tasks—in short, to survival.

WALKING IN SANJUÁN: THE VITAL DOMAIN METAPHOR

Walking as the paramount daily activity of Cotacachi Quichua emerges in expressive culture, not only in dance but in song text as well. Outside Cotacachi, in the *comunas*, walking is necessary for the survival of the *comunas* as well as for individual sustenance. Quichua community leaders frequently say that their particular *comuna* will succeed or fail depending on whether it can obtain outside aid. Rousing *comuna* residents to support the *comuna* and searching for assistance from provincial authorities demands footwork. Their view is that *comunas* will flourish only with persistent *purishpa* (walking) on their behalf. Moreover, on a personal level *purina* is to walk for one's educational benefit and to enable oneself to carry out family obligations. *Purina*, the inescapable daily activity of walking, becomes a positive metaphor in speech: it is behavior worthy of others' esteem because it is done on behalf of others; it is behavior leading to one's own enhanced self-respect.

In the text of sung *sanjuán*, the *purina* metaphor is "extended." In the metaphoric mechanism of extension, one takes experience from a domain where it is easily understood and uses it as the basis for domains more abstract and ambiguous. In sung *sanjuanes*, *purina* appears prominently in texts, notably as a verb of action. Figure 9–7 shows *sanjuán* verse couplets, with their primary (A) motives.

Purina in these *sanjuán* texts extends to emotion. The verses express either emotional release through walking ("I walk about crying and crying") or emotional involvement through walking ("I walk about because of you"; "Nights and nights I walk about"). *Purina* may be traced through its various metaphoric courses—from walking along the *chaki ñan* (footpath), to walking for the benefit of the *comuna* or for one's own betterment, to wandering, going about, for love, sadness, or as an outlet for other emotions. We notice how walking becomes extended to encompass the abstract, from physical movement for survival, to movement for broadly social purposes, to movement for personal emotional reasons.

In chapter 2 David McAllester calls certain Navajo great ceremonial chants "classic." One Cotacachi Quichua *sanjuán*, "Rusa María wasi rupajmi," qualifies as a classic in this region (ex. 9–12; fig. 9–8). "Rusa María" (recorded selection 56) is one of the most beloved *sanjuanes* of the Cotacachi Quichua *comuna*. In the recording, Gerónimo on vocal, Sergio on harp, and his father Miguel Armando on *golpe*, perform this *sanjuán* at a *wawa velorio* (Quichua child's wake) in January, 1980. You will hear noise as the microphone is passed back and forth from singer to harpist. "Rusa María" speaks of tragedy, drunkenness, and fright, as well as courting. The first double couplet suggests resignation in the face of a house fire disaster. Quichua homes higher up Mt. Cotacachi have thatched roofs, instead of tile, with wooden support beams. The family meal is cooked over an open hearth, and destruction by fire is an ever-present possibility. When I asked about this verse ten years later, in September, 1990, Imbabura Quichua musicians told me that "Rusa María's" home might well be small and old; she might be expressing both anger and the confidence that her neighbors, feeling sympathy, might build her a new home, larger and better. Quichua families are accustomed to disaster, relating both to property and to infant death.

Alcoholic beverages can be another source of social tragedy. Most alcohol

a. Kanta nishpami shamuni | I come speaking of you
Kanta nishpami *purini* | I walk speaking of you

b. Wawagumantallamari | Indeed just because of the baby
Wakai wakai *purini* | Do I walk about crying and crying

c. Solo kampa muchitawan | Only with your kiss
Ayunashka *purini* | Nourished, do I walk about

d. Wata wata *purini* | I walk about years and years
Kanta nishpa muyuni | I go this and that way speaking of you

e. Wakai wakai *purinki* | You (will) walk about crying and crying
Llaki llaki muyunki | You (will) go this and that way very sad

f. Na pimanta *purini* | Not for whomever do I walk about
Kanmantami *purini* | I walk about because of you

g. Tikumantami shamuni | I come from (the *comuna* of) Tiku
Kanta nishpalla *purini* | I walk about only speaking of you

h. Ima nishpalla *purinki* | Just why do you walk about?
Mana nimanta *purinki* | You don't walk about for nothing

i. Llaki llakilla *purijuni* | I am walking about very sad
Wakai wakailla *purisha* | I shall walk about crying very much

j. Karu karuta *purishpa* | Walking very far
Llaki llakilla muyujun | He is moving this way and that, very sad

Fig. 9–7. *The Quichua verb, purina, in Cotacachi sanjuán couplets.*

k. Juyaimantalla *purini*   I walk about just because of love
   Llakimantalla muyuni   I go this and that way just because of sadness

l. Kanmantallami *purini*   I walk about just because of you
   Tutai tutailla *purini*   Nights and nights I walk about

Fig. 9–7.   (Continued)

consumed in the Cotacachi countryside is cane alcohol (*trago*), brought as contraband from another region of Ecuador. Frequently, the owners of the small stores in the *comunas* mix this alcohol with water, berry juice, or other substances, and the effects can be unpredictable. Consumption of cane alcohol or other alcohol is vital in Cotacachi rituals (such as a child's wake) and in Andean rituals in general throughout Peru and Bolivia. Yet, overconsumption of *trago* can produce hallucinations, strongly emotional behavior, and in the case of adulterated *trago*, even blindness or death.

"Rusa María" refers also to courting. *Wambra* and *kwitsa* may mean either young man and young woman, or boy and girl. Courting begins in the schoolyard and elsewhere at age twelve or thirteen. Quichua often marry in their mid- or late teens.

"Rusa María" speaks of the inevitable in Cotacachi Quichua life: the natural environment, ritual practice in conflict with economic exploitation, and cultural expectation and human instinct. "Rusa María" is a song—danced to on festive occasions; it is a source of joy and pride to all *indígenas* of Cotacachi.

The traditions of the Quichua of Cotacachi—the people, the language, the dress, the material culture, the character of *sanjuán* and the harp that plays it—have been preserved for hundreds of years. *Cada llajta* (individual character of the community) ensures the uniqueness of many aspects of their expressive culture. However, the Cotacachi Quichua share some traits with other regions and cultures of Latin America. One of these is the wake ritual for a dead child. Let us look at *wawa velorio* to see how it accommodates *cada llajta* with broader beliefs and practices that transcend cultural and political boundaries.

WAWA VELORIO

In Imbabura as elsewhere in Latin America, infants struggle to survive. In three consecutive months in 1979–1980 I witnessed three *wawa velorio* rituals on

Ex. 9–12.   Sanjuán, "Rusa María wasi rupajmi."

Rusa María wasi rupajmi	Rusa María's house burning
Mas ki rupachun nishkashi,	So let it burn, she seems to have said,
Rusa María wasi rupajmi	Rusa María's house burning
Mas ki rupachun nishkashi,	So let it burn, she seems to have said,
Taita Manuilpash machashkamari	And Manuel, a father, very drunk
Manllarishkami wakajun,	Frightened, is crying,
Taita Manuilpash machashkamari	And Manuel, a father, very drunk
Manllarishkami wakajun,	Frightened, is crying,
Wambrakunapash kwitsakunawan	And young men and young women
Sirinkapajmi rishka nin,	Went to lie down together, they say,
Wambrakunapash kwitsakunawan	And young men and young women
Sirinkapajmi rishka nin.	Went to lie down together, they say.

Fig. 9–8. Lyrics to "Rusa María."

Cotacachi's slopes. I observed a fourth child's wake there in August, 1990. The infant mortality rate in Ecuador continues to be very high; deaths are caused in large part from intestinal and respiratory diseases. The death of young children in Ecuador—and throughout Latin America—is a daily tragedy which through its very frequency ironically serves to preserve dozens of unique regional traditions of genre, instrument, and dance.

After nightfall, Sergio, the harpist contracted to provide music for the wake, (ill. 9–7), his younger brother and apprentice-harpist César, and their family leave their Tikulla home for the home of the deceased. After more than an hour's uphill winding journey on *chaki ñanes*, father-golpeador Miguel Armando bearing the family harp, they arrive. At about 9:30 Sergio sits down with his harp next to the platform bearing the deceased infant. A few candles illuminate the casket and the home. After tuning, Sergio plays a strongly percussive music, called *vacación* (recorded selection 57; ex. 9–13). The all-night *wawa velorio*—the wake for the deceased child—has begun.

Vacación (the same term is used for both the genre and the title itself) differs audibly from *sanjuán*. First, *vacación* does not require a *golpeador* but is performed by the harpist alone. Second, it is not sung but is purely instrumental. Where *sanjuán* is in simple meter, *vacación* lacks the regular stresses that characterize a particular meter. *Vacación* is not built, like *sanjuán*, in eight-beat phrases but in long, descending cycles. *Sanjuán* is dance music; *vacación* is not.

Sanjuán is performed throughout the night at *wawa velorio*, accompanying the dancing of family and guests. *Vacación* is tied to two special ritual moments: at the outset of the wake, and whenever behavior centers around the deceased child. Harpists informed me that they play *vacación* at the beginning of the ritual in order to drive out the *demonio*, or devil, from beneath the platform supporting the deceased child. The second ritual moments include late-evening adorning of the corpse, and dawn closing of the casket.

Before playing *vacación*, after playing it, and periodically throughout the night, the harpist and his family are offered food and drink—bananas, home

Ill. 9–7. *Harpist Sergio.*

made bread, barley gruel, maize gruel, stewed corn and *trago*. We have mentioned the central importance of *trago* consumption in ritual settings both in Cotacachi and throughout the Andes. In *wawa velorio*, most of those present consume the drink.

The man (never a woman) with the *trago* bottle and plastic cup goes around the room, offering a *copa* (cup) of *trago* to each man and woman: *"Ufyapai!"* ("Drink!"), he says; the one being offered the *copa* usually first asks him to drink—which he does—then accepts the offer him- or herself.

Until approximately midnight, Sergio performs mostly *sanjuanes*. By 10:30 P.M. he has played some five to ten *sanjuanes*, including perhaps "Carabuela," "Llakishamari nirkanki," "Ilumán Tiyu," and "Rusa María." Occasionally, to keep the dancing going, he changes from one *sanjuán* to another without stopping. There is a distinctly regular and nearly metronomic tempo sense about this

Ex. 9–13. *Transcription of vacación, played by harpist Sergio at child's wake.*

father-son duo. Miguel Armando's *golpe* is solid and reliable, invariant, and Sergio's rhythm is strong and regular. Vocalists for the duo may be Sergio's companions, Roberto and Gerónimo. One sings with Sergio. The voice-harp duo performs typically-texted *sanjuanes*, including "Rusa María," "De Cayambe a Wachala," and "Ruku kuskungu." To enhance the *alegre*, or happy, character of the festive ritual, the harpist likes to have near-constant chatter together with his music and *golpe*.

At around 10:30 P.M. in the middle of playing a *sanjuán*, Sergio suddenly stops and shifts into *vacación*. Now the child, in its casket, is removed from the platform where it has been prominently displayed and placed on the floor for adorning and crowning. The infant is usually given to its mother, who mourns the loss of her baby with a lament. This sobbed music uses the principal notes of *vacación*: D–C–A (scale degrees 8–7–5 of the D-minor key). A crown of flowers is put on the baby's head. Its waist and wrists are wrapped in ribbons and bouquets of flowers are placed alongside the body in the casket. During this entire time, Sergio plays *vacación*, and he stops only when the infant and its casket are again placed on the platform.

Although dancing to *sanjuán* was slow to start, by 1:30 A.M. everyone is dancing. The godmother and the father might begin to dance, prompting Sergio to shout a pleased "*Achi mamaka kallarinka ña!*" ("The godmother will begin [to dance] now!"). Gerónimo shouts: "*Shinlli shinlli bailapankich' kumarigukuna!*" ("Dance strongly, dear comadres!"). Sergio now hardly stops for small talk, immediately following one *sanjuán* with another.

He now begins to alternate *sanjuán* with *pareja*, a slightly faster music, also for dancing but usually without text.

Very late, at about 3:00 A.M., Sergio leaves the harp and asks his younger brother César to take over (ill. 9–8). With very few people still awake, César plays a string of short *sanjuanes*. There is no banter between César and his *golpeador*-father, as there had been more naturally between musicians of the same generation, such as Sergio and Gerónimo. This is *sanjuán* without reaction—functional dance music with little function, since no one is dancing.

At about 5:00 A.M. everyone is awake and shares a morning meal of boiled potatoes. Before sunrise (an hour later) Sergio again takes over the harp, tuning and playing a *pareja*. Suddenly he shifts into *vacación* and the casket is taken outside into the patio. Sergio stops quickly, picks up the harp, and heads outside. Recorded selection 58 begins with Sergio performing *vacación* as the casket is taken outside. He then remarks, ". . . sacando para afuera" ("[they're] taking [it] outside"). He heads at once outside and there the mother begins to sing her lament.

The mother bids farewell to her child for the final time. She heard cycles of *vacación* for a few minutes just prior to the casket's removal outside. Now, as if on cue, and almost precisely at sunrise, she expresses her grief in a lament which, as in the night before, uses almost exclusively the same three important pitches from *vacación*: D–C–A. In Sergio's actual tuning these

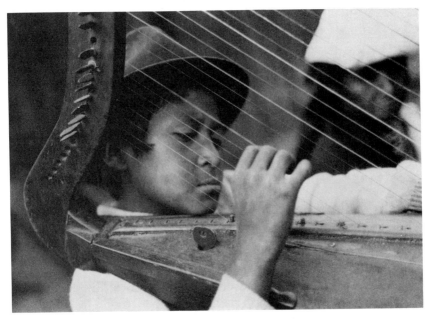

Ill. 9–8. *Harpist César.*

pitches are G♯–F♯–D♯. Soon after she begins, Sergio, also near the casket, repeats *vacación* on the harp. Both musical expressions are *of* the child: the mother's *to* the infant, the harpist's *about* the infant. The infant is open to view for only a few more minutes and so the focus of everyone's attention is on her (referring here to a January 12–13, 1980 ritual for a 2-year-old girl). Although *vacación* does not "accompany" the mother's lament (they are simultaneous but independent musical expressions), nevertheless they are together in time and object focus, and are close in musical pitch and structure. Like *vacación*, the lament is cyclical in form, always beginning with the G♯ and descending through the F♯ to the D♯.

Example 9–14 is a transcription of a part of this lament. The transcription shows note heads only because the lament is not strictly metrical. The mark "⌒" over the pitch indicates that it is held longer than the surrounding notes. At this point the mother sing-sobs alone. On this particular January 1980 morning, her sobs make it difficult to render most of the words precisely. Clearly she is addressing her baby daughter, whom she calls "*warmiku*" ("little woman"). In many ways this woman's lament is close in character to the Rumanian solo lament (recorded selection 27) discussed in chapter 5. First, both expressions are specifically addressed to the deceased. Both are sobbed-sung in short phrases that ultimately descend to the lowest pitch. Remarkably, both the Rumanian woman and the Ecuadorian Quichua woman sing not only the same intervals (essentially a descending major second, then a descending minor third) but even the same actual pitches: G♯, F♯, D♯.

Ex. 9–14. *Transcription of mother's lament for her baby daughter.*

Lamenting at dawn, the mother caresses her child's face or entire wrapped body one last time. Then the *golpeador* hammers on the lid of the casket and when the child is no longer visible Sergio stops playing *vacación*. Just after 6:00 A.M. the godfather hoists the casket to his shoulder and everyone walks down the mountain to the town of Cotacachi, where the child is buried in the cemetery. After the burial the party adjourns to a *cantina* (tavern) where Sergio continues to play *sanjuanes* on the harp for dancing throughout the day.

Dancing, all night, at a child's wake. On Cotacachi's slopes and throughout

Latin America *wawa velorio*—or *velorio de angelito*—is a celebration. We find this surprising, perhaps. We might feel some of the confusion of a French baron, Jean Charles Davillier, who came upon a festive child's wake while traveling in the Spanish Mediterranean in the 1870s (see ill. 9–9). He could not understand the merrymaking—in this case a couple dancing a *jota*, accompanying themselves with castanets. One of the relatives informed him, "Está con los ángeles" ("She is with the angels"). In Roman Catholicism, baptism confers a vital regeneration in Christ and thus an unconditional promise of salvation to a baptized child dying in infancy. In Catholic Spain and Latin America, the deceased infant is believed to be an angel. This is cause for rejoicing.

Indeed, the symbolic treatment of the child suggests her or his transformation into an angel. In various Latin American countries in this century, one finds that the infant is not only present but *raised*: lying on the elevated platform, seated on the table, tied to a ladder placed atop the casket, suspended from the roof, or pushed back and forth between poles. Each of these types of ritual gestures symbolizes the transformation into an angel and entry into eternity. Similarly, the infant is washed and dressed in the finest clothing available and is bedecked in ribbons, flowers, and paper or cardboard wings. Affixed to the child's shoulders or back, the wings are almost always present. Upon the child's head is a crown of real or artificial flowers, and this wreath is essential: the crown is both ubiquitous (in Latin American and Spanish child's wake) and ancient (the practice of crowning dead children dating back to the time of the ancient Greeks.) The atmosphere of the wake is always festive, with dancing, food, and alcoholic beverage.

Ill. 9–9. *A festive child's wake in the Spanish Mediterranean, 1870s.*

THE CAREER DILEMMA OF DON CÉSAR MUQUINCHE

We have seen how vital the harpist is in the Quichua child's wake in northern highland Cotacachi. The harpist is also very visible in the central highlands, especially Tungurahua. One talented individual artist, Don César Muquinche, is harpist of Illampu, a village in Tungurahua Province (ill. 9–10). His harp is considerably larger than the Imbabura harps. It is modeled on the harps of Paraguay; these instruments are distinguished by their substantial size and by

Ill. 9–10. *Don César Muquinche, harpist of Illampu, Tungurahua province.*

their neck shape—an inverted arch. The neck's tuning pegs are guitar-type mechanical tuning pegs, used also by the Paraguayans. The pattern of small, paired sound holes on either side of the column dates to Spanish harps of the seventeenth century.

An artist of national stature, Don César plays numerous musical genres, including *sanjuanito*, an adaptation of the Imbabura *sanjuán*. In recorded selection 59 we hear him playing an *albazo* called "Toro barroso." The *albazo* is well known among Spanish speakers throughout the highlands and even throughout the country. It is heard everywhere on the radio and at public and private celebrations.

Don César's decision to take up the harp was complicated. His father had been a professional harpist. Attending his father's performances as a child, the son witnessed the physical suffering that this career brought with it. César initially decided that he would apprentice as a hat maker. But his father, Don Francisco, advised his son that whatever César chose to do he should select something that would make him content and leave him with good memories. Ultimately, these words led César back to music. His decision to be a musician was also a reflection of Don César's great admiration and respect for his father—specifically for his father's ability to resist the temptations inherent in the harpist's career—and for his father's concern for him and serious advice to him.

In fact, both father and son followed similar paths. Both had a strong business orientation. Don César speaks of Naranjo's harp, and the services of Camilo Borja, Don Francisco, and himself as harpists as being "in some demand." Don César saw himself as being upwardly mobile; he disdained his own *indígena* roots. Yet both he and his father performed for both *indígena* and *blanco* (white) society. They bridged this cultural gap as performers. Both artists expanded their repertoires to meet the popular demands of both societies. Recall Mark Slobin's description of the adaptability that marked Miriam Nirenberg, the Yiddish folk singer (chapter 5). Also compare the comment by the Ghanaian Kasena musician, William Alban Ayipaga Connelly, that he saw himself as a "local" musician but wished to become a "general" one (chapter 3). Finally, both Don César and his father learned to play in ensemble as well as solo, and to adapt to changing performance arenas, such as radio and television.

We will see that both men appreciated playing as an art. They felt great pride in developing it both for their own self-esteem and for the satisfaction of their clients. Don César's highest compliment to artists or craftspersons was to call them "artists of quality."

In July 1980, after I had studied with him for several months, Don César Muquinche told me about the development of his artistic career. Let us look at the types of conflict he faced and how he finally resolved them, choosing harp music over hat making. Through his thoughts we can gain some insights into the reputation, the *fama*, of a harpist in Ecuador. I conducted the interview in Spanish and translated it into the English that follows:

Don César

I was born in 1920, here in Illampu (Tungurahua). My father, Francisco, was planning to become a tailor—to make men's suits. Well, he heard Camilo Borja play—a man who lived just alongside us—and, on hearing him play the harp, my father paid attention. And he said, "I would like to learn harp from this man."

My father then proposed to Borja that he teach him the harp. The man said yes and told him: "Let's make a deal: you make me trousers and I will give you harp lessons." My father told me that he had these lessons every day; he was very interested in learning quickly, taking advantage of the good will of the maestro.

When Borja saw that my father was beginning to play the harp fairly well, the maestro—who was in great demand at that time—told him he needed to buy his own harp. . . . There was a man . . . Segundo Alejandro Naranjo . . . who made fine instruments—very special harps. They had a fantastic resonance. . . .

My father told me that the harps made by this man were instruments in some demand and of very fine quality; there was no danger that the glue might loosen from the pieces. Even when the harp was hit hard the wood would not dent or come loose, as might happen today, with harps made of rough wood. . . .

My father was in demand in various places—in fiestas, in *wawas muertos* [dead children, i.e., *wawa velorio*]. . . . And with the rhythm of this beating upon the harp—they [the father and his *golpeador*] put on a fine show, without the need of other instruments.

[At children's wakes] the *golpeador* had to stay right there, by the harpist, all night long. Then, there were other events—matrimonio, patron saint fiestas. Among [indígenas], the matrimonio lasts three or four days. And the harpist has to be *there*. Day and night . . . It is the same in the fiestas—of devotion to some saint, for example.

They made a good ensemble. And ever since I could remember, my father was in great demand—as much among the *indígenas* as among the white people. He became an innovative, popular artist, who liked to entertain. [He played for] the people of society—a governor, a subtreasurer, here or beyond—in Quito [the capital], in different places. My father was very much in demand, very important: an artist of quality. He traveled to Quito, through the entire country. He became a very well-known artist . . . a very distinguished artist, for every class of society.

The musicians went to their engagements in a cart pulled by a horse. At times, they went on horseback, to Quito—carrying the harp, cushioned and secured with a scarf, or something else soft. There was a person who led the horses. [My father] told me about this.

Sometimes, traveling in this way was very trying. Finally my father said: "No, I won't travel like that. If we could go in those carriages . . . then I would go. I think I have been treating myself badly." And the people [provided what he requested], as they seemed to want my father's services greatly. Many times he went to Riobamba [capital of Chimborazo Province, just south of Tungurahua Province], I recall.

When I began growing up, I sometimes accompanied him, to see how he was treated, or how he might have been suffering. I saw that my father, being responsible, did not get drunk at the fiestas; he was careful to fulfill his responsibilities honorably. And whenever he went, the people paid him well. . . . But it is sad that he had to suffer a lot [due to the extremely long hours, the demands for continuous music, and the constant pressure to partake of alcohol with the guests] because the people never tired of enjoying themselves. So I felt bad for my father, and I said to him: "Now, father, when can I learn how to play, to help you?"

I lament the death of my father. But he left good memories, as an artist—very good memories. He died while still capable, surrounded by the profits of his labors. By contrast, [another] harpist of quality [that I knew] died poor because he was quite a womanizer. They say he squandered all he had earned, drinking with women. He died, poor, leaving his children poor. By contrast, my father said: "I have to extract a good inheritance from this profession [of harpist]. If the upper-class people occupy me well, pay me well, if the indígenas also pay me well, why not plant crops? Why not use [the money] for land, in things that are to serve me for life?"

My father thought about this very conscientiously. He [bought land and] worked the fields two or three days each week; he did not attend to the fields any more than that because he was in great demand in his career of music. My mother worked the fields more.

Now that I was becoming a young man, I had to think about it. There were harpists who went around poorly dressed, barefoot, dirty; I looked, and realized that my father took very good care of himself. There were other harpists, but awful ones. They got drunk and walked around looking like a mess—not even the instruments were well treated. And that's worse.

And so, I said no, I do not want to be a harpist because they get very drunk. Of course, my father is fine, he takes care of me; but I see that most people put pressure on the harpist—they say: "Drink, maestro," with great fervor. "Drink." They put it into your mouth. I said to myself, "Not me . . . I won't dedicate myself to the harp." My father, when they asked him to drink, said: "Don't force me to. I must carry out my responsibilities and earn my money. After I have completed my commitment, for which you have hired me, then I shall be delighted to drink. But I have to be responsible for my musical colleagues; they come with me, to earn a living. And, since I made the contract, I have to charge the patrón who has contracted me and, in turn, pay my *compañeros*, in order to assure their accompaniment in the future. If I get drunk, I can't discharge either my contract or my agreement to pay my *compañeros*, who came along expecting me to pay them. Thus, you are hurting me [by insisting that I drink and get drunk.]" This retort worked very well.

Nevertheless . . . I told my father that I did not wish to be a musician but rather a hat maker. I liked seeing young women or men who appreciated a truly elegant hat. And there was a hat maker of first quality, a man by the name of Segundo Villa Paredes, in Ambato [the provincial capital of Tungurahua]. I went there and learned all that the maestro had to teach—

how to make hats. I was there some two years, while I was young. I think I was already hat making by the age of fifteen years. By the age of eighteen or twenty I was a [hat-making] maestro.

I became independent and set up a workshop in Ambato. I worked for the "people of society," who liked my style of work. I had the confidence of these people and it went well for me. I had quite a nice workshop there in the city of Ambato.

When my father saw that I was a successful [hat-making] maestro, he told me: "Son, I congratulate you. You have distinguished yourself, now, don't you see? Now, I am going to recommend to you that you take advantage, in your *youth*, of your profession. Because of music, I have my fond memories. In the same way, I would recommend that you take advantage of, enjoy, your profession." I had to listen to my father, pay attention to him: he was making this recommendation for my own good.

Well, when I had become a very popular maestro, well esteemed and with plenty of work, there, in the city, guaranteeing me a good living, some people came to me on their own, to ask that I teach them the craft of hat making. Others came so that they might help me expedite my commitments to deliver the completed work. I accepted them as working assistants. I looked for those who already knew the craft. Others came and said: "Maestro, be so kind as to teach my son the profession." "Delighted" [I said.], and accepted them.

Soon I organized the work for those who had come to help and those who had come to learn, and I had some free time. Over there the people already knew—"You're the Muquinche—?" I said: "Yes." "Listen, and your father is a harpist of quality." I said: "Yes." "And you don't know anything?" "I too know a little bit." "And why don't you let us hear it? Why don't you bring a harp here to your workshop and play for us? Let us hear what your style is like, or how you play."

I thought: "Perhaps, yes, I must have a harp—as recreation from work."

Since the people had requested me to play the harp for them, I had a harp made. I brought it to my workshop, and I began to play it.

Meanwhile, some of the people continued talking with me: "Why not dedicate yourself to the harp?" At first I paid no attention to this. Of some people, I thought: "These [people] are going to do me harm." They sounded like those who had said [to my father]: "Look, maestro, you play beautifully; accept just one [drink]." I said: "No, I have my business—I have my workshop. I have this—how can I abandon my workshop?" When I put it this way, some withdrew their invitation; others continued asking me to play: "Play the harp, maestro." I said to myself: "Listen, this is bad; I am going to get hooked on this."

Well, as I was getting popular with my music, there came this man, I remember, from Radio Ambato, a man by the name of Villa Lobos, the manager of Radio Ambato. Juan Villa Lobos. Well, he said: "Maestro, can you do programs for Radio Ambato?" . . . I said: "Fine."

Well, then, I had to put attention into improving my art. And he said to me: "Maestro, would you be able to play together with other instruments, to make a nice *conjunto* (ensemble), with violins, bandolín, guitar, and flute?" I said: "Yes, sir, but only with the agreement that it is to be you who is in charge of getting these people together; if it is to be left to me to do this, then, no. I am busy." The man [did it], of course, since he liked the idea of organizing a *conjunto típico* (typical ensemble), as we called it . . . A very nice ensemble was thus created, along with the harp . . . it was a great hit with the people—"Such-and-such *Conjunto*, directed by . . ." They named me director of the ensemble.

We did the Radio Ambato programs Saturdays and Sundays—Saturdays in the afternoon and Sundays at midday. This was all the time, for some three years in a row. Every weekend.

This man Villa Lobos came to my hat workshop when I was about twenty-eight years old. . . . I was, by then, a harpist, no? By then, I had practiced my profession [of hat maker] for some eight years. When I came into popularity [as a harpist], I was twenty-eight years old . . .

My father visited me and said: "César, you came to like the harp?" I said: "Yes." He answered: "Very well, between the music and the hats, I think that you are going to become a rich man—for you are accumulating money." I confided to him that I did the same as he. With the monies that I earned—as much from the music as from the hats—I bought some small pieces of land. . . .

Well, trying to maintain the workshop, trying to fulfill my commitments, I came home from work at any old hour—at dawn, practically exhausted, wasted. To get the work done, I had to dig in and work myself.

I became ill. A fever, a lung infection, or a typhoid fever. This illness was very strong . . . it was in 1949. It was serious. I had to be hospitalized. Thank God, my hour had not yet arrived. I recuperated, my health restored. My father procured doctors to attend to me . . .

[One] doctor said: "You have to stop practicing one of your professions. If you continue at this rate, with the hats and the music, you won't do anything, neither the one nor the other. There is a danger that very easily you could drive yourself to complete exhaustion. Continue only with the music, or continue only with the hats." Of course I had to obey him. I said: "Very well. If I continue with the hats and the music, I'll be treating myself very badly." I had to pay attention to the doctor.

And so, I felt obliged to leave the profession of hat making.

ELSEWHERE IN ECUADOR

Let us conclude with a look at two other cultures and regions of Ecuador: the lowland Quichua of the Napo region of the eastern Ecuadorian jungle, and African-Ecuadorians of the Chota River Valley who live approximately two hours north of the Quichua of Cotacachi.

Recorded selection 60 is a curing song of a Quichua-speaking shaman of the jungle lowlands of eastern Ecuador. Among South American Indians in general, song is intimately connected to shamanism. The shaman is believed capable of communicating with spirits, in ecstatic "flights" entered into to cure patients but occasionally to cause illness as well (Olsen 1980: 368). The principal means for reaching this ecstatic state is through song, though certain cultures—including the Quichua-speaking peoples of the Napo River region—also use hallucinogenics to achieve the trance state believed essential to effect a cure. Many Native American shamans of Ecuador, Peru, and Venezuela are male, but the *machi*—the shaman of the Mapuche people of Chile—is female.

The history of shamans reaches back thousands of years. The word, *shaman*, comes from the Tungus language of Central Asia and Siberia; its root, *sam-*, has the idea of dance and leap, on the one hand, the notion of trouble and agitation, on the other. Chanting highly rhythmic music, accompanying himself or herself on a rattle, drum, or other beaten or shaken instrument (here a leaf bundle), the shaman travels back and forth between this world and a supernatural realm of souls and spirits. In this way, the shaman acquires the power needed to cure.

Jungle Quichua believe that the illness the shaman is requested to cure is created by "spirit projectiles" sent by another shaman. The curing shaman "sees" these darts, obtains the power to remove them from the patient, and sends them back to the shaman who induced the illness. In the recording, made in 1976, a sick woman was brought to the shaman's home. The Napo shaman has already entered the world of the spirits when he begins his song. Now he is able to "travel" between the spirit world and the world of his patient.

In this song, the shaman sings of a male jungle spirit—who then arrives. The shaman becomes this spirit and prepares to summon more spirits to him. Next, he experiences the sensation of soaring about; with this vision, he must fend off danger from multiple flying darts and lances. He chants that he is being protected by the shield of *Sungui*, master spirit of the water domain. Indeed, he is chanting while seated on a special stool, carved in the image of a water turtle to represent the seat of power of this *Sungui*. Ultimately, the shaman acknowledges several other arriving spirits, in addition to *Sungui*—all of which provide him, he says, with power to cure his patient. The Napo shaman believes that his chants come from the spirits he seeks to contact and that he is the vehicle by which the spirits may communicate with the world of humans (Whitten 1979:2–6). Example 9–15 shows one rendition in Western notation of part of the Napo shaman's song.

Notice first that the chanting is strongly rhythmic, dictated by the regular grouping of two eighth notes in the leaf-bundle rattle. Second, one pitch, G, is central, for the shaman always ends his musical phrases on this pitch. Selecting one, or perhaps two, pitches as an axis is characteristic of shamanic chanting in many Native American cultures of South America, among them the Napo Quichua, the nearby Shuar, and the Mapuche of Chile. Notice the pulsations of the shaman's voice. These are characteristic of this native South American's singing, as they were for certain types of singing among native North Americans, for example, the Iroquois and the Sioux (see chapter 2). The chant also has segments made up of three notes (D–E–G), and of four notes (G–A–B–high D); considered as a whole it has five different notes (D–E–G–A–B with the upper D replicating the lower D at the octave).

The music of a neighboring group, the Shuar, frequently uses only three different pitches (tritonic); and we know that the *sanjuanes* of highland Cota-

Ex. 9–15. *Transcription of part of curing song of Napo lowland Quichua shaman.*

cachi Quichua are prevailing five-pitched, or pentatonic. It is interesting that these lowland Quichua—who speak the same language (different dialect) as the highlanders but who share the jungle environment and shamanic curing belief system with the *Shuar*—use prominent elements of both musical systems.

Finally, although the recording does not provide a literal translation of the words of the shaman's song, its notes inform us that the shaman is relaying a tremendous amount of information in his chant. We alluded above to this wide range of "journey" experience; and this probably accounts for the fact that this and other lowland Quichua and Shuar shamanic chants have one musical note to one syllable of text—a "syllabic" style of singing words. This is an efficient means by which to convey in music a great deal of information—either experience or belief. In the tradition of the Western Roman Catholic Church, for example, the *Credo* section of the Mass ("I believe in one God...And in one Lord, Jesus Christ...And I believe in the Holy Ghost...") also conveys an enormously lengthy text and is also syllabic.

The music of the shaman of lowland Ecuador—and of Native American shamans throughout the length and breadth of South and North America—is incantation: it is a magical music that aims for a period of time to transform the world, to modify the course of events toward a particular desired end (Rouget 1985:131).

AFRICAN-ECUADORIAN MUSIC OF THE CHOTA RIVER VALLEY

When we think of Latin American regions that have large populations of African-Americans, Ecuador does not usually come to mind. Yet as much as 25 percent of the population of the country is African-Ecuadorian. They are heavily concentrated in coastal Esmeraldas Province which neighbors Imbabura Province. The first Africans arrived in Ecuador in the sixteenth century, after which Jesuit missionaries brought in large numbers of African slaves to work on plantations both on the coast and in the central highlands. The relatively small pocket of approximately 15,000 African-Americans in the Chota Valley, comprising ten to fifteen small villages, has an uncertain origin. The most widely accepted view is that the African-Ecuadorians of the Valle del Chota are descended from slaves held by Jesuits on their plantations in the highlands (Lipski 1987:157–158).

The best-known musicians today in the Valle del Chota are the guitarist-singers, Germán, Fabián, and Eleuterio Congo and their colleague, Milton Tadeo. Ten years ago they played mostly around their home village of Carpuela; today they are regional celebrities with regular weekend performances locally, on the coast, and in nearby Colombia. As of October 1990, they had recorded six long-playing records within 7 years. The Congo brothers are the third generation of composer-performers in their family.

In recorded selection 61, Fabián and Eleuterio Congo perform "Vamos pa' Manabí" ("Let's go to Manabi" [a coastal province next to Esmeraldas]). Both men play guitar; the voice is Fabián's (ill. 9–11). The text is reproduced in figure 9–9.

Notice first that, in contrast to the straight tone (without shake or vibrato in the voice) of the Quichua singers two hours down the road, Fabián's tone has substantial vibrato. Chapter 4 contains a good deal about the character and importance of improvisation in African-American music. In this African-

Ill. 9–11. *Fabian Congo, guitar player.*

Ecuadorian song, "Vamos pa' Manabí," you hear a distinctive freedom of expression in melody and rhythm—especially in the instrumental parts.

Fig. 9–9. *Lyrics for Chota Valley bomba, "Vamos pa' Manabí."*

Para no sufrir hagamos así (repeated) Vámonos de aquí para Manabí (rptd 3×) (Instruments alone)	So as not to suffer, let's do this: Let's go from here to Manabí.
Por donde yo estoy, muy lejos de tí (rptd) Siento el corazón, wambrita, por tí (rptd 3×) (Instruments alone)	Where I am, very far from you, I feel you in my heart, dear young woman.
Cuando yo estoy muy lejos de tí (rptd) Siento el corazón, wambrita, por tí (rptd 3×)	When I am very far from you I feel you in my heart, dear young woman.

(This text has been published; see Coba Andrade 1980:209.)

Contributing to the feeling of rhythmic freedom is the fact that Fabián regularly syncopates his rhythm—that is, he seems to sing "between" the beats of the guitars' pulse instead of with those strong beats. The guitars, too, play syncopated rhythm, especially in the "instruments alone" sections. After listening a few more times, try singing along with Fabián; the text is not long or complicated. See if you can begin to feel the subtle rhythm of the syncopated song; the more you practice, the closer you will get to this relaxed feeling and the more you will enjoy singing "Manabí."

We have been discussing the African-American character of "Manabí." One Ecuadorian ethnomusicologist has expanded this idea, referring to the *bomba* (the genre of which "Manabí" is an example) of Chota as an "Indo-Hispano-Afro-Ecuadorian" hybrid music (Coba Andrade 1980: 185). Where, then, is the "Indo," the Native American character? Recall from our discussion of nearby Cotacachi *sanjuán* that the accompaniment is often in the minor paired with the relative major key. In Fabián's and Eleuterio's "Manabí" two chords prevail: F major and its relative minor, D minor. We are reminded of *sanjuán* not only by this key relationship but also by the minor key arpeggiations of the guitar as at the beginning of the song. Recall that this type of introductory arpeggiation is also characteristic of *sanjuán* when played on the Imbabura harp. The "*T*" motive of Efraín's "Cascarón" is an example of this.

Finally, there is *wambrita* in the text of "Manabí." This word is Quichua, not Spanish. Depending on the region of the Ecuadorian highlands and on its context in a sentence, *wambra* (and its affectionate diminutive, *wambrita*) may mean either "young man" or "young woman." (In "Rusa María" it meant "young man.") In "Manabí" it means "young woman."

"Vamos pa' Manabí" of the Congo brothers is a rich musical expression of a border region: African-Ecuadorians, close to a major Quichua cultural zone, within a Spanish-speaking nation. It is not surprising to discover in this piece musical and textual characteristics associated with all three of these cultures. In this case, though, probably the sum of the parts does not create the whole: This *bomba* from Chota is unique not merely because of its several individual features but also because of the distinctive artistry of its performers, Fabián and Eleuterio—a quality that cannot be captured on paper.

DESPEDIDA, OR FAREWELL

You have heard music from many different parts of Latin America: the unmistakable razor's edge tempo and tension of Venezuelan *joropo*, the eloquent metaphors and profound sentiment of Víctor Jara, and the depth and richness of hocketing altiplano panpipes in ensemble. You have learned of the lifeways, harp, and songs of the Quichua of highland Ecuador, and you have witnessed the poignant Quichua ritual of *wawa velorio*—dancing at the wake of a child. Where Jara pointed to the plaiter of Lonquén and to Angelita Huenumán, we have singled out for recognition a number of individual "artists of quality," in Muquinche's phrase—artists who are probably among the forgotten persons of Latin America—including harpists Efraín, Sergio, and Don César himself, the Napo lowland Quichua shaman, and Eleuterio and Fabián Congo. In their own worlds of music, these artists are highly esteemed, for they practice music traditions—*sanjuán* and *bomba*, child's wake and shamanic healing, harp with golpeador—that their cultures prize highly and have preserved for hundreds of years.

Our own sense of community is bound up with our identification with our own music and music rituals. In one realm or another, we all obey the dictate of *cada llajta*: each of us, ultimately, is musically, linguistically, and certainly in many other respects, of a place.

REFERENCES CITED

Coba Andrade, Carlos Alberto
    1980   *Literatura Popular Afroecuatoriana.* Otavalo, Ecuador: Instituto Otavaleño de Antropología.
Davillier, Le Baron [Jean] Ch[arles]
    1874   *L'Espagne.* Illustrated by G. Doré. Paris: Librairie Hachette et Cie.
Harrison, Regina
    1989   *Signs, Songs, and Memory in the Andes: Translating Quechua Language and Culture.* Austin: University of Texas Press.
Jara, Joan
    1984   *An Unfinished Song: The Life of Victor Jara.* New York: Ticknor & Fields.
Lipski, John M.
    1987   "The Chota Valley: Afro-Hispanic Language in Highland Ecuador." *Latin American Research Review* 22(1):155–170.
Muquinche, César
    1980   Interview. July 12, Illampu, Tungurahua Province, Ecuador.
Obando, Segundo
    1988   *Tradiciones de Imbabura*, 3rd ed. Quito: ABYA–YALA.
Olsen, Dale A.
    1980   "Symbol and Function in South American Indian Music." In *Musics of Many Cultures: An Introduction*, edited by E. May, 363–385. Berkeley: Univ. of California Press.
Rouget, Gilbert
    1985   *Music and Trance: A Theory of the Relations between Music and Possession.* Translation from the French revised by Brunhilde Biebuyck, in collaboration with the author. Chicago: Univ. of Chicago Press.
Smith, Sandra
    1984   "Panpipes for Power, Panpipes for Play: The Social Management of Cultural Expression in Kuna Society." Ph.D. diss., University of California, Berkeley.
Whitten, Norman E., Jr.
    1976   *Sacha Runa: Ethnicity and Adaptation of Ecuadorian Jungle Quichua.* Urbana: Univ. of Illinois Press.

————, et alia

1979 "Soul Vine Shaman." I. Background Notes; II. Notes on the Recording. Sacha Runa Research Foundation Occasional Paper no. 5.

ADDITIONAL READING

Aretz, Isabel, Gérard Béhague, and Robert Stevenson

1980 "Latin America." In *The New Grove Dictionary of Music and Musicians,* S. Sadie, editor. Vol. 10, pp. 505–534.

Béhague, Gérard

1979 *Music in Latin America: An Introduction.* Englewood Cliffs, N.J.: Prentice-Hall.

————

1984 "Patterns of *Candomblé* Music Performance: An Afro-Brazilian Religious Setting." In *Performance Practice: Ethnomusicological Perspectives,* edited by G. Béhague, 222–254. Westport, Conn.: Greenwood Press.

Fairley, Jan

1985 "Annotated Bibliography of Latin-American Popular Music with Particular Reference to Chile and to Nueva Canción." *Popular Music 5: Continuity and Change,* 305–356. Cambridge: Cambridge Univ. Press.

List, George

1983 *Music and Poetry in a Colombian Village: A Tri-Cultural Heritage.* Bloomington: Indiana Univ. Press.

Olsen, Dale A.

1975 "Music-Induced Altered States of Consciousness among Warao Shamans." *Journal of Latin American Lore* 1:19–33.

————

1980 "Folk Music of South America: A Musical Mosaic." In *Musics of Many Cultures: An Introduction,* edited by E. May, 386–425. Berkeley: Univ. of California Press.

Robertson, Carol E.

1979 " 'Pulling the Ancestors': Performance Practice and Praxis in Mapuche Ordering." *Ethnomusicology* 23(3):395–416.

Seeger, Anthony

1987 *Why Suyá Sing. A Musical Anthropology of an Amazonian People.* Cambridge: Cambridge Univ. Press.

Stevenson, Robert

1968 *Music in Aztec & Inca Territory.* Berkeley: Univ. of California Press.

Turino, Thomas

1983 "The Charango and the *Sirena*: Music, Magic, and the Power of Love." *Revista de Música Latinoamericana/Latin American Music Review* 4(1):81–119.

ADDITIONAL LISTENING

Afro-Hispanic Music from Western Colombia and Ecuador
> 1967 Recorded and edited by Norman E. Whitten, Jr. Folkways FE 4376.

El Cancionero noble de Colombia
> 1962 Recorded by Joaquín Piñeros Corpas. Bogotá: Ministerio de Educación-Editorial Antares-Fontón. 3 discs. 36 pp. text.

Clásicas de la Canción Paraguaya: Alfredo Rolando Ortiz, Arpa
> n.d. (pre-1980) Industrias Famoso Cia., Ltda., Quito, Ecuador. LDF–1015.

Folklore de mi Tierra: Conjunto Indígena "Peguche" [Ecuador]
> 1977 Industria Fonográfica Ecuatoriana (IFESA). Guayaquil, Ecuador. Distributed by Emporio Musical S.A., Guayaquil and Psje. Amador, Quito. ORION 330–0063.

Los Grandes de la Bomba, con: Fabián Congo y Milton Tadeo.
> 1989 Novedades. L.P. 323102.

Indian Music of Mexico
> 1952, 1962 Recorded by Henrietta Yurchenko. Ethnic Folkways Library FE–4413. 4 pp. Introduction and notes, by Gordon F. Ekholm and Henrietta Yurchenko.

Mountain Music of Peru
> 1966 Recorded by John Cohen. Ethnic Folkways FE 4539.

Música Andina de Bolivia
> 1980 Recorded with comments by Max Peter Baumann. Lauro Records, LPLI/S–062. 36 pp. Booklet.

Música Etnográfica y Folklórica del Ecuador.
> 1990 Recorded by José Peñín, Ronny Velásquez, and Carlos Alberto Coba A. Instituto Otavaleño de Antropología, Otavalo, Ecuador. 2 discs. LP 5748, 5750. 5 pp. text.

Música Folklórica de Venezuela
> n.d. (post-1968) Enregistrements réalisés par Isabel Aretz, Luis Felipe Ramón y Rivera, et Álvaro Fernaud. International Folk Music Council, Anthologie de la Musique Populaire. OCORA OCR 78.

Ñanda mañachi 1 (Préstame el camino) [Ecuador]
> 197 LLAQUICLLA–Industria Fonográfica Ecuatoriana S.A. (IFESA). Guayaquil, Ecuador. 339–0501. Recorded in Ibarra, Ecuador. Produced by Jean Chopin Thermes.

T E N

◆ ◆ ◆

Discovering and Documenting a World of Music

DAVID B. RECK, MARK SLOBIN, AND JEFF TODD TITON

MUSIC IN OUR OWN BACKYARDS

All of us are familiar with the tale (or movie) of Dorothy and her adventures with the Tin Man, the Lion, and the Scarecrow in the fantastic land of Oz. But most of us have forgotten Dorothy's startling discovery once she got back to Kansas: home was where her heart was, a fascinating world of people, family, neighbors, and friends, and of things which before her adventures she had overlooked. This is a familiar theme in literature the world over. The hero or heroine (ourselves) travels to faraway places, sees and does fabulous things, meets incredible people, or searches for marvelous treasures. But invariably the rainbow leads home; the pot of gold is buried in one's own backyard; the princess is none other than the girl next door.

In our explorations of the world's musics we—both students and scholars—are fascinated by cultures and peoples greatly separated from us in geography or time, in sound and style, in ways of making and doing music. In a sense, for every one of us there is an Oz. But there is also a musical culture surrounding us, one that we see and hear only partially because it is too close to us, because we take it for granted, as fish do water. Our musical environment is held both in us (in our perceptions and memories) and by other members of our community, only a fraction of whom we may know. It expands *out* from us (and *in* to us) in a series of concentric circles that may include family, ethnic groups, regional styles, our hemisphere, and cultural roots (Western Europe, Africa, and so on). It is available to us live or mechanically reproduced. It comes to us out of history (the classical masterworks, old-time fiddle tunes, or bebop jazz) or it is a product of the here and now (the latest hit on the pop music charts or the avant-garde "new thing"). Our surrounding musical universe seems to us multifaceted and immensely complicated.

Gathering reliable information on contemporary music is what this chapter is all about. We want to encourage you to seek out a nearby musical world, to observe it in person, to talk with the people involved in it, to document it with tape recordings and photographs, and to present the information in a project that will make a contribution to the body of knowledge about contemporary musical activities. If this research project is part of a course, you should check with your instructor for specific directives. What follows is a general guide, based on the experience we and our students have had with similar projects at our colleges and universities.

Selecting a subject for your research is of course the first step in the project. Songs and instrumental music in our culture serve a great many purposes and occur in a staggeringly wide variety of contexts, from singing in the shower to the Metropolitan Opera, from the high school marching band to the rock festival, and from the lullaby to the television commercial jingle. Some of it is trivial, some of it is profound. It is all meaningful. To help you select a subject, let us impose order on our surrounding musical culture by means of a few organizing principles: family, generation, avocation, religion, ethnicity, regionalism, nationalism, and commercialization. As you read through the following brief survey you may find some subjects that interest you. Later we will give you some specific suggestions.

Family

As is true in all cultures, Americans first hear music in the context of family life (ill. 10–1). Much of that music comes from the records on the family ste-

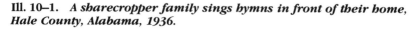

Ill. 10–1.   *A sharecropper family sings hymns in front of their home, Hale County, Alabama, 1936.*

Walker Evans. Courtesy of the Library of Congress

reo, radio, or television, and this "canned" music is especially important in developing children's musical taste. People often say they were very strongly influenced by the kind of music they heard before they were old enough to have their own records or choose the station on the family radio. Yet despite the parents' intentions, the youngster often rebels against his parents' taste in music and chooses to listen to what is favored by people his own age. There is usually some live music in the family as well. Many mothers and grandmothers sing lullabies, for example. These can be important since in North America, as elsewhere, lullabies not only lull but promise, praise, and teach cultural values. Sometimes lullabies are the only songs in a foreign language that American children with strong ethnic backgrounds hear, since people (particularly grandparents) often fall back on old, familiar languages for intimate songs.

Another important family context is the automobile, where families learn songs and sing together on weekends and vacations. This is not as surprising as it appears for the family car has become one of the basic centers of family experience, and it is one of the important places where the family gathers for an extended (some might say forced) period of time without outside distractions. The family used to have to choose between making their own music in the car or being force-fed by the radio, but the recent invention of automobile cassette recorders and compact disc players allows a family to have more control over what they hear when they drive.

In short, most Americans have an early layer of songs learned in childhood in a family setting. Often they are just songs for entertaining children, with no deep cultural message to impart. What they do teach is the musical tastes and orientation of the particular social group, whether rural Quebecois, California suburban, Illinois heartland, Appalachian mountain, or New York inner-city. Children then work in harmony with (or against) this basic musical background as a part of growing up and finding their individual identity.

Generation

Much American music making is organized along generational lines. Schools, church classes, scouting groups, sidewalk children's games, college singing groups, and many other musical situations include people of about the same age. Songs learned by these groups may stay with them as they grow older: imagine the twentieth or fiftieth college class reunion, where the aging ex-students keep singing the songs of their generation.

Yet the amount of generational mixing in American musical life has grown under the influence of television and records. In pop music, much of the music thought to belong only to the young in the 1960s, such as the music of the Beatles, appealed to older generations as well. Other styles, like country fiddling, which not long ago attracted only older musicians, have been picked up by young people, and now at a fiddle contest like the one held in Hartford, Connecticut, every year, the age spread of performers runs from eight to eighty.

In ethnic musics too, young people have taken to learning traditional songs from their grandmothers instead of laughing at the old folks' songs as they might have one or two generations ago.

Generational blurring is part of the process of musical homogenization we will see at work in still other areas of our music-culture. There is not as much difference between the sexes musically as there used to be. Just as women can now take up sports like race-car driving and become professional jockeys, so more females play instruments, like the drums and saxophone, that used to be largely limited to males. A whole genre that used to be male—barbershop quartet singing—now has a parallel female style, exhibited by groups such as the Sweet Adelines. We will see the effect of regional and ethnic blurring below.

Avocation

Music as hobby is an important part of American life. A barbershop quartet program lists the wives of the singers as "Thursday Night Widows"—perhaps one reason for the formation of women's quartets. Many Americans feel the need for a strong, group hobby, and of course some of this impulse is channeled into musical organizations. A local American Legion post, or an ethnic group like the Polish Falcons, may have a band; here the music making is part of the feeling of group solidarity. Being able to field a band for the local parade or festival brings the group visibility and pride. Individual members may find performing in a fife-and-drum corps or the Governor's Footguard Band (to use Connecticut examples) a very satisfying way to spend leisure time. Black youngsters in high school and college form extracurricular, informal singing groups whose repertoire includes soul or gospel music hits; sometimes these groups become semi-professional or even fully professional, as they get older. Most high schools and colleges can boast a few rock bands and possibly even a jazz group, as well as cocktail pianists, folk singing guitarists, and bluegrass ensembles.

Religion

Religion is one of the better-documented areas of North American musical life. We know about music's role in many religious movements, ranging from the eighteenth-century Moravians through the revival movements of the nineteenth century and the founding of new sects such as the Mormons. Much has been written about the appropriateness of certain types of music making in religious settings, such as organ playing in the Jewish synagogue or the introduction of folk and jazz elements to church services. The black spiritual is the object of scholarly study, while the tent revival preacher, the snake handler, and the ecstatic evangelistic churches receive attention from journalists (see ill. 10–2). But the musical activities of contemporary, mainline middle-class churches, synagogues, and mosques are little studied. Of interest also are the songs of new, unofficial religious movements, such as small meditation groups based on Christian or oriental religious thinking. These groups need to encourage solidarity

Ill. 10–2. *Music almost always accompanies formal rites of passage, such as this old-time river baptism. Slabtown, Virginia, 1930s.*

and teach their message, but they have no traditional music. Often they change the words of well-known songs as a way of starting, just as Martin Luther changed the words of German drinking songs 450 years ago to create a body of sacred songs we know as Protestant chorales. The new unofficial groups may also work hard on developing an "inner music" of their members, through which the individual believer reaches the desired state of tranquility.

Ethnicity

Ethnicity is the oldest consideration in the study of the American music-culture in the sense that America is a nation of immigrants. It is also one of the newest considerations because of the current interest in the public expresion of ethnic identity, a trend that gathered force beginning in the 1960s.

Throughout American musical history, ethnicity has played a major role. Whether in the dialect and songs of the French Acadians in New Brunswick, the heroic *corrido* ballads sung along the Rio Grande by Mexican-Americans, the retelling of the story of hard-hearted Barbara Allen by Anglo-American ballad singers, or the singing of a Yiddish lullaby in a Brooklyn tenement, Americans have maintained distinctive ethnic boundaries through music. Music's function as a sign of group solidarity and common ancestry is nowhere clearer than in the variety of songs, dances, and instrumental tunes that characterize the American ethnic mosaic. Students in the United States whose parents or grandparents stopped public singing of Old World songs on their way to becoming "one-hundred-percent Americans" now become enthusiastic about joining ethnic music groups or studying their group's heritage. Other parents and grandparents, of course, never stopped singing their native songs. American ethnic music has always involved transcontinental exchange. On the one hand, Greek-Americans may be influenced by new developments in popular music in Athens, while on the other, Polish-American records may find great favor among farmers in far-off mountain villages in Poland. American jazz and country music have spread around the world, from Holland to Russia and Japan. A very complicated interplay goes on between black music in the United States and the Caribbean (ill. 10–3). A single song may show layer upon layer of musical travel. A few years ago a style of pop music known as *reggae* developed in Jamaica, where it represented a blend of Afro-Caribbean and black U.S. soul music. This already complicated style came to America from England, where pop groups repackaged

Ill. 10–3.   *One of Boston's caribbean steel-drum bands performs at a women's prison, 1979.*

Jeff Todd Titon

it and exported it, and the cycle continues: *reggae* is now popular in some parts of Africa.

Much of the older ethnic music of North America has changed in ways described in chapter 5. For example, twentieth-century fiddle contests put a stress on prizes and public display of rural fiddle music, as opposed to the older tradition of playing the music at house parties and barn dances. Some New England contests include young fiddle players who have classical training, or who specialize in the "trick and fancy" category of virtuoso pieces instead of the old-time standard jigs, reels, and waltzes of the Northeast. Official events like open contests push style in directions that may be unfamiliar to older country performers, for whom fiddling meant a way to pass the time or to earn a night's pay by playing for eight solid hours of dancing.

On the other hand, folk festivals in the U.S. such as the Smithsonian Institution's Festival of American Folklife and the National Folk Festival seek out traditional singers, musicians, and craftspeople, and to present them insofar as possible in traditional contexts. Not that they are necessarily against change and progress, however; at the Bicentennial Festival of American Folklife, for example, one of the staging areas was called Old Ways in the New World. Here traditional performers from various Old World countries were flown to America and presented alongside their New World ethnic counterparts: Polish-American musicians alternated with folk singing and dancing groups from Poland; Louisiana Cajuns and French-Canadian fiddlers alternated with their counterparts from France; and all learned from the musical interchange.

Regionalism

Regionalism in North America is thought to have declined with the spread of the interstate highway system, chains of fast-food restaurants, and the spread of television, all of which began in the 1950s. But just as the ethnic groups never really dissolved into the so-called melting pot, so regional homogenization never really took place in American life. Regionalism crops up in the names of styles, like the Chicago blues sound, the Detroit "Motown" soul sound, or even within ethnic styles, like the distinction between a Chicago and East Coast polka type. The crisp bowing and up-tempo performance of a fiddle tune in the Northeast bears little resemblance to the same tune's performance in the Southwest, with its smooth bowing and more relaxed beat. In country music today, the Nashville sound can be distinguished from the Texas sound, reflecting earlier differences between country and country-western styles. Likewise, the same hymn tune shows considerable variation even within the same denomination in different parts of the country. One Indiana Primitive Baptist was overheard to comment on the slow, highly decorated tunes of her Primitive Baptist neighbors to the Southeast: "They take ten minutes just to get through 'Amazing Grace'!" There are also local preferences for types of ensembles. The Governor's Footguard Band, formed in Connecticut before the American Revolution, is unlikely to have a counterpart in Kansas. Connecticut's fife-and-drum corps can be found in many good-sized Connecticut towns, whereas the Midwest is the heartland of the marching band.

Like ethnicity, regionalism is coming back into fashion. There are now so many local festivals that books of listings are published. In some locales, mock battles are fought again and again for tourist throngs, with appropriate live or recorded music. One very visible regional music performance is the singing of "My Old Kentucky Home" at the May running of the Kentucky Derby. In a recent year 150 thousand spectators joined in, and millions of television viewers were on hand to link the song and event to the region of its origin. The media scour America each year for feature stories; in the process they turn what were once regional events, like the annual celebration of an admittedly obnoxious Appalachian vegetable called the ramp, into national news, thereby making regionalism a commercial product. However, musical boosterism is not always successful. In 1975 Los Angeles gave up looking for a city song to rival "I Left My Heart in San Francisco." The ten-year song search failed despite entries praising "sandy beaches free from leeches" and other unworkable solutions.

In summary, if only in terms of marketing advantage and a renewed desire for local color, regional diversity has not yet been replaced by a homogenized American music. The country is still too large and diverse to turn all music into brand names or to have the entire population respond equally to all music, and the search for revival or for novelty continues.

Nationalism

A breakaway colony that declared its independence and fought a war to preserve it, the United States long ago began seeking ways to establish a national musical identity. We have already commented upon its distinctive musical profile generated by ethnic and regional stylistic interactions. Popular national sentiment was also evoked by the frequent performance of patriotic songs, a tradition that has declined only in recent decades. Official music plays less of a part in American life now than when John Philip Sousa's band and its imitators played flag-waving tunes on the bandstand for Sunday promenaders, or when schoolchildren knew all the verses of the national anthem. When Gerald Ford was vice-president, he asked that the University of Michigan football fight song be played to greet him instead of a national ceremonial song—a sign of the decline of official music.

The change may also be seen by comparing the program for a large public concert in New York's Central Park in 1916 with one in 1976. For the earlier event, the composer Arthur Farwell produced a chorus of eight hundred and a full orchestra to accompany twenty-five thousand New Yorkers in classical music, people's hymns that Farwell wrote for the occasion ("March! March!" and "Joy! Brothers, Joy!"), well-known old-time favorites, such as "Old Black Joe," and patriotic songs. The event closed with the multitude singing "The Star-

Spangled Banner." In the 1976 event, the city shared sponsorship with an FM rock station. Only young people's music was played; there was no public singing. The crowd mingled, listened, and some danced; others relaxed and smoked. Marijuana was sold openly.

Perhaps our most obvious repertoire of national music consists of Christmas songs such as "Jingle Bells," "Deck the Halls," "Rudolf the Red-Nosed Reindeer," and the like. During the holiday season it is almost impossible to escape them. The curmudgeon who shoos away carolers from his front yard is said to lack the Christmas spirit, and he soon gains a neighborhood reputation as a Scrooge.

Commercial Music

Much of the music in our culture is supplied by paid professionals. It is remarkable that our complex culture continues to carry on the musical situations described earlier in non- or preindustrial societies. Though a genre like the funeral lament has largely dropped out of America, rituals like weddings and initiations (bar mitzvahs, debutante parties, senior proms) that mark a change of life still demand solemnization by music. A wedding may take place in a park with a Good Humor truck, balloons, and jeans instead of in a formal church setting yet music remains indispensable even if it consists of pop tunes instead of an official wedding march. There are other carryovers from early ritual as well. Elegant yacht clubs tend to schedule dances during full-moon evenings, continuing a practice of certain ancient cultures.

A great deal of the commercial music Americans come into daily contact with may be described as "disembodied," by which we mean that the listener does not feel the physical presence of the performer and many times cannot even see the original musical situation (ill. 10–4). Some of this music can be controlled partially by the listener who selects records from his or her collection to fit a mood. Choices are made from an entirely private domain of records over which the person has complete control regarding the selection of the music and the length of the listening experience. Although it is possible to imagine the original musical situation—concert or recording studio—there is no possibility of interaction with the performers, and the music sound is the same each time it is heard.

At the opposite end of the spectrum of disembodied commercial music is public background music. There is no logical connection between event and music in a supermarket such as there is in one's own room listening to a stereo. In the case of background music of the type used in offices and factories, the employer has chosen the music, which is manufactured by the supplier to have the effect of increasing worker productivity. This of course represents a particularly powerful type of unrequested music, and there is a split among the captive audience as to whether listeners appreciate its existence.

John Collier. Courtesy of the Library of Congress

Ill. 10–4. *Dancing to records on a juke-box, West Virginia, 1942.*

DOING MUSICAL ETHNOGRAPHY

Your aim in discovering and documenting a world of music is a *musical ethnography,* a written representation and description of a music-culture, organized from the standpoint of a particular topic. (Your writing may be accompanied by photographs, tape recordings, and even videotapes that you make while documenting the music-culture.) The goal of musical ethnography is to understand a music-culture or some part of it from a native's or insider's point of view (see Spradley 1979:3). What does that point of view encompass? Recall how in chapter 1 we divided a music-culture into four components: ideas, social organization, repertories, and material culture. Approaching a music-culture for the first time, you may feel overwhelmed; but if you organize your thinking about what you see and hear under the outline in Table 1–1, you will be well on your way to documenting the music-culture.

The music in the repertory can be recorded for later study and analysis. Much of social organization and material culture can be observed. By listening to insiders talk with each other, and by talking to them, you begin to understand their ideas about music, and through interviews you can learn more about those ideas, the repertory, social organization, and material culture. (After all, conversations and interviews formed the basis for the musicians' life histories in this book.) But discovering and documenting a world of music is not like examining an amoeba under a microscope. People will differ in how they behave, what they believe, and what they say to you. Different people will sing "the same tune" differently. Under these conditions, representing and describing a music-culture, even a single aspect of it, is a complex and subtle undertaking.

SELECTING A SUBJECT: SOME PRACTICAL SUGGESTIONS

It goes almost without saying that your field project will involve you in collecting, understanding, and organizing information about music in order to present it. It differs from the usual undergraduate research paper in that its focus is on a musical situation that you seek out from people rather than from books in a library. In ethnomusicology, as in anthropology and folklore, this in-person witnessing, observing, questioning, tape recording, photographing and (in some cases) performing, is called fieldwork: work "in the field" rather than the laboratory or library. This is not to say that library research is useless or should be avoided. It may be possible to find background information on your topic in the library, and you should not overlook the opportunity to do so, but the thrust of your project takes you into the field where you will obtain your most valuable and original information. Collecting, understanding, and organizing information about music are, of course, interrelated. You will begin with certain insights about the information you collect. As you organize it, you will gain new insights as you move toward an understanding of the musical situation from the web of information you have gathered.

You can approach the choice of a research subject in different ways. First, you might try to chart out the music which you hear daily:

1. Keep a log or journal of all the music heard through three or four days, or a week. Note the context, style, and purpose of the music. Calculate how much of your day is spent with music of some sort.

2. Record, videotape, or simply describe in words several television commercials that employ music. Note the style of the music and the image it attempts to project. How is the music integrated into the message of the advertisement? Is it successful? Offensive? Both?

3. Make a map of the uses of music in a motion picture or television drama as you watch it. For comparison, select a soap opera and a crime fighting show, or a situation comedy and a popular dramatic series.

4. Survey the stores in your area and their uses of background music. Interview salespeople, managers, owners, customers (always obtaining their permission). See what they say about music and sales.

5. Survey the contents of jukeboxes in bars and restaurants. Interview the manager about the content of his jukebox and the preferences of his clientele.

A second approach is to examine the music in your own background. Explore your memory of songs and music. Note how your racial, religious, and ethnic heritage influenced the music you heard and your current musical interests. How has your musical taste changed as you have grown older? Survey the contents of your record collection or preferences in radio listening. The same questions can be asked of your brothers and sisters, your parents, or other members of your family.

A third approach is to explore music in your community—college or home-town. Here you can interview people, listen to musical performances, possibly take part in them yourself, and gather quite a lot of information. Listed below are several possible subject headings:

Ethnic groups
Piano teachers
Private instrumental instruction (music stores, private lessons in the home)
Choir directors
Church organists, pianists, and so on
School music (elementary, junior high, high school)
Music stores
Musical instrument makers
Background music in public places
The club scene (discos, bars, coffeehouses, restaurants, nightclubs)
Musical organizations (community choral groups, bands, barbershop quartets, etc.)
Part-time (weekend) musicians
Professional or semiprofessional bands (rock, pop, jazz, soul, country, gospel, etc.)
Chamber music groups
Parades and music
Disc jockeys
Symphony orchestras

A fourth approach narrows the subject and concentrates on an individual musician's life, opinions, and music. Often we focus our attention on the musical superstars, but in the process we forget the many fine and sensitive musicians, many of them amateurs, who live in our communities. Senior citizens, teachers, owners of record or music stores, or tradespeople like the local barber, janitor, or factory worker have sometimes had rich musical experiences as professional or part-time musicians. To search out such people is not always easy. Try the musicians' union, ethnic organizations, word of mouth, school or college music teachers, radio station disc jockeys, the clergy, club owners, newspaper columnists and feature storywriters, or even local police stations and fire departments. Musicians can be approached directly at fairs, contests, festivals, concerts, and dances. Many colleges and universities have foreign student associations that include amateur musicians, and they can tell you about others in the area. Ethnic specialty restaurants and grocery stores are another resource.

The musical world that surrounds you is so diverse you may feel swamped, unable to focus your energy. But when it finally comes down to deciding on a subject for your project, two guiding principles will help you out: choose something you are interested in, and choose something you have access to. It will be hard to succeed if you are not curious about the music you examine, and you will have to be close to it to look at it carefully.

COLLECTING INFORMATION

Once you have chosen a subject, your next move is to immerse yourself in the musical situation, consider what aspects of it interest you, and select a topic. Then plan how you will collect information—what questions to ask when you talk to the musicians or others involved; what performances to tape record, and so forth. Almost always you will need time and the flexibility to revise your plans as you collect the information you need. Most people will be happy to tell you about their involvement with music so long as you show them you really are interested.

Gaining Entry

Musical activities usually have a public (performance) side and a private (rehearsal) side. The performance is the tip of the iceberg; you will want to understand what lies beneath, and that is best learned by talking to the people involved. If you must approach a stranger, it may be helpful to arrange an introduction, either by a mutual friend or by a person in authority. Protocol is important in some cases. If, for example, you will be talking with musicians in an ethnic organization, it is wise to approach the president of the organization and seek his advice. Not only is he (or she) in a position to give you good suggestions, but a president needs to know what is going on; it is expected of him. In other situations it is best to let the people in authority know what you intend to do, and why, but to avoid having them introduce you, particularly if their authority is legal only, and they do not belong to the same racial or ethnic group as the people whose music you will be studying.

The first contact is especially important because the way you present yourself establishes your identity and role. That is one reason why it is essential to take the time to be honest with yourself and others about your interest in their music and the purpose of your project. If you are a university student, you may find yourself being assigned the role of the expert. But this is a role to avoid. The people who give you information are the experts, and you are the student who wants to learn from them. Otherwise you would not seek their help. You hope they will be willing to let you talk with them, observe, and, if it is appropriate, participate in the music.

Selecting a Topic

Usually your subject takes in several music situations, and you will find yourself having to choose among them so as not to undertake a larger project than you can accomplish. If, for example, you are interested in Irish-American music in your community, you may find that there is so much going on that a survey of it all will be superficial, and so you will decide to concentrate on one aspect of it, perhaps the musical tradition of one family, or the musical scene in a particular club. Remember once again to choose something you are interest in and have access to.

The next step is one of the most difficult: selecting a topic. A topic is more than just a subject. It is a subject viewed from a particular angle, from a certain perspective, and with a limited goal in mind. "The Jewish cantor" is an example of a subject, something to investigate. "Musical training of Jewish cantors in New York City" is a topic. The cantor is viewed from a special perspective: his training. You want to understand what the training is and what the results are. Another example of a subject is "the Jelly Roll Bakers, a campus jazz band." A topic that involves the band might be "the repertoire of the Jelly Roll Bakers, a campus jazz band." Here the focus is on the band's choice of material; one goal is to determine why they choose certain songs and not others. By themselves, subjects cover too much ground. Topics focus your attention on specific questions that will help you organize the information you collect.

As you think about a topic, reread chapter 1 and see how the four-part model of the music-culture can help you select aspects of your subject that you are interested in. Do you want to focus on conceptions of music, social organization, repertories, or material culture? Of course, these aspects are interrelated, and it will be difficult to ignore any of them completely; nevertheless, concentrating most of your attention on one of them will help you select a topic you can manage, and it will give you some initial ideas to think about as you gather your information.

Library Research

Depending on the topic you have selected, it may be a good idea to visit the library at this point to see whether anyone has published research on your topic. The card catalog can be helpful; look under such headings as "music," "folk music," "popular music," and whatever categories are closely related to your subject. It may be useful to spend a couple of hours in the music section of the library stacks, looking at books on the shelves and opening any that might be centered in your subject, for it is almost impossible to know where to look for everything in the card catalog alone.

After you have checked the card catalog and the stacks, look in the reference section for such bibliographies as *The Music Index* and *RILM,* as well as specialized bibliographies and references works. The reference librarian can help you find these. If your library subscribes to *Ethnomusicology,* the professional journal of the Society for Ethnomusicology, you will find in each of its three yearly issues an invaluable guide to published research in the "Current Bibliography and Discography" section. It will be worth seeking this journal in other libraries nearby if yours does not subscribe to it.

In addition to *Ethnomusicology,* you may find some of the following periodicals helpful: *Latin America Music Review; Journal of Popular Music and Society; Journal of American Folklore; The Black Perspective in Music; Journal of Jazz Studies; John Edwards Memorial Foundation Quarterly; Living Blues; Stereo Review; Journal of Popular Culture; Yearbook of the International Council for Traditional Music; Foxfire; Southern Exposure; Southern Folklore Quarterly; Asian Music; Music Educators' Journal; Western Folklore; Journal of Country Music; American Music; World of Music; Popular Music; Frets; Black Music Research Journal; Bluegrass Unlimited; The Devil's Box; The Old Time Music Herald.*

Another good reason for visiting the library early in your project is that you may find a reference to a promising article or book that you will need to request on interlibrary loan. But avoid the temptation to read everything that looks as if it might somehow be relevant. The thrust of your project is outward into the field. Library research merely provides background information, and sometimes it cannot even do that—your subject may not have had attention in print, or the little that has been written may not be very useful. But if research on your topic has been published, you will be able to undertake a better project if you are familiar with it; and the people whose music you are studying will often be able to suggest good books and articles for you to read, thereby saving you time in your search.

Participation and Observation

Returning now to the field requires a basic plan of action. Which people should you talk with? What performances should you witness? Should you go to rehearsals? What about a visit to a recording studio? If you are studying a music teacher, should you watch a private lesson? Should the teacher teach you? Will you take photographs? Movies? Videotape? What kind of tape-recording equipment can you get? Who will pay for it? You probably have been thinking about these and many similar questions, but one more that you should pay attention to at this time is your personal relationship to the people whose music you will study. Should you act as an observer, as a detached, objective reporter? Or should you, in addition to observing, also participate in the musical activity if you can?

Participating as well as observing can be useful. (It can be quite enjoyable as well.) You hope to learn the music from the inside. You will come to know some of the musical belief system intuitively. You will not have to hang around the edges of the action all the time, depending on others to explain all the rules.

But participating has its drawbacks. The problem with being a participant-observer is that you sometimes know too much. It is like the forest and the trees: the closer you are to a situation, the less of an overall view you have, and in order to address your project to an outside reader, you will need to imagine yourself an outsider, too. We tend to filter out the regularities of our lives. If we had to remember every time we met a stranger whether our culture says we should shake hands, rub noses, or bow, we would be in constant panic, and if we had to think hard whether *red* means stop or go, driving would be impossible. This filtering process means that we take the most basic aspects of a situation for granted. So if you are participating as well as observing, you must make a special effort to be an outsider and take nothing for granted. This dual perspective, the view of the participant-observer, is not difficult to maintain while you are *learning* how to participate in the musical situation. In fact, when you are learning, the dual perspective is forced on you. The trouble is that after you have learned you can forget what it was like to be an outside observer. Therefore it is very important to keep a record of your changing perspective as you move from outsider to participant, and this record should be written in your field notes or spoken into your tape recorder as your perspective changes.

What if you work as an observer only, and forego participation? There are some advantages to doing so. It saves time. You can put all your energy into watching and trying to understand how what people tell you is going on matches what you can actually see and hear going on. You can follow both sides of "what I say" and "what I do" more easily with someone besides yourself. On the other hand, you do not achieve objectivity by keeping yourself out of the action. Your very presence as an observer alters the musical situation, particularly if you are photographing or tape recording. In some situations you will actually cause *less* interference if you participate rather than intrude as a neutral and unresponsive observer.

Ethics

There is an important ethical dimension, a right-and-wrong aspect about doing fieldwork. Most colleges and universities have a policy on research with human subjects designed to prevent people from being harmed by the research. If your research project is part of a course, be sure to discuss the ethics of the project with your teacher before you begin and, if things change, as you proceed. In any case, think carefully about the impact of what you propose to do. Understand that people have legal rights to privacy, and to how they look, what they say, and what they sing, even after it has gone onto your film or tape recorder. Be honest with yourself and the people you study about your interest in their music and the purposes of your project. Tell them right from the start that you are interested in researching and documenting their music. If you like their music, say so. If the project is something for you to learn from, say so. Explain what will happen to the project after you finish it. Is it all right with them if you keep the photographs and tapes you make? Would they like a copy of the project? (If so, make one at your expense.) Is it all right if the project is deposited in the college or university archive? Most archives have a form that the people (yourself included) will sign, indicating that you are donating the project to the archive and that it will be used only for research purposes. If this project is not merely a contribution to knowledge but also to your career (as a student or whatever), admit it and realize that you have a stake in its outcome. Ask the people whose music you are studying why they are cooperating with you and what they hope to achieve from the project, and bear that in mind throughout. And *never* observe, interview, make recordings or take photographs without their knowledge and permission.

Today many ethnomusicologists believe that it is not enough simply to go into a musical situation and document it. The fieldworker must give back something to the people who have been generous with their thoughts, their music, and their time. In some cultures, people expect money and should be paid. It is possible for the fieldworker to act not simply as a reporter or analyst but also as a cultural and musical advocate, doing whatever he can to help the music he is studying to flourish. Some excerpts from the 1978 brochure describing the Folk Arts Program of the National Endowment for the Arts illustrate the advocacy viewpoint:

> We define our responsibility as the encouragement of those community or family-based arts that have endured through several generations and that carry with them a sense of community aesthetic.... We attempt to help smooth the flow of cultural experience, so that all peoples can move confidently into their own futures, secure in the knowledge of the elegance and individuality of their own cultural pasts. [Program Description, Folk Arts Program, National Endowment for the Arts, Washington, D.C., June 1978]

Some ethnomusicologists in the United States work for arts councils, humanities councils, and other government agencies in "public sector" jobs where they are expected to identify, document, and present authentic folk and ethnic musicians to the public. Many taxpayers believe that if government supports the fine arts, it should also support folk and ethnic arts. In fact, most European governments do more than the United States and Canada to preserve and promote their folk and ethnic music. But not all ethnomusicologists agree that they should encourage the preservation of the music they study and admire. Some feel it is simply none of their business. Others believe that despite their good intentions, advocates ultimately do more harm than good. Ethnomusicologists, like all who deal with the arts, are open to charges of romanticism and bias, of course. But recently some have criticized public sector folklorists and ethnomusicologists for imposing their own ideas about authenticity, for propping up old-fashioned musics at the expense of emerging ones, and for interfering with the natural waxing and waning of music where they should leave well enough alone. Public sector workers reply that all is not "well enough." They hear a similar kind of commercial, popular music on radios and tapes throughout the world, and conclude that local musics—of which there are a great variety—are endangered. It is to humankind's advantage to have many different kinds of music, they believe. For that reason, they think advocacy and support are necessary in the face of all the forces that would make music sound alike the world over. This argument may at first seem remote to your project, but not when you think about your own involvement with the people and music you are studying.

Field Equipment: Notebook, Tape Recorder, Camera

The perfect fieldworker has all-seeing eyes, all-hearing ears, and total recall. But because none of us is so well equipped, we suggest you rely on written notes, tape recordings, and photographs that you yourself make in the field. These documents serve two purposes: they enable you to reexamine at leisure your field experiences when you write up your project, and, since they are accurate records of performances, interviews, and observations, they may be included in the final form your project takes. On the other hand, field equipment presents certain difficulties: it costs money, you need to know how to work it properly, and you may have to resist the temptation to spend much of your time fiddling with your equipment when you should be watching, thinking, and listening instead.

Fifty years ago, fieldworkers relied primarily upon notetaking, and today it is still indispensable. No matter how sophisticated your equipment is, you should carry a small, pocket notebook. It will be useful for writing down names and addresses, directions, observations, and thoughts while in the field. In the days before sound recording, music was taken by dictation in notebooks. While this is still possible, it is not advisable except when performances are very brief and you have the required dictation skills. Note that dictating a song puts the performer in an unnatural context and changes the performance. However, notebooks are especially useful for preserving information learned in interviews, particularly if a tape recorder is unavailable or awkward in the interview situation. In addition, you should make an effort to write down your detailed impressions of the overall field situation: your plans, questions, any difficulties you meet with; as complete a description as possible of the musical situation itself, including the setting, the performers, the audience, and the musical event from start to finish; and your reactions and responses to the field experience as it takes place. Your field notebook becomes a journal or diary that you address *to yourself* for use when you write up your project.

Most university music departments and many university libraries now loan inexpensive, portable cassette tape recorders to students for use in field collecting projects. Whether you use a tape recorder, and if so what type it is (microcassette, portable cassette, home stereo cassette deck, reel-to-reel, etc.) is largely a matter of the nature of your project and your and your instructor's expectations. The inexpensive portable cassette recorders are best suited to recording speech (interviews, for example). Although they come with built-in microphones, the sound quality can be improved dramatically if you use an inexpensive external microphone plugged into the recorder's microphone input jack. So equipped, a portable cassette tape recorder may be adequate for your needs. It should go without saying that you will want to be thoroughly familiar with its operation so that your recordings are accurate. But the portable cassette recorder is mechanically simple, and anyone can learn to operate it in just a few minutes. Most important, put the microphone in the right spot. If the sound is soft or moderate and it comes from a small area (a solo singer, a lesson on a musical instrument, or an interview, for example), place the microphone in close and equidistant from the sources of the sounds. If the sound is loud and widely spread out (a rock band or a symphony orchestra, for example), search out "the best seat in the house" and place or hold the microphone there. Make a practice recording for a few seconds and play it back immediately to check microphone placement and make certain the equipment is working properly. Take along spare batteries and plenty of blank tapes (see ill. 10–5).

If properly used, even the simplest cameras take adequate pictures of musical performances. A picture may not be worth a thousand words, but it goes a long way toward capturing the human impact of a musical event. An instant-picture camera is especially useful because you will be able to see the photograph immediately and correct mistakes (such as standing too far from the action) at once. A "portrait" or close-up lens placed in front of the regular lens will allow you to fill up the whole picture with a musical instrument. Instant pictures have another advantage: you can give them (well, not all of them) to the people you photograph.

Americans are in love with technology, even technology to get away from technology (backpacking equipment, for example). If you already know a lot about tape recording or photography and you own or can borrow high-quality equipment, by all means use it. Some of the photographs in this book and the accompanying recordings were made by the authors using professional equipment; after all, fieldwork is a part of our profession. But the more sophisticated our equipment is, the more difficult it is to use it to its full potential. There is a story (and it is a true story) about a photographer who went to a rock music festival and brought only his pocket instamatic camera. In the photographer's pit in front of the stage, he had maneuvered himself into the best position and was standing there taking pictures when a professional nudged him, saying, "Get out of here with that little toy!" The pro stood there with cameras hanging from his neck and shoulders, covering his body like baby opossums on a mama opossum. "Well," said the amateur, yielding his position, "I guess if you need all of that equipment you'd better stand in the right spot, too!"

Interviewing

Interviews with people (informants) whose music you are studying are a useful means of obtaining basic information and getting feedback on your own ideas. But be careful not to put words in your informants' mouths and impose your

James T. Koetting

**Ill. 10–5.   *A chief checks the quality of a recording of his musicians.
Kasena-Nankani Traditional Area, Ghana.***

ideas. The first step in understanding a world of music is to understand it as
much as possible in your informants' own terms. Later you can bring to bear on
the musical situation your perspective as an outsider. Remember that much of
their knowledge is intuitive; you will have to draw it out by asking questions, and
as an outsider you are well equipped to do so.

Come into the interview with a list of questions, but be prepared to let the talk
flow in the direction your informant takes it. In his 1956 preface to *Primitive*

Man as Philosopher Paul Radin distinguishes between two procedures for obtaining information: question-and-answer, and "letting the native philosopher expound his ideas with as few interruptions as possible." Your informants may not be philosophers, but they should be given the chance to say what they mean. Some people are by nature talkative, and you will be thankful of it. Others need to be put at ease; let the person know in advance what sort of questions you will be asking, what sort of information you need, and why. Often you will get important information in casual conversations rather than formal interviews; be ready to write down the information in your field notebook. Some people are by nature silent and guarded; despite your best intentions, they will not really open up to you. If you encounter that sort of informant, respect his or her wishes and make the interview brief.

Beginning fieldworkers commonly make two mistakes when doing interviews. First, they worry too much about the tape recorder, and their nervousness can carry over to the person they interview. But if you've already gotten the person's consent to be interviewed, it should not be hard to get permission to tape the interview. One fieldworker always carries her tape recorder and camera so they are visible from the moment she enters the door. Then she nonchalantly sets the tape recorder down in a prominent spots and ignores it, letting the person being interviewed understand that the tape recorder is a natural and normal part of the interview. Still ignoring the recorder, she starts off with the small talk that usually begins such a visit. Eventually the other person says something like, "Oh, I see you're going to tape record this." "Sure," she says steadily. "I brought along this tape recorder just to make sure I get down everything you say. I can always edit out any mistakes, and you can always change your mind. This is just to help me understand you better the first time." She says once they have agreed to be interviewed, nobody has ever refused her tape recorder. But she adds that if anyone told her to keep the recorder shut off, she would certainly do so.

A second problem is that beginning fieldworkers often ask leading questions. This makes the information they get unreliable. In other words, it is not clear whether the person being interviewed is expressing his or her own thoughts, or just being agreeable. In addition, leading questions usually result in short, uninteresting answers. Study this first dialogue to see how *not* to interview:

FIELDWORKER 1: Did you get your first flute when you were a girl?
INFORMANT: Yeah.
FIELDWORKER 1: What was the name of your teacher?
INFORMANT: Ah, I studied with Janice Sullivan.
FIELDWORKER 1: When was that?
INFORMANT: In college.
FIELDWORKER 1: I'll bet you hated the flute when you first started. I can remember hating my first piano lessons.
INFORMANT: Yeah.

The trouble here is that the informant gives the kinds of answers she thinks are expected of her. She is not really telling the fieldworker what she thinks. She is not even giving the conversation much thought. Now look what happens when another fieldworker questions the same informant.

FIELDWORKER 2: Can you remember when you got your first flute?

INFORMANT: Yeah.

FIELDWORKER 2: Could you tell me about it?

INFORMANT: Sure. My first flute—well, I don't know if this counts, but I fell in love with the flute when I was in grade school and I remember going down to a music store and trying one out while my father looked on, but I couldn't make a sound, you know!

FIELDWORKER 2: Sure.

INFORMANT: So I was really disappointed, but then I remember learning to play the recorder in, I think it was third grade, and I really loved that, but I didn't stick with it. Then in college I said to myself, I'm going to take music lessons and I'm going to learn the flute.

FIELDWORKER 2: Tell me about that.

INFORMANT: Well, I had this great teacher, Janice Sullivan, and first she taught me how to get a sound out of it. I was really frustrated at first, but after awhile I got the hang of it, and she would always tell me to think of the beautiful sounds I knew a flute could make. I used to think a flute could make a sound like water, like the wind. Well, not exactly, but sort of. And then Mrs. Sullivan let me borrow a tape of *shakuhachi* music—you know, the Japanese *flute*?—and I *heard* different kinds of water, different kinds of wind! I knew then that I would play the flute for the rest of my life.

Compare the two fieldworkers' questions. "Did you get your first flute when you were a girl?" is a leading question because it leads to the answer, "Yes, I got my first flute when I was a girl." Leading questions are questions with answers implied or embedded inside. What is more, fieldworker 1 implies that most people get their first flutes when they are girls, so the informant probably thinks she should answer yes. By contrast, the question of fieldworker 2—"Can you remember when you got your first flute?—is open-ended and invites reflection, perhaps a story. When the informant says "Yeah," fieldworker 2 asks for a story and gets a much better—and different—answer than fieldworker 1. Go over the rest of the first interview, see how fieldworker 1 injects her opinions into the dialogue ("I'll bet you hated the flute when you first started.") and fails to draw out the informant's real feelings about her lessons, whereas fieldworker 2 establishes better rapport, is a better listener, asks nondirective questions, and gets much fuller and truer answers.

If your project concentrates on a single informant, you may want to obtain his or her life story (Titon 1980). For this purpose a tape recorder is virtually a necessity. Since the way your informant views his life can be as important as the factual information he gives, you should try to get the life story in his own words as much as possible. This means refraining from questions that direct the story as you think it should go. What is important is how your informant wants it to go. Come back later, in another interview, to draw out specific facts and fill in gaps by direct questioning. In the initial interview, begin by explaining that you would like him to tell you about his life as a musician (or whatever is appropriate—composer, disc jockey, etc.) from the beginning until now. Once he starts, allow him plenty of time for silences to gather his thoughts. If he looks up at you expectantly, nod your head in agreement and try repeating what he has just said to show that you understand it. Resist your impulses to ask direct questions; write them down instead, and say you'll come back to ask questions later; for now you want the story to continue in his own words.

Not everyone will be able to tell you his or her musical autobiography, but if you are fortunate enough to find someone who can, it may turn out to be the most important part of your project. On the other hand, if your informant's life story is a necessary part of your project, but you cannot obtain it except by direct and frequent questioning, you should certainly ask the questions. If you get good answers, the result will be your informant's life *history*, a collaborative biography rather than an autobiography.

Interviews, then, with the people whose music you are studying (and perhaps with their audience) are important for obtaining factual information and testing your ideas. They are also important because through them you can begin to comprehend the musical situation from their point of view: their beliefs, their intentions, their training, their feelings, their evaluations of musical performance, and their understanding of what they are doing—what it is all about. Ultimately, since this is your project, you combine their ideas with your own when you write the project up using the information you have collected.

Other Means of Collecting Information

Another technique, often used in social science research, is the questionnaire. Its role in studying music is limited, but there are projects in which it can be helpful. Often this circumstance occurs when you wish to map out the general nature of a situation before moving into a specific sub-area to focus on. For example, to work on the meaning of pop songs in students' lives, it can be handy first to circulate a questionnaire to uncover the eventual sample you will study intensively. Questionnaires are most at home in studies of musical attitudes. To find out how shoppers react to supermarket background music, it would be hard to set up interviews but easy, if the store manager agrees, to arrange for distributing a questionnaire.

Aside from questionnaires, which seek out information, you might come upon information already gathered: autobiographical manuscripts, diaries, and tape recordings made by informants for themselves. Clubs, fraternities, schools, churches, and various organizations often store away old materials that shed light on musical activities. At concerts, the programs handed out can be rich in information, ranging from description of the music to the type of advertisers that support the concerts. Membership lists and patrons' lists may be included as well.

Newspapers are enormously helpful. Hardly a day passes without journalistic commentary on the musical environment, in news stories, reviews, and advertisements. Feature stories provide up-to-date information on current concerts, trends, and musical attitudes, both locally and nationally, while advertising can furnish insights into the ideals of the American musical world projected by the media, ideals that influence most of us one way or another. For example, an ad for an expensive home entertainment system designed to bring music into every home offers a direct connection between musical style and the rooms of the house: "101 Strings in the greenhouse, Bach in the bedroom, Frank Sinatra in the living room, Gershwin in the den, the Boston Pops on the patio, the Rolling Stones outside by the pool." What better brief description of middle-class musical taste could be found?

FINISHING THE PROJECT

After you have done all the hard work of organizing and collecting information, what do you do with it? Now is a good time to return to your original plan of action and list of questions you wanted to ask about the musical situation, particularly with reference to the four-part model that forms the basis of chapter 1. These questions and the information you have gathered offer a natural organization for your project. Specific advice on how to write it up and what form to present it in will be available from your instructor.

Be sure to keep in mind that you are not the only one affected by your finished project. Other people's feelings and, on occasion, social position are reflected in your work. Be clear in what you say about the people you worked with. Confidentiality may be important; if people asked you not to use their names or repeat what they said to you, respect their wishes. It is possible—even customary in many anthropological works—to change names of people or places to make certain no one is identified who does not want to be. Imagine the problems created for the member of a band who criticizes the leader if his words get back to the group, or for a school music teacher if he criticizes the school board to you in private and you quote him.

Checking back with informants is very helpful to clear up research questions. As you interview, collect information, and think about the musical situation you study, new questions always will occur to you. It is no different when you write up your project; you will probably find that it will be helpful to get back in touch with your informants and ask a few final questions so that you will be satisfied with your project when you have finished it.

In our Preface we wrote of our intention that our readers "experience what it is like to be an ethnomusicologist puzzling out his or her way toward understanding an unfamiliar music." A good field project inevitably provides just that experience. Valuable and enjoyable in and of itself, discovery and documentation of a world of music takes on added significance because it illuminates, even in a small way, our understanding of music as human expression.

REFERENCES CITED

Spradley, James P.
    1979   *The Ethnographic Interview.* New York: Holt, Rinehart, and Winston.

Titon, Jeff Todd.
    1980   "The Life Story." *Journal of American Folklore* 93.

ADDITIONAL READING

Collier, John, Jr., and Malcolm Collier
    1986   *Visual Anthropology: Photography as a Research Method.* Albuquerque: Univ. of New Mexico Press.

Georges, Robert A., and Michael O. Jones.
    1980   *People Studying People.* Berkeley: Univ of California Press.

Golde, Peggy, ed.
    1986   *Women in the Field: Anthropological Experiences.* 2nd ed. Berkeley: Univ. of California Press.

Goldstein, Kenneth.
    1964   *A Guide for Fieldworkers in Folklore.* Hatboro, Pa.: Folklore Associates.

Hattersley, Ralph.
    1978   *Beginner's Guide to Photographing People.* Garden City, N.J.: Doubleday.

Herndon, Marcia, and Norma McLeod.
    1983   *Field Manual for Ethnomusicology.* Norwood, Penn.: Norwood Editions.

Hood, Mantle
    1982   *The Ethnomusicologist,* chapters 4 and 5. 2nd edition. Kent, Ohio: Kent State Univ. Press.

Ives, Edward D.
    1980   *The Tape-Recorded Interview: A Manual for Fieldworkers in Folklore and Oral History.* Knoxville: Univ. of Tennessee Press.

Jackson, Bruce
    1987   *Fieldwork.* Urbana: Univ. of Illinois Press.

Karpeles, Maud
    1958   *The Collecting of Folk Music and Other Ethnological Material: A Manual for Field Workers.* London: International Folk Music Council and Royal Anthropological Institute.

Marcus, George E., and Michael M. J. Fischer
    1986   *Anthropology as Cultural Critique.* Chicago: Univ. of Chicago Press.

Rabinow, Paul
   1977 *Reflections on Fieldwork in Morocco.* Berkeley: Univ. of California Press.
Sanjek, Roger, ed.
   1990 *Fieldnotes: The Makings of Anthropology.* Ithaca, N.Y.: Cornell Univ. Press.
Spradley, James P. and David W. McCurdy.
   1972 *The Cultural Experience: Ethnography in Complex Society.* Chicago: Science
         Research Associates.
Wax, Rosalie.
   1971 *Doing Fieldwork: Warnings and Advice.* Chicago: Univ. of Chicago Press.

Index

I

J

CABRINI COLLEGE LIBRARY
610 KING OF PRUSSIA RD.
RADNOR, PA 19087-3699

DEMCO